AGRIPPA AND THE CRISIS
OF RENAISSANCE THOUGHT

AGRIPPA AND THE CRISIS OF RENAISSANCE THOUGHT

CHARLES G. NAUERT, JR.

55

ILLINOIS STUDIES IN THE SOCIAL SCIENCES

UNIVERSITY OF ILLINOIS PRESS • URBANA 1965

ACKNOWLEDGMENTS

More years ago than I like to count, the present study began as a doctoral dissertation in the Department of History at the University of Illinois. During the preparation of the dissertation, and during the years devoted to revising it for publication, I have received valuable assistance and learned counsel from great numbers of institutions and individuals. Professor William J. Bouwsma, now of the University of California at Berkeley, directed the thesis from which the present book is derived. I found him an ideal adviser, willing to let me work in my own way, yet always eager to give assistance when needed. Dr. Hans Baron of the Newberry Library in Chicago has encouraged the present study from a very early stage and has made valuable suggestions, both in detail and in general approach. Valuable assistance and encouragement also came from Professor Paul Oskar Kristeller of Columbia University. My many colleagues and friends at Bowdoin College, Williams College, and the University of Missouri have been sympathetic to my work and patiently willing to hear rather more about Agrippa von Nettesheim than I had any right to expect.

No scholar completes any work of this size without incurring indebtedness to great numbers of libraries and librarians. The University of Illinois Library was the first and principal center of my research, and I owe special thanks to Miss Isabelle F. Grant of the Rare Book Room and Miss Alma DeJordy of the Acquisitions Department. The libraries of Bowdoin College, Williams College, and the University of Missouri have been very helpful, and I particularly profited from the rare books of the Chapin Library at Williams College, and from the help of the curator, Dr. H. Richard Archer, and his assistants. I have been privileged to spend extended periods using the library collections of Harvard University, the University of Chicago, the University of California at Berkeley, and the Newberry Library. The authorities of the University Library at Wrocław, Poland, of the University Library of Würzburg, Germany, and of the Municipal Library at Lyons, France, have kindly permitted me to quote or publish manuscript materials from their collections.

The Department of History at the University of Illinois helped my study at a relatively early stage by awarding me the Kendrick J. Babcock Fellowship, which allowed me to spend a year of full-time work on my dissertation. The President and Faculty Research Committee of Bowdoin College made a grant to secure microfilms for my research, and the Research Council of the University of Missouri granted a subsidy for the typing of the manuscript. Miss Marie Taft of the University of Missouri Stenographic Bureau typed several chapters of the manuscript. My wife Jean helped with proofreading and indexing.

I also wish to thank the editors of the *Journal of the History of Ideas* for permission to use substantial portions of my article "Magic and Skepticism in Agrippa's Thought" in the present study. The editors of *Studies in the Renaissance* likewise have permitted me to draw heavily on my article "Agrippa in Renaissance Italy: The Esoteric Tradition."

It is a great pleasure to recall the kindness of these and many other persons, and I can only hope that I have had the wit to profit by their assistance.

Columbia, Missouri
20 April 1965

CONTENTS

Chapter Twelve

AGRIPPA AND HIS AGE

"To the Reader"—*Ad Lectorem,* as authors said in so many early printed books—is due some explanation of the reasons for this effort to recall to memory the life and thought of a man who, whatever his fame in the sixteenth and seventeenth centuries, has not retained that fame like his greater contemporaries, Luther and Erasmus. Heinrich Cornelius Agrippa von Nettesheim (1486-1535) has indeed been thoroughly forgotten, or at least reduced to that level of dim awareness indicated by a rather brief entry in the *Encyclopaedia Britannica,* or a short footnote intended to identify for the careful reader of Marlowe's *Doctor Faustus* the sorcerer whom Faustus takes as his model when he decides to conclude the pact with the Devil. Yet Agrippa has not always been so obscure. The literary reference in Marlowe's play is but one example of the fact that the name of the sorcerer and doubter Agrippa was indeed one to conjure with in the man's own century. As a later chapter will show in more detail, references to Agrippa, or influences from his thought, are frequent in Renaissance literature. Yet the main purpose of the

1

present book is not merely to expand those little editorial footnotes which identify the Agrippa of Marlowe, the Her Trippa of Rabelais, or a principal literary source of Montaigne's famous "Apology for Raymond Sebond."

The real justification for this study of the life and thought of this long-forgotten man, Agrippa, is rather that as much as any man of his time, he felt keenly the religious and intellectual problems, and even the political and social problems, of the early sixteenth century. His numerous surviving books and letters, therefore, offer the historical investigator a clear and fresh view into the period when the Northern Renaissance was attaining its full development, and when the Lutheran Reformation was shaking the consciences of all thinking men. Agrippa saw the problems of his age in a way which differed in certain respects from his more famous contemporaries, Erasmus, Thomas More, and Luther. Yet his way of seeing the world was perhaps as typical of his contemporaries as was theirs. Indeed, one of the special values of a study of his thought is that it represents certain elements in the mind of the early sixteenth century (most notably the study of occult traditions and the pessimistic questioning of the value of all human learning) which are very prominent in the intellectual life of the Renaissance, but about which Erasmus, for example, is reticent. Indeed, one recent student of Renaissance culture hits sharply at the conspiracy of silence by which modern scholarship has passed over without mention those elements in sixteenth-century thought, such as magic, which may not suit the taste of those who want to make the Renaissance the enlightened and reasonable starting-point of our own supposedly enlightened and reasonable age. In reality, these neglected parts of sixteenth-century culture represent no mere extravagances of a lunatic fringe of men devoted to exorcisms and the invocation of demons, but rather an important and widely held view of the world and of man's place in the world.[1] A study of Agrippa's thought can do much to illuminate this element in Renaissance thought. Thus perhaps it can even suggest some reinterpretations of the position of the whole period in the history of Western civilization, reinterpretations which are sadly needed after two generations of assault on the whole concept of Renaissance by medieval scholars who, in their eagerness to show the presence of sup-

[1] Eugenio Garin, *Medioevo e Rinascimento: Studi e ricerche* (Bari, 1954), pp. 172-73.

posedly "Renaissance" and "modern" elements in the civilization of the High Middle Ages, have begged the whole question of what Renaissance men thought they were accomplishing by their attacks on medieval "barbarism," and why they thought it.[2]

Optimism, progress, and liberation of the human spirit from the shackles of tradition have been traditional themes of those who have written the intellectual history of Europe in the early sixteenth century. Western man, aided by the rediscovered treasures of ancient learning and by the rise of new, self-confident, inquisitive middle classes, free from bondage to the ways of the past, became suddenly creative in all fields of endeavor, in literature, in religious reform, in government, in economic activities, in the mastery of his environment by the accomplishments of the rising natural science. These themes of optimism and self-confidence, of reform and renewal, of discovery and invention, were certainly present in the age. There are few better illustrations of this triumphant Renaissance mood than the famous letter of Erasmus to Agrippa's friend Capito, written in February of 1517.[3] But these optimistic elements were not the only ones, and perhaps not the dominant ones, in the European mind of the early sixteenth century. Later ages have looked back in the light of the subsequent remarkable expansion and development of European civilization and have seen in the Renaissance era the germ of their own liberal and enlightened period: hence their use of the term "renaissance," or "rebirth," to characterize the age, a term which in many of its implications has been justly subjected to criticism by more recent historians, but which has become irrevocably fixed as a part of the historical vocabulary.

The men who did the actual living of the early sixteenth century felt quite differently about their age. Their moods of optimism were matched (perhaps even outweighed) by dark moods of pessimism. They saw the dominant intellectual systems of medieval scholasticism degenerating into mere arid trifling or into intellectual despair and appeals to blind faith; in the case of a Latin Aristotelian like Pomponazzi, even into what many regarded as rank infidelity. Acquaintance with rediscovered ancient literature was often unsettling as well as intellectually stimulating. The ferment of religious reform when one actually had to live through it meant galling dis-

---

[2] *Ibid.*, pp. 102-6.

[3] *Opus epistolarum Des. Erasmi Roterodami*, ed. P. S. Allen [and H. M. Allen and H. W. Garrod] (12 vols.; Oxonii, 1906-58), II, 487-92 (No. 541).

satisfaction with existing conditions and the most acute mental anguish for those who could not rest satisfied with the church as it was and yet could not tear themselves away from the traditional ecclesiastical institution. The rise of new classes often meant social disorganization, the ouster of traditionally privileged groups by new men, the widespread adoption of new standards of behavior that scandalized those whose attitudes had been formed under the influence of older patterns of conduct. The rise of national states in Western Europe brought a temporary end to civil strife but led to a long series of international conflicts that left the national governments weakened and impoverished and, by the late sixteenth or early seventeenth century, ready for a new series of internecine struggles. At the same time the exaltation of royal power over all other elements in the traditional society outraged the sense of propriety and decency even of those classes which benefited from the increased effectiveness of central government. Thus there was a dark side as well as an optimistic side to the condition of Renaissance Europe; and those great heroes of the traditional interpretation of the Renaissance as an age of progress and hope, Erasmus and Sir Thomas More, felt the problems of their time keenly enough to produce two satires, *The Praise of Folly* and the *Utopia*, which are far less the confident prophecies of a new age than bitter complaints against the failures of a present one.

Erasmus and More were not the only ones to feel this darker side of life along with the optimistic awareness of new opportunities. If the Renaissance mood included a sense of possibilities still unexplored by modern men, there was also a sense of having lost security of belief and action, a sense of being adrift, with a vision of the world which sharply repudiated the traditional medieval cultural heritage (repudiated it bitterly, even while at times plagiarizing it ruthlessly and without acknowledgment),[4] but which at the same time had few reassuring certainties of its own except its shrill negation of the "barbarism" of the recent past. This darker side of Renaissance culture has been variously seen as a "false Renaissance," a "Counter-Renaissance," a "classical reaction." [5] The

[4] For a striking illustration of this practice on the part of Boccaccio, see Jean Seznec, *La survivance des dieux antiques* (London, 1940), p. 188 *et seq.*
[5] The quoted passages come, respectively, from Ludwig von Pastor, *The History of the Popes* (40 vols.; St. Louis, Missouri: B. Herder, 1894-1953), I, 38; Hiram Haydn, *The Counter-Renaissance* (New York, 1950), *passim;* and Lynn Thorndike, *A History of Magic and Experimental Science* (8 vols.;

important point, however, though many recent interpreters of the Renaissance have overlooked it because of its very obviousness, is that this criticism of late-medieval thought and society merits study in its own right. Whether the humanists' criticism of scholastic philosophy, of medieval religious tradition, of the social conditions of early commercial capitalism, of the activities of the newly strengthened monarchies, was arrogant, ill-informed, reactionary, and in every way ill-founded, is not, after all, the only historical consideration. It should not even be the historian's primary consideration. Justified or not, this humanistic repudiation of traditional medieval learning and attitudes is a historical fact. It is clearly present in the thought of many of the leading men of the fifteenth and sixteenth centuries. Hence for the historian, it ought to become in its own right an object of study, not an object of rebuttal and reproach.

The following chapters of this work will attempt to portray in the life and thought of Agrippa the career of a personage who shared many of the hopes and still more of the fears of his age, and who also, in his widely influential appeal from bankrupt human reason to the wisdom of an occult antiquity, represents an important reaction of Renaissance thinkers to their intellectual predicament,[6] yet a reaction which is not prominent in the writings of Erasmus, More, and Luther, and which has been only occasionally mentioned as a prominent element in the thought of important leaders of thought in the period.[7]

Even the biography of Agrippa von Nettesheim is instructive for one who wishes to understand the problems of the Renaissance. He is a good example of a man who sought to make his career not in the traditional medieval channels of the church, the universities, or the legal and medical professions, or through lifelong participation in civil or military administration, but through his reputation for

New York, 1923-58), V, 3-4. For this whole aspect of the period, see the illuminating essay of Eugenio Garin, "Interpretazioni del Rinascimento," in his *Medioevo e Rinascimento,* especially pp. 90-92, 100-6; also the brilliant study of decadence as a factor in the culture of Renaissance Germany by Rudolf Stadelmann, *Vom Geist des ausgehenden Mittelalters: Studien zur Geschichte der Weltanschauung von Nicolaus Cusanus bis Sebastian Franck* (Halle, 1929), *passim* (including considerable attention to Agrippa).

[6] Garin, *op. cit.,* pp. 98-99, 153-54, 167-68.

[7] Aby Warburg, "Heidnisch-antike Weissagung in Wort und Bild zu Luthers Zeiten," *Gesammelte Schriften* (2 vols.; Leipzig, 1932), II, 490-535; cf. Erwin Panofsky, *Albrecht Dürer* (2 vols.; Princeton, 1943), I, 168-70.

profound erudition in strange and wonderful fields of learning. It was not an easy or secure existence. Rather, the life of Agrippa was like that of many another wandering and insecure Renaissance scholar, for even such an internationally famous personage as Erasmus experienced sharp vicissitudes of fortune. The life of Agrippa was one of great expectations and bitter disappointments, of questing for security and failing to gain it, of awareness of the spiritual crises of his age and inability to resolve them. His was the life of a wanderer: France, Spain, England, Italy, Switzerland, the Low Countries, and his native Germany were the scenes of his life. Indeed, part of the interest of his biography is that he was involved in the intellectual currents of not just one or two places, but of a whole succession of *milieux*. Except for his boyhood, he resided in no country more than seven years, in no city as much as four. He lived on the outer fringes of the society of the great and powerful, and twice thought he was about to gain influence at a great royal court; but his hopes were repeatedly frustrated. Wars in Germany and especially in Italy plagued his existence. Religious controversy and the outbreak of the Reformation made his situation precarious. The failure of medieval learning to solve his intellectual problems drove him to a search for older sources of truth; and the failure of these sources to satisfy his needs completely pushed him, at least in certain moments, to the brink of intellectual despair. The earlier chapters of the present study will attempt to sketch the outlines of his biography and to suggest the influence on his thought of the associations which he formed during each period of his life.

This agitated, constantly changing external career was in part a cause and in part a reflection of the even greater agitation of Agrippa's intellectual world. It was partly his travels and exposure to so many intellectual traditions that made him accumulate a stock of learning noteworthy even in that age of universal men, made him also grope tentatively in directions followed by many of the bolder spirits of the next two or three generations. The later chapters of the present book will undertake to analyze his thought and to show, as suggested above, the importance of a strong pessimism about human learning in his thought. They will also suggest certain ways in which Agrippa sought to escape his own tendencies toward intellectual despair, such as his widely influential studies in the occult arts. Finally, while the present writer makes no pretense of having exhaustively searched the literature of subsequent centuries for every chance literary reference to Agrippa, a concluding chapter will suggest ways in which the figure of Agrippa (both as reality and as myth) affected and reflected the thought of succeeding generations.

CHAPTER ONE

THE MAKING OF A SCHOLAR

Agrippa's life began, as it ended, in obscurity; but it is possible to determine something of his experiences in the years prior to 1507, date of his earliest surviving letter. He regarded Cologne as his *patria*, and he still had a mother and a sister living there in the mid-1520's. Sixteenth-century biographers commonly dated his birth 14 September 1486; and the year, at least, is very likely right.[1]

[1] The place of origin was clearly Cologne. See letter of Ioannes Rogerius Brennonius to Agrippa, Metz, 12 February 1520, printed in *De beatissimae Annae monogamia ac unico puerperio* . . . (n.p., 1534), fols. P4r-P7r, and also printed as *Epistolarum Liber II*, xliv, in Agrippa's *Opera* (2 vols.; Lugduni, n.d.), II, 759-62. (Henceforth the latter collection will be cited as *Epist.*) Also Amicus [Claudius Cantiuncula] ad Agrippam, Basel, 23 February 1519, *Epist.* II, xvi; and Agrippa to Senate of Cologne, Bonn, 11 January 1533, *Epist.* VII, xxvi. A letter sent to Agrippa from Antwerp in 1527 (*Epist.* V, xv) is of no real authority, but has caused many older biographers to suppose that while Agrippa was born in Cologne, his ancestors came from the Low Countries. This gratuitous assumption appears in Johann Georg Schelhorn, *Amoenitates literariae* (2nd ed.; 14 vols. in 7; Francofurti, 1726-30), II, 555, and in Ioannes Iacobus Mullerus, *Ex historia literaria de Henrici Cornelii Agrippae eruditorum portenti vita fatis et scriptis* (Vitembergae Saxonum, 1726), p. 5. The year of his birth depends on his *De beatissimae Annae monogamia*, fol. B6r: "Nam anno humanae salutis millesimo quingentesimonono, aetatis meae uicesimosecundo primum in dola Burgundiae publica lectura sacras literas professus sum. . . ."

Agrippa's matriculation at the University of Cologne lists his father's name as "Henricus de Nettesheym, citizen of Cologne"; after the father's death in 1519, Agrippa's mother and sister are the only relatives mentioned in his correspondence.[2] The social rank of his parents is uncertain, but one may guess that they came from the upper bourgeoisie or lower nobility resident in the city. Agrippa claimed to belong to a family of distinguished rank with long traditions of service to the Hapsburgs; but these claims may well have been aimed solely at gaining the favor of patrons.[3] Even his family name is uncertain, but it was as Agrippa or Cornelius Agrippa that his own and succeeding centuries chiefly knew him.[4] On the title pages of books which he published during his own lifetime, his name appeared as "Henricus Cornelius Agrippa ab Nettesheym," or simply as "Henricus Cornelius Agrippa."

Of Agrippa's early education very little is known. He confesses that he learned astrology from his parents, but this reference may be only to belief in it and not to formal study. In any case, his

[2] The death of his father is reported in a letter of Agrippa to the Bishop of Cyrene, coadjutor of the archdiocese of Cologne, written from Metz, 6 February 1518 (1519, n.s.). This letter is in Lyons, Bibliothèque Municipale, MS. No. 48, fol. 29v, and also is printed as *Epist.* II, xix. *Epist.* II, xliv, mentions his mother and a sister living in Cologne in 1520, and there are occasional later references.

[3] These claims usually appear in petitions to rulers. Agrippa to Imperial Council at Malines, Brussels, 1531, *Epist.* VI, xxii: "Sum enim non solum ingenuus, sed et spectabilis genere, nec tantum clarus imaginibus avitis, sed et propriis titulis militia doctrinaque partis. . . ." Same to Eberhard Cardinal van der Mark, Ghent, 12 May 1531, *Epist.* VI, xviii: "sunt avitae nobilitatis imagines, militaria insignia, scholastici tituli. . . . Proinde et pater et avi et atavi et tritavi Caesarum Romanorum Austriacorumque Principum a longo aevo ministri fuerunt." Cf. same to Mary of Hungary, Bonn, n.d. [1532], *Epist.* VII, xxi. Yet judging from *Oratio IV*, in *Opera*, II, 1091, Agrippa regarded it above his social status to associate with great princes: "a publicis negotiis principumque ultra sortem meam familiaritate."

[4] Auguste Prost, *Les sciences et les arts occultes au XVI siècle: Corneille Agrippa, sa vie et ses oeuvres* (2 vols.; Paris, 1881-82), I, 119-27, thinks that "Nettesheim" was a village near Cologne, and that "Cornelius" may be a surname. Cf. *ibid.*, II, 431-36, Appendices I and II. Prost is unaware of the use of "Nettesheim" in the matriculation of Agrippa at the University of Cologne, and thinks it an unauthorized later addition intended to give a noble ring to the name. But see *Die Matrikel der Universität Köln*, ed. Hermann Keussen (3 vols.; Bonn, 1892-1931), II, 473. "Agrippa" was a personal name taken because of his origin in Cologne, *Colonia Agrippina*. His children and grandchildren living in France used "Corneil-Agrippa" as their surname, according to Luc Maillet-Guy "Henri Corneil Agrippa, sa famille et ses relations," *Bulletin de la Société d'archéologie et de statistique de la Drôme*, LX (1926), 208.

interest in astrology and other occult arts began very early; and consideration of his life makes it abundantly clear that study of the occult arts formed not only a persistent interest, but also his chief title to fame and favor wherever he went. He matriculated in the University of Cologne on 22 July 1499, still a minor. His master in the faculty of arts was Petrus Capitis de Duunen, who that same year had received the licentiate in theology. Agrippa himself received a licentiate in arts on 14 March 1502. Whether he ever received any further degree from Cologne or any other university is uncertain. There is no evidence except his own oft-repeated claim of doctorates in canon and civil law and his less frequent claim of a doctorate in medicine. His biographer Prost flatly denies his claim to a degree in medicine and casts serious doubts on the legal doctorates; and one must admit that Agrippa never gave any details of where and when he took his degrees, although there is a hint that he may have taken a degree during his stay at the University of Pavia in Italy.[5]

Several considerations make it likely that Agrippa was telling the truth about his education, particularly in the case of the legal doctorates. First, there is the element of time. So little is known about Agrippa's life up to 1507 and again from 1511 until his departure from Italy for Metz in 1518 that one cannot be positive, as Prost thinks, that there is no period when Agrippa could have completed his studies for a degree. Second, it is clear that Agrippa spent much of this period in university towns and in touch with university circles. Third, there is no doubt that Agrippa was commonly acknowledged a doctor, at Metz, for example.[6] Finally, it is un-

[5] For the date of his enrollment and of his degree from Cologne, see *Matrikel*, ed. Keussen, *loc. cit.* The claim to the triple doctorate is not uncommon. For example, Agrippa to Theodoricus, Bishop of Cyrene, Metz, 6 February 1518, in Lyons, Bibliothèque Municipale, MS. No. 48, fol. 32r-v: ". . . Post vtriusque iuris ac medicine (vt meorum desiderio satisfacerem: qui me doctorem malunt quam doctum) acceptis scholastico more tiaris et annulis, ad sacras literas quamuis sero toto me studio contuli. . . ." The substance of this letter is printed as *Epist.* II, xix. Cf. *Epist.* VI, xxii; VII, xxi; and *De beatissimae Annae monogamia*, fol. M8r. Prost, *op. cit.*, I, 127 *et seq.*; II, 70-94, 441-51. The hint of a doctorate from Pavia in his lecture on the *Pimander*, in *Opera*, II, 1083-84: "Vosque celeberrimi viri me in armis militem, in literis nunc doctorem, vobisque devotum addictumque pectus meum benigno animo suscipite." If "nunc doctorem" refers to a formal title rather than merely the function of teaching, "nunc" would suggest that the degree was very recent. The letter of a friend written in 1522 (*Epist.* III, xv) suggests an Italian education for Agrippa, who is called "oriundus Colonia, educatione Italus."

[6] Prost, *loc. cit.*, is probably right in discounting the appearance of the legal doctorates in the imperial license printed on the verso of the title page of *De occulta philosophia libri tres* (Coloniae, 1533), for the imperial chancery

deniable that he possessed considerable knowledge both in medicine and in law; and while his practice of medicine may have been based on his broad general knowledge, especially in alchemy, as Prost claims, his ability to cite points of law and to draw up legal briefs, as well as the probable demands of his public duties as *orateur* of the city of Metz, make it likely that he had formal legal training.[7] Even in the case of his claim to a medical doctorate, the frequent gaps in knowledge about his earlier years, even as late as his departure from Italy in 1518, would leave plenty of time for him to have taken a degree. Medical degrees in the early sixteenth century were often given within a few months after matriculation,[8] and Agrippa's multifarious learning on questions of natural and occult philosophy would doubtless have enabled him to qualify far more rapidly than the great majority of those who studied in the medical faculties. The question of his doctorates cannot be answered with a positive affirmative, but neither can it be decided with so firm a negative as Prost claims. Whatever degrees he may have possessed, Agrippa certainly acquired a mastery of the traditional four faculties: arts, medicine, law, and even theology (a field in which he claimed special studies but no formal degree). Like Faust he mastered all fields of learning and found all of them equally dissatisfying.

In any case, there is no doubt that Agrippa was exposed to the influence of the arts faculty of Cologne. This university was one of the chief centers of Thomism in the late fifteenth century. Although there was a factional split in the faculty, this was not, as at Paris

---

may have written his titles just as he proposed them, without investigating their validity. But the records of Metz, printed by Prost himself, *op. cit.*, II, 473-74 (Appendix XIII), regularly refer to Agrippa as "maistre Henry Cornelis, docteur," "maistre Henry Cornelis, di Agrippa, orateur et licencié en chacun droit," and "maistre Henry Cornelis, le docteur." Cf. H. Follet, "Un médecin astrologue au temps de la Renaissance, Henri Cornelius Agrippa," *Nouvelle Revue*, XCVIII (1896), 307.

[7] For Agrippa's medical knowledge, see *Contra pestem antidota*, in *Opera*, II, 578-82, and incidental references in his correspondence. His legal knowledge appears in his briefs defending the accused witch of Woippy, 1519, printed in *De beatissimae Annae monogamia*, fols. R1r-R7v, and R7v-S5v. These documents appear greatly abridged in *Epist.* II, xxxviii-xxxix. Cf. also the remark of his friend Theodoricus Wichwael in a letter of 29 November 1509, *Epist.* I, xxi: "quando apud nos causas ageres." Could this refer to the study of law, as well as to pleading of cases?

[8] V. L. Saulnier, "Médecins de Montpellier au temps de Rabelais," *Bibliothèque d'Humanisme et Renaissance*, XIX (1957), 432, shows that at Montpellier many students received their diplomas in six months or less, and the great majority within less than two years after matriculation.

and elsewhere, between the Thomists (*antiqui*) and the Terminists (*moderni*) but between the Thomists, who generally had the upper hand, and the Albertists, those who preferred the authority of the great native doctor, Albertus Magnus.[9] Perhaps it was from this Albertist influence that Agrippa drew his lively interest in the natural world and the occult connections between its parts, for Albert was much interested in natural philosophy. Agrippa himself strengthens this conjecture by tracing his magical studies back to his earliest youth and naming Albertus' *Speculum* as one of the first texts that he studied on this subject.[10]

His occultist works also drew very heavily on the *Natural History* of Pliny the Elder; and very likely his introduction to this important ancient scientific encyclopedist occurred during his youthful studies at Cologne. In his later denunciation of the Cologne faculty, one of the charges he made was that the masters had compelled the learned Johannes Rack von Sommerfeld (Aesticampanus, 1460-1520) to suspend his lectures on Pliny and even to leave the city. Since Sommerfeld spent the early years of the sixteenth century lecturing at various German universities, including Cologne, Agrippa may well have derived some of his enthusiasm for Pliny from hearing him lecture, even though he did not specifically call Aesticampanus a former teacher of his.[11]

It is highly probable that during these early studies at Cologne or during his brief return to that city in 1507 Agrippa first learned of a writer who influenced his approach to both human reason and natural science, Ramon Lull. In the preface to his *In artem brevem Raymundi Lullii*, Agrippa reveals that his teacher in this Lullian art was Andreas Canterius, one of a Frisian family whose members were the wonder of their age for learning, a learning which Agrippa attributes to their mastery of Lull. This Andreas Canter, already

[9] For conditions at Cologne in this period, see Johann Meurer, *Zur Logik des Heinrich Cornelius Agrippa* (Bonn, 1913), pp. 2-4.

[10] Agrippa to Theodoricus, Bishop of Cyrene, Metz, 6 February 1518 (1519, n.s.), in Lyons, Bibliothèque Municipale, MS. No. 48, fols. 31v-32r: "En tute in parte nosti, quemadmodum post dialecticam; naturaliumque rerum peruestigationem, insuper totam celorum militiam perlustrarim: ducibus duabus illis magnis magni alberti sapientiis; quas in speculo suo; opusculo non admodum laudato: describit."

[11] Agrippa to Senate of Cologne, Bonn, 11 January 1533, *Epist.* VII, xxvi. On Rack von Sommerfeld, see Ludwig Geiger, art. "Aesticampanus, Joh. Rhagius," *Allgemeine deutsche Biographie*, I, 133-34, and *Matrikel*, ed. Keussen, II, 44. Cf. Paola Zambelli, "A proposito del 'De vanitate scientiarum et artium' di Cornelio Agrippa," *Rivista critica di storia della filosofia*, XV (1960), 171. Aesticampanus lectured at Cologne on both Pliny and St. Augustine.

such a marvel for learning that matriculation fees were waived, entered the University of Cologne on 14 July 1491, and he was still living at Cologne in 1509.[12] Thus he was quite possibly in touch with Agrippa during the latter's undergraduate years from 1499 to 1502.

The Nettesheimer had very little to say about the university itself until 1533, when, finding that some of the professors were instrumental in impeding publication of his *De occulta philosophia*, he directed against the university a violent diatribe addressed to the senate of the city. Then he described the doctors of the university as slavish followers of Aristotle and Averroes, two pagan philosophers most hostile to Christian teachings, and of Thomas and Albert, who taught the doctrines of the same pagans. The faculty members were mere sophists. "What is surprising, therefore, since your university is in the hands of this kind of trunks and posts, if all good arts are compelled to flee from your city?"[13] The Dominicans and other theologians at Cologne, he charged, had conspired to drive all good letters from Germany. No longer did students from abroad flock to study there. This bitter attack also decries the general ignorance and depraved morals of the masters of Cologne and gives examples from Agrippa's personal knowledge of their ignorance and vice. But all this was written in 1533, and one cannot be sure that already at the turn of the century Agrippa had such hostile feelings toward the university.

Despite Agrippa's later attack on the university, his experience there left him with interests that persisted throughout his life. He must have become familiar with scholastic philosophy. He probably

[12] The Canter family is celebrated in the anonymous *Die Cronica van der hilliger stat van Coellen 1499*, printed in *Die Chroniken der deutschen Städte*, ed. C. Hegel (Leipzig, 1877), XIV, 876-77; and in Johannes Butzbach, *Auctarium Joan. Boutzbachii de scriptoribus ecclesiasticis*, partially edited by Karl Krafft and Wilhelm Crecelius, "Mittheilungen über Alexander Hegius und seine Schüler, sowie andere gleichzeitige Gelehrte, aus den Werken des Johannes Butzbach, Priors des Benedictiner-Klosters am Laacher See," *Zeitschrift des bergischen Geschichtsvereins*, VII (1871), 273-75. A good brief summary of knowledge about this celebrated family is in P. S. Allen's note to a letter of Erasmus to a brother of this Andreas, *Opus epistolarum Des. Erasmi Roterodami*, ed. P. S. Allen [and H. M. Allen and H. W. Garrod] (12 vols.; Oxonii, 1906-58), I, 125-26 (No. 32). None of these accounts mentions the Lullian art.

[13] Agrippa to Senate of Cologne, Bonn, 11 January 1533, *Epist.* VII, xxvi (*Opera*, II, 1035): "Quid mirum ergo, cum in ejusmodi truncorum et stipitum manibus vestra Vniuersitas consistat, si omnes bonae artes a civitate vestra exculare cogantur?"

studied the logical works of Ramon Lull and so came into touch with an extreme form of rationalism, a rationalism that Lull himself and his disciples applied to occult sciences. Also, the influence of Albertus Magnus doubtless had much to do with arousing in him an interest in natural philosophy and especially in magic. Despite all his intellectual struggles, this interest never left him. Finally, his enthusiasm for Pliny the Elder, from whom he drew much material for *De occulta philosophia*, went back to the Cologne period.

Agrippa's activities from his graduation in 1502 to the beginning of his surviving correspondence in 1507 are, with one exception, a total blank. His biographers have often guessed that he entered the service of the Hapsburg family as an undersecretary or as a soldier and that if he really did receive knighthood as he claimed, it may have been in this period.[14] It is quite possible that he stayed on in Cologne as a student, perhaps of law or medicine. But these are mere conjectures unsupported by any evidence.

Sometime prior to 28 March 1507, when an Italian fellow student, Landulphus, wrote him "ex Academia Parisiaca," Agrippa transferred his studies from Cologne to the University of Paris. On that particular date, Agrippa was in Cologne; but he intended to return to France and sent greetings to friends there. His letters and writings contain no hint of what he studied at Paris, but one student of Agrippa's thought has noted certain traces of Parisian philosophical influence in his commentary on the Lullian art. In general, this work depends on logical doctrines common to most of the scholastics; but his usage of certain terms betrays the influence of Duns Scotus and even of Occamite nominalism as taught by the strong Terminist faction at the University of Paris.[15] This acquaintance with the Occamist tradition was one factor in Agrippa's later elaboration of skepticism.

That economic considerations forced Agrippa's return to his native city is just another of the many conjectures of his biogra-

---

[14] Henry Morley, *The Life of Henry Cornelius Agrippa von Nettesheim* . . . (2 vols.; London, 1856), I, 15, 17-19, 21-23, gives a largely imaginary account of Agrippa's service to the Emperor Maximilian in this period and suggests that even in Paris he was an imperial agent posing as a student. Joseph Orsier, *Henri Cornélis Agrippa, sa vie et son oeuvre d'après sa correspondance (1486-1535)* (Paris, 1911), pp. 11-12, is unclear but apparently thinks that Agrippa spent much of the period 1501-07 in military service. He did claim to have been in imperial military and diplomatic service, but these claims probably refer to later periods, especially his years in Italy.

[15] Meurer, *op. cit.*, p. 56. The correspondence with Landulphus is printed as *Epist.* I, i-iii.

phers, although it is clear that while there he tried to win the favor of an unnamed but wealthy patron.[16] It may be that he returned to Cologne to study. Whether this was his motive or not, it is most probable that while there he heard the lectures of the celebrated legal scholar, Peter of Ravenna, who began teaching at Cologne at the very end of 1506 and continued there till just after Easter of 1508, when he left for Mainz, partly because of the controversies in which the jealousy of the native doctors, especially the theologian Jacob Hochstraten, had involved him. Agrippa later denounced the Cologne faculty for its attacks on this legal scholar, whom he described as "formerly my teacher." [17] Since Peter probably died at Mainz in 1508 or early in 1509 without returning to his native Italy, their contact must have occurred during the scant year and a half that Peter spent in Cologne.

What followed Agrippa's return to France at some uncertain date, probably in early 1508, is one of the most puzzling episodes in the man's biography. It is clear from the letters of Agrippa and his friends Landulphus and Galbianus for 1508 and early 1509 that an expedition to Spain, which they had planned as early as 1507, really did materialize. Agrippa's own account of this adventure clearly refers to a military expedition intended to seize a fortified place near Barcelona from a band of rebellious peasants. The expedition fell between April, 1508, when Agrippa was about to set out, and December 20 of the same year, by which time he was safe in Avignon after searching Catalonia, Valencia, Naples, and the Ligurian coast for traces of friends whom the failure of the enterprise had forced to flee. No one has been able to identify satisfactorily either the events or the local place-names in Agrippa's account of the adventure; but even the skeptical Prost, while doubting the accuracy of Agrippa's relation of events, is not willing to regard the whole episode as apocryphal.[18]

[16] *Epist.* I, ii.
[17] *De beatissimae Annae monogamia*, fol. M5v: "quondam praeceptorem meum Petrum Rauennatem." On Peter, see the extensive article by Eisenhart in *Allgemeine deutsche Biographie*, XXV, 529-39. He was also famous for his writings on mnemonics, according to Paolo Rossi, *Clavis universalis: Arti mnemoniche e logica combinatoria da Lullo a Leibniz* (Milan, 1960), pp. 27-30.
[18] The narrative appears in correspondence between Agrippa and his friends, *Epist.* I, iv-x, especially *Epist.* I, x. Morley, *op. cit.*, I, 15-57, has identified the various events and places with the use of much imagination but little evidence. Prost, *op. cit.*, I, 132-52, and II, 466-69 (Appendix XI), reports his failure to identify the place-names, despite the aid of the Spanish historian Don Manuel Milá y Fontanals.

Two facts of some significance stand out clearly amid all the confusion of this Spanish episode. One is that Agrippa and his associates had hoped to gain great fame and wealth by their service in Spain and had also intended to continue their co-operation by going to Italy. The other is that their short-lived military success had depended on contrivances of some sort by means of which Agrippa had been able to capture the fortification which had been the object of the enterprise.[19] All else is obscure. One cannot even be sure that the king in whose name Agrippa and his companions were acting was Ferdinand of Aragon, although this conjecture seems likely. Despite the reference to the proximity of Barcelona, Castile rather than Aragon is the probable locale of the adventure. Certainly Castile in this period, after the deaths of Queen Isabella and Philip the Handsome, and before King Ferdinand had firmly re-established his own control, was the scene of many political intrigues on the part of France, the Papacy, and the Empire. Not until 12 December 1509 did the Emperor Maximilian I abandon his intrigues with the nobility of that country.[20] This general area may be the locale of Agrippa's expedition. It is also possible that the adventure took place in the Pyrenean kingdom of Navarre, for this region, too, was the scene of military and political intrigues throughout the first decade of the century. The best guess is that Agrippa had with the aid of explosives or other fruits of his alchemical studies helped his

[19] Plans for the trip to Spain and then to Italy went back to 1507: *Epist.* I, iii. For Agrippa's mention of his military contrivances, *Epist.* I, x. Antonio Bernárdez, *Enrique Cornelio Agripa, filósofo, astrólogo y cronista de Carlos V* (Madrid, 1934), pp. 22-23, conjectures that Agrippa had put down a peasant revolt "con el empleo de métodos destructores de pirotecnia, cuyo secreto ofrecieron a Fernando V."

[20] Kurt Kaser, *Deutsche Geschichte zur Zeit Maximilians I (1486-1519)* (Stuttgart, 1912), for general historical background on Maximilian. Helda Bullotta Barracco, "Saggio bio-bibliografico su Enrico Cornelio Agrippa di Nettesheim," in Rome, Università, Istituto di Filosofia, *Rassegna di Filosofia*, VI, No. 3 (luglio-settembre, 1957), 223-24, states flatly that the king whom Agrippa was serving was Ferdinand of Aragon. This is a sensible conjecture. Less convincing is her statement that Agrippa was still in Ferdinand's service during his flying visit to Italy and Provence. Her conclusion that Agrippa became a knight (*auratus eques*) at this time is possible, but she is flatly wrong in equating this title with membership in the exclusive Order of the Golden Fleece. On the disturbed political conditions in Castile at this period, see Antonio Ballester y Beretta, *Historia de España y su influencia en la historia universal*, V (2nd ed.; Barcelona, 1946), 285-98. On the disturbed situation in Navarre, *ibid.*, V., 320-24. Cf. Roger Bigelow Merriman, *The Rise of the Spanish Empire in the Old World and in the New* (4 vols.; New York, 1918-34), II, 318-34.

friend Janotus suppress a local uprising of peasants on the latter's estates somewhere in northern Spain.[21] What larger significance this exploit had, if any, remains a matter for conjecture.

After making good his escape from the rebellious peasants, Agrippa, in the company of an aged man, Antonius Xanthus, who had been an interpreter for the Turks and may have been a Greek refugee, sought news of Landulphus, first at Barcelona, and then at Valencia from "Comparatus the Saracen, a skilled philosopher and astrologer, and formerly a disciple of Zacutus." [22] Since the friends had originally planned to go from Spain to Italy, Agrippa made a brief but fruitless trip to Italy, seeking Landulphus at Naples and then returning along the Ligurian coast to Avignon, where he finally learned from a merchant that his friend was safe at Lyons.

The letters of this early period prove that Agrippa and his associates had formed some kind of secret society which probably went back to their student days at Paris. The very earliest letters contain hints of deep secrets not to be entrusted to writing, as well as alchemical phrases that probably reflect one of the chief interests of the group. The society appears to have been a mutual-help association pledged to the enrichment of its members in both worldly and intellectual goods. Out of these associations grew the Spanish adventure. That the society was a brotherhood with definite organization and secrets is clear from Agrippa's report that, finding his companion Xanthus trustworthy, he had instructed him and admitted him "into the oath of our society," [23] as also from the following recommendation of a candidate for membership by Landulphus:

[21] The friend Janotus, who was central to the whole affair, was apparently a Basque: *Epist.* I, ii. Others of Agrippa's friends at Paris, not all of them involved in the adventure, were "D. Germanum Ganeum, et Carolum Focardum, D. de Molinflor . . . D. de Charona," the Italian Landulphus, and Galbianus, Bovillus, Clarocampensis, Brixianus, Adam, Fascius, Wigandus, Perrotus, and Stephanus. Some of these names may be Spanish. (In the quoted portion, I have dropped a comma which Agrippa's *Opera* prints after *Germanum*.)

[22] *Epist.* I, x. The reference to Zacuto reflects the occultist interests of the Agrippan circle, for he was a noted astronomer of the period (see *The Jewish Encyclopedia*, XII, 627). One of Agrippa's closest friends later in Italy, Augustinus Ritius, was also a pupil of Zacuto, according to François Secret, *Le Zôhar chez les Kabbalistes chrétiens de la Renaissance* (Paris, 1958), pp. 11-12. The name Xanthus sounds as if this friend were a Greek.

[23] Agrippa to Landulphus, Avignon, 20 December 1508, *Epist.* I, viii: ". . . Quem ego iam comprobatum instructumque, in nostri sodalitii sacramentum ascivi."

And he is a curious investigator of arcane matters, and a free man, restrained by no bonds, who, impelled by I know not what reputation of yours, wishes to search through your secrets also. Hence I want you to explore the man thoroughly, and so that he reveals to you the scope of his mind; indeed, in my opinion, his aim is not far from the mark, and experience of great things is in him in certain respects. Then, therefore, fly from north to south, on all sides winged with Mercurial wings, and if it is permitted, embrace Jove's scepters and make him, if he wants to swear to our rules, an initiate of our society.[24]

Small wonder that Agrippa has seemed a founding father to later secret and occultist groups! Apparently he was the central figure of the confraternity.

These earliest surviving pieces of Agrippa's correspondence show that in company with a brotherhood of like-minded persons, Agrippa was seeking to make his career on the basis of his growing reputation for profound knowledge of ancient sources of wisdom. The brotherhood was secret because ancient wisdom would be dangerous to society unless confined to the restricted circle of true lovers of learning. This "gnostic" or occultist attitude, the belief that certain kinds of knowledge might be safely studied by a tightly knit group of initiates, but must be kept from the view of the ignorant and depraved masses of humanity, was quite common in that age. In particular, Neoplatonists like Marsilio Ficino conducted studies of antique (or pseudo-antique) sources which they admitted would be dangerous to religion and to society if not carefully kept from the hands of the profane—an attitude fully shared by Agrippa and his own circle of friends.[25] Magical, astrological, alchemical, and cabalistic studies were almost always regarded as esoteric, that is, unsuited to public disclosure. Indeed, such occult knowledge regularly tended to develop semireligious expressions that could hardly be reconciled with strict Christian orthodoxy, try as the occultists might to effect such a reconciliation. In a few extreme cases, in fact,

[24] Landulphus to Agrippa, Lyons, 4 February 1509, *Epist.* I, xi: ". . . Estque rerum arcanarum curiosus indagator, et homo liber, nullis irretitus vinculis, qui, nescio, qua fama tua impulsus, tuum quoque perlustrare cupit abyssum. Vellem ergo profunde virum explorares, atque tibi ut suae mentis indicaret jaculum. non procul siquidem a scopo, meo judicio, sagittat, et magnarum rerum experientia apud eum in aliquibus extat. Tum ergo ab Aquilone in Austrum vola, undique Mercurialibus pennatus alis, et Iovis si lubet, sceptra amplectere, atque illum, si in nostra velit jurare capitula, nostro sodalitio adscitum face."

[25] D. P. Walker, *Spiritual and Demonic Magic from Ficino to Campanella* (London, 1958), p. 51; Paul Oskar Kristeller, *The Philosophy of Marsilio Ficino,* trans. Virginia Conant (New York, 1943), pp. 25-27.

interest in ancient esoteric wisdom produced overt expressions of mystical, semipagan, syncretistic religious faith that was only tenuously Christian. A good example of this tendency is the appearance in Rome and in Florence of the obscure but fantastic figure of Mercurio da Correggio in the late fifteenth century.[26] There is nothing to show that Agrippa and his own occultist friends went so far as did Mercurio and his disciple Ludovico Lazzarelli, for that pair and their followers constituted what amounted to a secret religious sect.[27] But Agrippa and his young associates in France and later in Italy,[28] if not quite a Hermetic religious sect, did form a fairly well-defined secret group of investigators of an ancient wisdom thought to be concealed in such texts as the Hermetic literature, the Cabala, the Orphic hymns, and Neoplatonic philosophy.[29] This brotherhood produced, in the form of Agrippa's own *De occulta philosophia*, one of the most important and influential pieces of Renaissance occultist literature.

The objectives of such occultist groups as Agrippa's easily passed beyond mere attainment of knowledge about ancient sources of wisdom, and beyond mere religious exaltation. The ties of the initiates based on their common studies would become so intimate that the members of the brotherhood would help one another in all sorts

[26] Walker, *op. cit.*, pp. 30-35, argues that even in the thought of Ficino and his disciple Francesco Cattani da Diacceto, pursuit of esoteric knowledge and the accompanying astrological and magical practices came near to involving non-Christian religious rites. In the case of Mercurio da Correggio and Lazzarelli, this heterodox religious element became explicit, as Mercurio re-enacted the role of Christ and declared himself to be a reincarnation of the divine *Pimander* of Hermetic literature. See Paul Oskar Kristeller, "Marsilio Ficino e Lodovico Lazzarelli: Contributo alla diffusione delle idee Ermetiche nel Rinascimento," in his *Studies in Renaissance Thought and Letters* (Rome, 1956), pp. 227-32, 236-40; *idem*, "Ancora per Giovanni Mercurio da Correggio," *ibid.*, pp. 249-57; *idem*, "Lodovico Lazzarelli e Giovanni Mercurio da Correggio, due ermetici del Quattrocento, e il manoscritto II.D.I.4 della Biblioteca Comunale degli Ardenti di Viterbo," in Biblioteca degli Ardenti della Città di Viterbo, *Studi e ricerche nel 150° della fondazione* (Viterbo, 1960), pp. 13-37.
[27] Kristeller, *Studies*, p. 229.
[28] Paolo Zambelli, ed., "Cornelio Agrippa di Nettesheim: Testi scelti," in *Testi umanistici su l'Ermetismo*, ed. Eugenio Garin *et al.* (Rome, 1955), pp. 110-11; cf. *eadem*, ed., "Agrippa di Nettesheim, *Dialogus de homine*," *Rivista critica di storia della filosofia*, XIII (1958), 53, and my article, "Agrippa in Renaissance Italy: The Esoteric Tradition," *Studies in the Renaissance*, VI (1959), 197, 202-4.
[29] For discussions linking the whole concept of Renaissance, as viewed by contemporaries, with the attempt to revive Neoplatonic philosophy and the various occult traditions associated with it, see Kristeller, *Philosophy of Marsilio Ficino*, pp. 20-29, and D. P. Walker, "The Prisca Theologia in France," *Journal of the Warburg and Courtauld Institutes*, XVII (1954), 204-59.

of practical ways. Immediately on Agrippa's arrival in Avignon late in 1508, and repeatedly during his many later changes of residence, his fellows smoothed his way and promoted his worldly success by helping him find patrons and gainful employment.

This fraternal sense that linked Agrippa and his friends was not, however, the only tangible gain supposed to grow out of their association. The study of such ancient wisdom as was contained in the Hermetic books, the Orphic hymns, the Cabala of the Hebrews, and similar traditions, was no mere literary exercise. Occult study implied elevation of the soul by ancient truth, and not just acceptance of that truth. This fact was the real reason for the religious or semireligious expressions which often accompanied esoteric studies. But the aims of studying the occult went beyond elevation of the mind and praise of God. Neoplatonism and the many forms of occultism that were related to it taught clearly that once the mind of man had been illuminated by ancient wisdom and elevated to a state of religious exaltation, that mind became endowed with vast powers and was even able to draw down celestial power from above. In a literal sense, knowledge was power. Holding such beliefs, the occultists of the Renaissance naturally and easily passed from study and exaltation to attempts to make practical application of the vast reserves of human and celestial energy that the illumined human soul had at its disposal. Magical and alchemical operations, both of which occupied Agrippa and his friends at various times throughout his life, were attempts to win such practical benefits—wealth, fame, and power over mankind and over nature—from the wisdom available in ancient sources. Those sources offered not just practical details of correct procedure for magical incantations or alchemical experiments, but far more important, the spiritual power needed for works which were ordinarily beyond human capabilities.[30]

The identification of Agrippa's earliest occultist friends in France

[30] For an illuminating discussion of the relation of magic to Renaissance culture, with treatment of Pico della Mirandola and the Agrippan circle, see Eugenio Garin, "Magia ed astrologia nella cultura del Rinascimento," in his *Medioevo e Rinascimento: Studi e ricerche* (Bari, 1954), pp. 150-69, and "Considerazioni sulla magia," *ibid.*, pp. 170-91. Kristeller, *Studies*, p. 257, has shown that Lazzarelli, if not himself a practitioner of alchemy, was a pupil of the alchemist Joannes Richardus de Branchiis of Burgundy. He also shows, *ibid.*, p. 226, that Lazzarelli was accused of magical practices. For all his circumspection, even Ficino believed that the illuminated soul has both prophetic and magical powers (Kristeller, *Philosophy of Marsilio Ficino*, pp. 309-15). D. P. Walker, *Spiritual and Demonic Magic*, pp. 12-24, 45-53, insists that Ficino himself engaged in rites like the singing of Orphic hymns which were intended to have magical effects.

is exceedingly difficult, even though the early portions of his published correspondence are full of suggestive clues. Certain names, such as those of his Italian friend Landulphus, or Galbianus, Antonius Xanthus, Carolus Focardus, Adam, and Fascius, doubtless belonged to obscure friends whose identity is lost forever.[31] The identity of others is relatively easy to establish, such as the noted court painter Jean Perréal, whose presence at Lyons is mentioned in a letter that Agrippa wrote from Dôle in 1509, and to whom Agrippa sent friendly greetings much later while he himself lived at Fribourg and at Lyons.[32] Likewise the Geoffroi Brulart, French royal treasurer, whom Agrippa saw at Berne in 1523 and described as an enthusiast for occult learning and as a friend of "more than twenty years'" standing, is an identifiable historical figure, member of an important family of *noblesse de la robe*, and intendant for the province of Champagne.[33] This connection is significant because it shows Agrippa's early acquaintance with one of that group of official families with whom he was in close touch while he lived at the French court in the 1520's. Certain other identifications of his friends can be made only tentatively, largely on the basis of similarity of name. During his Spanish adventure, for instance, Agrippa had a companion surnamed Perrotus. Could this man be that Émile or Miles Perrot who in the early 1520's was a humanistic teacher of grammar at the Collège du Cardinal Lemoine, and who was a friend of the reformer Guillaume Farel? This identification is purely conjectural and is based entirely on similarity of name.[34] But if Agrippa did know this man or some close relative of his, it would establish an early link between him and the reform-minded French humanists whom he certainly knew at a later date.

Other associations of Agrippa with French humanists at this early

[31] Yet the family name Landolfo does occur in the records of the University of Pavia, and a certain Rafaello Landolfo of Pavia became professor of civil law there in 1520: *Memorie e documenti per la storia dell' Università di Pavia e degli uomini più illustri che v'insegnarono* (3 vols.; Pavia, 1878), I, 73.

[32] *Epist.* I, xvii; III, liv; V, vii-viii. The Ioannes Parisiensis Pictor with whom Agrippa was friendly must have been Perréal, who was known as "John of Paris."

[33] *Epist.* III, xl: "mihi ante annos viginti semper amicissimus." Cf. M. Prévost, art. "Brulart," *Dictionnaire de biographie française*, VII, col. 487-88.

[34] *Epist.* I, x. For Perrot, see Pierre Imbart de la Tour, *Les origines de la Réforme* (4 vols.; Paris, 1905-35), III, 182-83, and Jean Jalla, "Farel et les Vaudois du Piémont," in [Comité Farel], *Guillaume Farel, 1489-1565* (Neuchâtel, 1930), p. 289; cf. *ibid.*, pp. 114-16. One difficulty with this identification is that Émile Perrot was a student of law at Turin from 1528. Could he have been old enough to participate in the adventure of 1508?

date have frequently been suggested by his biographers through similar conjectural identifications of his circle of friends. If true, they should contribute to an understanding of occultist tendencies within early Gallic humanism. It does seem possible that Agrippa's friend Ganaeus was the humanist Germain de Ganay, that his Brixianus was the Hellenist Germain de Brie, and even that his Bovillus was the well-known humanist Charles de Bouelles.[35] The latter certainly would have attracted Agrippa by his combination of mathematical, philosophical, and theological learning; and his work may have brought the writings of Trithemius of Sponheim to Agrippa's attention, even though his own attitude to the magic of Trithemius was so hostile that his attack on the Abbot of Sponheim gave rise to a notable scandal.[36] All these conjectures about Agrippa's earliest French friends are made more probable by yet another hypothetical identification. This is the conjecture that the friend whom Agrippa calls *Clarocampensis* was that prolific popularizer of humanistic ideas, Symphorien Champier. There is far more evidence for this identification than for the others, even though *Champerius*, not *Clarocampensis*, was the usual Latinized form of *Champier*. Evidence

[35] These names occur in Latinized form in Agrippa's letters for 1506-09: *Epist.* I, ii, viii, ix, x, xii. These identifications are purely conjectural, though Morley, *op. cit.*, I, 54-55, makes them with confidence. With rather greater reservations, he identifies Agrippa's friend Wigandus (*Epist.* I, viii) with the Dominican Wirt or Wigandus who was burned at Basel in 1509 for denying the Immaculate Conception. In *Epist.* I, ix, Bovillus' Christian name appears as Supplicius, not Carolus.

[36] In 1509, Bouelles issued an attack on Trithemius for commerce with demons which he claimed to have discovered in the abbot's *Steganographia*. This letter of Bouelles was addressed to Germain de Ganay, who may be identical with Agrippa's French friend Ganaeus. See Walker, *Spiritual and Demonic Magic*, pp. 86-87, and Paola Zambelli, "A proposito del 'De vanitate scientiarum et artium' di Cornelio Agrippa," *Rivista critica di storia della filosofia*, XV (1960), 176-77, and the preface to Signorina Zambelli's edition of some Agrippan texts in *Testi umanistici su l'Ermetismo*, p. 111. Ganay was also the recipient of another letter expressing concern about the orthodoxy of magical practices, this one from Ficino's pupil Francesco da Diacceto, expressing doubt about the "spiritual" magic which he had derived from Ficino: Walker, *Spiritual and Demonic Magic*, pp. 34-35. Agrippa himself knew of Ganay's attack on Trithemius, for a friend, probably Johannes Lagrenus, guardian of the Franciscan friary of St. Bonaventure at Lyons, in 1522 referred to it and sought his judgment on Trithemius: *Epist.* III, xxxiii. Agrippa possessed a manuscript of the *Steganographia* (which was not printed until 1606): Agrippa to Brennonius, Cologne, 20 June 1520, *Epist.* II, lvii. Despite his attack on Trithemius, Bouelles (who himself may have been one of Agrippa's circle of French friends) was interested in occult wisdom, as shown by Walker, "Prisca Theologia," *loc. cit.*, 214-17.

to support this association between the youthful Agrippa and Champier is varied. For one thing, not only were both men active in introducing Italian ideas into France, but both later became members of the faculty of the University of Pavia in Italy at the same time, in 1515, Agrippa in the arts faculty and Champier in the faculty of medicine.[37] Second, Champier himself in a work published in 1508 gave a valuable list of his friends. Among his teachers he listed a German, Cornelius, who may be Agrippa, though this identification is not very likely.[38] Finally, it is significant that Champier was one of the leading French enthusiasts for Neoplatonic and occultist learning; that his own works were published along with the texts of Hermes Trismegistus, Ludovico Lazzarelli, and Jacques Lefèvre d'Étaples in the edition which Agrippa must have used; and that in Champier's thought there are even traces of Agrippa's peculiarly ambivalent attitude toward magic and the powers of human reason.[39] The whole French humanistic school, which was led by Lefèvre and which included Champier, Bouelles, Brie, and Ganay, shared the occultist enthusiasms of late fifteenth-century Italian humanism, though with far greater reservations than the Italians

[37] For Champier, see *Memorie e documenti*, I, 122. For Agrippa's connection with Pavia, see the next chapter.

[38] *De triplici disciplina* (Lugduni, 1508), fol. C7v: "Primum inter amicos locum preceptores nostri iure optimo sibi vendicant . . . . In artibus et philosophia. Cornelius ostendit germanus." Paola Zambelli, "Umanesimo magico-astrologico e raggruppamenti segreti nei Platonici della Preriforma," in *Umanesimo e esoterismo: Atti del V convegno internazionale di studi umanistici, Oberhofen, 16-17 settembre 1960*, ed. Enrico Castelli (Padua, 1960), p. 154, flatly states that this Cornelius was Agrippa. This is not very likely, for there is no other evidence that Agrippa taught prior to his appearance at Dôle in 1509; and James B. Wadsworth, *Lyons 1473-1503: The Beginnings of Cosmopolitanism* (Cambridge, Massachusetts, 1962), p. 94, n. 6, notes that this Cornelius has been tentatively identified as Cornelius Oudendyk. Yet Champier's list does include others whom Agrippa certainly knew before he moved to Lyons in 1524, such as André Bryau, the royal physician; Jacques Lefèvre d'Étaples; and the physician Denys Thurini of Lyons; also the royal physician Jean Chapelain, his best friend at the French court between 1525 and 1528. So some acquaintance with Champier is likely, even if Agrippa was not the Cornelius who taught Champier. On Champier, Bryau, and the intellectual life of Lyons in the early sixteenth century, see Wadsworth, *op. cit.*, especially pp. 73-93, 156-60.

[39] In fact, Champier later, under Lutheran influence, showed a tendency akin to Agrippa's rejection of all learning except the Gospel: Walker, "Prisca Theologia," *loc. cit.*, 204-8, 210-12, 231, 234-35, 253-54. Cf. Kristeller, *Studies*, pp. 224-27, for the Hermetic editions. For Champier's authorship of a critique of magic entitled *Dialogus in magicarum artium destructionem*, see Dr. Zambelli's article on Agrippa in *Rivista critica di storia della filosofia*, XV, 176-77. Cf. Wadsworth, *op. cit.*, pp. 80-93.

showed.[40] Merely on the strength of this fact alone, one would expect Agrippa to have sought out these individuals during his earliest period of travel and study in France. Hence even though the evidence for his connection with Champier, Bouelles, and others is not absolutely conclusive, the likelihood is fairly strong. Such connection would also explain why later at Metz he rushed to the defense of Lefèvre, whom he had never met.

Agrippa's first concern on reaching Avignon was to get in touch with the members of this secret society, whoever they may have been. Before he could join them, however, he had to get money, for he had reached Avignon in poverty. He informed Landulphus that he had set up "our usual alchemical shop" [41] and that he planned to keep working until he had enough money to reach Lyons. Such activities would hardly have given him the necessary resources, unless perchance Bernárdez is right in identifying his alchemical work as false coinage.[42] It is more likely that Agrippa really was trying to secure the quintessence or *spiritus mundi* from gold and use it to make more gold from base metals, a procedure which he later claimed to know perfectly but which, he admitted, did not yield more gold than the quantity from which he had originally taken the *spiritus mundi*. His experiments along these lines continued throughout his life. At Metz and in Switzerland he associated with persons who regularly conducted alchemical experiments. At Lyons in 1526, he apparently still hoped to grow gold from certain seeds that a friend had brought him; and his letters for the summer of 1529, when he was residing at Antwerp, are full of reports on the progress of alchemical experiments, which he regarded as successful but not so lucrative as he had hoped.[43]

---

[40] Zambelli, in *Rivista critica di storia della filosofia*, XV, 169-70; Walker, "Prisca Theologia," *loc. cit.*, 204.

[41] Letter of 24 January 1509, *Epist.* I, x (*Opera*, II, 687): "instructa solita nostra chrysotoci officina."

[42] Bernárdez, *op. cit.*, pp. 44-45.

[43] Agrippa, *De occulta philosophia libri tres* (Coloniae, 1533), Bk. I, ch. xiv, p. xix. Agrippa's friends at Metz, especially Tyrius, were most interested in alchemy; and while Agrippa laughed at Tyrius' excesses, he also wanted to be kept informed of the results of his work. See Agrippa to Brennonius, Cologne, 15 June 1520, *Epist.* II, lii, and other letters of the same period. In 1526, Agrippa was still receiving reports about Tyrius: Brennonius to Agrippa, Metz, 23 July 1526, *Epist.* IV, xxvii. For his hopes of growing gold from seeds, see Agrippa to Chapelain, Lyons, 21 October 1526, *Epist.* IV, lvi. He was still busy with alchemical work at Antwerp in July, 1529 (*Epist.* V, lxxiii). In August, he sadly

If his work in this art really did solve his financial problems, it was by attracting patrons, not by producing gold from base metals. His fellow members of the secret society appear to have helped him attract the interest of several prospective benefactors. It is possible to interpret their attitude as that of a group of impostors who sought with magic arts to deceive the gullible. Thus one friend wrote to Agrippa that a certain nobleman of Châlons offered an excellent chance for gain but warned that Agrippa should give the appearance of prosperity and should grant no requests until overwhelmed by many favors. He added, "The man is hot; you must strike while the iron is hot." [44] But Agrippa's whole career makes this interpretation of the letter improbable. Although he doubtless counted on his alchemical work to attract interest and perhaps was not above intimating that his work was more successful than it really was, it is likely that Agrippa was as earnest in his efforts to transmute metals as in his search for a patron.

Several opportunities seemed about to open up for Agrippa at this time. As early as May of 1509, he apparently had the favor of the abbot of the monastery of St. Symphorien at Autun, for he was then enjoying that lord's favors. At this period he also hoped for advantage from his connection with Jean Perréal, the painter. But his chief opportunities seemed to lie in winning the favor of Margaret of Austria, governor of Franche-Comté and the Low Countries, and of other persons who could help him secure an academic position. One such person was Antoine de Vergy, Archbishop of Besançon and chancellor of the University of Dôle, who, according to a friend of Agrippa's, boasted "that he will show you some things which perhaps not even you know." [45] It was probably the favor

---

reported only very small success: "successit optatum, et inventum est lucrum, sed non quantum tantis laboribus et longi temporis operi satis responderet." (*Epist.* V, lxxxii.)

[44] Amicus amico [to Agrippa], n.p., n.d. [about 1509], *Epist.* I, xx: "calet homo, dum calet ferrum, cudendum est."

[45] Landulphus amico suo [Agrippae], Dôle, 18 June [1509], *Epist.* I, xiii: " . . . Nonnulla jactat se tibi ostensurum, quae nondum etiam tibi forte cognita sunt." Prost, *op. cit.*, II, 152-60, argues that this letter and the following reply do not involve Landulphus, since the salutations used do not correspond to the intimate terms used in their other correspondence, but suggest an older and highly placed man living at Dôle. For Antoine de Vergy and his relation to the university, Nicolas-Antoine Labbey-de-Billy, *Histoire de l'université du comté de Bourgogne et des différens sujets qui l'ont honorée. . .* (2 vols.; Besançon, 1814-15), I, 161. Cf. Pius Bonifacius Gams, *Series episcoporum*

of this man which gave Agrippa the opportunity to give a course of lectures at the University of Dôle, on Johann Reuchlin's cabalistic work *De verbo mirifico*. These lectures aroused much interest and were attended by Simon Vernerius, dean of the church in Dôle, vice-chancellor of the university, and doctor of civil and canon law, and also by members of the faculty and of the parlement of Dôle. Agrippa claimed that he gave these lectures *gratis* in honor of Princess Margaret and of the university, and that because of them, "received into the college by the doctors of this university, I was besides presented with a professorship and stipends." [46] There was a logical connection between his desire for academic renown and his attention to the governor, Margaret of Austria. Since the reform of the university in 1503, royal confirmation was necessary not only for stipendiary professors as formerly, but for all; and nomination of professors had been taken away from the college of professors and put into the hands of the *distributeurs*, nonacademic appointees who were the channels for governmental supervision of the university.[47] The historians of the university assume that Agrippa held a regular chair of theology during his short stay there, as, indeed, he directly claims in his *Expostulatio contra Catilinetum*.[48]

These university lectures were not Agrippa's only effort in the year 1509 to win the favor of Margaret of Austria. At about the same time, on the urging of a friend who advised him not to confine himself to transitory public lectures but to write and so win lasting

---

ecclesiae catholicae (2nd ed.; Leipzig, 1931), for my identifications of bishops. For Agrippa's connection with the Abbot of St. Symphorien, see Agrippa to Landulphus, Autun, 28 May 1509, *Epist.* I, xii. For Jean Perréal, see *Epist.* I, xvii, where Agrippa warned his correspondent not to claim that Agrippa possessed any superhuman powers, "sed ut humanitatis nostrae mediocritatem plane agnoscatis." Cf. Léon Charvet, "Correspondance d'Eustache Chapuys et d'Henri-Cornélius Agrippa de Nettesheim," *Revue savoisienne*, XV (1874), 47-48.

[46] *De beatissimae Annae monogamia*, fol. B6r: ". . . Ab huius studij doctoribus in collegium receptus, insuper regentia et stipendijs donatus sum. . . ." Cf. his *Expostulatio contra Catilinetum*, in his *Opera*, II, 510. For the success of his lectures, see dedication of *De foeminei sexus nobilitate et praecellentia* to Maximilianus Transsylvanus, Antwerp, 16 April 1529, in *Opera*, II, 513-15.

[47] F. B. H. Beaune and J. d'Arbaumont, *Les universités de Franche-Comté, Gray, Dôle, Besançon: Documents inédits publiés avec une introduction historique* (Dijon, 1870), pp. lxxv-lxxvi; cf. p. xxxvi. The university was then in a state of decay; and even at its peak, it never had more than five hundred students in this period.

[48] *Ibid.*, p. cxxix, and Agrippa, *Opera*, II, 511: "nam haec lectura in causa fuit cur me in collegium receperunt, ac lectura ordinata simul et regentia et stipendiis denoverunt."

fame, as Reuchlin, Pico, and Valla had done, Agrippa composed a startling little work, much reprinted and translated later in the century, though not made public until twenty years after its composition. Its theme was the superiority of the feminine sex. The treatise seeks to prove woman's superiority, not just her equality in intellect and final beatitude; and it does so with numerous arguments. First, her name is superior, for *Eva* means life and *Adam*, earth; besides, *Eva* has more affinity with the ineffable name of God, *JHVH*. (Such an argument should hardly be surprising, especially since its author was at the very same period interested in Cabala and was lecturing on Reuchlin's earliest cabalistic book. Indeed, not only Cabala, but many of the other systems of occult learning current at that time, would have agreed with the idea underlying Agrippa's argument, that the names of things are not purely conventional, but are true reflections of the essence of the objects to which they refer. This relationship was held to be particularly true of words in ancient languages, and true of Hebrew above all other tongues.) Second, woman is more perfect because she was the last of creatures and was created in Paradise, not by intermediary creatures as man was, but directly by God. (This thesis also shows cabalistic and Neoplatonic ideas of a hierarchy of emanations through which the physical universe was created.) Third, woman's body is more comely and shows greater modesty in the location of the genitals, nor is her face disfigured by a beard. Fourth, the mother contributes more of her substance and intelligence to offspring than the father does. Fifth, females have conceived without males, although the Virgin Mary is the only human female to have done so. Sixth, women are more eloquent speakers, and there is hardly a recorded instance of a mute woman. Seventh, Adam, not Eve, committed original sin; hence Christ the Redeemer was born a man; hence priests are male. Eighth, the best creature was the woman Mary, while men, with the worst creature, Judas, among them, have been first in every sin and are much more incontinent. Ninth, women, when permitted, have excelled in all fields, even becoming popes (Pope Joan) and warriors (Joan of Arc, among others). Indeed, Agrippa concludes, only masculine tyranny and monopoly of education prevents women nowadays from equalling the exploits of the great women of the past.[49]

[49] *De nobilitate et praecellentia foeminei sexus*, printed as appendix to *De incertitudine et vanitate scientiarum et artium declamatio* (Hagae-Comitum, 1662), and also in *Opera*, II, 518-42.

An attack by Jean Catilinet, provincial superior of the Franciscans in Burgundy, ruined Agrippa's hopes for academic success and favor at court. One result of this attack on the orthodoxy of his lectures on Reuchlin was that Agrippa did not present his treatise on feminine superiority to Margaret until almost twenty years later. Another result was that he left the university and Franche-Comté, whether voluntarily or not one cannot tell. Judging from Agrippa's *Expostulatio contra Catilinetum*, the attack on him took the form of a denunciatory Lenten sermon given not in Franche-Comté but before the whole court of the Low Countries in Flanders. He has accused me, Agrippa explained, of being "a judaizing heretic, who have introduced into Christian schools the criminal, condemned, and prohibited art of Cabala, who, despising the holy fathers and Catholic doctors, prefer the rabbis of the Jews, and bend sacred letters to heretical arts and the Talmud of the Jews." [50] Although Agrippa vehemently denied that he was a heretic or that he condemned Catholic doctors, he added that he still did not despise rabbinical learning. But most of the apology (which, unlike some of his later controversial writings, is measured in tone) consists only of complaints that Catilinet's public denunciation has jeopardized the young man's career and that it would have been more agreeable with Christian charity if he had admonished him privately.

Considering the suspicion in which Hebrew studies in general and cabalistic and talmudic studies in particular were held at this time, just a year before the outbreak of the Pfefferkorn-Reuchlin controversy, one should hardly be surprised to find Agrippa having trouble at Dôle, a university where the theological faculty "tried to make up for its numerical inferiority by its zeal for orthodoxy" and was encouraged and even pushed in this direction by the parlement, the Estates, the city council, and the intolerance of the masses.[51] This same extremely conservative religious attitude dominated the whole of the Franche-Comté. Although Agrippa himself had won the favor of Antoine de Vergy, Archbishop of Besançon, on account of his reputation for occult learning, the Archbishop was a pillar of orthodoxy and a few years later, during the Reformation, vehemently led the fight against the spread of Lutheran

---

[50] *Expostulatio*, in *Opera*, II, 509: "haereticum judaisantem, qui in Christianas scholas induxerim scelestissiman, damnatam ac prohibitam cabale artem, qui contemptis sanctis patribus et catholicis doctoribus praeferam rabinos Iudaeorum, et contorqueam Sacras literas ad artes haereticas et thalmuth Iudaeorum."

[51] Beaune and d'Arbaumont, *op. cit.*, pp. cxxx-cxxxii.

THE MAKING OF A SCHOLAR 29

doctrines. Nearby at Neuchâtel, the Archbishop's aunt, Guillemette de Vergy, regent of that principality, gained her nephew's assistance in excluding Reformed doctrines from her domains. Many years later, in 1536, the canons of the cathedral at Besançon tried to out-law entirely the study of Greek on the grounds that it was an in-citement to heresy; and in that same year, only the intervention of the civic authorities of Neuchâtel and Berne was sufficient to gain the release of a goldsmith who was guilty of owning a French Bible —even though the Bible was not the version of the heretic Olivétan, but the conservative and widely approved one of Lefèvre d'Étaples.[52] This was hardly the region in which a young scholar could expound the dark mysteries of Jewish Cabala without exposing himself to attacks by the champions of orthodoxy.

Even before the hostility of the Franciscan Catilinet ruined his hopes of academic success at Dôle, Agrippa, never a man to have but one string to his bow, had sought alternative means of advance-ment. It was while at Dôle that he sought the favor of the rich nobleman of Châlons, already mentioned. Also at this period, a friend of his translated his little treatise on female superiority (or perhaps the text of his lectures on Reuchlin) into French and made it known in France, not only to the royal painter Jean Perréal, but also to certain learned circles at Lyons, a city where Agrippa later lived, and where perhaps even at this early period he had ties with influential families like the Laurencins, the Bohiers, the Brularts.[53]

Agrippa also retained his contacts in Germany, particularly in his native city of Cologne, which he had probably last visited in 1507. By late November of 1509, he was receiving urgent requests for his return, expressed in letters which spoke glowingly about his extensive wanderings and his exploits in both the military and the literary fields. These requests came from old friends who were at-tracted by his reputation for occult learning. One of these, Theo-doricus Wichwael, was titular bishop of Cyrene and administrator of the archdiocese of Cologne from 1504 down to his death in 1519. His particular interest was in Agrippa's opinion of judicial astrology, in the light of Pico della Mirandola's famous attack on that pseudo-science, the *Disputationes adversus astrologiam divinatricem*, and of the subsequent defense of astrology by Lucius Balancius, or Bellan-tius. The Bishop complained that during Agrippa's earlier visits,

---

[52] [Comité Farel], *Guillaume Farel*, pp. 145-46, 253, 376-77.
[53] *Epist.* I, xvi-xviii.

while he had been pleading a lawsuit (or perhaps studying law under Peter of Ravenna?), Agrippa's expressions of opinion about astrology had been vague.[54] A second Cologne friend, not identified by name, likewise was interested in Agrippa's studies of occult science, particularly in his investigation of ancient sources and "sacred letters." This same friend's letter suggests that Agrippa had at Cologne a whole circle of occultist acquaintances who wished to spend long hours in discussion with him, as they had in the past.[55]

Since Germany seemed so hospitable and Burgundy so hostile to his learning, Agrippa returned to his native land at the end of 1509 or very early in 1510. He visited the famed student of occult lore, Trithemius of Sponheim, in the latter's monastery of St. James at Würzburg during that winter, for sometime before 8 April 1510, he penned the dedication of his first major work, *De occulta philosophia*, in honor of Trithemius. Doubtless Agrippa drew from the learned abbot further encouragement for his studies, for his dedicatory epistle refers explicitly to a recent *(nuper)* conversation between them on occult matters.[56] In fact, there must have been a series of conversations, extending over several days.[57] It is probable, though there is no direct evidence, that Agrippa also visited his family and occultist friends at Cologne early in 1510. He certainly was there later in that year.

Throughout his early years, however, Agrippa pursued an active as well as a studious life; and he was as anxious to gain the favor of the powerful as he was to win the respect of the learned. In fact, his reputation as a scholar was his chief title to princely patronage. There is at least some evidence that Agrippa's trip to Germany at the beginning of 1510 had more tangible benefits in view than the stimulus of scholarly conversation with Trithemius, with Bishop

[54] Theodoricus Wichwael, Bishop of Cyrene, to Agrippa, Cologne, 29 November 1509, *Epist.* I, xxi: "cum, quando apud nos causas ageres, ambiguus nobis visus fueras. . . ." For the identity of this Theodoricus, with whom Agrippa was again in touch on his return from Italy in 1518 and 1519, see Conradus Eubel *et al.*, eds., *Hierarchia catholica medii et recentioris aevi* (2nd ed.; 4 vols.; Monasterii, 1913-35), IV, 345.

[55] *Epist.* I, xxii.

[56] For the dedication and Trithemius' reply, *De occulta philosophia*, fols. aa3r-v and aa4r [the latter folio is incorrectly signed as a4r]; also printed as *Epist.* I, xxiii-xxiv. On Trithemius, see Walker, *Spiritual and Demonic Magic*, pp. 86-90.

[57] Würzburg, Universitätsbibliothek, MS. M.ch.q.50, fol. 1ʳ: "Sed quum interim tecum in herbipoli per paucissimos dies conuersatus fuissem. . . ." This passage does not appear in the printed text of Agrippa's letter.

Theodoricus, and with other students of the occult. An unnamed German or Burgundian friend, probably writing from France, sent him the latest military news from Italy, and in return expected the latest news about the activities and plans of the Emperor, and about the Imperial Diet which had been summoned on 13 January, and which actually met at Augsburg from early March until May. The tone of this letter would suggest that the Nettesheimer was in touch with political circles.[58] Perhaps this period marks the beginning of his service to the Hapsburg ruler, Maximilian I.

Yet Agrippa did not spend all of 1510 in Germany. His *Expostulatio contra Catilinetum* bears the dateline London, 1510. Elsewhere, Agrippa reveals that while in England he studied the Epistles of St. Paul with the learned and virtuous John Colet and "with him as teacher, I learned many things." [59] These studies with the Dean of St. Paul's are important because they show that Agrippa was early exposed to that emphasis on a simple Biblical religion (yet one within the Roman tradition) that characterized not only Colet but many of the northern humanists. Very probably there was a direct connection between Agrippa's Biblical studies at London and his enthusiasm for occult learning, with cabalistic exegetical methods serving as the link between the two kinds of study. Colet, unlike Agrippa, was reserved and even doubtful in his expressions of opinion on the Cabala and on the magical or semimagical implications of Florentine Neoplatonism. Yet he was interested in these studies and followed the writings of Reuchlin and other students of esoteric literature.[60] Thus contact between Colet and the young lecturer on Cabala is not at all surprising.

The cause of Agrippa's going to England, however, was not his desire for a brief period of study with Colet, but "a certain quite

[58] Amicus Agrippae suo, n.p., n.d., *Epist.* I, xix. The letter refers to the French defeat of the Venetians' river attack on Ferrara on the night of 21-22 December 1509. See John S. C. Bridge, *A History of France from the Death of Louis XI* (5 vols.; Oxford, 1921-36), IV, 47. The dates of the Imperial Diet come from Leopold von Ranke, *Deutsche Geschichte im Zeitalter der Reformation* (5th ed.; 6 vols.; Leipzig, 1873), I, 127. The letter must be later than the battle it reports, and probably later than the Emperor's convocation of the Diet on 13 January 1510. It is probably earlier than the opening of the Diet on 6 March, and must be earlier than May, when results of the Diet would have been common knowledge. The nature of the news related suggests a French or Burgundian source, but the place of composition remains unclear.

[59] *De beatissimae Annae monogamia*, fol. B6v: "illo docente multa didici. . . ."

[60] Joseph Leon Blau, *The Christian Interpretation of the Cabala in the Renaissance* (New York, 1944), pp. 33-35.

different and most secret affair [that] I was conducting then." The nature of this business is most uncertain; but if the conjecture is correct that Agrippa was in the service of the Emperor from early 1510, then perhaps his secret business had to do with one of the many busy political intrigues which Maximilian was always spinning. This is the guess of the biographer Morley; and unlike most of his conjectures, this one is not unlikely. Certainly Agrippa was in imperial service less than two years later. Maybe he was in 1510. It is a matter of record that Maximilian did send a political mission to England in September.[61]

Fresh from his secret mission and Biblical studies in London, Agrippa returned to Cologne, where "before the whole university and the whole theological company, I declaimed, by no means untheologically, theological opinions (which you [scholastic theologians] in a term not quite Latin, call *quodlibeta*)." [62] The probable date of this theological disputation is late 1510, or perhaps early 1511.

The most important event of 1510, however, was neither the trip to London nor the disputation at Cologne. The late winter or early spring of that year marks the completion of the first version of Agrippa's *De occulta philosophia*, and its dedication to Trithemius. This treatise, which was perhaps the most famous of Agrippa's writings, shows (if further evidence were needed) how deeply he and his enthusiastic and admiring friends had gone into the study of magic. His several days of conversation with Trithemius encouraged him to collect together his wide knowledge of magical lore, to seek to redeem magic from its ill-repute by purging it of dangerous and superstitious elements, and finally to write it all down in the form of a treatise on magic or occult philosophy. The version which he sent to his distinguished friend does not, however, represent the more extensive form in which the book was published two decades later. *De occulta philosophia* continued to grow throughout its author's life and received some revision in the period immediately before it was printed. Study of what is probably the original manuscript copy sent to Trithemius in the late winter or early spring of

---

[61] *De beatissimae Annae monogamia*, fol. B6v: ". . . longe aliud, et occultissimum quoddam tunc agebam negotium." Morley, *op. cit.*, I, 228-29. Maximilian did send a messenger to Henry VIII on 2 September 1510 (*Letters and Papers, Foreign and Domestic, Henry VIII*, I, 182), but there is no proof that Agrippa was part of this mission.

[62] *De beatissimae Annae monogamia*, fol. B6v: "coram uniuerso studio, totoque theologico coetu, theologica placita (quae uos uocabulo non admodum latino, quodlibeta dicitis) haud non theologice declamaui."

1510 shows that although the later version included the materials of the earlier, the book had undergone extensive rearrangement and many additions.[63]

Trithemius praised his young friend's efforts highly and urged him to continue his studies, but he warned that such matters must be communicated only to trusted associates. This magical treatise in fact did circulate only in manuscript until the printing of Book One in 1531, and did not appear in full until 1533. Even then, in his preface, Agrippa excused its publication by alleging fear of unauthorized publication of one of the garbled manuscript versions then in circulation.[64]

The year 1510 stands at the end of this earliest period of Agrippa's life. Already the pattern for the rest of his years had been set. His repeated wanderings, from Germany, to France, to Spain, to Italy, to Burgundy, to England, were only the beginning of a lifetime of restless moving about in search of rich and powerful patrons. His studies, not only of the regular academic subjects but, still more, of the occult sciences, were to continue to his very latest days. Those studies were repeatedly to attract to him enthusiasts for ancient wisdom, just as they already had done at Paris, at Dôle, at Cologne, and elsewhere. Learning, and the reputation for learning, in all fields but especially in the traditions of occult antiquity, was already his open sesame to the chambers of princes and nobles, to the libraries of the studious, and to the lecture halls of universities. Agrippa's restless search for knowledge, for power, for wealth, was subsequently to take him to Italy, to Switzerland, to the Low Countries, and on more than one occasion, back to the German Empire and the Kingdom of France. Already deeply versed in cabalistic, Neoplatonic, patristic, and Biblical learning, and probably already advanced in the study of law and medicine, certainly the possessor

[63] Würzburg, Universitätsbibliothek, MS. M.ch.q.50. Comparison of a microfilm of this manuscript with a photographic reproduction of the only known holograph of Agrippa, Breslau, MS. Rehdigeriana, 254.4 (now a part of the Universitätsbibliothek at Wrocław), a letter of 1532 to Erasmus, suggests that the hand is not Agrippa's. The presentation copy may well have been prepared by an amanuensis, for at times Agrippa kept a copyist in his employ. A comparison of the manuscript and printed texts of De occulta philosophia is Josef Bielmann, "Zu einer Handschrift der Occulta Philosophia," Archiv für Kulturgeschichte, XXVII (1937), 318-24.

[64] De occulta philosophia, fol. aa2v (for this leaf, which is missing from the University of Illinois copy ordinarily used, I cite a photocopy of the University of Chicago copy, which, however, represents a closely similar but distinct edition, also issued at Cologne in 1533).

of at least a university degree in the liberal arts, Agrippa opened the second phase of his life with his departure for Italy. There he spent seven years deeply immersed in political and military adventures, and still more deeply immersed in discovering the learning of Renaissance Italy.

CHAPTER TWO

AGRIPPA IN RENAISSANCE ITALY

The next recorded event in Agrippa's life after the completion of *De occulta philosophia*, the trip to England, and the disputations at the University of Cologne is his departure for Italy. Probably this occurred sometime in 1511; in any case, it is certain that after convoying imperial gold to the army at Verona by way of Trent, he was at Borgo Lavezzaro in northern Italy on 5 April 1512.[1] He spent about seven years in the peninsula before his departure for Metz early in 1518.

This lengthy Italian period of Agrippa's life is significant not merely for the career of the man himself, but principally because

[1] His presence at Borgo Lavezzaro on 5 April is proved by a letter of that date, printed in his *Opera* (2 vols.; Lugduni, n.d.), II, 706-7, as *Epistolarum Liber I*, xxix. (Henceforth this collected correspondence will be cited as *Epist.*) An undated letter, *Epist.* I, xxv, reveals his presence in Trent convoying imperial gold to Verona. Since he claimed to have participated in the Council of Pisa, which he must have attended during its stay at Milan in early 1512, he must have been in Italy for several months before the letter of 5 April. Arrival in 1511 would agree with his claim to Mary of Hungary in 1532 that he spent seven years serving Maximilian in Italy (*Epist.* VII, xxi), and would not clash with a remark in his lecture of 1515 that he had just spent three years in military service (*Oratio II*, in *Opera*, II, 1073-74).

it is a concrete example of the influence of Renaissance culture on a northern scholar who even before his arrival there was receptive to many of the intellectual interests which flourished in the cities of northern Italy. The inquisitive northerner who was attracted by the culture of Italy was, indeed, one of the most significant types of the late fifteenth and early sixteenth centuries. This significance stems in part at least from the importance of the transfer of cultural influences from south to north of Europe. Italy was then a rich source of ideas and attitudes for the rest of the Continent, and many travelers into the peninsula were active in transmitting Italian influences to the lands north of the Alps. The northern visitor to Renaissance Italy is also important for the historian of European thought because he offers a fresh insight, from outside as it were, into conditions within that country. Certainly the northern humanistic visitor to Italy was already a well-established type even as early as 1506, when the most famous such visitor, Erasmus, began his own three-year stay there. Erasmus, in fact, was only following the example of his English friends, the Oxford Reformers. One recent student of Erasmus' Italian connections even suggests that by his time, the great day for such cultural contacts was already ended, and that a mature humanist like Erasmus had little to learn from the Italian Renaissance, which had already passed its intellectual zenith with the premature deaths of the great Florentine generation in the 1490's.[2] Nevertheless, the flow of visitors from the north continued. Italy remained profoundly attractive to all who sought to keep abreast of the latest movements of thought. It still had much to offer, if not to an already mature Erasmus, then certainly to younger and less sophisticated men. Agrippa was not the only northerner of note to make the pilgrimage across the Alps after Erasmus. Another German who made the same journey about the same time under

---

[2] Augustin Renaudet, Érasme et l'Italie (Geneva, 1954), pp. 46, 75. On the other hand, for an effective argument that the generation of Erasmus and Agrippa still relied heavily on Italians and refugee Greeks for its knowledge of Greek language and literature, see Deno J. Geanakoplos, "Erasmus and the Aldine Academy of Venice: A Neglected Chapter in the Transmission of Graeco-Byzantine Learning to the West," Greek, Roman, and Byzantine Studies, III (1960), 107-34, and more generally, idem, Greek Scholars in Venice: Studies in the Dissemination of Greek Learning from Byzantium to Western Europe (Cambridge, Massachusetts, 1962). Unfortunately, Agrippa's references to his acquaintances are too vague to reveal whether he was in personal touch with any of the major Italian or Greek Hellenists. Apparently he never visited either Venice or Padua, the two chief centers from which Greek learning spread in this period.

rather similar circumstances, though his stay was relatively brief, was Ulrich von Hutten, whose budding German patriotism was stimulated by what he saw in Italy.[3] Agrippa's contact with Renaissance Italian culture in its homeland was far longer in duration, and far more significant for his own development, than was the case with either Hutten or Erasmus.

The special interest of Agrippa's residence in Italy thus derives partly from the considerable length of his stay, and partly from his close contacts with Italian persons and movements of thought. These contacts occurred mainly in the university towns of Pavia (where he lectured in philosophy and married an Italian wife) and Turin, and in other places of northern Italy, notably Milan and the court of the Marquis of Monferrato at Casale.

The occasion for Agrippa's coming to Italy was not scholarship, but service, probably, as he claimed, military in nature, to the Emperor Maximilian, who at this period was allied with the French in opposition to Venice and to Pope Julius II. The letters of Agrippa in this period show him first of all engaged in bringing a shipment of gold from Germany to Verona by way of Trent. The precise nature of his other services to Maximilian is uncertain, but Agrippa's own claim to have fought and to have won knighthood in battle is not quite so far-fetched as his chief biographer contends.[4] There

[3] Hajo Holborn, *Ulrich von Hutten and the German Reformation,* trans. Roland H. Bainton (New Haven, 1937), pp. 45-46.

[4] *De beatissimae Annae monogamia ac unico puerperio* . . . (n. p., 1534), fol. B6v: "Exinde a Maximiliano Caesare contra Venetos destinatus, in ipsis castris, hostiles inter turbas plebemque cruentam. . . ." He repeated the claim in his letter of 1532 to Mary of Hungary (*Epist.* VII, xxi): "hinc avo tuo divo Maximiliano Caesari a prima aetate destinatus, aliquandiu illi a minoribus secretis fui. deinde in Italicis castris septennio illius stipendio militavi: postea varia legatione functus, nunc literis, nunc militia. . . ." He certainly did not spend all of his seven years in Italy soldiering for the Emperor. Cf. also *Epist.* III, xix, and *Oratio in praelectione* . . . *Trismegisti,* in *Opera,* II, 1076. His claim to knighthood appears in his letter of 6 February 1518 (1519, n.s.), written from Metz to his friend Theodoricus Wichwael, Bishop of Cyrene, in Lyons, Bibliothèque Municipale, MS. No. 48, fol. 30v, and printed as *Epist.* II, xix. See also *De beatissimae Annae monogamia,* fol. B7r; *Epist.* VI, xxii; and *Epist.* VI, xviii. At one point he later lamented having abandoned a military career: *Querela super calumnia ob editam declamationem de vanitate* . . . in *Opera,* II, 441-42. The biographer Auguste Prost, *Les sciences et les arts occultes au XVI siècle: Corneille Agrippa, sa vie et ses oeuvres* (2 vols.; Paris, 1881-82), I, 221-23, II, 44-70, 436-39, is on this, as on so many points, hypercritical. He makes ridiculous on Agrippa's use of the title *eques auratus* by supposing that here Agrippa was making the obviously absurd claim to membership in the exclusive Order of the Golden Fleece. Actually, the phrase *eques auratus* implies nothing more than a simple claim to knighthood, and is a synonym for *miles.*

is an air of secrecy in Agrippa's letters to his Italian friends that suggests that part of his service was as an agent engaged in the complex political negotiations which were then in progress, as the unstable German emperor first supported the French and their schismatic Council of Pisa and then shifted gradually to the side of the Pope. Certainly Agrippa claims to have had contact with the abortive council through the person of its most distinguished adherent, Bernardino Carvajal, Cardinal of Santa Croce. This relationship could hardly have begun before the autumn of 1511, when the council opened, and must be dated before June, 1512, when the schismatic council, having already taken shelter at Milan, moved its sessions first to Asti and then to Lyons, where it gradually passed out of existence.[5] At this period, Maximilian was engaged in negotiations for a truce with Venice; and his drift to the side of Pope Julius II was already evident in his granting permission for the Swiss allies of the papacy to cross his territories in April, 1512, and in his withdrawal from French service of all the German infantry who had formed the core of the French army and had made a great contribution to such earlier French victories as the Battle of Ravenna (11 April 1512). Agrippa may have had some part in these negotiations with the Swiss and the papacy, if not in 1512, then the next year. A papal brief dated at Rome 12 July 1513 commends Agrippa for his devotion to the Holy See, as reported to the new pope, Leo X, by Ennio Filonardi, Bishop of Veroli and nuncio to the Swiss.[6] Even toward the late pope, Julius II, Agrippa did not long maintain the hostility which his participation in the schismatic Council of Pisa might imply. A letter which he wrote, probably in 1513, praises a certain Candiotus for his satire against the late pope. But the praise is given in most equivocal terms and includes a clear rebuke for carping against the dead.[7]

Whatever the precise nature of Agrippa's services to the Emperor and to the new pope, the important thing is that the excitement and adventure of Maximilian's Italian policies had brought Agrippa, as they did Hutten about the same time, into Italy. Agrippa's itinerary for the year 1512 can be traced with a fair amount of precision.

[5] De beatissimae Annae monogamia, fol. B6v. Ludwig von Pastor, The History of the Popes (40 vols.; St. Louis, Missouri, 1894-1953), VI, 415.

[6] Epist. I, xxxviii; Pastor, op. cit., VI, 412-14.

[7] Agrippa to Candiotus, n.p., 1512, Epist. I, xxviii. The year given by Agrippa's editor is wrong unless based on a calendar that begins the new year later than 1 January, for Julius II lived until February, 1513.

His letters show that after reaching Verona he must have traveled westward and must have spent much of that year in the vicinity of Novara, at Pavia, at Casale Monferrato, at Vercelli, and at Milan.[8] The same letters show that Agrippa did not devote all his time and energy during 1512 to his official duties, but was already in contact with occultist students, with whom he exchanged cabalistic books (unfortunately not further specified), and who did their best to be of service to him.

In particular, there is evidence to show that Agrippa had appeared in that year as a lecturer at the University of Pavia, probably in the spring; that he was in Pavia during June, when French power collapsed amidst popular uprisings against their rule throughout the Milanese territories; and that, after having been briefly held captive by Swiss troops in early July, he finally decided to leave Pavia and the Milanese territory and secure the patronage of the ruler of Monferrato. This decision was taken some time in September, 1512.[9] For whatever reason, however, Agrippa did not settle at Casale as planned; the surviving letters for the years 1513 and 1514, while very few, suggest that he had been engaged on some sort of business with the Swiss previous to March, 1514, and had been in Switzerland and perhaps in touch with the papal legate, Filonardi.[10] Bishop Filonardi was the center of the pro-papal faction in Switzerland. But Agrippa also had some connection, not made clear in his correspondence, with Franciscus Supersaxo, son of the leader of the pro-French faction in the same country.[11] These letters, together with the papal brief of July, 1513, suggest that Agrippa must still have been in official service of some sort, possibly still as an agent of the Emperor, although there is no reference to Maximilian in the letters. It is certain that Agrippa spent much of these years in Lombardy. In August, 1514, however, an anonymous correspondent was writing to him of plans for a trip to Rome. That such a trip to south and central Italy actually occurred is shown by a letter of Agrippa written from Brindisi on 5 February 1515, by which date he was already planning a speedy return to the north.[12] The purpose of the trip to Rome

[8] *Epist.* I, xxvii-xxxviii.
[9] *Epist.* I, xxvii, xxxi, xxxii. Cf. *Memorie e documenti per la storia dell'Università di Pavia e degli uomini più illustri che v'insegnarono* (Pavia, 1878), I, 169.
[10] *Epist.* I, xl, xliv.
[11] *Epist.* I, xxxii; cf. Alexandre Daguet, "Agrippa chez les Suisses," *Archives de la Société d'histoire du canton de Fribourg*, II (1858), 133-38.
[12] *Epist.* I, xlii, xliii, xlvi.

and to Brindisi remains unclear. Apparently it had no connection with service to the Emperor, and quite possibly he was no longer in imperial service at all by the end of 1514; the latest clear reference that shows Agrippa still actively engaged in service to the Emperor is dated 15 March 1514.[13] The unsettled state of life suggested by these travels is further proved by his continued search for new patrons. His friends were trying to win for him the assistance of Alessandro Laudi, Count of Ripalta, whom he had met at Piacenza.[14] These negotiations were still pending in the early fall of 1514, before the trip to the south, but evidently they did not come to success.

With his return to northern Italy early in 1515, Agrippa began the most important part of his Italian residence. This was the period when, thanks in part to his marriage, his existence became more settled and his numerous contacts with Italian students of occult learning assumed a more regular form, as he lived first at Pavia as a lecturer on the *Pimander* of Hermes Trismegistus, and later, after the French invasion of Lombardy had made that city unsafe and had caused the loss of all his household goods through looting, at Casale Monferrato. Agrippa's marriage was perhaps the decisive force in his attempt to build a more settled academic career at Pavia. The earliest reference to his first wife, who was a native of that university town, occurs in a letter dated 24 November 1515. Sometime before the spring of 1517, she bore him a son. Judging from Agrippa's letters, his wife was a person of some social position in Pavia. In 1519 he praised her as "a noble maiden, a well behaved and beautiful young woman, [who] lives so to my taste that up to now not a harsh word has passed between us, and, I trust, never will." [15]

Aside from his wife and her family, who were Agrippa's contacts at the University of Pavia? There is no clear evidence on this point, for no letters survive for this period of residence there. Earlier letters, however, show that Agrippa had already, while in Switzerland

---

[13] *Epist.* I, xl.   [14] *Epist.* I, xlii-xliii, xlv.

[15] Agrippa to Theodoricus, Bishop of Cyrene, Metz, 6 February 1518 (1519, n.s.), Lyons, Bibliothèque Municipale, MS. No. 48, fol. 31r-v. The first wife is first mentioned in a letter of 24 November 1515, *Epist.* I, xlviii, which makes it clear that her parents resided at Pavia. Philippe de Vigneulles, *La chronique de la ville de Metz*, ed. Charles Bruneau (4 vols.; Metz, 1927-33), IV, 332, describes the impression made by this tiny and colorfully dressed native of Pavia on the inhabitants of Metz. Their son is mentioned in a letter of 13 March 1517, *Epist.* II, iii. The name "Ascanius" applied to the boy in *Epist.* II, xli, is probably only a poetic one.

in 1513 and 1514, been associated with some agent of Massimiliano Sforza, whom the Swiss maintained as duke of Milan between 1512 and the French invasion of 1515. Thus court influence may well have helped Agrippa secure permission to lecture in the university. This conclusion is supported by the surviving fragment of Agrippa's teachings at Pavia, the inaugural lecture on the Hermetic *Pimander*. Here he gave fulsome praise to the incompetent puppet duke, as well as to the well-known *condottiere*, Francesco Gonzaga, Marquis of Mantua, who appears to have been in the audience.[16]

With only two exceptions, Agrippa's printed correspondence reveals nothing about the names of the occultist enthusiasts with whom he associated in Italy. The editor of a recently rediscovered work of this period, his *Dialogus de homine*, suggests that Agrippa must have known Paolo Ricci, the converted Jew who was an important religious controversialist and a translator of the cabalistic *Sha'are Orah* and of a part of the talmudic literature. But although Agrippa certainly did know some of this Ricci's translations, it is not so certain that he knew the man himself. Ricci, a native of Germany, had left Pavia by 1514 to settle in Augsburg; and by 1516 he was serving as physician to the Emperor Maximilian.[17]

The two identifiable personages with whom Agrippa was in close touch in Italy both shared his interest in the study of ancient learning, especially the Cabala. One was the man who seems to have been his intermediary in winning the favor of the Marquis of Monferrato, Agostino Ricci. This Ricci, with whom Agrippa corresponded and from whom he sought advice on the publication of his *Dialogus de homine*, was another converted Jew and probably was a brother of the other Ricci, Paolo. At least the French humanist Symphorien Champier regarded them as brothers. In any case, Agostino Ricci was the author of a book on astronomical and cabalistic subjects, *De motu octavae sphaerae*, which had been published in 1513. Many years later, he served as physician to Pope Paul III.[18] The second associate of Agrippa who can be identified by name was a Swiss

---

[16] *Epist.* I, xliv; *Oratio in praelectione . . . Trismegisti*, in *Opera*, II, 1077.

[17] Paola Zambelli, "Agrippa di Nettesheim, *Dialogus de homine*," *Rivista critica di storia della filosofia*, XIII (1958), 52-53; for the date of Ricci's removal to Germany, see *Opus epistolarum Des. Erasmi Roterodami*, ed. P. S. Allen [and H. M. Allen and H. W. Garrod] (12 vols.; Oxonii, 1906-58), II, 500n.

[18] Zambelli, *loc. cit.*, 53; Lynn Thorndike, *A History of Magic and Experimental Science* (8 vols.; New York, 1923-58), V, 264, 284. That Agostino Ricci shared the cabalistic interests of Paolo and of his friend Agrippa also appears

pupil of his at Pavia, Christoph Schylling of Lucerne, one of "so
many of our Germans then studying arcane letters at Pavia." [19]
In 1518 or 1519, after leaving Italy, Agrippa inquired after this
Schylling in the hope that he had salvaged a copy of his teacher's
commentary on the Epistles of St. Paul which had been lost during
Agrippa's precipitate flight from Pavia after the French victory at
Marignano in 1515. At that later period, Agrippa learned that
Schylling had continued his study of Hebrew and of cabalistic
learning by becoming a pupil of the famed Christian Hebraist and
cabalist, Johann Reuchlin, at Tübingen in Germany. Agrippa re-
joiced to discover the name of this former student mentioned in
Reuchlin's book *De accentibus*.[20]

The little that can be discovered about the persons with whom
Agrippa associated while in Italy suggests certain conclusions about
his own activities and studies there, and also about the cultural
milieu in which he lived while in northern Italy. The implication is
strong that he spent most of his time not in official military or political service to the Emperor, the Pope, or any other authority, but
rather in study and teaching at Pavia and elsewhere. This inference
is further confirmed by many of Agrippa's letters from the years
in Italy. However tantalizingly vague the references may be, they
make it clear that Agrippa and various unnamed friends were exchanging books on Cabala and other texts which they believed to
contain ancient wisdom. But there is more to learn from Agrippa's
seven years of residence in Italy than the mere fact that he and his
friends were students of ancient wisdom, and that the cultural world
of early sixteenth-century Italy was conducive to such interests.
It is possible to determine with some precision the character of the

---

from the title of his own book, *De motu octaue sphere: opus mathematica atque
philosophia plenum, vbi tam antiquorum quam iuniorum errores luce clarius
demonstrantur; in quo et quamplurima platonicorum et antique magie (quam
cabalam hebrei dicunt) dogmata videre licet intellectu suauissima* (In oppido
Tridini, 1513).

[19] Agrippa, letter in Lyons, Bibliothèque Municipale, MS. No. 48, fol. 40v:
"nuper cum quodam discipulo meo heluetio lucernensi christophoro Schyllingo
nomine: quem inueni inter tot germanos nostros tunc papie studentes archana-
rum literarum." In place of "inueni," MS. may have written "iuuenem," the
reading given in the edition of Zambelli, *loc. cit.*, 50. This letter is a variant of
Epist. I, xlix, which, however, lacks the reference to Schylling.

[20] *Epist.* II, xv, xxxvii. Cf. Ludwig Geiger, *Johann Reuchlin: Sein Leben und
seine Werke* (Leipzig, 1871), p. 108, and Reuchlin, *De accentibus, et orthographia, linguae hebraicae* (Hagenoae, 1518), fol. XI^r.

ancient wisdom which drew him to Italy, and also the character of the circles in which he moved.

Unlike his more famous predecessor in Italy, Erasmus, Agrippa found the chief attraction of the peninsula not in its flourishing philological studies but in certain other studies which were also flowering at the same period. These studies, like philology, had to do with the recovery of ancient learning. But for the circles in which Agrippa moved, this ancient learning was not chiefly grammatical and philological, but was a body of esoteric lore, the writings of an occult antiquity which was very generally believed to have possessed learning so profound and so true that it was of great value even for the understanding of Christian religion. In short, Agrippa was in touch with persons given over to the study of such traditions as the Hermetic literature and the Cabala. This occultist study, almost always intimately associated with the practice of magic and divination, was carried on by scholars who regarded themselves, not unjustifiably, as heirs of the esoteric interests of Marsilio Ficino and Giovanni Pico della Mirandola in the preceding century.[21] Such interests in ancient esoteric lore were often strangely combined with tendencies toward fanatical religious enthusiasms. In the generation before Agrippa's visit to Italy, such interests had produced a Hermetic sect which took its inspiration from a fanatical prophet, Giovanni Mercurio da Correggio, and from a disciple of his, Ludovico Lazzarelli, a minor humanist who died in 1500 and whose writings Agrippa knew and cited. This Hermetic enthusiasm not only survived in Italy during Agrippa's own stay there, but also spread its influence to France, where it affected the thought of Symphorien Champier and Jacques Lefèvre d'Étaples, two persons with whom Agrippa himself had some connection.[22]

Agrippa not only got in touch with Italian students of occult antiquity, but even made himself the leader of an admiring group of occultists, including both Italians and foreigners like himself. True, he was a barbarian from the north, as he modestly admitted; yet he reminded his Italian audience at Pavia that "even barbarians

[21] Renaudet, *op. cit.*, p. 51; Zambelli, *loc. cit.*, 47-71; for Christian cabalism, Joseph Leon Blau, *The Christian Interpretation of the Cabala in the Renaissance* (New York, 1944), and the sharply divergent interpretation by François Secret, *Le Zôhar chez les Kabbalistes chrétiens de la Renaissance* (Paris, 1958).

[22] Paul Oskar Kristeller, *Studies in Renaissance Thought and Letters* (Rome, 1956), pp. 221-47, 249-57. Cf. Chapter One, above.

are rational men." [23] He had already won friends and fame, if not fortune, through association with similar groups in France and at Dôle in the Franche-Comté. Now in Italy he won by his lectures, his conversation, and his writings a reputation which was still alive several years after he returned to northern Europe.[24] These enthusiasts for the "wisdom" being rediscovered in various obscure texts which either stemmed from ancient times or were believed to do so, were a tightly knit group, virtually a secret society, all of whom had certain common interests in ancient lore. Toward outsiders who did not share their veneration for ancient wisdom, this group felt the exclusiveness and hostility which might have characterized a gnostic sect of the early Christian centuries.[25]

In a negative sense, the common interest felt by Agrippa and his Italian associates implied a keen dissatisfaction with the officially accepted body of theological and philosophical science, which they felt to be both fruitless and wicked. Yet they were not, in their repudiation of scholastic theology and philosophy, intending to turn against what they conceived to be the Christian religion, for the positive, constructive side of their common interests lay in a trust that religion and philosophy could be restored from corruption to sound health through learning. Even such extreme and unorthodox

[23] Agrippa, Oratio in praelectione . . . Trismegisti, in Opera, II, 1076: "Quod si quem vestrum scandalizet, barbarum hominem in Lizeto [sic] gymnasio bonas literas interpretari, is sciat barbaros etiam homines esse rationales, et frui coelo. . . ."

[24] Amicus ad Agrippam, Strasbourg, 1523, Epist. III, lv.

[25] Zambelli, loc. cit., 53, argues that this group of Agrippa's followers constituted a definite and organized secret society. Elsewhere, in Testi umanistici su l'Ermetismo, ed. Eugenio Garin et al. (Rome, 1955), pp. 110-11, she argues that his warnings in his public lectures that the profane should be kept at a distance are to be taken literally as a command to keep their studies from the uninitiated, who might cause them trouble with church authorities despite Agrippa's repeated assertions of submission to the church. See Oratio in praelectione convivii Platonis, in Opera, II, 1062: "Absint autem hac veneranda lectione, quicunque terrenis obvoluti sordibus, Baccho atque illi hortorum deo mancipati, Amorem ipsum divinum munus, porcorum atque canum ritu in lutum prosternunt." Cf. II, 1072, for fear of being denounced for false teaching. Cf. also Oratio in praelectione . . . Trismegisti, in Opera, II, 1080-81: "Vos igitur illustrissimi candidissimique viri, vos qui virtutem colitis, vos ad mea tantum dicta aures adhibite, animosque intendite vestros: Contra, qui sanctas leges contemnitis, hinc vos effugite, et procul hinc miseri, procul ite prophani. Vos autem qui divina amatis, quique rerum arcanarum estis percupidi, et circa abditioris philosophiae symbola, ac mirbilium [sic] dei operum reconditas vires, plenissimasque mysteriorum antiqui seculi traditiones curiosi estis exploratores, vos inquam adeste foeliciter. . . ."

manifestations of this occultist spirit as the Hermetic prophet Mercurio da Correggio at least tried to establish the compatibility of their teachings with Christian orthodoxy. And there is nothing to show that Agrippa and the other latter-day followers of Mercurio's visionary preachings went so far from the pale of Christian orthodoxy as he. Certainly other successors of this Hermetic tradition, such as Lefèvre d'Étaples, were discreet and orthodox. Insofar as one can judge from Agrippa's own writings of this period, he and his circle of friends shared the common reform program of the humanism of their day and did not go far beyond Erasmus and Lefèvre in their proposals for reform of the church and of all learning.

What distinguished Agrippa and his friends at Pavia and Casale Monferrato from Erasmian humanists was that they believed, more clearly than the latter, that the way to such a restoration of pure and holy theology and philosophy was pointed out by certain writings which were being brought to light and studied in their own day after centuries of neglect. These rediscovered books were in every case treatises which claimed to teach profound and ancient mysteries, stemming ultimately from a divine source. In short, these newly recovered sources were esoteric. Agrippa himself clearly set forth his friends' attitude toward these ancient books in his various treatises written in this period, such as the inaugural lecture of his course on the Hermetic *Pimander*, delivered at Pavia in 1515; his undated *Oratio in praelectione convivii Platonis;* the *Dialogus de homine,* of late 1515 or 1516; and the *De triplici ratione cognoscendi Deum,* of 1516. The governing idea in all four of these works is the faith that the Hermetic writings, long neglected but now restored through the work of Ficino and others, and the cabalistic writings, the restoration of which had begun with Pico and was continuing with the work of Reuchlin and Paolo Ricci, were the gateway to true wisdom. Ancient and occult writings, long neglected by an ignorant and impious humanity, would bring men back from intellectual pride and intellectual despair to a humble acknowledgement of the goodness of God. Far from undermining religious faith, as the vain and contentious learning of the traditional schools did, this newly recovered but ancient and venerable knowledge would provide the key to a profound and truly religious understanding of the truth revealed in the Christian Scriptures. Both Hermetic and cabalistic books, Agrippa and his friends believed, were from God; both traditions would provide new insights into the real meaning of

Biblical texts. Agrippa and his friends taught that "even the Gospel, like the Mosaic law, has one meaning on the surface for the more simple, another in its core, which has been separately revealed to the perfect." Thus Agrippa regarded his lectures at Pavia on the Hermetic writings as being truly "theological," for they expounded books which would open the way to an understanding of this inner meaning of the Bible.[26]

The most important benefit of this recovery of the true interpretation of Scripture, and of the accompanying reconstruction of human knowledge on its basis, Agrippa maintained, would be eternal happiness, eternal salvation. Ignorance of God since the sin of Adam he regarded as the source of death and of human misery, for God had withdrawn the light which till then had illuminated man and which had prevented the decomposition of the essentially compound, and so essentially mortal, human nature. Having turned away from the knowledge of eternity, having preferred his own pitiful rational light to the powerful illumination of God, man had become not only mortal, but also the prisoner of his own unbridled lusts, which could never be satisfied, and which reduced him to the miserable, restless, and transitory existence of a brute.[27] But if, by knowledge gained through the occult revelations, withheld from the vulgar mob but granted to the truly wise and virtuous in the form of the Cabala and the Hermetic books, man could restore his knowledge of the divine truth, then he could regain justice and virtue and happiness.[28] The occult writings, therefore, offered man knowledge, and through it, both happiness in this life and eternal beatitude in the world to come.

This theme is evident in all of Agrippa's works of the Italian period, but most directly in his longest and most significant treatise of these years, De triplici ratione cognoscendi Deum. The object of this entire treatise is to show how man may win the desired knowledge of God. As the title suggests, there are three ways, each being

[26] De triplici ratione cognoscendi Deum, cap. V, in Opera, II, 493: "Habet etiam Evangelium, quemadmodum Lex Mosaica, aliud in cortice propositum imbecillioribus, aliud in medulla, quod segregatim revelatum est perfectis"; De beatissimae Annae monogamia, fol. B6v.

[27] Dialogus de homine, Lyons, Bibliothèque Municipale, MS. No. 48, fol. 55 [sic; recte 56]. This text is now printed, with indication of the original manuscript pagination, in Zambelli, loc. cit., 57-71. Cf. De originali peccato, in Opera, II, 554, 558, and De triplici ratione, in Opera, II, 481-82.

[28] Oratio in praelectione . . . Trismegisti, in Opera, II, 1079-80; De triplici ratione, cap. II, in Opera, II, 482.

more nearly perfect than the preceding one. The first way is the knowledge of God from nature. This knowledge is sufficient to make inexcusable the neglect of the divine, even by a pagan who never heard the name of Christ. It can lead man to the two essential beliefs of any religion, piety toward God and justice toward his fellow man.[29] Yet in the opinion of Agrippa, this knowledge of God from His creatures is imperfect, and can never lead to true goodness and true happiness. It is only preparatory to the second path to the knowledge of God, the Mosaic law. This is a traditional and hardly original assertion, to be sure! But Agrippa goes on to deny that the literal meaning of the Hebrew law is the true one. "Nothing could be more absurd," [30] he writes, than the law if taken only literally. But when God revealed this law to Moses, He also revealed a secret interpretation of it, not to be divulged to the masses, but to be restricted to the wise few. This knowledge was eventually written down in the Jewish Cabala, while Hebrew contacts with ancient Egypt explain why the same truths are found in the Hermetic books. This true and profound interpretation of the Pentateuch, Agrippa insists, points directly to the coming of the Messiah in the person of Jesus Christ, and so to the third way of knowing God. The first two ways to God are a mere preparation for the Christian revelation, which is the third and perfect way. But this revelation, like the Mosaic one, must be interpreted in the light of the esoteric writings, which will reveal to the wise its hidden inner meaning. This general notion, that the Hebrew revelation, as understood in the light of the Cabala, led directly into the Christian religion, actually led a number of Jewish scholars in Agrippa's own time to be converted to Christianity. Among them were Paolo Ricci, translator of the cabalistic treatise *Sha'are Orah,* and his brother, Agrippa's close friend Agostino Ricci.

If knowledge of God and eternal happiness were the most important fruits of the studies carried on by Agrippa and his friends, there were nevertheless also immediate and practical advantages to be gained from their occultist brotherhood. Agrippa's own biography shows clearly that one of these benefits was simply the mutual aid which persons bound by the close ties of occultist fraternity

[29] *De triplici ratione,* cap. III, in *Opera,* II, 486.
[30] *Ibid.,* cap. IV, in *Opera,* II, 489: "Quod si solum literalem sensum legis apprehendas, absque spiritu futurae lucis, veritatis et perfectionis, nihil erit lege magis ridiculum, et anilis fabulae . . . similimum."

offered one another. From his days at Paris through his Italian years and even down to his return to his native Cologne in the 1530's, it was Agrippa's occultist brethren who sought to win the patronage of princes for him and who offered him shelter and encouragement.

Far more important, however, was the practical utility which Agrippa believed would come from the knowledge which he and his friends pursued. The enlightened soul, the soul which had attained a true understanding of God's revelation, would not only regain mastery over its own body but would also win power over all nature. Thus the study of the Cabala and the Hermetic literature led into the study of magic—white magic, of course, involving the aid not of demons but of good spirits and of the occult powers of the soul itself. "For the basis of all miracles is knowledge, and the more things we understand and know, the more readily and efficaciously do we work." [31] It was precisely this power over nature which Adam had lost by original sin, but which the purified soul, the *magus*, now could regain.[32] This magical knowledge had long been associated with the Hermetic tradition; and while the main current of medieval Jewish cabalism had been hostile to any such attempt to associate mystical illumination with magic, yet the cabalists had firmly believed that the enlightened soul did possess great power. They had not been entirely free from the corrupting attempt to make use of this knowledge for magical practices.[33] It is worth recalling that Agrippa had already produced an early version of his *De occulta philosophia*, his treatise on magic. And there is conclusive evidence that this work (although not printed in its entirety until 1533, and then in a much expanded form) was circulating in manuscript among Agrippa's former disciples at Pavia in 1523.[34]

Agrippa's belief that the truly illuminated soul could perform works of magic which seemed miraculous even led him into an attack on the corruption of the church in his own day. The early

[31] *Dialogus de homine*, MS. fol. 52v [*sic; recte* 53v]: "Omnium enim miraculorum radix cognitio est, quanto enim plura intelligimus ac cognoscimus, tanto maiora et promptius, et efficatius operamur. . . ."
[32] *De triplici ratione*, cap. V, in *Opera*, II, 492-93.
[33] Gershom Gerhard Scholem, *Major Trends in Jewish Mysticism* (New York, 1946), pp. 99-100, 144-45.
[34] *Epist*. III, lv, lxxvii (the latter from a person who came from Italy to Lyons because of Agrippa's fame for occult learning).

church, he argued, had been aided by the miraculous works of the apostles and of their immediate successors, who were able to perform these miracles precisely because they did possess the pure and spiritual knowledge of the revelation contained in the Bible. Properly, Agrippa felt, the prelates of the church ought always to be gifted with such wonder-working powers based on true knowledge. If present-day theologians and prelates were unable to perform any such miracles (and they were unable), that inability was merely further proof of their corruption and lack of faith. Their error was that they founded their knowledge on reason instead of on faith. They were adulterating the Word of God with their own attempts to bend it to the demands of human reason.[35]

Agrippa's writings during this Italian period demonstrate one further belief which he and his friends at Pavia and Casale shared. Because of the darkness caused by Adam's sin, the human mind cannot know the true nature of God by reason,[36] but only by esoteric revelation. The use of reason in an attempt to get this knowledge about God had only led man into sin. In his little book *De originali peccato*, written either at the very end of his stay in Italy or else, more probably, shortly after he moved to the imperial city of Metz early in 1518, Agrippa suggests that in an allegorical sense, Adam in the Book of Genesis represents Faith, which is misled by Eve, the personification of Reason, which in turn has been misled by sensory experience, the Serpent. Truth in religion is based on faith, not on reason, Agrippa argues, for God is above all human knowledge, and "therefore in order truly to know Him, dialectics and philosophy are unable to ascend, being checked by reason, which is hostile to holy faith." "For only faith is the instrument and means by which alone we can know God." The rational theology of his own day, on the other hand, Agrippa regards as vain and contentious learning.[37] There is no question which modern theologians do not presume to settle by reason, or rather, by reason

---

[35] *De triplici ratione*, cap. V, in *Opera*, II, 493-95.

[36] *Ibid.*, cap. III, in *Opera*, II, 482.

[37] *De originali peccato*, in *Opera*, II, 554-55. *De triplici ratione*, cap. V, in *Opera*, II, 491: "Ad illum igitur vere cognoscendum, dialectica et Philosophia nequeunt ascendere, impeditae ratione, quae est inimica sanctae fidei." *Opera* here reads "queunt," but I have corrected it to "nequeunt" on the basis of MS. Lat. 16,625 of the Bibliothèque Nationale at Paris. *Ibid.*: "Sola enim fides instrumentum est et medium, qua sola possumus Deum cognoscere. . . ." Cf. *ibid.*, p. 496.

to involve in a labyrinth of futile reasonings and partisan quarrels. "What is worse, if there are any who do devote themselves to this ancient theology and religion, they are called madmen, ignorant, irreligious, sometimes even heretics, and (as Hermes says) are held in hatred, even the threat of capital punishment is held over them, they are insulted, [and] often they are deprived of life." [38] Thus Agrippa's attack on the use of reason in theology had led him to a defense of all the Biblical humanists of his time against denunciations by their scholastic enemies. Like the other humanists, he upheld the ideal of a return to the pure, undefiled faith of the early church, in opposition to the contentious wrangling of scholastic theology. To the proud rationalism of the professional theologians, Agrippa and his friends contrasted the firm and humble faith of the true believer, who praises God for illuminating man by grace, and who prepares himself for enlightenment with vigils, fasts, and a life lived in imitation of Christ. Only to such persons, Agrippa felt, will God grant knowledge which is beyond the reach of human investigation, the knowledge of the true mysteries of religion, which are contained not in the external revelation but in its inner meaning. [39]

Thus Agrippa and his friends at Pavia, Casale, and elsewhere were deeply immersed in the study of the Hermetic writings, which had been re-edited and retranslated a generation or two earlier by Marsilio Ficino, the leading philosophical figure among fifteenth-century Florentines. They were also continuing Agrippa's earlier interest in cabalistic studies, already evident in his Dôle lectures of 1509 on Reuchlin's *De verbo mirifico*, and continued now with the aid of Paolo Ricci's translation of *Sha'are Orah*, entitled *Portae lucis* in Latin, and also with the aid of the cabalistic studies of Agrippa's good friend Agostino Ricci. Quite conformably to their interest in such ancient sources as the pseudo-Hermes and the Cabala, Agrippa and his friends were profoundly affected also by the esoteric coloration given to ancient thought in the works of leading scholars of

[38] *Ibid.*, p. 500: "quod deterius est, si qui sunt qui huic pristinae theologiae ac religioni se dedicant, insani, ignari, irreligiosi, interdum etiam haeretici vocantur, atque (ut inquit Hermes) odio habentur, etiam periculum capitale in eos constituitur, contumeliis afficiuntur, saepe vita privantur." Cf. Ludovico Lazzarelli, *Crater Hermetis*, in *Testi umanistici su l'Ermetismo*, p. 68, and *Corpus Hermeticum*, ed. A. D. Nock, trans. A. J. Festugière (4 vols.; Paris, 1945-54), I, 97 (IX, 4). Cf. *De potestate et sapientia Dei* [i.e., the *Pimander*] (Paris, 1494), fol. CI[v], for phrasing that suggests that Agrippa used the translation by Ficino: "interdum etiam odio habentur: contumeliis afficiuntur: vitaque priuantur."

[39] *De triplici ratione, loc. cit.*, 490, 493-94.

the preceding century, such as Ficino, Pico, and Lazzarelli, and by the writings of their own contemporaries, such as Johann Reuchlin. These literary influences on Agrippa's thought form the subject of a later chapter.

The French reconquest of the Milanese district after their triumph at Marignano in September, 1515, forced Agrippa and his family to flee, with the loss of property, books, and income from university lectures.[40] The immediate result was Agrippa's moving to Casale Monferrato, where the Marquis, Guglielmo IX Paleologo (1494-1518), offered him a pension, and where he spent most of 1516 and part of 1517. This minor Italian prince had created a reputation for himself as a patron of men of letters and had founded at Casale an Accademia degli Illustrati, where men met to discuss philosophy, laws, and natural sciences.[41] To him Agrippa dedicated both the *Dialogus de homine* and the *De triplici ratione*. But the pension he received was probably too modest for Agrippa's ambitions. His dissatisfaction with this pension led him to undertake several negotiations for more lucrative positions. One of these was with a certain Master Hannibal, whose favor a priest living at Vercelli tried to secure for Agrippa. This wealthy man spoke encouragingly of granting him a pension of two hundred ducats, probably far more than what he got from the Marquis. The same intermediary also assured him of the benevolence of Ludovico Cernole, also of Vercelli, who offered to find him a residence in that city until Master Hannibal came to terms. But although these negotiations were still in progress on 2 June 1516, nothing ever came of them, and Agrippa remained at Casale.[42] Nevertheless, he had other prospects for an advantageous change of residence and of patron. He had apparently been looking for the favor of the Duke of Savoy during the interval between his flight from Pavia and his decision to go to Casale, a decision taken probably in 1516. His interest in Savoyard favor continued. At some time between late 1515 and 1517, he lectured on "theology" at the University of Turin.[43] Perhaps these lectures were on the Epistles of St. Paul, in which his interest went back to his studies with John Colet in 1510 and on which he had

[40] *Epist.* I, xlix.
[41] [Antonio?] Sancio, *Cenno storico intorno ai marchesi del Monferrato di stirpe Paleologa* (Casale, 1835), pp. 55-60.
[42] Letters concerning these negotiations are in *Epist.* I, xl-II, i.
[43] *Epist.* I, liv-lix; *De beatissimae Annae monogamia*, fol. B6v.

written the commentary which he lost during the sack of Pavia in 1515. On the other hand, since he regarded the Hermetic writings also as sacred, his "theological" lectures at Turin may have dealt with those books. The University of Turin had welcomed Erasmus in 1506, and it may have been either there or at Pavia that Agrippa met Eustache Chapuys, who was later to befriend him while an episcopal official at Geneva in the early 1520's and again while imperial ambassador to England at the end of the 1520's.[44]

Agrippa was certainly at Chambéry in Savoy in the spring of 1517.[45] He soon decided, however, that his hopes in Savoy were vain and that the continuing state of political unrest, which made travel dangerous for his friends and himself,[46] would make it wise to leave Italy altogether. His surviving correspondence for 1517 shows that while he was still in touch with Savoy, he also had friends who were urging him to accept positions at Avignon, at Geneva, at Metz, and even in France. His most influential friends in this search for a new patron and a new residence were the Lyonese family of Laurencin, the head of which was in the French fiscal service, while one son, Jean de Laurencin, was commander of the order of Saint-Antoine de Riverie, and another, Ponce de Laurencin, was governor of the order of St. John at Metz. To the former, Jean, he dedicated his commentary on the *Ars brevis* of Ramon Lull, quite possibly at this very time (1517).[47] The latter was one of the envoys sent by the city of Metz to negotiate the terms under which Agrippa finally departed from the Italian peninsula to settle at Metz as *advocatus* of the city government.[48] Some time before mid-January of 1518, Agrippa had taken his decision to return to the north, and by mid-February he had arrived in Metz.[49]

---

[44] Garrett Mattingly, "Eustache Chapuys and Spanish Diplomacy in England (1488-1536): A Study in the Development of Resident Embassies" (unprinted Ph.D. thesis, Harvard University, 1935), pp. 7-10, 47-56, 625-29.

[45] *Epist*. II, v.   [46] E.g., *Epist*. II, ii.

[47] The date of this dedication is uncertain. A letter of 1523 (*Epist*. III, xxxvi) provides a *terminus ad quem* by mentioning the commentary. Agrippa apparently came in touch with the Laurencin family in 1516 or 1517, but he could have met them much earlier, since he had already been in France at least twice. The treatise on Lull may antedate the dedication to Laurencin, for the dedication suggests that Agrippa had had it for some time before he inscribed it to Laurencin (*Opera*, II, 333).

[48] Prost, *op. cit.*, I, 299-307, 309; II, 473-74.

[49] *Epist*, II, xi; cf. Prost, *op. cit.*, II, 473-74, for documents which tend to support his selection of mid-February, 1518, as the time of Agrippa's arrival in Metz.

Despite its many hardships, Agrippa's Italian experience was one which he always cherished. When in 1518 he wrote a letter of advice to the young legal scholar Claudius Cantiuncula, who was winning distinction at the University of Basel, he concluded with the recommendation to visit Italy, after which "every other country will seem vile, if you compare it to this one." [50] On a later occasion, despite the fact that he had studied both at Cologne and at Paris, he was described as "an Italian by education." [51] Even though he was destined never to return to Italy, his connection with those Italians who shared his occult interests continued for the rest of his life. His removal from Lyons to Antwerp in 1528 was accomplished with the aid of an Italian merchant, Augustinus Furnarius, who did business at Lyons and Antwerp, and an Italian Augustinian friar, Aurelius ab Aquapendente, both of whom shared his intellectual interests.[52] Agrippa's contacts with Monferrato must have survived, for in a letter written from Antwerp in 1529 after the death of his second wife from plague, he spoke of an offer from "a certain Marquis who formerly knew me," and who begged him to move back to Italy.[53] During Agrippa's most troubled period in the Low Countries, he found protectors in two Italian members of the household of Cardinal Campeggio, Bernardus Paltrinus and Lucas Bonfius. These friends continued to correspond with Agrippa after they had moved to Germany and then to Italy. One of them wrote from Bologna in December, 1532, reporting excitedly that he had been privileged to have a brief personal interview with Francesco Giorgi Veneto, who was a disciple of Pico, and that he had spoken of Agrippa to this learned man. Giorgi had given Agrippa's friend permission to read his book *De harmonia mundi*. The same letter shows that Agrippa's friend was trying to buy the library of the late general of the Augustinians, Egidio di Viterbo, but was beaten by another purchaser, Girolamo Aleandro, Archbishop of Brindisi since 1524.[54] This correspondence proves that Agrippa's friends in

[50] *Epist.* II, xiv: "Demum hortor te, ut post visam Germaniam ac Galliam, totamque illam barbarorum nostrorum colluviem, tandem in Italiam te conferas: quam si aliquando apertis oculis introspexeris, omnis alia patria turpis vilisque erit, si ad hanc contuleris."
[51] Amicus [Wolfgang Fabricius Capito] ad Agrippam, near Basel, 23 April 1522, *Epist.* III, xv: "Agrippa, inquit, est oriundus Colonia, educatione Italus...."
[52] *Epist.* V, xx-xxiii.
[53] *Epist.* V, lxxxiv. This Marquis could not have been Guglielmo IX, who died in 1518; but it was probably a successor who had known Agrippa.
[54] *Epist.* VII, xxii.

Italy kept him supplied with books and with news concerning matters of occultist interest.

Thus Agrippa's ties with the occultist circles of northern Italy and his interests in Italian thought survived even after he had been absent for many years. Italy had not created those interests, and his position while there was more that of a master than of a disciple of the Italian Renaissance. But contact with the well-developed occultist movement in Italy, with the coterie of avowed disciples of Pico, the enthusiasts for the Cabala and for Hermetic books, had certainly enriched Agrippa's acquaintance with these traditions. And his success in building up a loyal following in Italy must have aided his later success in becoming, in each of the many places where he later resided, the center of a small group of bold spirits who sought to use occult truth, the concealed wisdom of the ages, for the purification and reform of their present world.

CHAPTER THREE

IN THE WORLD OF PRE-REFORM

Sometime before mid-January of 1518, Agrippa accepted the offer to come to the free imperial city of Metz as *orator* and *advocatus*, a position which apparently presupposed legal training and which required him to conduct negotiations with neighboring principalities and to pronounce official speeches of welcome to visiting dignitaries.[1] Agrippa received generous treatment: forty *écus au soleil* for traveling expenses to Metz and a salary of 120 livres a year, as compared with a maximum of 72 livres for any earlier incumbent. In addition to relieving what was probably a very great financial embarrassment, the new job at Metz made possible a far more settled way of living than was possible at the court of Guglielmo Paleologo or of any other Italian prince. He probably owed

[1] For the legal side of his duties, see the documents printed by Auguste Prost, *Les sciences et les arts occultes au XVI siècle: Corneille Agrippa, sa vie et ses oeuvres* (2 vols.; Paris, 1881-82), II, 473-74 (Appendix XIII, No. 3), from records of the city of Metz. His diplomatic and oratorical functions appear in *Orationes* V, VI, and VIII, in his *Opera* (2 vols.; Lugduni, n.d.), II, 1092-96.

this position to his friendship with the Laurencin family of Lyons, for Ponce de Laurencin, a brother of Jean and governor of the order of St. John of Metz, was one of the two envoys sent to Savoy to negotiate with "maistre Hanry Cornelis, docteur." Agrippa's address to the city council on his arrival makes special mention of his friendship with the family of Laurencin.[2] Agrippa may also have already known another person high in the ecclesiastical hierarchy of Metz, Theodore de Saint-Chaumont, Abbot of Saint-Antoine de Viennois, the same who later as vicar-general of the absentee bishop of Metz, the Cardinal of Lorraine, played a prominent role in the arrest and execution of the reforming preacher Jean Châtelain. At least this Theodore was one of the French clergymen who partici- pated in the schismatic Council of Pisa in 1512.[3] Agrippa himself claimed to have attended this gathering and possibly made contact with Theodore there, just as he may well have had his earliest con- tact with the Laurencin family group through the same church as- sembly. On the other hand, Agrippa nowhere mentions Theodore by name. So this man may or may not have been one of Agrippa's early patrons at Metz. The probable date of the Nettesheimer's arrival in Metz is mid-February, 1518.[4]

This removal took Agrippa and his family from the exciting and vital culture of Renaissance Italy into the very different but also ex- citing and vital culture of northern Europe on the very eve of the Reformation. In Metz from 1518 to early 1520, then in his native Cologne during much of 1520, next in Geneva from the spring of 1521 to early 1523, and finally at Fribourg (Suisse) from March of 1523 until April of 1524, Agrippa was living in or near the western fringes of the German Empire at the very period when the intellec- tual stirrings of pre-Reformation humanism were beginning to be-

[2] For his financial treatment, Prost, op. cit., I, 299-307, 309; II, 473-74. For additional material on the Laurencin family, Léon Charvet, "Correspondance d'Eustache Chapuys et d'Henri-Cornélius Agrippa de Nettesheim," Revue savoisienne, XV (1874), 46-47. Agrippa's speech to the council is Oratio IV, in Opera, II, 1091-92.
[3] L. Sandret, "Le concile de Pise (1511)," Revue des questions historiques, XXXIV (1883), 436-38.
[4] A Genevan friend had heard of his decision for Metz by 16 January 1518: Epistolarum Liber II, xi, in Opera, II, 728. (Henceforth this correspondence will be cited as Epist.) Prost, op. cit., gives no justification for his dating of the first document recording payments to Agrippa; but careful study of this and the other financial records which he prints makes his date very probable. The documents are in his Appendix XIII, op. cit., II, 473-74.

come magnified and deflected by the early teaching and preaching of Luther and his adherents. Although all of these places in which Agrippa spent the early Reformation years were to be profoundly affected by the new religious upheaval, and although one of them, Geneva, in the generation following Agrippa was destined to replace Wittenberg as the center of world Protestantism, it is important to note now a point which will come up again in the special chapter on Agrippa's relation to the Reformation. This point is that the prevalent spirit of Metz, Cologne, Geneva, and Fribourg was that of pre-Reformation humanism, not the new evangelical spirit of Wittenberg. Agrippa and his humanistic friends throughout this period followed the Lutheran movement with a lively interest, often with a warm sympathy, and yet increasingly with a vague but disturbing sense of disquietude. Their interests, their demands, their programs for reform and renewal often were closely akin to those of the Reformers. Yet it is important to observe that these interests, demands, and reform programs were, in the case of Agrippa, already formulated before 1517. If Agrippa and his friends sometimes *agreed* with Luther, that does not at all prove that they *followed* Luther. Although their humanistic program lacked the profound depth and emotional vigor of Luther's, it at least had a breadth of interest and universality of outlook signally lacking in the great German Reformer.

This mood of pre-Reform, accompanied by a close interest in the Wittenberg teachings, was clearly present in Agrippa's circle of friends at Metz. For at Metz, despite his burden of official duties, which required him to be absent from the city from time to time, Agrippa quickly developed intimate contacts with other seekers after ancient wisdom and a renewal of learning, much as he had already done in France and in Italy. Together with his friends, he kept abreast of the latest publications of "advanced" thinkers, including the new and exciting literature of the Protestant Reformation. At the same time, Agrippa's interests in natural philosophy, including alchemy and occult literature, filled much of his leisure. This fact can be conclusively demonstrated despite the scarcity of such topics in his surviving letters for the years at Metz, since his correspondence during later years with his former companions in that city shows that his most intimate associates spent much of their time in alchemical and other secret studies. Even more than in Italy, Agrippa seems to have been the boldest and most adventure-

some spirit of them all, willing and eager to assume and defend
extreme viewpoints which alarmed even his friends. For example,
sometime before February, 1519, Agrippa wrote a treatise on original
sin, *De originali peccato*, which shocked some of his friends because
of its opinion that original sin had been an act of sexual intercourse
between Adam and Eve, a view which was not original with Agrippa
but wh:ch certainly had never been the received opinion of the
church.[5] Yet this questionable teaching did not cause him nearly

[5] A letter of Claude Dieudonné, undated but probably of 1519, shows that
some of his fellow Celestine monks at Metz had been scandalized by Agrippa's
views. See Agrippa, *De beatissimae Annae monogamia ac unico puerperio . . .*
(n.p., 1534), fol. N2r (also printed as *Epist.* II, xxi). Agrippa's good friend
Theodoricus Wichwael, Bishop of Cyrene, also had doubts about the orthodoxy
of his opinion. See his letter and Agrippa's reply in Lyons, Bibliothèque Municipale, MS. No. 48, fols. 27r-39r. The reply, which bears date 6 February 1518
(1519, n.s.), sets a *terminus ad quem* for Agrippa's treatise. These letters are
printed, though in incomplete form, as *Epist.* II, xviii-xix. The origin of
Agrippa's own view is difficult to trace. He explicitly states on fol. 1ʳ of the
Lyons manuscript that he did not find this opinion in any other author. Nevertheless, the idea must have come to him as a result of his readings. The doctrine
that original sin was sexual is an obvious outgrowth of the Gnostic repudiation
of corporeality, and especially of sexual relations. This doctrine was especially
common in Manichean religion. See F[rancis]. Legge, *Forerunners and Rivals
of Christianity: Being Studies in Religious History from 330 B.C. to 330 A.D.*
(2 vols.; Cambridge [England], 1915), II, 299-304, 329. Cf. K. Kessler, art.
"Mani, Manichäer," in *Realencyklopädie für protestantische Theologie und
Kirche*, XII, 209-10, for variants. Agrippa himself probably derived the notion
from the Church Fathers, for these writers, especially the Latins, emphasized
the sensuous nature of sin, according to O. Kirn, art. "Sünde," in *Realencyklopädie für protestantische Theologie und Kirche*, XIX, 138-39. There are hints
of it in such relatively obscure texts as the *Acta disputationis Archelai* and the
Catecheses of Cyril of Jerusalem. Far more likely, however, is dependence on
Augustine's *De Genesi ad litteram*, Lib. XI, Cap. 41 (*Corpus Scriptorum Ecclesiasticorum Latinorum*, XXVIII¹, 376), where the great Bishop of Hippo
discusses (and rejects) precisely such an interpretation of original sin. As for
the figurative interpretation which Agrippa joins to this sensuous one, St. Ambrose suggests that the sin might be regarded as the deception of *mens* (Adam)
by *delectatio corporis* (the Serpent) working through *sensus* (Eve): *De para-
diso*, 15:73-74 (I 179 A-C) (*Corpus Scriptorum Ecclesiasticorum Latinorum*,
XXXII¹, 331). St. Ambrose in turn refers back to a possible nonpatristic source,
Philo Judaeus. Finally, it may be significant that Agrippa wrote *De originali
peccato* just before or just after his departure from Italy, a period when he
was under strong Hermetic influence. The *Pimander* of Hermes Trismegistus,
while not mentioning Adam and Eve, does, at least in its Latin version as
known to Agrippa, associate human procreation with the fall of man from a
state of perfection: *De potestate et sapientia Dei* [i.e., the *Pimander*] (Paris,
1494), Cap. 1, fol. a4ᵛ: "Homo autem cum considerasset: in tempore suo rerum
omnium procreationem ipse quoque fabricare voluit[.] Unde a contemplatione
patris: ad speram generationis delapsus est." Cf. *Corpus Hermeticum*, ed. A. D.

so much trouble as two other theological or ecclesiastical questions which became the subjects of two heated controversies which pitted Agrippa against certain influential members of the regular clergy at Metz. These controversies raised up many enemies and so made his continued residence at Metz increasingly uncomfortable.

In one of these controversies, Agrippa was able to score a considerable victory. This was his justly celebrated defense of an aged peasant woman of Woippy who had been accused of witchcraft. He claimed that a group of drunken conspirators having no authority broke into the woman's home in the middle of the night and dragged her before the *officialis* or judge of the ordinary's court at Metz. They had the aid of the Dominican inquisitor, Nicolaus Savini, whom Agrippa charged with complicity in a plot to seize the victim's property. Agrippa claimed that they bribed the judge to permit them to take the victim back to the village, where they starved and tortured her. After several days, the judge went to the village and, contrary to the law, proceeded by way of inquisition and permitted her accusers to put her to the torture. At length word of these proceedings reached the cathedral chapter at Metz; and the judge, falling ill, confessed on his deathbed that the woman had been unjustly treated. Despite the demand of the inquisitor for a renewal of the torture, the chapter excluded him from the case; and the vicar not only freed the woman but fined her accusers heavily. This is Agrippa's account of the case.

In the course of his defense of this woman, Agrippa prepared two briefs, one for the vicar and one for the new new judge. The nature of his defense is of considerable interest for the student of his thought. There is no attack on the reality of witchcraft itself, a procedure which in any case would hardly have been effective. The dominant note is the recurring charge of irregular and illegal procedure: unauthorized arrest, conspiracy between the accusers and the inquisitor, abandonment of the accused to the custody of her adversaries, the vagueness of the charges, simultaneous following of two contradictory forms of procedure, the admission of questionable witnesses. Next there is the question of jurisdiction. Agrippa

---

Nock, trans. A.-J. Festugière (4 vols.; Paris, 1945-54), I, 10-11 (Traité I, No. 13), where, however, the modern translation gives a quite different sense. If Agrippa knew the Zoharic treatise *Bereshith*, he would have found there a story that Adam had intercourse with evil spirits, though no suggestion that the sin of Adam was anything of the sort. See *The Zohar*, trans. Harry Sperling and Maurice Simon (5 vols.; London, 1931-34), I, 83 (19b).

admits that the *officialis* is the ordinary judge for the case. What right, he asks, did the inquisitor Savini have to participate? If he acted as assessor to the court, his appointment was improper because of his association with the accusers; and in any case it expired with the death of the first judge. If his participation rested rather on his position as inquisitor, then there was a serious jurisdictional error, for inquisitors have power only in open and indisputable cases of heresy, while in this case the facts are disputed, and the issue is not properly heresy but witchcraft. To these legalistic arguments, Agrippa joined a theological counterattack: the defendant's accusers themselves were heretics! One of their major proofs was that the defendant's mother had been burned as a witch and, even if she had not begotten her by a demon, had certainly dedicated her to Satan. Does not such an argument, asked Agrippa, undermine the efficacy of the sacrament of baptism, as if in vain the priest said, "Exi immunde spiritus"? Are not such accusers guilty of the heresy of Donatism? [6]

If these arguments do not prove that Agrippa denied the possibility of witchcraft (and they certainly do not prove it), they at least show that he was cautious about its application in a specific case. As early as 1510, though he admitted that demons had commerce with witches, he attributed the witches' errors also to senility.[7] A letter of September, 1520, suggests strongly that his close friend Brennonius thought the victims of a renewed witch-hunt to be nothing but eccentric old women.[8] Agrippa's attitude on this question, as well as his unusual views on original sin, well illustrates his willingness, even eagerness, to investigate and uphold views other than the commonly received ones.

This witchcraft case won for Agrippa some friends, including

[6] For this episode, see Agrippa's letter to Henricus, imperial councillor of Luxembourg, in *De beatissimae Annae monogamia*, fols. S5v-S7v, and an almost identical letter to Claudius Cantiuncula, *Epist.* II, xl. The two defense briefs appear in *De beatissimae Annae monogamia*, fols. R1r-R7v, R7v-S5v, and also in abridged form as *Epist.* II, xxxviii, xxxix. See also Brennonius' three letters to Agrippa, one undated, one probably from June, 1520, and one dated 27 September 1520, *De beatissimae Annae monogamia*, fol. P8r-v (*Epist.* II, xlvi); *Epist.* II, liii; *De beatissimae Annae monogamia*, fols. Q7r-R1v (*Epist.* II, lix).

[7] *De occulta philosophia*, I, 31, in Würzburg, Universitätsbibliothek, MS. M.ch.q.50, fol. 24r: "maleficis mulieribus . . . quae quidem anilis dementia sepe in eiusmodi flagicijs errare deprehenditur." This is printed in *De occulta philosophia libri tres* (Coloniae, 1533), Bk. I, ch. xxix.

[8] Brennonius to Agrippa, 27 September 1520, printed in *De beatissimae Annae monogamia*, fols. Q7r-R1r, and as *Epist.* II, lix.

the defendant, but also many powerful enemies. His second controversy at Metz raised up still more enemies and did not offer him
the possibility of a clear-cut decision in his favor, as did the witchcraft case. Unlike the latter case, this controversy involved an issue
directly related to the cause of reform-minded humanism, one which
had already pitted humanist reformers against conservative churchmen who upheld old church traditions against critical attacks by
humanistic scholarship. This dispute concerned the monogamy of
St. Anne. To the old legend of St. Anne, who was said to be the
mother of the Virgin Mary, medieval tradition had added embellish-
ments, among them the belief that after bearing the Virgin and after
the death of her first husband, Joachim, she had married twice more,
once to Cleophas and once to Salome, by each of whom she had a
daughter. All three daughters were named Mary; and they married
Joseph, Alpheus, and Zebedee, bearing, respectively, Jesus Christ;
St. James the Less, Joseph the Just, Simon, and Jude; and James
the Greater and the Apostle John.[9] The attack on this belief came
first of all from the greatest figure among French humanists, the
linguist, theologian, and philosopher, Jacques Lefèvre d'Étaples.
Agrippa became involved in this controversy only because he had
defended Lefèvre's views in discussions at Metz, notably with the
aristocrat Nicole Roucel, and then, according to the baneful custom
of the times, which he had already experienced at Dôle and which
many another humanist had also felt, had been publicly denounced
from the pulpit as a rank heretic. In response to this accusation,
Agrippa drew up a brief treatise based on Lefèvre's discussion of
the question, *De tribus et una.* His foes, in turn, composed articles
of refutation, to which Agrippa wrote a point-by-point rebuttal.
His chief adversaries were Dominicus Delphinus of the observant
Franciscans, Nicolaus Orici of the Minorites, and, above all, Claudius
Salini, prior of the Dominican friary at Metz and a recent doctor
of Paris. All three, be it noted, were members of the regular clergy,
which had already taken up the defense of tradition against the
humanists in the notorious Reuchlin controversy earlier in the same
decade.

This controversy gave rise to an exchange of letters between
Lefèvre and Agrippa. On 23 May 1519, Lefèvre wrote to thank
Agrippa for sending his little treatise, delivered by the Celestine
monk Claude Dieudonné. The French humanist reformer sent to

[9] *De beatissimae Annae monogamia,* fols. A7v-A8r.

his new friend certain other literature on the topic. At the same time, however, he began urging the Nettesheimer to avoid controversy if possible. In a later letter he pointed to Reuchlin as an example of how a pious and good man could suffer if he became involved with the monks. He urged Agrippa not to think of his (Lefèvre's) honor but only of the glory of the Virgin and of St. Anne. Apparently he had some reservations about his young adherent's Latin style, for he also warned him, if he must produce more controversial literature, to be sure to write elegantly.[10] Agrippa did continue the controversy, which did not even cease with his departure from Metz. One authority relates that Agrippa left the city on the very day of a public debate on the issue. Agrippa's friend Brennonius carried on the controversy with some success after Cornelius' departure.

This man, whom Agrippa generally calls Brennonius but whose real name was Jehan Rogier, curate of the parish of Sainte-Croix at Metz, was Agrippa's closest associate in the city and continued to correspond with him for a number of years after his departure. He shared Agrippa's interest in occult literature and reported to him, not without considerable amusement but also not without interest in the results, the alchemical enthusiasms of another, more obscure friend, Tyrius, keeper of the city clock. He not only carried on the St. Anne controversy but even sued one of his Dominican adversaries for slander after the latter had publicly denounced him in the city square. Like his friend Agrippa, like many another member of the secular clergy, he resented the invasion of his rights as a parish priest by the mendicants and became involved in another lawsuit when he called them to account for their exorbitant claims to superiority over the secular clergy. In addition to their common interests in the occult and in religious problems, he and Agrippa shared an active interest in learning of all kinds. When in 1522 a Roman inscription was unearthed at Metz, it was this learned priest and another friend of Agrippa, the young aristocrat Nicole de Heu, who deciphered it. Brennonius continued his disputatious ways in religion and during a Lutheran-scare in 1525 was one of several clergymen imprisoned for a time.[11]

[10] The Agrippa-Lefèvre correspondence appears *ibid.*, fols. N7r-O7r. On St. Anne, cf. *Lexikon für Theologie und Kirche*, I, 451.

[11] Philippe de Vigneulles, *La chronique de la ville de Metz*, ed. Charles Bruneau (4 vols.; Metz, 1927-33), IV, 332, tells of their close association and describes Agrippa's departure on the day of the disputation. For Brennonius' connection with the Roman inscription and for his later imprisonment, *ibid.*,

Another of Agrippa's friends at Metz was Claude Dieudonné, a Celestine monk who met Agrippa when the latter was a dinner guest in his monastery near Metz. His first letter to Agrippa asked for spiritual counsel, surely an odd request to come from a monk to a layman, but a good example of the way in which Agrippa was able to impress a new acquaintance with his profound learning. What especially attracted Dieudonné's attention was Agrippa's bold treatise on original sin—good evidence that the Nettesheimer's appeal was felt especially by those bolder spirits who liked to investigate the most recondite subjects, and to discuss the most daring and extreme viewpoints. Dieudonné's fellow monks opposed his association with his new friend, and he once wrote that he dared not confide the copying of one of Agrippa's works to any of his brethren. Agrippa communicated to Dieudonné not only his own unprinted manuscripts but also some of the writings of Luther. The biographer Prost thinks that it was a desire to remove him from Agrippa's influence that led his order to transfer him first to Paris and then to the new Celestine monastery at Annecy. At Paris, he delivered Agrippa's earliest letter to Lefèvre, and from Annecy he corresponded with Agrippa during the latter's stay at Geneva. Eventually, his interest in new religious ideas, which had been fostered by Agrippa, led him to abandon his order and to become a Reformed pastor in Switzerland.[12]

A friendship of even greater importance for Agrippa's intellectual development was that with Claude Chansonnette, or Cantiuncula, a young jurisconsult who won the praises of the legal scholars Zasius and Alciati. His parents resided at Metz, and it was probably through them that Agrippa met him. Apparently the city of Metz had aided in his education at the University of Basel, and there was some hard feeling when he refused to return to his native city but instead accepted a professorship and, despite his youth, the rectorate in his university. Agrippa originally wrote him partly to encourage

---

IV, 435, 548. The bitterness of the controversy is reflected in Brennonius' letter of 12 February 1520, printed in *De beatissimae Annae monogamia*, fols. P6v-P7r, and as *Epist.* II, xliv. Agrippa was also embittered by the controversy: Agrippa to Brennonius, Cologne, 19 February 1520, in *De beatissimae Annae monogamia*, fol. P3r-v, also printed as *Epist.* II, xliii.

[12] Letters from Dieudonné are in *De beatissimae Annae monogamia*, fols. N2r-N3r, and *Epist.* II, xxi, xxii. Cf. Prost, *op. cit.*, I, 358-73, and Charvet, *loc. cit.*, 33-34, for his career at Annecy and his subsequent conversion to Protestantism.

him to study humane letters and Scripture, partly to urge him to broaden his education by a trip to Italy, but chiefly to ask him to seek out his former student, Schylling, who had rescued his incomplete commentary on the Epistles of St. Paul from the plunder of his home at Pavia in 1515. The correspondence shows the development of a close personal friendship, but its chief interest is its reflection of how closely Agrippa followed the writings of Reuchlin, Erasmus, and the Lutherans. From the publishing center of Basel, Cantiuncula kept his friend supplied with both news and books.[13]

Only two members of the tightly closed oligarchy that ruled Metz, Nicole de Heu and Nicole Dex (or d'Esch), appear in the list of Agrippa's intimates in the city. Both of them belonged to families sympathetic to the cause of reform, and from 1524 on, Nicole d'Esch was the leader of the Evangelical group in the city.[14] His other friends were all men of the middle and intellectual classes, and most of them shared his interest in the occult and in the religious crisis: Tyrius, keeper of the great city clock, a man already mentioned; Baccaretus, Tilmannus, Andreas and Jacobus Carboneius, Mischaulus, and the physician Renaldus, men of whom only the names are known; and Jacobus the bookseller, who suffered exile for Lutheran beliefs. At a later period, their mutual friends at Metz brought Agrippa into indirect contact with the popular German writer on medical and astrological subjects, Lorenz Fries.[15]

Agrippa's residence at Metz, in addition to confirming his claim to possess an education in the law, was important chiefly because it brought him back into the milieu of northern humanism just at the moment when the figure of Martin Luther was about to precipitate a great crisis within the ranks of the humanists. His defense of an accused witch and his support of Lefèvre in the St. Anne controversy show how he aligned himself with the "advanced" school of thought at a time when the Reformation had not yet clearly un-

[13] On Cantiuncula, see Prost, *op. cit.*, I, 343-56; *Allgemeine deutsche Biographie*, III, 767-68; Alexandre Daguet, "Agrippa chez les Suisses," *Archives de la Société d'histoire du canton de Fribourg*, II (1858), 141-46, 154, 158; and two works by Guido Kisch, *Humanismus und Jurisprudenz: Der Kampf zwischen mos italicus und mos gallicus an der Universität Basel* (Basel, 1955), especially ch. I and p. 121, n. 23, and *Erasmus und die Jurisprudenz seiner Zeit: Studien zum humanistischen Rechtsdenken* (Basel, 1960), ch. 4, 6.

[14] [Comité Farel], *Guillaume Farel, 1489-1565* (Neuchâtel, 1930), pp. 137, 472-74, 476-80; cf. Maurice Thirion, *Étude sur l'histoire du protestantisme à Metz et dans le pays Messin* (Nancy, 1884), p. 43.

[15] *Epist.* IV, xxviii, lviii; on Fries, see Lynn Thorndike, *A History of Magic and Experimental Science* (8 vols.; New York, 1923-58), V, 430-34.

folded but already had added a new element to the existing ferment
of religious reform. The religious discontent and anticlericalism
which were already evident in certain of the treatises he wrote in
Italy were naturally accentuated in these surroundings. The period
in the imperial free city was also one of continued interest in occult
sciences.

The city of Metz itself was alive with diverse spiritual and
intellectual crosscurrents during Agrippa's time there; and he participated in many of them. The government of the city was in the
hands of a tightly closed aristocracy, which was itself sharply split
into two factions. The family of Heu led one faction; and Agrippa
was friendly with them and with the family of Esch, which supported them. As so often in the Reformation period, political rivalry
became further inflamed by religious controversy, since the families
of Heu and Esch favored reform and included a number of out-and-
out Lutherans, while the rival family of Gournay defended the
traditional church.[16] The politico-religious strife was heightened by
the corruption and weakness of the church authorities, whose head,
the bishop, was not only an absentee and a mere youth, but also a
member of the House of Lorraine whose head as Duke of Lorraine
constituted a threat to civic independence. In fact, the bishop was
Jean de Lorraine, the later cardinal, who years later became titular
godfather of one of Agrippa's sons born at Lyons. Just as at Geneva,
the church of Metz was crippled by a corrupt and absentee leader-
ship, and by its association with dynastic forces which posed a
threat to civic independence. These conditions already in the fourteenth and fifteenth centuries had generated a tradition of religious
unrest and anticlericalism among the citizens; and during Agrippa's
residence there, this tradition was beginning to be revived by the
spread of humanistic and Lutheran reform ideas.[17] Agrippa's own
associates were mostly from the group that favored the cause of
reform. It was only after his departure, however, that the growing
religious and social unrest generated by the Lutheran movement led
to a real crisis, beginning with the spread of Lutheranism among the
ruling classes from 1521 on. By 1524 a friend of Agrippa, the runaway French Franciscan reformer François Lambert,[18] and another

---

[16] [Comité Farel], *op. cit.*, p. 472; Thirion, *op. cit.*, pp. 21-24 (a sketch of the
constitution of Metz in this period).

[17] Thirion, *op. cit.*, pp. 7-20, 25-29.

[18] *Ibid.*, pp. 33-35; Roy Lutz Winters, *Francis Lambert of Avignon (1487-
1530): A Study in Reformation Origins* (Philadelphia, 1938), pp. 50-53.

ex-Franciscan preacher, Jean Védaste, invaded the city to preach new doctrines. The climax came in the years 1524-25. In the first of these years, an evangelical but probably orthodox reforming preacher, Jean Châtelain, caused such uproar by his sermons against clerical corruption that he was arraigned in the episcopal court and then, when the reforming nobles proved strong enough to prevent his conviction, was lured outside the city jurisdiction into territory of the Duke of Lorraine, was arrested as a heretic, and on 12 January 1525, despite his affirmations of Catholic orthodoxy, was burned at the stake. News of his execution set off violent popular riots against Theodore de Saint-Chaumont, Abbot of Saint-Antoine, vicar-general of the absentee bishop, and against others involved in the betrayal of Châtelain. So severe was this crisis that the rulers felt the whole aristocratic system to be endangered by the popular turmoil, and employed armed force to re-establish their control.[19] The brutal and summary execution of Châtelain caused quite a stir among partisans of reform as well as among the citizens. Whether Agrippa knew Châtelain is not entirely certain; but after his departure from Metz, his letters refer to some business involving a man of that name (Castellanus).[20] On the other hand, Agrippa's own letters for 1525 and 1526 make no mention of this notorious case.

Another striking scandal at Metz in the year of 1525 did involve a person who beyond all doubt was a close friend of Agrippa. Châtelain's preaching had been followed up by other evangelization of undeniably Protestant character, for in 1525 both Pierre Toussain and the uncompromising Guillaume Farel entered the city and made abortive attempts to preach. The new ideas were spreading, and in June of 1525 the authorities had to reprimand a conventicle of women who called themselves *Évangéliennes* and met privately to discuss Scripture. A high-ranking personage, son-in-law of one of these women, on his deathbed refused to make confession to a priest. The Reformation became the sole topic of conversation in the city. In the face of this rising tension, the conservative faction arrested two priests on charges of heresy, Didier Abria and Jehan Rogier. Rogier was curate of Holy Cross, and Agrippa's most intimate friend in the city. He had not long before been involved in bitter jurisdic-

---

[19] Thirion, *op. cit.*, pp. 35-42.
[20] See the letters exchanged between Agrippa and Brennonius during 1520, *Epist.* II, xlv, xlvii, xlix, l, lxi.

tional disputes with the regular clergy;[21] but fortunately for him, both he and Abria were released for lack of evidence.

The excitement of these events had hardly died down before a still more shocking scandal occurred, again involving friends of Agrippa. About Easter, 1525, a wool-carder of Meaux, Jean Leclerc, had arrived in the city. He had been exiled from Meaux for radical Protestant actions, including the posting of placards proclaiming the Pope to be Antichrist. At Metz he was in touch with Agrippa's friends the bookseller Jacques and Nicole d'Esch; and in the house of the latter he met Guillaume Farel during that man's brief visit to Metz in June. The scandal occurred on 23 July, when in the company of Jacques and another man, Leclerc entered the cemetery of Saint-Louis and in an iconoclastic fury mutilated two statues of the Virgin despite the pleas of his two companions. Arrested for this outrage, Leclerc boasted of his deed. On 29 July, he was burned at the stake. Jacques the bookseller, though innocent of the actual mutilation, suffered the loss of his ears, the pillory, and perpetual exile. A few days later, the city authorities formally prohibited the assertion of Lutheran doctrines, and the possession of heretical books.[22] Agrippa's comment in a letter written nearly a year later from Lyons was hardly sympathetic: having asked Brennonius to greet other friends, he also sent greetings to "the ears of Jacques the bookseller, for (as I hear) he himself on account of his Lutheranism left only them at Metz. . . ."[23]

Agrippa at Metz was obviously in touch with partisans of reform as well as with students of occult lore. But it is important to remember that he left the city in 1520, at a time when the whole movement for church reform was amorphous and undifferentiated. In 1520, none of his friends really could have been a Lutheran yet. After he left the city some of them, Nicole d'Esch and Jacques the bookseller, for instance, developed into Lutherans in the proper sense of the word. Others, including the man who was by far the closest to Agrippa, and the only one (except for the Erasmian re-

[21] Brennonius kept Agrippa informed of these events: *Epist.* II, xliv, xlix, lix (covering Brennonius' controversies, but not his arrest).
[22] On the Metz religious crisis of 1525-26, see Thirion, *op. cit.,* pp. 33-53, and [Comité Farel], *op. cit.,* pp. 472-84.
[23] Agrippa to Brennonius, Lyons, 23 June 1526, *Epist.* IV, xx: "auriculas Iacobi librarii. nam (quod audio) ipse pro Lutheranismo illas solas Metis reliquit. . . ." This letter also shows that there had been a two-year lapse in their correspondence.

former Chansonnette) with whom he kept in touch fairly regularly, Rogier-Brennonius, retained their desire for reform but did not abandon the traditional church. This is true even of the unfortunate Châtelain, assuming that he was the Castellanus of Agrippa's letters. Even though Agrippa at Metz had the reputation of a partisan of Luther, his religious orientation while there was not distinctively Lutheran, but followed the lines of humanistic reform, with overtones of occultism and esoteric learning as shown by his treatise on original sin, *De originali peccato*. With such later extremist tendencies as the iconoclasm of Leclerc, Agrippa had no sympathy: witness his cruel humor over the mutilation of his old friend Jacques.

It is not likely that Agrippa's associations with the reforming element at Metz, as distinguished from his own involvement in the witchcraft and St. Anne controversies, made his official position in the city untenable, for his successor, Jean Bruno de Niedbruck (or Pontigny), was another advocate of reform and was associated with a group of innovators who included Didier Abria and Pierre Toussain. Niedbruck retained his connection with Metz, and Agrippa was friendly to him, for in 1534 from Bonn he wrote him a letter of greetings.[24]

It did not take Agrippa more than a year to become tired of Metz. On 6 February 1519, he described the city in a letter as "the stepmother of all good letters and virtues,"[25] doubtless referring to the prevalent hostility to the ideas of Erasmus and especially, as shown above, of Lefèvre d'Étaples. In June, he wrote to a native of Metz, Cantiuncula, "I am stuck in this place, fastened by I know not what nail, but so fastened that I can't imagine either how I shall stay or how I shall leave. I was never ever anywhere from which I would depart more gladly than from this city of Metz, stepmother (I would say by your leave) of all arts and sciences."[26] There was considerable delay in getting a release from his obligations to the city; but by 19 February 1520, Agrippa was in his native Cologne, where he had apparently arrived only a few days before.[27]

[24] Printed in *De beatissimae Annae monogamia*, fols. A2r-A4v, and in *Opera*, II, 583-86.
[25] Lyons, Bibliothèque Municipale, MS. No. 48, fol. 39r: "ex ciuitate metensi, sed omnium bonarum literarum virtutumque nouerca."
[26] *Epist.* II, xxxiii: "Ego hoc loci nescio quo clavo defixus haereo: sed taliter defixus, ut neque quomodo maneam, quomodo abeam, cogitare valeam. Nunquam unquam alicubi locorum fui, unde abirem libentius, quam ab hac omnium bonarum literarum virtutumque noverca (pace tua dixerim) civitate Metensi."
[27] *Epist.* II, xliii, establishes Agrippa's arrival in Cologne by 19 February 1520. A whole series of letters exchanged between him and Brennonius that winter

Agrippa had no specific plans on his departure for Cologne. Apparently he intended to spend several months there and then to go to Savoy, where he hoped to secure a pension from the Duke.[28] He still had relatives living in Cologne, his mother and a sister. Furthermore, in his native city as in all other places where he lived, he had close friends among persons interested in humanistic and occultist studies. His closest such friend, Theodoric Wichwael, Bishop of Cyrene and administrator of the archdiocese of Cologne, had died in 1519,[29] probably not long after the death of Agrippa's own father. But there is evidence that Agrippa was in touch with such other enthusiasts for ancient wisdom as Johannes Potken, the prefect; Johannes Caesarius, the physician, philosopher, and Greek scholar; and Count Hermann von Neuenar, dean of the cathedral and the central figure among those humanists who supported Reuchlin and Erasmus against the conservative theological faculty of the city.[30]

Agrippa's letters show that during his stay in his native city he continued his earlier interests. He closely followed Brennonius' prosecution of the St. Anne controversy at Metz and wrote of plans to publish his own writings on the subject. He also followed the scientific activities of his friends at Metz, such as an all-day search for an herb supposed to have marvellous powers, or Tyrius' efforts to transmute metals, or the efforts of the entire circle to discover from its owner the formula of an efficacious (or at least lucrative) cure for the French pox. He had also left certain business affairs in Brennonius' hands at Metz, apparently not in good condition.

---

and spring confirms this date. A document printed by Prost, *op. cit.*, II, 473-74 (Appendix XIII, No. 7), shows that the city paid his salary for what would be the first quarter of 1520. But it appears not among ordinary expenses, as do Agrippa's earlier wages, but among extraordinary expenses, apparently because it was a goodwill terminal payment. One letter contradicts these dates, since it was written "Ex civitate Mediomatricum, ipso die Conversionis Pauli, anno 1520" (30 June): *Epist.* II, xlii. This letter reports receipt of the license to depart from Metz. The weight of the other evidence compels the conclusion that this letter is misdated.

[28] Agrippa to Brennonius, Cologne, 16 June 1520, *Epist.* II, liv.

[29] Conradus Eubel *et al.*, *Hierarchia catholica medii et recentioris aevi* (2nd ed.; 4 vols.; Monasterii, 1913-35), IV, 345.

[30] All these persons appear in Agrippa's letters of this period, except Count Hermann, who is mentioned in a letter of 11 January 1533, *Epist.* VII, xxvi. On Caesarius' activity at Cologne, see *Allgemeine deutsche Biographie*, III, 689-91. For the importance of Count Hermann, *ibid.*, XXIII, 485-86, and Franz Joseph von Bianco, *Die alte Universität Köln und die späteren Gelehrten-Schulen dieser Stadt*, I. Theil (Cologne, 1856), pp. 386-87.

During the spring, summer, and fall of 1520, Agrippa impatiently awaited the arrival of Brennonius for a visit, first set for Pentecost but much delayed. Aside from personal affection, the primary purpose of this visit was joint study of certain rare and esoteric books. Brennonius had a copy of a recently discovered manuscript work attributed to one Marcus Damascenus, *De variis admirandisque animae humanae naturis*. Agrippa was impatient to see this treatise, but his friend's trip was repeatedly put off and probably did not occur until the fall of 1520. As an inducement to hasten Brennonius' arrival, Agrippa wrote that he had certain abstruse propositions drawn from books left to him "by the will of Trithemius." [31] Later he indicated that he had a copy of the late abbot's *Steganographia* and that he had an amanuensis at work on another copy of the treatise.

Other examples of the varied nature of his interests also come from this temporary residence in Cologne. He gave advice on magical operations to a friend of the philosopher, physician, and Greek scholar Caesarius. Cantiuncula sought his friend's opinion of his new book on civil law, the *Topica*.[32] And a letter from a servant of Theodore, Count of Manderscheidt, showed Agrippa's reputation for being *au courant* concerning mechanical contrivances by asking him for information about certain ingenious mills said to be in use at Metz.[33] Also during this period, Agrippa engaged in an obscure quarrel with one of his servants, whom he finally accepted back into his service.[34]

Agrippa planned to leave Cologne in the spring of 1521 and, after visiting Brennonius at Metz, to proceed to Geneva in hopes of using his connections there to secure a pension from the Duke of Savoy. After some delay caused by an illness of his wife, they set out for Metz, where his wife suffered a relapse and died and was buried in the church of Brennonius. Agrippa then proceeded, either alone or with his son, to Geneva, which he reached sometime late in the spring of 1521. Throughout the summer, Brennonius sent to him

[31] Agrippa to Brennonius, Cologne, March-April 1520, in *De beatissimae Annae monogamia*, fol. Q1v, also *Epist*. II, xlviii. The identity of Marcus Damascenus is uncertain. Prost, *op. cit.*, II, 4, guesses that he was some unknown Gnostic writer of that name.

[32] Cantiuncula to Agrippa, Metz, 22 July 1520, *De beatissimae Annae monogamia*, fol. P2r-v, also *Epist*. II, lviii.

[33] *Epist*. III, i.   [34] *Epist*. III, ii-iii.

reports on arrangements for the care of his wife's grave at Metz
and on the health of his relatives at Cologne, together with news of
the doings of the Reformers and of military operations in the
vicinity of Metz.[35]

At Geneva sometime before 25 November 1521, and probably
as early as mid-September, Agrippa married his second wife, with
whom he lived happily until her death during an epidemic at Antwerp in 1529. Describing their compatibility, Agrippa wrote,
"There was never anger between us upon which the sun set." In
1524 he called her noble and beautiful and said that she lived so
that he could not decide whether she or his first wife was more
loving and obedient.[36] Her name, Latinized into "Iana Loysa Tytia,"
has been preserved in an epigram of the humanist Hilarius Bertulph
and two of Aurelius ab Aquapendente. Apparently she had some
relationship with the seigneurs d'Illens or Eylens, nobles of the Pays
de Vaud, and with Guillaume Furbity of Montmélian, who will
appear again in a later chapter. This second wife bore to Agrippa
one daughter, born at Fribourg and soon dead, and five sons, Aymon,
Henri, Jean, and two whose names are unknown, all born at Lyons
except the first, native to Geneva, and the last, born at Antwerp.
Aymon, Henri, and Jean assuredly survived their father, for legal
records show that the family was established at Saint-Antoine in
the Viennois, where it survived into the early seventeenth century.[37]

Agrippa already had influential acquaintances in Geneva before
he arrived, for while he was still in Savoy in 1517, a friend had

[35] On 21 March 1521, only the wife's illness was delaying their departure for
Metz (*Epist.* III, vi). There is a three-month gap in Agrippa's correspondence;
and at its end, he was already at Geneva (*Epist.* III, vii). Brennonius' letter of
19 July proves that the wife was buried at Metz: *Epist.* III, viii.

[36] Agrippa ad Amicum [Guillaume Furbity], Antwerp, 1529, *Epist.* V, lxxxi.
The comparison between the two wives is in a letter of 20 August 1524 to
Brennonius (*Epist.* III, lx).

[37] The verses giving her name are in *Opera*, II, 1150-52. Prost, *op. cit.*, II,
451-59, prints documents on Agrippa's wives and children. See also Henri Naef,
Les origines de la Réforme à Genève (Geneva, 1936), pp. 321-24. For the later
history of his children, see also Luc Maillet-Guy, "Henri Corneil Agrippa, sa
famille et ses relations," *Bulletin de la Société d'archéologie et de statistique de
la Drôme*, LX (1926), 120-44, 201-25. For the family of Illins, Illens, or Eylau,
Prost, *op. cit.*, II, 486-87, and Charvet, *loc. cit.*, 85-88. A *terminus ad quem* for
the date of the second marriage is set by a letter which mentions "my wife's
uncle" as the bearer, and which is dated from Geneva on 25 November ("ipso
die Catharinae") 1521: *Epist.* III, xi. Another letter strongly suggests mid-
September, 1521, as the date of the marriage: *Epist.* V, lxxxi.

urged him to settle in that city. One historian conjectures that this friend was a member of the cathedral clergy, probably Pierre Alardet, Dean of Annemasse, who later became Bishop of Lausanne. Whoever this person was, his letters also reveal that Agrippa already knew Eustache Chapuys, who as *officialis* or judge of the episcopal court since 1517 was the most important civil official in the city. Chapuys had probably met Agrippa while a student in Italy, either at the University of Turin or at the University of Pavia.[38] Since Chapuys was the agent of the Bishop of Geneva, Jean de Savoie, who co-operated with his relative, the Duke of Savoy, in a joint dynastic effort to establish effective control of the city in opposition to the elected municipal officials, his friendship was a valuable aid in Agrippa's desire for a pension from the Duke. Sometime in the spring of 1522, Agrippa visited the court of the Duke. His friends at Geneva and at the capital of Savoy, Chambéry, worked to help his cause. But the Chancellor of Savoy, Claude d'Estavayer, Bishop of Belley, was slow to fulfill the vague promises which the Duke had made, even though Agrippa tried to speed action by claiming to have been offered a pension by France also.[39] This was not to be his last experience with bureaucratic procrastination.

If Agrippa's friends at Geneva were unable to fulfill his Savoyard hopes, however, they could at least advance his well-being in the city itself. On 11 July 1522, the city fathers made a free grant of citizenship to "the honorable lord Henricus Cornelius Agrippa, doctor of arts and medicine, from Cologne on the Rhine, now of the parish of Saint-Gervais." [40] Chapuys as *officialis* was the Bishop's deputy in control of the Genevan hospital and also had supervisory powers over physicians and barber surgeons. Hence he was able to license his friend to practice medicine in Geneva, and even, according to one biographer of Chapuys, placed him in charge of the city

[38] Amicus ad Agrippam, Geneva, 16 November [1517], *Epist.* II, x, urging Agrippa to come to Geneva and advising him to write to Chapuys, who is offended at his silence. Naef, *op. cit.*, pp. 315-17, conjectures that this correspondent was Alardet. Certainly Alardet knew Agrippa at a later date. See Bertulph's verses on Agrippa, dedicated to Alardet, in *Opera*, II, 1152-53. Cf. Garrett Mattingly, "Eustache Chapuys and Spanish Diplomacy in England (1488-1536): A Study in the Development of Resident Embassies" (unprinted Ph.D. thesis, Harvard University, 1935), pp. 9-10, 42-56. Robert Centlivres and Otto Strasser, in [Comité Farel], *op. cit.*, p. 173, note that a certain Pierre d'Illens was prior of the Augustinian friary at Aigle up to 1526.

[39] For these negotiations, *Epist.* III, xviii, xxi-xxii, xxiv-xxvi, xxix-xxx, xxxii.

[40] Geneva, Conseil General, *Registres du Conseil de Genève* (12 vols.; Geneva, 1900-36), IX, 193; Naef, *op. cit.*, p. 314.

hospital. In any event, there is documentary proof that Agrippa was involved in some way in the care of the sick and needy at Geneva, for on Tuesday, 16 July 1521, the city council issued an order for the care of a pauper "for whom Master Agrippa interceded."[41] Chapuys' political influence probably had much to do with the city's grant of citizenship to his friend.

The position of Agrippa in Geneva, however, was not merely that of suitor for ducal favors and practitioner of medicine. Medicine was closely akin to astrology and others of those same occult sciences which Agrippa had already pursued in France, in Italy, and at Metz. And so, as one might reasonably expect, Agrippa once again became an active leader of those persons in the city who shared his enthusiasm for ancient wisdom—that is, for humanistic study of Antiquity in general, and in particular, for that important part of the ancient heritage that concerned such occult sciences as magic, astrology, or the Hermetic and cabalistic books. The continuation of these interests on the part of Agrippa is clearly established by the fact that he prepared and published one of the popular astrological calendars for the year 1523, a surviving fragment of which has been discovered in the present century.[42]

The friends of Agrippa must have constituted a lively and influential circle of liberal-minded humanist students of all sorts of ancient learning, including the occult learning in which Agrippa specialized. Again, as in each of the other cities were he resided, the Nettesheimer appears to have become a considerable personage among such circles, greatly respected for his strange and omnifarious learning. Because of the capital importance of Geneva in the second period of the Reformation, historians of the origin of Protestantism in that city have long viewed this humanistic circle gathered round Agrippa in the early 1520's as the seedbed of the Reformed faith. Certainly Agrippa and his friends followed the dramatic career of Martin Luther and his adherents closely and with considerably sympathy.[43] Futhermore, since he was already following the literature of the Reformation closely even at Metz, and stayed in touch with his friend Cantiuncula at the publishing center of Basel, Agrippa probably played an important role in purveying the new doctrines among his friends. Certainly many, perhaps most,

---

[41] *Registres du Conseil de Genève*, IX, 93; IX, 97; Mattingly, *op. cit.*, pp. 47-48.
[42] *Registres du Conseil de Genève*, IX, 93n.; Maillet-Guy, *loc. cit.*, 225.
[43] E.g., *Epist.* III, xxx.

of those who survived into the 1530's became supporters of the Reformation. In these early years of religious upheaval, such a sympathy was common among humanists. Agrippa and his Genevan associates welcomed and helped the runaway Franciscan friar, François Lambert, who later became an active leader of the Reformation in Hesse; and Agrippa helped him on his way with a letter of recommendation to his humanist friend Cantiuncula at Basel.[44] But while there is value in studying Agrippa and his circle as precursors of the Genevan Reformation, as sowers of the doctrinal seed which Farel and Calvin were to reap two decades later, it is just as important to realize that Agrippa and his friends were no crypto-Protestants, and that if they regarded themselves as precursors of anything, it was as precursors of the enlightenment of mankind through the spread of classical literature, ancient magic, and the simple, trusting, "untheological" faith of the first Christian century, not as precursors of Luther, still less as precursors of the religious and social radicalism which was evident among the more extreme Reformers. This whole question merits fuller discussion in a later chapter on Agrippa's relation to the Reformation; but it is worth observing that for every one of Agrippa's Genevan friends who became a Protestant, there was at least one who distinguished himself in the defense of the old religion.

Several of this liberal humanistic circle can be identified by name as persons of considerable importance in the political and religious history of French Switzerland. Alardet was one of them. Chapuys was another, and formed so high an opinion of Agrippa's learning and abilities that many years later, when he was imperial ambassador to England, he made repeated efforts to have his old Genevan associate Agrippa write a treatise upholding the cause of Catherine of Aragon against the famous divorce suit of Henry VIII. The chief patron of learning among Agrippa's friends was the Maecenas of Genevan humanism, Aymon de Gingins, Abbot of Bonmont, a Cistercian abbey in the Pays de Vaud nearby, who had been named bishop-elect and designated successor to Jean de Savoie, and who also served as vicar-general of the diocese. Bonmont never became bishop, however, for the pro-Savoyard faction managed to substitute Pierre de la Baume as coadjutor in the see and to win for him

[44] Winters, *op. cit.*, *passim*, and *Realencyklopädie für protestantische Theologie und Kirche*, XI, 220-23. For a more complete discussion of this episode, see Chapter Seven below.

the reversion of the episcopal office on the death of Jean de Savoie in February, 1522. Gingins opened to his friends the treasures of the abbatial library. His personal closeness to Agrippa is amply demonstrated, not only by the fact that he was godfather to Agrippa's infant son, who bore the same name, Aymon, but also by the fact that he cared for this child for more than two years after Agrippa had left the city.[45] In addition, he appears to have tried to help his new friend win the patronage of the Duke of Savoy.[46]

Round this high church official, Bonmont, the civil administrator Chapuys, and Agrippa, gathered many other enthusiasts for good letters from Geneva and the surrounding territory. Jean, Seigneur de Lucinge, a scholar, poet, and soldier of fortune, friend of Erasmus and of the ill-starred Duke Ulrich of Württemberg, urged Agrippa to write advice on studies to Philibert de Lucinge, a young relative who had gone to study at Basel.[47] The historian Henri Naef has also argued convincingly that two anonymous letters contained in Agrippa's surviving correspondence were from the future Reformer and chronicler of the overthrow of the old system in Geneva, François Bonivard. This man at this period was in political disgrace, having been involved in the political collapse of the anti-Savoyard faction, the *Eidguenots*. The pro-Savoyard faction, the *Mamelus*, or "Egyptian slaves," as their foes called them, had decisively overcome the *Eidguenots* in 1519, and in that year Bonivard had fled the city in a vain effort to escape imprisonment. He was nevertheless arrested and held in captivity until 1521. At the period of Agrippa's residence in Geneva, he appears to have been living outside the city at his native Seyssel, but was engaged in efforts to recover his priory at Saint-Victor. On 25 June 1522, he wrote to Agrippa from Seyssel and seems to have been awaiting an astrological prognostication, or nativity, promised by Agrippa, which was to be delivered by Jean Duchat, former *quêteur* of his priory.[48] Though his involvement in anti-Savoyard political schemes might seem to preclude close association with Agrippa, a suitor for a pension from the Duke, and with Chapuys, the highest civil representative of the ducal and episcopal interest in the city, Bonivard appears

[45] Mattingly, *op. cit.*, pp. 798-99; *Epist.* III, xxxviii, xxxix, xlix, lviii, lxiii, lxviii, lxxiv, lxxvi, lxxviii.

[46] *Epist.* III, xxiv, xxv.

[47] Mattingly, *op. cit.*, pp. 48-52; *Epist.* III, xxxi. According to Naef, *op. cit.*, pp. 317-18, this Sieur de Lucinge was named Bernard, not Jean.

[48] Naef, *op. cit.*, pp. 318-20; *Epist.* III, xix.

to have been on intimate terms with the Genevan humanists, and most particularly with Chapuys, with whom his friendship went back to their student days at the University of Turin prior to 1512.

Another member of the Agrippan circle at Geneva was Louis Beljaquet, rector of the city school. That he shared the scientific interests of Agrippa is suggested by the fact that in May of 1523 he abandoned teaching for the profession which Agrippa was practicing there, medicine.[49] Probably the religious discussions among the Genevan humanists were an early cause of the spiritual evolution which later made Beljaquet an adherent of the Reformed faith, much admired by Calvin and his associates.

If Beljaquet was a member of the humanistic group who many years later became a Protestant, there were others who, whatever their desire for reform, never wavered in their loyalty to the traditional faith. One such was Guillaume Furbity, of Montmélian, a Dominican or Cistercian, a doctor of the Sorbonne, and a relative of Agrippa's Genevan wife, a man who later was an outspoken foe of the Reformers, preaching and disputing publicly in opposition to Farel and Viret in the early 1530's until he was arrested and imprisoned. This is apparently the same Furbity who as titular Bishop of Alexandria became suffragan to Claude d'Estavayer, Bishop of Belley and Chancellor of Savoy, in 1535.[50] Since he later appears to have been associated with the Bishop of Belley, this Furbity may have been one of those on whom Agrippa was counting to further his cause with the Chancellor and the Duke of Savoy. Agrippa also met a visiting humanist, a former fellow student of Juan Luis Vives, Hilaire Bertulph of Leyde, when this youth visited Geneva in 1521. Bertulph soon became secretary to Erasmus at Berne, and later a member of the household of the French King's sister, Margaret of Alençon (later Queen of Navarre). This warm admirer of Agrippa was the author of a complimentary epigram on the Nettesheimer's wife.[51]

Agrippa's correspondents during this period included many of his old friends. Among them were an anonymous of Annecy, almost

[49] Naef, op. cit., p. 320.

[50] Charvet, loc. cit., 93-95; Eubel, Hierarchia, III, 342; Mattingly, op. cit., pp. 48-52; Naef, op. cit., pp. 321-24. Charles Borgeaud, in [Comité Farel], op. cit., p. 316, identifies the Furbity who clashed with Farel as Guy, not Guillaume.

[51] [Comité Farel], op. cit., pp. 124-26; Naef, op. cit., pp. 313-31; Opus epistolarum Des. Erasmi Roterodami, ed. P. S. Allen [and H. M. Allen and H. W. Garrod], (12 vols.; Oxonii, 1906-58), V, 13, n. 13.

certainly Dieudonné; Brennonius; Capito, who within a short time
was to become Bucer's chief co-worker in the Reformation at
Strasbourg; and Cantiuncula, whose failure to respond to his friend's
letters during much of the Swiss period appears to have been the
result of loss or theft of a number of letters, no uncommon occur-
rence in days when there was no organized postal service except for
governments. Agrippa was also in touch with the guardian of the
Franciscan friary of St. Bonaventure at Lyons, Jehan de la Grène
(Lagrenus), who expressed interest in *De occulta philosophia* and
asked Agrippa, as a pupil of Trithemius, to comment on an attack
(perhaps that of Charles de Bouelles) made on the Abbot of Sponheim as a magician and familiar of demons.[52]

The close association among Agrippa, Chapuys, Bonmont, and
Bonivard may well be the key to understanding an episode in the
experience of Agrippa at Geneva that has puzzled most of his biographers until the careful study of Chapuys and his friends made a
number of years ago by Garrett Mattingly. The problem is the
interpretation of a puzzling letter of 1522 in which Eustache excused
his absence from a dinner given by Agrippa because his public position required him to act discreetly. Some biographers have denied
that Chapuys could have written this letter, arguing that since the
Savoyard faction in Geneva had already triumphed decisively, the
references in the letter to some persecution which the author was
undergoing do not fit the situation of Chapuys. The biographer of
Chapuys, however, has discovered that during 1522 Chapuys was
in such political difficulties that for a time he even found it discreet
to withdraw to Annecy. What is more, it was precisely his attempts
to use his official position to help his humanistic friends that seem to
have contributed most to his temporary fall from favor. He had
become involved in a dispute with the *procureur fiscal* through his
attempts to defend a certain Allardet (perhaps the humanistic canon
who had first helped introduce Agrippa at Geneva) in a tax delin-
quency matter. In such a tense period, Chapuys may well have
hesitated to fraternize publicly with his fellow enthusiasts for humanistic learning. Furthermore, at this period, the Swiss city of Fribourg was exerting its influence on Geneva in an effort to undo the
Savoyards' success in setting aside the claim of Chapuys' friend, the

---

[52] *Epist.* III, xxxiii (dated 27 October 1522). Agrippa refuted these charges
against Trithemius in an indirect reply written at Fribourg, 20 January 1524,
Epist. III, liv.

patron of the Genevese humanists, Abbé Bonmont, to the succession
to the episcopacy. As a councillor of Duke Charles III of Savoy and
as a career member of the administrative bureaucracy of the Savoy
dynasty, Chapuys was obliged to support the claim of Pierre de la
Baume, a partisan of Savoy, to the office of bishop. Naturally, as
he was striving to win the confidence of this new bishop, under
whom he held his public office as *officialis*, Chapuys must have had
to be discreet in his association with the humanists centered around
the disappointed claimant to the bishopric, Abbé Bonmont.[53] It may
also be true that Agrippa's reputation for overboldness in religious
questions, and for sympathy with the early stages of the Lutheran
Reformation, made Chapuys, already compromised by his attempt
to favor Allardet, avoid close association with his humanistic
friends.[54] It has also been suggested with great probability that the
Agrippan circle was interested in alchemy, like Agrippa's friends
in other places where he lived; and, with less probability, that the
Genevan authorities suspected these alchemical operations of being
a cover for false coinage. It has been established that a young friend
of the group, Jean Maillard, was arrested for counterfeiting; but
this was in October of 1523, long after the disgrace of Chapuys,
and even many months after Agrippa himself had left the city of
Geneva. Thus the suggestions that Chapuys avoided his friends because they were suspected of false coinage, or that Agrippa's own
departure was under duress or conditions of disgrace, is quite unfounded.[55] Actually, Agrippa for many years maintained close
friendships in Geneva—with the Abbé Bonmont, guardian of his
son Aymon, for instance. Furthermore, even after Chapuys had
advanced to the responsible position of imperial ambassador to England and had become the legal adviser of those who upheld Catherine of Aragon's claim to be lawful queen of England, he still sought

[53] *Epist.* III, xxviii, speaks in the third person of Eustochius' regret that dis-
cretion prevents his attendance. The whole affair, which puzzled earlier scholars
like Charvet, *loc. cit.,* 25-30, 36, and Daguet, *loc. cit.,* 141, appears to have been
settled by Mattingly, *op. cit.,* pp. 53-56, 798-99, who has clarified the attribution of certain letters, and has proved that *Epist.* III, xxviii, really does concern
Chapuys, who was in some difficulty through his intervention in a tax delin-
quency case. For the suggestion that some unpleasantness may have resulted
from Agrippa's association with the counterfeiter Jean Maillard, see Henri
Denkinger, "Henri Corneille Agrippa," *Dictionnaire historique et biographique
de la Suisse*, I, 125.
[54] Naef, *op. cit.,* pp. 324-31.
[55] *Ibid.,* pp. 341-42; Denkinger, *loc. cit.,* I, 125.

out his old friend Agrippa as a respectable and talented scholar whose pen could be of service in behalf of the unfortunate spouse of Henry VIII.

Agrippa had not intended to settle permanently in Geneva; and after it became clear that his hopes in the direction of Savoy were futile, he began casting about for another position. In particular, he appears to have had hopes for an offer from France, where he had friends willing to help him.[56] But when he left Geneva about the beginning of 1523, he did not go to France but, via Payerne and perhaps Lausanne, to the Swiss city of Fribourg, where he arrived sometime before 20 March. In a letter written on that day to Chapuys, he described his friendly reception "by my lords of Fribourg," and attributed it not a little to the favor in which they held Chapuys. Although Agrippa's own letters are vague concerning the nature of his duties, indirect references in missives addressed to him show that he was town physician, a conclusion also proved by the archives of the city of Fribourg, which show that his wages were 127 livres, plus a large house and allowances of grain and wine.[57] His duties as well as his family responsibilities were confining, but he was able to make one short trip to Berne late in April, 1523, when he talked with a man whom he described as an old friend, Godefroi Brulart, a French royal treasurer who was staying there with a man whom he called General Nurbec. Although Agrippa called Brulart a devotee of occult studies, some students have regarded him and his host at Berne as secret agents of Charles, Duke of Bourbon, and so have concluded that Agrippa was in touch with the rebellious vassal of Francis I even at this early date.[58]

Even if the object of his conversations with Brulart at Berne was political rather than occultist, there is plenty of other evidence that, just as in earlier years, Agrippa studied occult sciences while at

[56] For an offer to help him if he came to Lyons, *Epist.* III, xxxiv.

[57] Agrippa was at Payerne on 6 January 1523: *Epist.* III, xxxviii. He had friends at Lausanne, including the bishop (*Epist.* III, xlviii, 1); but aside from this fact, there is no support for the conclusion of Naef, *op. cit.*, pp. 342-43, that he stopped in that city. He describes his reception at Fribourg in *Epist.* III, xxxviii. An anonymous friend wrote him that the city treasurer, Johannes Reiff, had reported "tuam excellentiam in Friburgensem Aesculapium esse assumptam" (*Epist.* III, lv). The information about his wages at Fribourg is printed from the treasury records by Daguet, *loc. cit.*, 146.

[58] *Epist.* III, xl-xli. Daguet, *loc. cit.*, 154-55, conjectures, on what evidence I know not, that the meeting with Brulart concerned not occult learning but political intrigue with agents of the Duke of Bourbon.

Fribourg. It was desire to receive instruction in that field that prompted a letter from a Strasbourg friend of the city treasurer, Hans Reiff. Agrippa commissioned the latter to explain to his correspondent a summary of *De occulta philosophia* which he sent with his reply. To the same Strasbourg admirer Agrippa mentioned plans to edit the treatise of Marcus Damascenus which he had secured from Brennonius. He also asked his friend's opinion on certain astrological questions. Another admirer, Claude Blancherose, the same who in the Lausanne disputation of 1536 was to oppose the Reformers Farel and Viret, wrote Agrippa twice in 1523 from Annecy, attracted by Jean de Laurencin's praise of Agrippa and also by reading his commentary on the Lullian art. Agrippa's friend Antoine Pallanchi, notary at Fribourg, was commended to a friend as a curious seeker after occult knowledge. Finally, an unnamed associate of the Bishop of Lausanne desired to visit Agrippa in order "to talk about the loftiest secrets of things." [59]

The letters of the period also reflect a continuing interest in the Reformation. Agrippa still was in touch with Cantiuncula, from whom he expected news of the doings of Luther, Erasmus, and the other public figures of the age. His contact with the Erasmians at Basel was not only through Cantiuncula, but also through Bertulph, whom he had probably met at Geneva in 1521. It was probably this secretary of Erasmus who wrote from Basel a letter describing Erasmus' favorable comments about Agrippa. Those who had praised the Nettesheimer were, in addition to Bertulph, Cantiuncula, Philibert de Lucinge (the Genevan youth to whom Agrippa had given advice on studies), and the philosopher Thomas Zegerus.[60] Early in 1524, Agrippa recommended to Cantiuncula as "an evangelical man" one Thomas Gyrfalk, who by 1527 was openly a Protestant. Other friends at Fribourg who were interested in the Reformation were the musician and cantor of the cathedral chapter, Vannius, or Hans Wannenmacher, who despite his friendship for Zwingli held onto his position until 1530, when he was tortured and banished. There was also a friend named Ulrich, the only one of Agrippa's correspondents to use the standard greeting of the

[59] Amicus ad Agrippam, Lausanne, 6 November 1523, *Epist.* III, l: "ac de altissimis rerum arcanis colloqui. . . ." For the rest of this paragraph, see *Epist.* III, xxxvi-xxxviii, xl, xlii, lv-lviii.

[60] Amicus [Bertulph?] ad Agrippam, Basel, 10 November [1523], *Epist.* III, xliv.

Protestants, "Gratia et pax a Deo patre et domino nostro Iesu Christo." Naef guesses that this man was Uli Techtermann, whose father disinherited him for his short-lived adherence to Protestantism.[61]

Of course not all of Agrippa's friends at Fribourg favored the Protestants. His friend Hans Reiff, the city treasurer, some years later was a determined foe of Guillaume Farel's efforts to evangelize the village of Grandson.[62] Also during this period, Agrippa corresponded with the physician Claude Blancherose of Annecy. Although Blancherose sympathized with the humanistic type of religious reform, he had no use for schism or for doctrinal heresies. Years later, in the Lausanne religious disputation of 1536, he was one of the tiny handful of Roman Catholics, mostly devout laymen, who sought in vain to make up for the incompetence of the official spokesmen of the church, and to defend the old faith against attacks by Farel, Calvin, Viret, and other Reformed preachers.[63]

The significance of these connections with persons of Protestant or at least Erasmian leanings will form the subject of a later chapter; but for the present, it is important to observe that such friendships must have made life unpleasant for Agrippa in such a strictly Roman Catholic city as Fribourg, where from 1522 onwards the city government had taken severe measures against religious innovators, culminating in an act of 11 December 1523, confiscating all Lutheran books, and the act of early January, 1524, requiring all residents to swear to a profession of faith. Perhaps it was with this narrow orthodoxy in mind that Agrippa called Fribourg "bare and destitute of the cultivation of all sciences." [64]

These conditions were, however, at most a contributory cause of Agrippa's departure from Fribourg. Agrippa voluntarily resigned his position as town physician on 9 July 1523, probably because he

---

[61] For Gyrfalk, see Agrippa to [Cantiuncula], Fribourg, 5 January 1524, *Epist.* III, liv; Naef, *op. cit.*, pp. 343-45; Daguet, *loc. cit.*, 152. For Vannius and the conjectural identification of Uli Techtermann, see Amicus ad Agrippam, Fribourg, 7 August 1524, *Epist.* III, lxxx; and Naef, *op. cit.*, pp. 343-47.

[62] [Comité Farel], *op. cit.*, pp. 269-70.

[63] For Agrippa's exchange of letters with Blancherose, *Epist.* III, xxxvi, xxxvii; cf. [Comité Farel], *op. cit.*, p. 345. The correspondence suggests that Agrippa and Blancherose met through their mutual friends, the Lyonese family of Laurencin.

[64] *Epist.* III, lvi: "Ex Friburgo Helvetiorum, omnium scientiarum cultu deserto ac destituto. . . ." Naef, *op. cit.*, pp. 347-51.

found his duties burdensome; and when he was ready to leave Fribourg, the city council demonstrated its good will by granting him a *viaticum* of six florins.[65] The obvious reason for his resignation but continued residence in the city was that he wanted to be free of encumbering obligations so that he could accept some richer offer.

[65] Prost, *op. cit.*, II, 40-44.

CHAPTER FOUR

GALLIC PERFIDY

Up to his departure for France in the spring of 1524, the dominant tone in Agrippa's life was one of hope for success in his
worldly affairs. Of course he felt the intellectual and religious problems of his age keenly even in this earlier period; but his personal
expectations, though seldom fulfilled in complete measure, were
high. This personal optimism vanished soon after his arrival in
France. The bitter disappointments and actual want which he experienced first in France and then in the Low Countries during this
later period of his life must have stimulated those pessimistic elements which, as later chapters will show, were not absent even in
his earlier thought. The earlier period produced Agrippa's major
writings in the occult field, although his interest in occultism never
left him even in his most despairing hours. The later period, however, produced the work which is the fruition of all his earlier
doubts and uncertainties as well as the product of his personal disappointment in the summer of 1526, *De incertitudine et vanitate
scientiarum declamatio inuectiua.*

Yet when the richer offer he had been awaiting at Fribourg finally came from the French court early in 1524, Agrippa's hopes were still high. On 5 January 1524, he wrote to Cantiuncula that he was planning to leave Fribourg for France; but he did not actually arrive there until 3 May 1524, when in a letter to Aymon's guardian, Abbé Bonmont, he described his arrival in Lyons in Vergilian terms: "Per tot varios casus, per tot discrimina rerum tandem venimus Lugdunum." He reported that he was in the company of old friends, that he expected a fixed pension from the King, and that he had already received money for the settling of his household.[1]

As usual, Agrippa did not clearly state the nature of his new duties. Probably he was not certain. After talking with Jacques d'Illens, a relative of Agrippa's Genevan wife, a friend writing from Lompnes (probably Bonivard) believed that Agrippa's duties would be military. He warned him to wear into battle some distinguishing mark so that his friend Chapuys, who was in imperial service with the army of Bourbon, could recognize him. The Nettesheimer himself later claimed that he brought over to the French cause two thousand infantry led by his wife's relatives, the lords of Illens. Finally, in his letters to the Abbé de Bonmont, guardian of his son Aymon, he claimed not only to be in frequent touch with royal councillors but even to be himself admitted to the transaction of public business.[2] The uncertainty about his new position is not surprising, for he entered France at a period of great uproar. The year before, the greatest nobleman of the realm, the Duke of Bourbon, had fled the country to escape arrest for his treasonous relations with the Emperor Charles V. The prosecution of Bourbon (*in absentia*, of course) and of his fellow conspirators was still in progress. In that spring and summer of 1524, the French armies

---

[1] As early as 19 September 1522, while still seeking the patronage of the Savoyard court, Agrippa claimed that he had received an offer from France: *Epistolarum Liber III*, xxiv, in his *Opera* (2 vols.; Lugduni, n.d.), II, 794-95. (Henceforth this collection of letters is cited as *Epist.*) His letter to Cantiuncula is *Epist.* III, lii. That reporting his arrival in Lyons and his bright prospects is *Epist.* III, lviii.

[2] Henri Naef, *Les origines de la Réforme à Genève* (Geneva, 1936), pp. 318-20, identifies the anonymous of Lompnes as Bonivard; cf. *Epist.* III, lix. The claim to have brought over troops is in a letter to Brennonius, Lyons, 26 September 1524, printed in *De beatissimae Annae monogamia ac unico puerperio . . .* (n.p., 1534), fols. S7v-S8r, and in *Epist.* III, lxii; also in a letter to Chapelain, Lyons, 3 November 1526, *Epist.* IV, lxii, where he sets the number of troops at four thousand. His claim to be admitted to state secrets was his excuse for not writing more often to his friends in Geneva, which he regarded as a hotbed of anti-French intrigue: *Epist.* III, lxiii, lxviii.

beat off a multiple invasion led by the renegade duke. During the whole period, the King's main energies went into preparations for the ill-starred invasion of Italy which began in the early autumn of 1524 and culminated in the disaster of Pavia on 24 February 1525. While Agrippa waited at Lyons, the King himself moved in and out of the wartime capital, and the rest of the court, headed by the Queen Mother, Louise of Savoy, as regent, moved about in central France at such places as Blois, Romorantin, Amboise, and Bourges. Not until September, 1524, was the Regent at Lyons; and not till 17 October did she definitively establish herself there, making the fortified Abbey of St. Just and later the Celestine convent the center of her war administration.[3] Yet another factor which must have delayed the assignment of definite duties to Agrippa, and which helps also to explain his later difficulties in getting paid, was the commencement of a far-reaching reorganization of the royal financial system. This reorganization had begun in January, 1523, and culminated in the trial and execution of the great treasury official, Semblançay, in 1527.[4]

Despite his claims of high connections and the prospect of important official duties, Agrippa had to wait until after the court settled down at Lyons in October, 1524, to get a clearly defined position at the court of the Regent;[5] and when it came, the new employment turned out to be that of personal physician to Louise, who was in chronic ill health. Doubtless there was a considerable lack of clarity about his duties; and doubtless he expected to be able to gain influence in affairs of state.[6]

It is a certainty that Agrippa came to France because of promises

---

[3] For an account of these disturbed political events, see Paule Henry-Bordeaux, *Louise de Savoie: Régente et "Roi" de France* (Paris, 1954), pp. 180-293; Pierre Jourda, *Marguerite d'Angoulême, Duchesse d'Alençon, Reine de Navarre: Étude biographique et littéraire* (2 vols.; Paris, 1930), I, 87-89, 90-96; and Ernest Lavisse, ed., *Histoire de France depuis les origines jusqu'à la Révolution* (9 vols.; Paris, 1900-11), V[1], 217-23.

[4] Henry-Bordeaux, *op. cit.*, pp. 201-6, 213-15, 343-66; Lavisse, *op. cit.*, V[1], 230-38.

[5] In August, 1524, Agrippa claimed to be receiving wages from the King (*Epist.* III, lx); a letter of 26 September (*Epist.* III, lxii) suggests that his future was still uncertain; on 22 November he made his claim to be in touch with official business, but still complained that the costs of the war kept him from being rich except in promises (*Epist.* III, lxiii).

[6] For the real nature of his position, see Agrippa to Chapelain, Lyons, 3 November 1526, *Epist.* IV, lxii, where he bitterly described himself as "Principis tuae scatophagum medicum"; cf. his letter of 1532 to Mary of Hungary, *Epist.* VII, xxi. Henry-Bordeaux, *op. cit.*, p. 234, and Jourda, *op. cit.*, I, 90-92, show that Louise of Savoy was in chronic ill health.

of friends to find him lucrative and honorable employment at court. Very likely his actual position, which in the opinion of the Queen Mother included astrological prediction of political events as well as medical advice, was below the expectations which his patrons at court had aroused during 1522 and 1523. The identity of these friends who urged him to come to France and gained for him his court appointment is a problem which admits of at least partial solution. Agrippa must have had friends surviving from his youthful residence in France prior to 1510. Very likely he still was in some sort of touch with the circle of Symphorien Champier, though his correspondence for this period contains no trace of this. He frequently sent greetings through friends to the humanist Lefèvre d'Étaples, but that relationship was not close enough for Lefèvre to have been one of Agrippa's chief patrons. He also continued to send warm greetings to the royal painter and honorary royal chamberlain Jean Perréal during the French years. There is no proof, however, that Perréal was one of those who brought him to France.

Those who actually had most to do with bringing Agrippa to Lyons were very likely members of the wealthy and influential Laurencin family, some of whom were money-changers and royal treasury officials in France, others of whom had entered the church. Agrippa knew members of this family at least as early as 1517, for they had been active helpers in his pursuit of patronage at the court of Savoy and at the court of the papal legate in Avignon. Even at that time, there had been some mention of Agrippa's coming to Lyons. His appointment at Metz was gained largely through their influence; and he dedicated his Lullian commentary to Jean de Laurencin of Lyons, preceptor of the commandery of Saint-Antoine de Riverie in the military and hospital order of St. Anthony. Another member of this family was his brother, Ponce de Laurencin, preceptor of the commandery of St. John of Metz.[7] Its head, who also favored Agrippa, was Claude I de Laurencin, a wealthy Lyonese money-changer who in 1513 purchased the barony of Riverie near Lyons, and appears in Agrippa's letters under the title *dominus Ripuariae baro*. Yet another Laurencin mentioned in the letters

[7] Léon Charvet, "Correspondance d'Eustache Chapuys et d'Henri-Cornélius Agrippa de Nettesheim," *Revue savoisienne*, XV (1874), 47-49; F. M. Rudge, art. "Orders of Saint Anthony," *Catholic Encyclopedia*, I, 555-56. For Agrippa's dedication, see his *Opera*, II, 331-33. Another work of his, *Sermo de inventione reliquiarum Beati Antonii Heremitae, pro quodam venerabili ejus ordinis religioso*, in *Opera*, II, 573-77, may well have been dedicated to Jean de Laurencin.

for 1517 was "magnificum dominum thesaurarium Laurentinum"—
probably Claude II de Laurencin, who in 1522 held the office of
receveur-general de tailles for the Lyonnais.[8] Closely linked with
this Lyonese family was the man who served as one of Agrippa's
most loyal advocates at court throughout the years in France,
Symphorien Bullioud, Bishop of Bazas. Bishop Bullioud's sister
Sibille was married to Claude I de Laurencin; hence he was the
uncle of Agrippa's friends the brothers Laurencin.[9] Although he
successively held the bishoprics of Glandèves, Bazas, and Soissons,
Bullioud was really a professional bureaucrat. It is even possible
that he was the first of the Laurencin family connection that
Agrippa met, for in 1509 he replaced Charles II d'Amboise as
French governor at Milan; in 1512 he was associated with the schismatic Council of Pisa, which Louis XII employed as a weapon in
his struggle with Pope Julius II, and with which Agrippa claimed
to have been associated. Later, when the French King abandoned
his own council and adhered to the Fourth Lateran Council, Bullioud attended the conclave that elected the new pope, Leo X,
in 1513. Quite probably Agrippa learned to know him in this period;
certainly he was a close friend and loyal advocate of Agrippa between 1524 and 1528. Another member of this Bullioud-Laurencin
family grouping who aided Agrippa at Lyons was a cousin of the
Bishop of Bazas, Pierre Salla. Association with this group of *noblesse
de la robe* is harmonious with Agrippa's known friendship with an
avowed enthusiast for occult arts, Geoffroi Brulart, intendant for
the province of Champagne,[10] and with Henri Bohier, seneschal of
Lyons, another high royal financial official.[11] The financial aristocracy of early sixteenth-century France formed an influential and
tightly knit class of families; and some of Agrippa's best advocates

[8] *Epist.* II, iii, iv, ix, from the spring of 1517. In 1523, a friend from Annecy,
probably Claude Blancherose, had discussed Agrippa with the eldest of the
four Laurencin brothers ("Dominus de Rivo-everso") and with "dominus
Ripuariae baro," that is, apparently, with Claude II de Laurencin and his father,
Claude I (*Epist.* III, xxxvi, xxxvii). For help with the identities of the members
of the Laurencin family, I wish to thank Dr. Natalie Zemon Davis of the
University of Toronto.

[9] On the Bishop of Bazas, Charvet, *loc. cit.*, 47-49; Roman d'Amat, art. "Symphorien Bullioud," *Dictionnaire de biographie française*, VII, col. 663; and
Tabaraud's sketch in *Biographie universelle*, VI, 259.

[10] Agrippa ad Amicum [Christoph Schylling], Berne, 27 April 1523, *Epist.*
III, xl; cf. M. Prevost, art. "Brulart," *Dictionnaire de biographie française*,
VII, col. 487-88.

[11] M. Prevost, art. "Bohier, Henri," *ibid.*, VI, col. 782.

were of this group. Other, more shadowy friends mentioned in the correspondence of Agrippa between 1524 and 1528 appear also to have had treasury connections,[12] though of course, he also had enemies among this class, such as Barguin, and Thomas and Antoine Bullion, the officials whom he blamed for his difficulties in drawing his salary.

Another class of men with whom Agrippa had close connections (some of whom may have helped persuade him to settle at Lyons and seek royal patronage) were his fellow physicians. Certainly the most intimate of these was his colleague as physician to Louise of Savoy, Jehan Chapelain. Chapelain was the principal physician of the Regent, for he accompanied her when the court left Lyons at the beginning of February, 1526, leaving Agrippa behind, and his letters show that he was continually and actively concerned with the state of Louise's health. During Agrippa's period of disfavor at court, Chapelain and the Bishop of Bazas worked together as his most loyal and persistent advocates. Chapelain remained in the service of the Queen Mother up to her death in 1531, and afterward became physician to King Francis until his own death in 1543.[13] Whether Agrippa knew Chapelain before he came to Lyons is uncertain, though the closeness of the friendship, and the extent to which Chapelain was willing to push Agrippa's cause even when their royal mistress felt sharp resentment against the Nettesheimer, might suggest a friendship of long standing. In any event, Agrippa certainly knew some Lyonese physicians before coming to France in 1524, and it is very likely that some of these had much to do with bringing Agrippa to court. On 20 January 1524, Agrippa wrote a letter from Fribourg to a certain Dionysius concerning occult matters. In this letter he upheld the reputation of his master Trithemius against a slanderous attack, obviously the one made several years earlier by Charles de Bouelles. He expressed his hope to come to Lyons soon, and greeted by name two friends, Jean Perréal and a certain Master Andreas, royal physician.[14] This Master

---

[12] Such as Martin de Troyes (mentioned repeatedly in Book IV of Agrippa's correspondence), the Seigneur de Ryans (*Epist.* IV, ix), Adhemar de Beaujeu (Bellojocus) (*Epist.* IV, xxv), Jean Laurinus (*Epist.* IV, li), Chalendatus (*Epist.* IV, lx, lxi) and Vauzelles (*ibid.*), Ponterasius (*Epist.* V, iii), and an anonymous correspondent from Condrieu (*Epist.* IV, lx-lxi).

[13] V. L. Saulnier, "Médecins de Montpellier au temps de Rabelais," *Bibliothèque d'Humanisme et Renaissance,* XIX (1957), 452-53.

[14] *Epist.* III, liv.

Andreas was very probably that André Briau (or Briellus) who served as physician to both Louis XII and Francis I. This man, who died in 1530, was a friend of Symphorien Champier, who was himself a physician as well as a popularizer of humanistic learning.[15] The recipient of this letter from Agrippa very probably was another Lyonese physician, Denis Thurini, on whose behalf Agrippa later wrote a letter seeking favorable action in a case pending before the Parlement of Paris.[16] Finally, Agrippa had close relations with other French physicians whom he may have met only after coming to that country, such as Guillaume Cop of the noted family of humanists and physicians; Jérôme de Monteux, a well-known medical writer with whom he exchanged information, and several lesser-known figures.[17]

After coming to Lyons, and perhaps before, Agrippa also was acquainted with various individuals of the official classes in addition to the Laurencin group. Testimony taken in a lawsuit of 1560 reveals the identity of some of these individuals. One witness in the case, which involved the claim of Agrippa's sons Henri and Jean to the privileges of persons nobly born, was Ginette Chicquam, widow of the royal notary Benoît Joyet. She claimed to have been a friend of "Mᵉ Henri Corneille Agrippa et demoiselle Jane Loyse (Tyrstie) sa femme. . . ." [18] Agrippa himself had claimed that the godparents of his son Jean were Jean, Cardinal of Lorraine, and the Dame de Sainte-Prie. The testimony of 1560 shows that some other gentleman represented the Cardinal as proxy, and that Dame Claude Remye, wife of Jehan Bruyères, "procureur ez cours de Lyon," was the godmother—perhaps also acting as proxy for the Dame de Sainte-Prie or some other lady of noble rank.[19] The godparents of the elder son born to Agrippa at Lyons, Henri, were Henri Bohier, seneschal of Lyons, and Dame Claude (or Claudine) Dumas, pro-

---

[15] Saulnier, loc. cit., 451-52. Dr. Natalie Zemon Davis suggested the identity of this Andreas, a conclusion also reached by Charvet, loc. cit., 48.

[16] Epist. V, viii.

[17] For Cop, Epist. IV, xxxvii, xlii, xliv, xlviii, lxii; V, iii. For Jérôme de Monteux, Epist. IV, lxxi. Epist. IV, xviii, shows Agrippa's relations with a number of physicians. Also in this period, he was in touch with foreign physicians, such as the noted German medical writer Lorenz Fries (Epist. IV, xxviii, lviii), and a physician of Annecy named Vincentius (Epist. V, i).

[18] Auguste Prost, Les sciences et les arts occultes au XVI siècle: Corneille Agrippa, sa vie et ses oeuvres (2 vols.; Paris, 1881-82), II, 455 (Appendix VIII).

[19] Ibid., II, 456-57. Cf. Agrippa ad Amicum [the Abbé de Bonmont], Lyons, 24 July 1525, Epist. III, lxxvi.

prietress of the Logis du Charriot-d'or. Although these were less distinguished than the other pair of titular godparents, the names of Henri's sponsors in baptism are of considerable interest because Claudine Dumas, herself a subsequent convert to Protestantism, was related by marriage to Hélcuin Dulin, an early evangelical leader at Lyons and director of the influential Collège de la Trinité.[20] Perhaps mutual religious interests formed a link between this Dumas family and the Laurencins. At least three sons of Claude II de Laurencin, François, René, and Claude III, later became Protestants.

This association with elements of the Lyonese populace who later became Protestant suggests that Agrippa had a connection with circles of humanistic and even evangelical tendency, as well as with occultists, though such a statement does not prove that Agrippa was anything more than a humanistic sympathizer with reform. His letters to the Bishop of Bazas and to Chapelain at times have a vaguely evangelical and reformist ring; and the chief literary product of these years, *De vanitate*, complains bitterly about church corruption and closes on a note of evangelical (but not distinctively Protestant) trust in Scripture.

There are other associations which further illustrate these relationships with reform-minded humanists in France. Decidedly the most distinguished was the king's own sister, Marguerite d'Alençon, who already in this period was beginning to stand forth as the patron of reforming churchmen and of the new humanistic literary movement. To her Agrippa dedicated his work *De sacramento matrimonii* in the spring of·1526, obviously in the hope of winning her sympathy and so regaining the favors of his own patron, the Queen Mother Louise of Savoy. In return for this dedication, the Duchess sent Agrippa a gift of twenty *écus d'or*;[21] but he never became a member of her inner circle. Agrippa may not have won her as his own patron, but he certainly had many connections with her circle. When some courtiers criticized his *De sacramento matrimonii*, he wrote to the closest associate of Marguerite in her church reform interests, Michel d'Arande, who had just become

---

[20] I owe this information to Dr. Natalie Z. Davis, whose doctoral dissertation, "Protestantism and the Printing Workers of Lyons: A Study in the Problem of Religion and Social Class During the Reformation" (University of Michigan, 1959), led her to identify the names and relationships of many early Lyonese Protestants.

[21] Jourda, *op. cit.*, I, 140-41.

Bishop of Saint-Paul-Trois-Chateaux,[22] asking Arande to take up his defense. Arande had been an extremely active reforming preacher in Marguerite's service, subject to bitter attacks from the conservatives, and often regarded by Protestant reformers as one of themselves. Though Agrippa doubtless knew Arande, he was probably closer to two other persons whom the Duchess favored, his Metz friend Claude Chansonnette, whose translation of Erasmus' *Manière de soy confesser* (1524) was one of the first humanistic works to stir Marguerite's conscience deeply,[23] and Hilaire Bertulph, who entered her service in November, 1524, and whom Agrippa had known in Switzerland.[24] Via his friend Chapelain, Agrippa also sent frequent greetings to Lefèvre d'Étaples, who was the spiritual father of most early French reformers, and to the humanistic scholars Cop and Budé.

Friendship with such humanistic and reforming figures harmonizes well with Agrippa's close associations with medical men, treasury officials, and other bureaucrats, since the new learning penetrated most rapidly among precisely these sections of the French people. Agrippa's title to their friendship and patronage rested on his reputation for learning in all fields, and especially on his proficiency in the occult arts and on his open sympathy for the cause of church reform, a cause which in France was still amorphous enough that humanists, Catholic reformers, and out-and-out Protestants were not clearly differentiated. Hence Agrippa could on the one hand attract the interest of such churchmen as Jean Lagrène, the occultist-minded guardian of the convent of St. Bonaventure at Lyons,[25] the Dominican Pierre Lavin of Mâcon (also a person with occultist interests),[26] and Jean de Foix, Archbishop of Bordeaux,[27] while on the other

[22] Lyons, 7 May 1526, *Epist.* IV, vii. Arande had fled to Strasbourg along with Lefèvre d'Étaples and Roussel in 1525 to escape persecution by the Parlement of Paris; but the favor of Marguerite d'Alençon and of Louise not only secured his recall but also gained him his bishopric, which the Pope confirmed on 8 January 1526. After assuming his position on 17 June, he seems to have moderated his early radicalism, though he undertook the reform of his diocese and retained some ties with the Meaux group of reformers. See Roman d'Amat, art. "Arande, Michel d'," *Dictionnaire de biographie française*, III, cols. 227-30, who insists that Arande never was a Lutheran.

[23] Jourda, *op. cit.*, I, 92-96.

[24] *Opus epistolarum Des. Erasmi Roterodami*, ed. P. S. Allen [and H. M. Allen and H. W. Garrod] (12 vols.; Oxonii, 1906-58), V, 13, n. 13.

[25] Lagrène was probably one of Agrippa's earliest advocates at Lyons. Agrippa knew him as early as October of 1522: *Epist.* III, xxxiii; cf. *Epist.* III, liv.

[26] *Epist.* IV, xvii, xix, xxxiv, xlv.   [27] *Epist.* IV, lxx, lxxv, lxxvi; V, xxii.

hand he was in touch not only with humanistic reformers like Lefèvre and Michel d'Arande, but also with openly Protestant figures such as the exiled François Lambert of Avignon, and the reformer Antoine Papilion.[28] Agrippa stood between the religious camps, clearly hostile to the conservatives who dominated the Sorbonne, but not fully associated with those extreme reformers who were willing to break finally with the Roman church.

The true golden age of sixteenth-century French humanistic scholarship and literature had not yet arrived during Agrippa's residence there; but already in the middle classes and in court circles, there were signs of what was to come later.[29] Louise of Savoy was interested to some extent in learning and in a Catholic reform of the church; her son Francis at least toyed with the same interests; while her daughter Marguerite had already begun to attract the attention of scholars and reformers of all sorts, though she was not yet the dominant cultural figure which she became later in life.[30] For all the ill fortune, unhappiness, and want that he experienced in France, Agrippa had the good luck to be in Lyons, which was the principal center of the new intellectual and spiritual movements, favored as it was by the frequent presence of the royal court, the growth of active and cultured commercial and administrative classes, its geographical proximity to both Italy and Germany, and the remoteness of such strong conservative forces as the Sorbonne and the Parlement of Paris. He played a prominent role in the intellectual life of this milieu, enjoyed friendships with persons of both political and intellectual importance, and for a time, at least, felt his French residence to be prosperous and highly advantageous. His position was sufficiently dignified that later, when he began to lack money, he complained that his honors merely made his poverty all the more disgraceful and hard to bear.[31]

---

[28] *Epist.* III, lxxxii, where Lambert returns greetings sent to him through Papilion. On Papilion, cf. Jourda, *op. cit.*, I, 98-99. On the other hand, Agrippa's correspondence betrays no connection with such evangelical leaders as the almoners of Marguerite d'Alençon, Gerard Roussel and Pierre Toussain, nor with active preachers of the time such as Étienne Lecourt, Pierre de Sébiville, Martial Mazurier, Aymé Meigret, Anémond de Coct, or Pierre Caroli, nor yet with the humanist martyr Louis Berquin. Agrippa's associations were not chiefly with open partisans of the German reformers, but with reform-minded clergy and laymen who sympathized with the Protestants and complained about church abuses, but refused to abandon the traditional institution.

[29] Lavisse, *op. cit.*, V[1], 297-99.

[30] Jourda, *op. cit.*, I, 23-24, 44-46, 92-96, 98-102; II, 1075-80.

[31] Agrippa to Chapelain, Lyons, 15 July 1526, *Epist.* IV, xxv.

Agrippa stayed at Lyons from early 1524 to late 1527, his longest
residence in any one place since childhood. His stay falls into two
periods, one of moderate prosperity and great hopes, and the other
of deepening despair and real poverty. The departure of Louise of
Savoy for Blois and then the Spanish border without him in early
February, 1526, is a convenient dividing line between these periods.
Even before her departure, he was richer in promises than in actual
benefits. He complained of this less than a year after his arrival,
explaining that "these wars for the most part snatch their munifi-
cence itself away from me." Later he wrote that, like Pandora, he
still had hope but little else.[32] By April, 1526, Agrippa had begun
to pester Chapelain to have the Queen Mother do something to
alleviate his want; and this request grew into a barrage of letters,
gradually increasing in bitterness. Aside from the fact that he was
not permitted to follow the court after its departure from Lyons,
his complaint was that the promised pension went unpaid. The man
to whom the king had entrusted his payment on leaving Lyons was
dead, and the various treasurers to whom he applied for money
claimed either to have no pay warrants for him or to lack funds
for the payments. Agrippa insinuated that his friends at court had
played him false; and in fact one of them, the seneschal Bohier,
did commit an indiscretion which increased the obvious disfavor
into which Agrippa had fallen at court. By the summer and fall of
1526, Agrippa, plunged into deepest despair, was threatening—
and this in letters addressed to courtiers—to join the King's enemies.
Finally on 7 October 1526, an agent of the treasurer Barguin informed him privately that his name had been stricken from the roll
of pensioners. Agrippa's bitterness and denunciation of rulers in
general and female rulers in particular became even more savage
than before. He even had difficulty getting his back pay for the
period up to his dismissal. Only by having the wife of a cousin of
the Bishop of Bazas, Pierre Salla, steal the papers of the treasurer
Thomas Bullion was he able to force that man to pay, a procedure
not far from blackmail. He received his "posthumous money," as
he called it, in mid-November, 1526. Despite the efforts of his
friends to restore his favor at court, he never again received a
French pension.[33]

[32] Agrippa ad Amicum [Bonmont], Lyons, 22 November 1524, Epist. III,
lxiii; Same to Same, Lyons, 8 June 1525, Epist. III, lxxiv.
[33] For these efforts to get paid, see the printed correspondence of Agrippa
for 1524-26, passim. As a matter of fact, the payment procedure used by the

Naturally, one asks what was the cause of Agrippa's disgrace. Doubtless the fiscal difficulties of the crown in its wars with the Hapsburgs were one cause, for Agrippa was not the only courtier to complain of delay in payment. Another cause, once his disgrace had begun, must have been his indiscretion in denouncing the perfidy of the court. But the fundamental causes of his fall from favor were three. One, an incident of the summer of 1526, was his reluctance to draw up an astrological prognostication for Francis I as the Queen Mother had asked. The request was not surprising, since astrology and medicine were commonly linked in that century. Louise, in fact, believed strongly in portents and predictions, and from 1508 to 1522 kept a peculiar sort of journal to record events in her life and especially in the life of her son. The form of this journal suggests that she kept it for consultation by prognosticators.[34] Holding such views, she must have found the Nettesheimer's reaction to her request offensive. Agrippa wrote his friends to urge the Queen to put his talents to better use than on what he called "astrological superstition"; and the seneschal Bohier indiscreetly showed to Louise a letter in which Agrippa not only insinuated that she was superstitiously abusing astrology but also remarked that in any case the stars were favorable not to Francis I but to his archrival, the Duke of Bourbon. Evidently Agrippa's indiscreet handling of this royal request for a prognostication was coupled with the still greater indiscretion of letting his unfavorable predictions and his charges of superstition become generally known. The chronicler Claude Bellievre recorded that in May of 1527 Agrippa said that the stars menaced King Francis with death within six months.[35] For Agrippa to refuse to prophesy when asked was unwise; for him to predict evil fortune for his patron's son was still more unwise; but for him to let word get about that his prophetic learning revealed the impending death of the King was sheer folly. No Renaissance state would tolerate prophecies of the king's death. Henry

---

crown did make it important to get a "favorable" assignment, i.e., to get a warrant drawn on a treasury official who was both willing and able to pay. See Lavisse, *op. cit.*, V^1, 231. Even a favorite of Marguerite d'Alençon, the poet Marot, repeatedly complained of being ill-assigned, and hence of going unpaid.

[34] For a discussion of this journal, see Henri Hauser, "Le *Journal* de Louise de Savoie," *Revue historique*, LXXXVI (1904), 280-303.

[35] Claude Bellievre, *Souvenirs de voyages en Italie et en Orient; Notes historiques; Pièces de vers*, ed. Charles Perrat (Geneva, 1956), p. 11.

VIII of England regarded such prophecies as constructive treason; and in an age when astrological predictions carried great prestige and were commonly used for propaganda purposes by governments, Agrippa was fortunate that his indiscretions caused him no more harm than the loss of royal favor.

This incident so angered Louise that Agrippa's friends obviously hesitated to speak too warmly in his behalf. Furthermore it must have increased certain suspicions which formed the other main cause of Agrippa's disgrace. The prediction of success for Bourbon seemed to confirm suspicion, probably going back to Agrippa's earliest days at Lyons, that he was a secret adherent of the rebellious duke. Cornelius himself admitted freely that he had had offers from Bourbon before coming to France; and soon he was complaining openly that if he and his relatives, the lords of Illens, had only accepted those offers, they would now be rich from the spoils of the French. His threats to follow evil courses if not restored to favor must have appeared like evidence that he was meditating treason if not already involved in it. Such suspicions must have been further strengthened by his friendship with Chapuys and other members of the Savoyard faction at Geneva, and by the fact that from time to time he sent his secretary to Germany and to Savoy. In September, 1526, he admitted to the Bishop of Bazas that he had had offers from other princes, including hostile ones, though he said that he had rejected them.[36]

A third probable cause of Agrippa's disgrace was his reputation for religious radicalism. Though Agrippa himself was closer to humanistic reformers than to real Protestants, and though the Regent herself was rather anticlerical and her daughter Marguerite a reputed heretic and an ardent promoter of humanistic and even semi-Protestant evangelization, the time of troubles that followed the military disaster of Pavia (1525) was one of great danger for all partisans of reform, whether Protestant or not. The Sorbonne and the Parlement of Paris had long since been pressing for an active persecution; and in the eyes of the religious conservatives who dominated those institutions, there was no difference between liberal

[36] The astrological incident is mentioned frequently in the letters of the summer and early fall of 1526, especially *Epist.* IV, xxix, xxxvi-xxxvii, xl, li. Agrippa himself realized that suspicions of sympathy for Bourbon (or worse) contributed to his fall from favor; see his letter of 3 November 1526 to Chapelain, *Epist.* IV, lxii. His admission that he had received offers from the enemy is in a letter of 29 September 1526 to the Bishop of Bazas, *Epist.* IV, xlix.

humanistic reformers and avowed Lutherans. Already in the second half of 1524 several of Marguerite's favorite church reformers had been prosecuted for heresy; and while Marguerite herself continued to intervene in favor of her personal favorites, the general policy of the government turned unfavorable to the reformers. The reasons for this new line of policy were chiefly political. The primary reason was the fear that the new religious ideas would create social unrest as they spread among the lower ranks of the population. Contemporaneous events in Germany, the Knights' War and the Peasants' Revolt, were further underlined by the spread of open heresy in French court circles, and of both theological and social unrest among conventicles of persons from the lower classes, especially in Lyons and other great towns. There were even open anticlerical outbursts at Meaux and other centers of the humanistic religious reform movement.[37] Political events soon made the danger even greater for anyone known to sympathize with reform. The government under the stress of the war emergency had already shown that it would tolerate no unrest in the war capital of Lyons. But from early 1525, the disasters of the Pavia campaign helped stir up a popular frenzy against church reformers on account of their foreign orientation, while the political crisis prevented the government from making the clear distinction between Lutherans and humanists which the Regent probably would have preferred to make, and which her daughter Marguerite certainly wished to maintain. The King, to whose authority Marguerite had appealed in the past in order to secure the release of her friends, was in captivity from 25 February 1525 to 17 March 1526. During this period the Regent, Louise, had to assume the full burden of government. Several of the Parlements proved difficult to keep in check; and careful management was necessary to control them, and also to prevent the princes of the blood, in particular the Duke of Vendôme, from challenging her title to the regency. In such conditions, Louise and Marguerite could hardly afford to jeopardize the co-operation of the Parlements and the peers by resisting the popular clamor for the repression of heresy. Even those closest to Marguerite, Lefèvre, Roussel, and Arande, had to flee to Strasbourg in order to escape persecution;[38] and not until the return of King Francis was it possible for Marguerite to win more than a momen-

[37] Pierre Imbart de la Tour, *Les origines de la Réforme* (4 vols.; Paris, 1905-35), III, 164-95, 243-46.
[38] Iourda, *op. cit.*, I, 140-41.

tary respite from persecution for her reformer-friends.[39] In such circumstances, Agrippa's ties with foreign humanists, and even with such avowed Protestants as Lambert and Capito, must have weighed against him, though the principal causes of his loss of favor at court were doubtless his unwillingness to make predictions and the suspicion that he was a partisan of Bourbon.[40]

Agrippa's correspondence contains proof that his threats to go over the enemy were not without substance. Sometime in 1526, a relative urged him to take revenge for Gallic perfidy by joining Bourbon and the imperial army. Early in 1527, Agrippa was in direct correspondence with Bourbon, sending him information of some sort, gratefully declining an army command, and assuring him that the heavens favored his cause. His letters to Bourbon seem to presuppose earlier correspondence which has not survived.[41] If any hint of these relations reached the court, it is small wonder that even Agrippa's most loyal friends there were somewhat hesitant about identifying themselves too closely with him.

Growing disfavor did not prevent Agrippa from seeking by literary work in the spring of 1526 to restore his favor at court. To Marguerite, Duchess of Alençon, later Queen of Navarre, he dedicated what was, with one minor exception, probably his first book since he left Metz in 1520. This treatise, *De sacramento matrimonii*, aroused criticism rather than praise from certain persons at court, who objected to its teaching that marriage might be dissolved for adultery and to its exaltation of the physical side as well as the religious side of marriage. Hence it did Agrippa little good at court even though he defended its orthodoxy and decency and prepared a translation into the vernacular.[42] The following summer, he sought to attract the interest of the Queen Mother and of King Francis

[39] *Ibid.*, II, 137-38, 140-41, for Marguerite's efforts on behalf of Berquin and of the Meaux reformers.

[40] His fear of the religious attitude of the court is evident in his letter of 16 September 1526 to Chapelain, *Epist.* IV, xliv.

[41] Amicus ad Agrippam, Montluel, n.d., *Epist.* IV, lxv. Agrippa to Bourbon, Lyons, 26 February and 30 March 1527, *Epist.* V, iv, vi. Prost. *op. cit.*, II, 152-56.

[42] The treatise is in his *Opera*, II, 543-52. Its dedication to Marguerite is *Epist.* IV, i; for its reception at court, *Epist.* IV, ii-iii, vii. On the translation, *Epist.* IV, iv. The only trace of literary work between *De beatissimae Annae monogamia* (1519) and the treatises of 1526 is a surviving fragment of a calendar for 1523, printed at Geneva by Jacobus Diniand, with the legend "Autore Henrico Cornelio Agrippa": Luc Maillet-Guy, "Henry Corneil Agrippa, sa famille et ses relations," *Bulletin de la Société d'archéologie et de statistique de la Drôme*, LX (1926), 225.

himself by writing about his projected work on engines of war, *Pyromachia*, a treatise which he probably never completed and which does not survive. Somewhat later, in the fall of 1526, just before he learned of the cancellation of his pension, he sought in vain the reversion of a rich office at Lyons.

After the double blow of losing his pension and learning that the desired office was already filled, he almost abandoned further efforts to regain favor. His correspondence henceforth was full not of begging for intercession but of vituperation of the perfidy of courtiers, querulous hints that his own friends had let him down, coarse puns directed against the French, threats to desert to the enemy and to publish his correspondence and so reveal how shabbily Louise had treated him, and demands for the names of those who had slandered him at court. By the summer of 1527, he was urgently seeking a clear release from his obligations to the Queen Mother and was haughtily telling his friend Chapelain, whom he regarded as living in Hell (the court), "Besides, we have no further need of Proserpina or Pluto." [43] The reference is to Louise and Francis.

Out of this period of most profound despair came two of the most important of Agrippa's works. The first, *Dehortatio gentilis theologiae*, is of uncertain date but was dedicated in June of 1526 to the Bishop of Bazas. The pessimistic tone and fideistic attitude of this little treatise are even more fully developed in a book which he wrote in the late summer of 1526, *De incertitudine et vanitate scientiarum declamatio inuectiua*, perhaps the most frequently printed of all his works and beyond question the most significant of them. This book contains the renunciation of all human arts and sciences, including those which he had treated in *De occulta philosophia;* it is also a mordant social satire; and it concludes by stressing the superiority of the Christian Gospel to any human learning. Quite probably the depression of his fortunes during the period of composition influenced the mood which this book reflects; but, as a later chapter will show, the germ of its leading ideas is evident even in his earlier works.

The composition of *De vanitate* in the discouraging summer of 1526 might lead one to expect a lessening of interest in occult matters, since the book appears to deprecate its author's earlier studies.

[43] Lyons, 12 August 1527, *Epist.* V, x: "Caeterum nobis nec Proserpina, nec Plutone ulterius opus est."

Except for letters in which Agrippa chides one or two friends for excessive devotion to astrology,[44] no such lessening of occultist interest really occurred. During his first year in France, a friend in Basel asked him in the name of the printer Johann Froben to seek a manuscript of Pliny's *Natural History* at Lyons.[45] Throughout the period, Agrippa's letters show that he was trying to borrow copies of such treatises as Aristotle's *Mechanics*, cabalistic and Lullian writings, Trithemius' *Steganographia*, his own *Geomantia* (his only copy was with Brennonius at Metz), and Ptolemy's *Cosmographia*. Friends from Fribourg and other places were eager to study occult sciences under him; and on at least one occasion, Agrippa admitted such a student to his service.[46] He also sought and gave out medical advice. Not many months before he became so reluctant to cast the horoscope of Francis I, he had sent some predictions to a friend in the household of the Queen Mother, probably Chapelain.[47] He not only continued to receive news of Tyrius' alchemical work at Metz and to demand news of the experiments of his friend Natalius of Toulouse, but also conducted alchemical operations of his own on one occasion, hoping to grow gold from seeds which a friend had brought him.[48] Furthermore, he received and answered requests for interpretations of certain prodigies, which, he thought, portended further French defeats and grave danger from the Turks.[49] His desire to get occultist books was so great that it even

[44] Agrippa ad Amicum, n.p., n.d., *Epist.* IV, viii; Petrus Lavinius, O.P., to Agrippa, Mâcon, 13 June 1526, *Epist.* IV, xvii; Agrippa to Lavinius, Lyons, 18 June 1526, *Epist.* IV, xix. Cf. also the burlesque prognostication recently discovered and attributed to Agrippa by Paola Zambelli, in "Umanesimo magico-astrologico e raggruppamenti segreti nei platonici della preriforma," in *Umanesimo e esoterismo: Atti del V convegno internazionale di studi umanistici, Oberhofen, 16-17 settembre 1960*, ed. Enrico Castelli (Padua, 1960).

[45] [Cantiuncula?] to Agrippa, Basel, 12 November 1524, *Epist.* III, liv.

[46] Agrippa ad Amicum, Lyons, 19 August 1525, *Epist.* III, lxxxi; cf. *Epist.* III, lxv, lxvii, lxx, lxxv, lxxvii. Whether at this period Agrippa read Greek occultists in the original is uncertain. Latin texts of Aristotle and Ptolemy were available, and he certainly read Latin more readily than Greek.

[47] [Chapelain?] to Agrippa, Cognac, 26 May 1526, *Epist.* IV, xii.

[48] For Tyrius' experiments, *Epist.* IV, xvii. For Natalius, *Epist.* IV, xxxv; V, xii, xiii. For the seeds of gold, *Epist.* IV, lvi. For another example of interest in alchemy, see his letter to Jérôme de Monteux, Lyons, 23 November 1526, *Epist.* IV, lxxi; and cf. Maillet-Guy, *loc. cit.*, 134-44. Monteux was a medical doctor of Montpellier then residing at Saint-Antoine de Viennois, and a writer on natural philosophy.

[49] Chapelain to Agrippa, Chambourg, 26 September 1526, *Epist.* IV, xlviii; Agrippa's reply, Lyons, 11 October 1526, *Epist.* IV, lv.

gave occasion for an untrustworthy courier to extort money from
him before delivering treatises sent by Brennonius.[50]

The ferocity of Agrippa's attacks on the French court after the
cancellation of his pension shows clearly that he was looking abroad
for patrons. Had he had any serious hopes of staying in France, he
surely would never have written such indiscreet attacks on Francis
and his mother. By early 1527 at the latest, as we have seen, he was
in touch with the archenemy of the King and his mother, the exiled
Duke of Bourbon; and in 1532, he claimed that this duke and the
imperial chancellor, Mercurino Gattinara, had persuaded him to
leave France.[51] He may have received vague encouragement from
such persons; but two avid students of the occult, rather than great
officers of state, really persuaded him to abandon France for the
Low Countries. These two were a Genoese merchant who had
houses in Lyons and Antwerp, Augustinus Furnarius, and an Italian
Augustinian friar residing chiefly at Antwerp, Aurelius ab Aquapendente. It is difficult to tell just when he came in touch with these
men, but he probably knew Furnarius before the completion of
De vanitate in 1526. His increasingly haughty tone toward his
friend Chapelain in the summer of 1527 suggests that by that time
the prospect of a move to Antwerp had been broached. The plan
to leave Lyons took definite shape in the fall of 1527, and he
and his family probably left that city on 5 December, reaching
Paris by water along the rivers Loire and Seine shortly before 1
January. There Agrippa hoped to secure his release from royal
service and a military pass and escort to the frontier, and then to
move himself and his family to Antwerp.[52]

Like so many of his hopes, this one was thwarted. As weeks
stretched into months, Agrippa got repeated promises of his release
and even renewed offers of royal patronage, but no release. Living
at an inn consumed money faster than he could earn it, probably
by the practice of medicine. Not until 17 March 1528 could he

[50] The correspondence with this youthful adventurer, Ioannes Paulus Fla-
mingus, occurred in the summer and fall of 1526: Epist. IV, xxviii, xxxiii, xxxviii,
lviii, lxiii, lxvii-lxviii.

[51] Agrippa to Mary of Hungary, Bonn, n.d. [1532], Epist. VII, xxi.

[52] In his letter of 16 September 1526 to Chapelain, reporting completion of
De vanitate (Epist. IV, xliv), Agrippa mentioned that he had dedicated it to
a newly found patron. The dedication as printed at Cologne in 1531 and in
other editions is to Furnarius. Thus, unless there was a change in dedication,
he must have known Furnarius before 16 September 1526. For Agrippa's trip
to Paris, Epist. V, xx-xxiii.

nform Furnarius that he had recently got his letters of dismissal, and those without any accompanying gift from the avaricious Queen Mother.[53] Since by this time he had exhausted the funds which Furnarius had advanced, he tried everywhere but without success to borrow. To make matters worse, when friends presented his letters of safe-conduct for the signature of the commander on the northern border, the Duke of Vendôme, that prince tore them up, angrily declaring that he would never sign in favor of a diviner.[54] By May, he had his safe-conduct from the French but was still delayed by unsettled conditions on the border and above all by lack of money. In the middle of June, news of an arrest of French goods at Antwerp caused him concern for the property he had send ahead there, especially his books. Finally a friend, probably Furnarius, sent him money. Then, shortly after learning that Louise of Savoy was so angry at him that he was in danger of arrest, he set out alone, leaving his family behind. The journey occurred between 16 July and 23 July, on which latter day he reached Antwerp.[55] His family had to join him later. His household at this period consisted of himself, his wife, four sons, and four servants, a figure which suggests that in addition to the daughter born at Fribourg, one of his sons, probably the one by the first wife, was dead.[56]

The months spent waiting in Paris, from late 1527 to July of 1528, were a time of anxiety and of financial distress. Nevertheless, in a letter of this period Agrippa reported that he was enjoying the company of friends old and new, men of occultist interests from whom he could learn many new things.[57] Although his announced intention of taking up residence in enemy country, at Antwerp, caused many French to shun him, his friends at court

[53] *Epist.* V, xxviii.
[54] Agrippa ad Amicum, Paris, 31 March 1528, *Epist.* V, xxx.
[55] For the dates of his trip and his fear of arrest by the Queen Mother, see *Epist.* V, xlix-li.
[56] Agrippa to Chapelain, Paris, 6 May 1528, *Epist.* V, xliii. Since his son Aymon had probably been sent up from Geneva at the end of the summer of 1525 (*Epist.* III, lxxiv, lxxviii), Prost, *op. cit.*, II, 87-96, is correct in noting that one son is missing. Maillet-Guy, *loc. cit.*, 212, proves that Aymon, Henri, and Jean survived their father; hence the missing son must be the one by the first wife, or possibly the third of the sons born at Lyons.
[57] Agrippa to Augustinus Furnarius, Paris, 17 March 1528, *Epist.* V, xxviii: "inveni praeterea istic veteres amicos, et conquisivi novos, etiam viros arcanarum literarum eruditissimos, didicique et vidi permulta, quae hactenus ignoravi."

were still working to regain royal favor for him, and he claimed to have been approached with rich offers which he spurned because of his eagerness to join his new friends in the Low Countries.[58] The court at this period was nearby at St.-Germain; and Agrippa was still in touch with his friends Chapelain, Bohier, and the Archbishop of Bordeaux.[59] His other relationships, those with the occultist friends, were obviously more pleasant, for they were less involved with the bitterness and rancor between Agrippa and the Queen Mother. The only identifiable figure in these circles is the Paris mathematician Oronce Finé, who at this period was teaching at the Collège de Maître Gervais, a position which he held from 1524 until his appointment to the chair of mathematics at the new Collège Royal in 1530. It was probably Finé to whom Agrippa (who was extremely fond of dogs) presented a puppy while at Paris. Finé and Agrippa were busy about certain calculations, doubtless astrological, which Finé was exchanging with a certain Master Nicolas. Finé must have been the person who invited Agrippa to dine with a friend learned in mathematics, along with Master Nicolas and the principal of Finé's college. Later, on 1 June 1528, Agrippa wrote to Finé, who had left the city for a time, and requested a copy of the work *De motus octavae sphaerae calculo*, probably meaning his new book *La theorique des cielz, mouvemens, et tomes practiques des sept planetes, nouuellement et tresclerement redigee en langaige francois*. This work was very likely based on Agostino Ricci's *De motu octavae spherae*, which Finé had edited at Paris in 1521.[60] Finé was an important personage in the intellectual life of Paris in the later 1520's; and at his home Agrippa would naturally have met those occultist friends, old and new, to whom his earlier letter alluded. Whether he knew Finé before this sojourn at Paris is uncertain. In any event, his unhappy stay there must have been relieved by these contacts with prominent students of mathematics and the occult sciences.

The residence in France had been a time of bitter disappointment for Agrippa. His bright hopes had turned to an increasingly uncon-

[58] *Epist.* V, xxiii-xxiv, xxvii, xxxiii.

[59] Chapelain to Agrippa, St.-Germain, 31 December 1527, *Epist.* V, xxii.

[60] I owe the reference to a Finé edition of Ricci's work to Zambelli, *op. cit.*, p. 151, n. 22. On Finé, see Delaulnaye, art. "Finé (Oronce)," *Biographie universelle*, XIV, 542-44; and cf. Agrippa to Orentius, Paris, 1 June 1528, *Epist.* V, xliv. The other letters attributable to Finé, and a reply of Agrippa declining a dinner invitation on grounds of ill health, are *Epist.* V, xxxix-xlii.

trolled rage at the way in which the French court had treated him. Likewise his writings of this period, especially *De vanitate*, represent stark despair with the intellectual, religious, moral, and social conditions of European civilization. Yet the literary expression of this despair was in itself an important achievement. If he had died on leaving Switzerland, he would have been a far less significant figure in European intellectual history than he is. If he had died on leaving France, he would have held very nearly the place which now is his due. His most significant work during the rest of his life was the preservation of his writings by their publication and the further illumination of certain aspects of his thought in apologetic treatises and letters.

CHAPTER FIVE

CLOSING YEARS

Two crises faced Agrippa within a few weeks of his arrival in Antwerp. The first was financial, for his new patrons, Furnarius and Aurelius, were both absent from the city on business; and for a few days he feared that he had again been abandoned. The return of these friends solved this problem for a time. The second crisis involved getting his family across the border and was aggravated by a serious illness which struck his wife, who was again with child. Thanks to the care of a relative of hers, probably Guillaume Furbity, she was able to rejoin her husband in early November.[1]

The months following Agrippa's reunion with his family were one of the few placid periods in his life. He engaged in the practice of medicine and spent much of his time with his occultist friends, chiefly Furnarius, Aurelius, and one or more scholar-servants of his own household, discussing the secrets of nature, performing alchemical operations in his laboratory, and preparing astrological calcula-

---

[1] Agrippa to Ludovicus ————, Antwerp, 5 November 1528, *Epistolarum Liber V*, lx, in his *Opera* (2 vols.; Lugduni, n.d.), II, 935-36. (Henceforth this correspondence will be cited as *Epist.*)

tions. On occasion, wealthy persons called him to Louvain and Malines for medical consultation; and during an outbreak of the plague in the late summer of 1529, Agrippa claimed to have been active in the care of the sick. His only failure during this period was in his hope to become physician to Margaret of Austria, governor of the Low Countries.[2]

This prosperity and happiness ended with the death of his wife on 17 August 1529.[3] She had already been seriously ill at Paris; and the birth of her last son on 13 March 1529 left her in poor health. She contracted the plague, which also carried off several of the servants. Agrippa's children were cared for by friends, and he himself had to stay at an inn.

Once Agrippa had begun to recover from this blow, several possibilities seemed open to him, offers from the King of England, from Mercurino Gattinara, imperial chancellor, from a marquis he had known in Italy (probably the son of his former patron, the Marquis of Monferrato), and from the court of Margaret of Austria, a position less lucrative than the others, but honorable.[4] Sometime late in 1529, he accepted the latter offer, which made him imperial archivist and historiographer. His official writings consist of a history of the coronation of Charles V as king of the Lombards and emperor of the Romans at Bologna in February, 1530, a work which merely lists the order of processions; a funeral oration composed later in 1530 for his patron, Margaret of Austria; and a speech of welcome to the Emperor written for the latter's nephew, Prince John of Denmark.[5] None of these works is of much significance.

[2] Amicus ad Agrippam, Malines, 16 January 1529, *Epist.* V, lxvi.

[3] Reported in his letter to Guillaume Furbity, Antwerp, 1529, *Epist.* V, lxxxi. The letter is dated 7 August, but there is a reference to an illness that began on the day of St. Lawrence (10 August). Auguste Prost, *Les sciences et les arts occultes au XVI siècle: Corneille Agrippa, sa vie et ses oeuvres* (2 vols.; Paris, 1881-82), II, 451-54 (Appendix VIII), concludes that the latter date is less subject to errors in transcription and hence ought to form the basis for dating the wife's death. I follow his date.

[4] Agrippa to [Furbity], Antwerp, 4 October 1529, *Epist.* V, lxxxiv.

[5] The historical work, *De duplici coronatione Caesaris apud Bononiam historiola*, is in his *Opera*, II, 1121-45. The funeral oration for Margaret of Austria is *Oratio X*, printed *ibid.*, II, 1098-1120. The oration written for the son of Christiern, exiled King of Denmark, is *Oratio IX, ibid.*, II, 1097-98. Prost, *op. cit.*, II, 259-61, casts doubt on Le Glay's conjecture that Agrippa was tutor to this boy. Aside from the existence of this oration, which is not conclusive evidence, there is no proof that he was. The date of Agrippa's appointment as historiographer was 27 December 1529, at wages of forty livres. See H. Follet, "Un médecin astrologue au temps de la Renaissance, Henri Cornelius Agrippa," *Nouvelle revue*, XCVIII (1896), 307, 309, for the relevant docu-

As historical works they cannot compete with two letters written by Agrippa in 1527 concerning Germanic antiquities.[6] With one minor exception, there is no evidence that Agrippa had any of his works printed until his arrival in the Low Countries. But books in that age still circulated widely in manuscript; and Agrippa's letters show that at least some of his works did so circulate, adding to the very great reputation for learning which he had enjoyed since youth. But only the printing of his books could allow him to address the learned of his day. To this work of publication he now turned. With the exception of his minor work on geomancy, the majority of his letters, and the surviving fragment of *Dialogus de homine*, all of Agrippa's extant writings were printed during his lifetime, some of them repeatedly. This fact exercised a decided influence on the author's later career, for publication of some of his books, especially *De vanitate*, aroused bitter opposition.

The first printed book of Agrippa concerning which there is reliable information is an edition of several small tracts that appeared at Antwerp in 1529 from the press of Michael Hillenius.[7] During 1530 and 1531, Agrippa must have been very actively engaged in printing his works. On 12 January 1529 (probably 1530, n.s.), he received an imperial license granting him exclusive right to publish *De occulta philosophia, De vanitate, In artem brevem Raymundi Lullii et Tabula abbreviata*, and *Quaedam orationes et epistolae*. In the course of 1530, he published at Antwerp *De duplici coronatione;* and *De vanitate* appeared in September from the press of Grapheus at Antwerp. In 1531, the same Antwerp house put out an edition of Book I of *De occulta philosophia*. Several editions of *De vanitate* and another of the first part of *De occulta philosophia* appeared that year at Antwerp, Paris, and Cologne.[8]

---

mentation from the Archives du Nord at Lille. For Margaret's funeral oration, he received twelve livres, according to a document from the Brussels archives printed by Léon Charvet, "Correspondance d'Eustache Chapuys et d'Henri-Cornélius Agrippa de Nettesheim," *Revue savoisienne*, XV (1874), 98.

[6] Agrippa to Franciscus ―――, Lyons, 3 January 1527, *Epist.* V, i; Agrippa ad Amicum, Lyons, 16 September 1527, *Epist.* V, xi.

[7] On this edition, see John Ferguson, "Bibliographical Notes on the Treatises *De occulta philosophia* and *De incertitudine et vanitate scientiarum* of Cornelius Agrippa," *Proceedings of the Edinburgh Bibliographical Society*, XII (March, 1924), 1-23, an article representing a posthumous fragment of a projected bibliographical study of Agrippan editions.

[8] The license to print appears on the verso of the title page of the 1533 Cologne edition of *De occulta philosophia*. On editions in Agrippa's lifetime, see Ferguson, *loc. cit.*, and Prost, *op. cit.*, I, 39-45.

Agrippa's favor at the court of the Low Countries did not last very long, and his publications had much to do with his loss of grace. Although later he was to claim that Margaret of Austria had been most favorable to him, he confided to a friend that she had been so outraged by the publication of *De vanitate* (or, as he put it, by the slanders of the monks against that book) that if she had not died, he would have been prosecuted for impiety. The minds of the Emperor and of Ferdinand, King of Hungary, had also been alienated. Indeed, although Agrippa probably did not know this, the examination and condemnation of *De vanitate* by the theological faculty of Louvain, of which he so bitterly complained, was the result of an order by Margaret that the faculty examine the book.[9]

Partly as a result of the poverty of the crown, which was too busy with wars to pay for such luxuries as historiographers, but chiefly because of the criticism aroused by *De vanitate*, Agrippa for the second time in his life experienced trouble in getting paid by a princely employer. Just as in France, he responded to the crisis first by pleading for his money and then by vague threats of evil courses if his disfavor continued. He was not without highly placed advocates: Lorenzo, Cardinal Campeggio, the papal legate; Lucas Bonfius and Bernardus Paltrinus, the legate's secretary and steward, intimate friends of Agrippa and colleagues in the study of the occult; Joannes Dantiscus, Bishop of Culm and ambassador of the King of Poland; and Eberhard, Cardinal van der Mark, Prince-Bishop of Liége. But these patrons were able to do little except secure an imperial order forbidding prosecution of Agrippa by his creditors, and to effect his release when despite this order one of his creditors violently seized him and threw him into debtors' prison.[10] His financial problems were made worse by the necessity of leaving his family at Malines, whither he had moved from Antwerp after becoming historiographer, and following the court from place to place in quest of his pay.

[9] Agrippa ad Amicum, Malines, 19 January 1531, *Epist.* VI, xv. For a document proving that Margaret of Austria sent a copy of *De vanitate* to the Louvain theological faculty on 11 September 1530 (immediately after its appearance) because its orthodoxy was suspect, see an extract from the Archives du Nord at Lille printed by Follet, *loc. cit.*, 309-11.

[10] For Agrippa's patrons, see his letter of 12 May 1531 to Cardinal van der Mark, *Epist.* VI, xviii. His financial trouble is shown by many letters of 1531, including two petitions to the imperial council (*Epist.* VI, xxi-xxii). For his brief imprisonment for debt in August, *Epist.* VI, xxiii-xxvii. These letters make it clear that he was imprisoned for debt, not for writing *De vanitate*, as some older biographers thought.

During these financial difficulties, which arose chiefly out of the controversy over *De vanitate*, Agrippa declined a splendid chance to get into another fight. His old Genevan friend, Eustache Chapuys, was now imperial ambassador to England. In a flattering letter describing how all learned men in London praised *De vanitate* and *De occulta philosophia*, this friend repeatedly urged Agrippa to write a defense of the marriage of the Queen, Catherine of Aragon. A section of the chapter on prostitution in *De vanitate*, containing thinly veiled reference to Henry VIII's repudiation of Queen Catherine, encouraged Chapuys to hope that Agrippa would comply with his request; but the latter already felt burdened by his disfavor at the imperial court and was not willing to incur the enmity of another ruler unless he received an explicit request from Charles V or his sister, Mary of Hungary, to write in behalf of Catherine. Apparently there was some rumor in England that Agrippa was about to come out in defense of Henry's divorce, but it is probable that he wanted to hold himself aloof unless he received some sure commitment from one side or the other. The passage in *De vanitate* suggests that his personal inclination was to oppose Henry.[11]

By December of 1531, Agrippa had controversial works of his own to produce. As an anonymous friend had warned him, the faculty of the University of Louvain had prepared a set of articles denouncing *De vanitate* as scandalous, impious, and heretical. A still greater authority, the Sorbonne, condemned the Paris edition of the work on 2 March 1531; and even his friends frankly told him that most people felt that his unbridled tongue was the main

---

[11] *De incertitudine et vanitate scientiarum declamatio inuectiua* (Coloniae, 1531), ch. lxiii, fol. N1r. (Henceforth this work will be cited as *De vanitate*, and by chapter only, as there are numerous editions.) The reference to Henry VIII's divorce, incidentally, is clear proof that Agrippa continued to revise the text of the book after he completed the basic text in 1526. The letters of Chapuys began on 26 June 1531, and are printed as *Epist*. VI, xix-xx, xxix, xxxiii, xxxv. In a long autobiographical letter of 1532 to Mary of Hungary (*Epist*. VII, xxi), Agrippa sought to win favor by claiming to be at work on such a treatise. On 10 September 1531, as he had promised his friend, Chapuys included in his official dispatch a statement that Queen Catherine wanted Agrippa to be asked to write in her behalf. See *Letters and Papers, Foreign and Domestic, Henry VIII*, V, 204-5 (No. 416). On 1 March 1532, the English agent at Antwerp, Stephen Vaughan, wrote to Thomas Cromwell, "I hear that Agrippa has written a book in favor of the King's great matter, which has not yet come forth. I do not greatly believe it." (*Ibid.*, V, 402 [No. 843]).

source of his troubles.[12] The imperial privy council referred the Louvain articles against him to the parlement at Malines. Not until 15 December 1531 was Agrippa able to secure from the head of the privy council, Jean Carondelet, Archbishop of Palermo, a copy of the charges. Instead of recanting as Carondelet said the Emperor wanted him to do, he wrote two defenses, an *Apologia* in which he refuted the charges point by point, and an earlier *Querela* in which he attacked the "theosophists" who had made the charges against him. On 6 February 1532, in a letter to one of his friends in the retinue of Campeggio, Agrippa characterized the *Apologia* rather well: "I have replied to the Louvain slanderers modestly of course, but not without salt and vinegar and even mustard. . . ."[13] When he found that the parlement of Malines procrastinated instead of reaching a judgment which he felt would clear him of suspicion, he dedicated the *Apologia* to Cardinal Campeggio and sent it to Cratander at Basel to be printed, although the refusal of Cratander to bring it out delayed its publication until 1533.

Just at the height of this controversy, Erasmus wrote his first letter to Agrippa, intending merely to recommend to Agrippa a student of the occult whom he himself had not been able to satisfy. He courteously added that *De vanitate* had caused Agrippa's name to be on the lips of all. Erasmus had not read it but had heard that it was rather free. Agrippa hastened to write Erasmus, asking him for his own opinion of *De vanitate* and assuring him that he himself was a loyal Erasmian and also, in all he wrote, an obedient son of the church. This correspondence opened in the fall of 1531, but Erasmus put off giving an opinion until April, 1533. Then, although praising the book and assuring its author that it contained nothing at which virtuous monks and clergymen could take offense, he strongly advised Agrippa to avoid further controversy, pointing to the burning of Louis Berquin as an example of a virtuous man who perished merely because of liberty in talking of the monks. He added, "Above all, beware not to involve me in this business. I am

---

[12] The anonymous and undated warning is *Epist.* VI, xxx. Prost, *op. cit.*, II, 464 (Appendix X), prints most of the text of the Paris censure. The admonition from a friend, probably Bernardus Paltrinus, is dated Ratisbon, 25 March 1532, *Epist.* VII, vii.

[13] *Epist.* VII, iii: "Respondi Lovaniensibus calumniatoribus modeste quidem, sed non sine sale et aceto etiam atque sinapi. . . ." The *Apologia* and *Querela* appear in Agrippa's *Opera*, II, 257-330, 437-59.

overwhelmed with more than enough ill-will. That would both burden me and harm you more than it would help you." [14] This letter suggests that Erasmus feared that association with Agrippa would only get him involved in new troubles. A few days later, in a letter to Abel Closter, he praised Agrippa's mental endowment, wide reading, and memory but added that there was greater profusion than wise selection in his book. He expressed displeasure at Agrippa's self-proclaimed war on the monks because he could see no reasonable expectation of gain from such attacks and feared that the Nettesheimer would accomplish nothing but to arouse the monks against good men. [15]

Agrippa's loose talk of war on the monks was not for Erasmus' ears alone. On 17 September 1532 he used the same expression in a letter to the Protestant leader Melanchthon, whom he asked to greet "that unconquered heretic Martin Luther, who, as Paul says in Acts, serves God according to the sect which they call heresy." [16] In this letter he also greeted Georg Spalatin as an old friend; and about the same time, he wrote of his war on the monks to his old friend Cantiuncula. These books and letters in defense of *De vanitate* militate strongly against any interpretation which would discount that book as nothing but a *jeu d' esprit*, a mere rhetorical exercise.

The bitterness which marked the French period of Agrippa's life found only temporary alleviation during his stay in the Low Countries. Once again he made the mistake of staking his fortunes on the favor of a royal court; and once again, he found his hopes disappointed. He continued his alchemical and other magical studies

---

[14] Erasmus to Agrippa, 21 April 1533, *Epist.* VII, xl. Also printed in *Opus epistolarum Des. Erasmi Roterodami*, ed. P. S. Allen [and H. M. Allen and H. W. Garrod] (12 vols.; Oxonii, 1906-58), X, 203 (No. 2796).

[15] *Opus epistolarum Erasmi*, X, 209-11 (No. 2800).

[16] Agrippa to Melanchthon, Frankfurt-am-Main, 17 September 1532, *Epist.* VII, xiii: "invictum illum haereticum Martinum Lutherum, qui, ut in actibus ait Paulus, seruit Deo secundum sectam quam haeresim vocant." Agrippa probably met Spalatin while the latter was in Cologne with the Elector Frederick of Saxony in September, October, and November of 1520, a period which was marked by the interview of the Elector and the Emperor Charles V in Cologne. At this period also, Erasmus was in Cologne as a member of the imperial council. The acquaintance with Spalatin could hardly have been intimate, for Spalatin was a principal adviser of the Elector, and was deeply involved in intricate negotiations with the Emperor and with the papal nuncios. See Irmgard Höss, *Georg Spalatin, 1484-1545: Ein Leben in der Zeit des Humanismus und der Reformation* (Weimar, 1956), pp. 178-83. Throughout this period, Agrippa was temporarily residing in Cologne.

and experiments as before but also continued to defend and expound his skeptical treatise *De vanitate*. The importance of this period, aside from his further explanation of certain points in his earlier writings, lies chiefly in the printing of his writings, almost all of which were in print before his death.

The first hints that he was losing favor at the imperial court in the Low Countries caused Agrippa to begin to seek a new patron, the reform-minded Archbishop of Cologne, Hermann von Wied. By 10 January 1531, Agrippa had already dedicated the forthcoming Antwerp edition of Book One of *De occulta philosophia* to that prelate; and a friend had shown Archbishop Hermann five quaternions which were already off the press. Agrippa must have had several advocates at the archiepiscopal court, among them the imperial bureaucrat Cornelius Scepper.[17] The Archbishop later received the dedications of Book Two and Book Three of the same treatise. After more than a year of negotiation and correspondence, the Archbishop on 1 February 1532 invited Agrippa to visit Cologne, a trip which he made in March, probably staying somewhat longer than a month.[18] Agrippa claimed that the purpose of this trip into Germany was chiefly to gather materials for official histories which he planned to write of the Italian campaigns of Charles of Bourbon and of the Emperor's campaigns against the Turks. Despite these claims and his argument that he had maintained a household at Malines, Agrippa found that the imperial treasurer had used this journey outside the Low Countries as an excuse for refusing to pay his small pension. Angrily, he sent letters of complaint to the new governor of the Low Countries, Mary of Hungary, and to her secretary, Johannes Khreutter. To the latter he played the tune of German national resentment against the predominance of Burgundian foreigners at the imperial court. Finding that these appeals were fruitless, and perhaps fearing renewed prosecution by his creditors now that his pension had been suspended, Agrippa decided to accept the offer which Archbishop Hermann made. In-

[17] See, in addition to the dedicatory epistles attached to the three books which comprise the work, the letter of an unnamed friend to Agrippa, Cologne, 10 January 1531, *Epist.* VI, xiv.

[18] The Archbishop's invitation was dated 1 February 1532: *Epist.* VII, i. Agrippa received it on 10 February and at once promised to come at his earliest opportunity: *Epist.* VII, v. Agrippa to Erasmus, 17 March 1532, *Epist.* VII, vi, reveals that at that date he was visiting the Archbishop at Cologne, and that he planned to stay about a month before returning to the Low Countries.

deed, he may have returned to the Low Countries only to prepare to move to Cologne, a step which he took, apparently in considerable haste, sometime in June of 1532.[19]

Agrippa's principal residence during the next months was with the Archbishop at Bonn, although he was at Frankfurt-am-Main on 17 September, when he wrote his letter to Melanchthon. He had not renounced his claim to the title and salary of imperial historiographer, for he denied that the position obliged him to reside only in the Low Countries. Doubtless these renewed efforts were as fruitless as his earlier demands for payment. So he stayed at the archiepiscopal court, and the last surviving letters in his printed correspondence show him enjoying the baths of Bertrich in the company of the Archbishop and inviting friends to come with good books and participate in their delights.

Even in the company of the tolerant archbishop-elector of Cologne, who ended his days in the Evangelical confession and resigned his see rather than subject the principality to internecine strife, Agrippa was not free of controversy. The issue this time was the printing of all three books of De occulta philosophia, only the first part of which had appeared in the editions of 1531. His adversaries, as usual, were the Dominicans. The work of printing was under way before the middle of November, 1532; but shortly before Christmas, the Dominican inquisitor, Conrad Colyn of Ulm, denounced Agrippa's book as suspect of heresy and unfit to be printed. The senate or council of the city of Cologne forced the printer, Soter, to suspend work; and it impounded the quaternions already completed. At the urging of the publisher, Godfried Hetorp, and of Soter himself, Agrippa sprang to the defense. He probably did not help matters by his long letter of 11 January 1533 to the city council, roundly denouncing the Cologne faculty and indirectly reflecting on the city for tolerating such ignoramuses and for following their advice to interrupt printing of the book. He also alleged the imperial license of 1530, although that document probably implied no approval of the contents of the book as he now claimed. He feared that the inhibition would cause his book to miss the next Frankfurt fair. He also feared that the inquisitors would impound the printer's manuscript, which probably was his only copy of the last two books. Finally his efforts to have the

---

[19] Prost, op. cit., II, 328, attributes the evident haste of his departure to fear of his creditors.

Archbishop permit publication were successful, though the two
nearly identical editions that finally appeared in the summer of
1533 lack name of printer or place, perhaps because of the difficulties surrounding the publication.[20]

During his residence with the Archbishop, Agrippa kept in touch
with his friends Paltrinus and Bonfius, who had accompanied
Cardinal Campeggio first to Ratisbon and then to Italy, and with
Augustinus Furnarius, who had also returned to Italy. Although
these letters contain much discussion of Italian politics and of
Agrippa's efforts to secure his pay from Charles V, the most interesting portion is that concerning occult matters, for the letters show
that Agrippa continued to follow keenly those occult studies which
he had pursued throughout his earlier career. Paltrinus reported
his interview with Francesco Giorgi of Venice, the disciple of Pico
della Mirandola, and his efforts to secure copies of rare cabalistic
and other esoteric books.[21] Friends closer at hand, too, such as a
Heidelberg admirer of Agrippa's skill in transmutation and natural
science,[22] continued to correspond with him on occult matters.

Lacking any letters for the period after mid-1533, Agrippa's
early biographers described his final years and death in the wildest
terms imaginable. Out of the welter of legends which surround
Agrippa's death, most of them going back to the account in Paolo
Giovio's *Elogia doctorum virorum*, one could make little sense if
it were not for Johann Wier, who as a young man lived and studied
with Agrippa, probably while the latter still resided in the Low
Countries. In addition to refuting stories that the devil in the shape
of a dog accompanied Agrippa and was present while the wretched
man lay on his deathbed, Wier relates several facts which help
round out the story of Agrippa's life. His account is the only proof
that Agrippa took a third wife, a woman of Malines, but repudiated
her while living at Bonn in 1535. In the same year, he continues,
Agrippa went to Lyons, where Francis I had him arrested for
writing against the late Queen Mother. Friends secured his release,

[20] See the letters for early 1533, especially *Epist.* VII, xxiv, xxxi, xxxiv, and
xxxix, for the troubles concerning publication of *De occulta philosophia.*
Agrippa's fiery remonstrance to the Senate of Cologne, dated from Bonn, 11
January 1533, is *Epist.* VII, xxvi.

[21] See, for example, Agrippa to [Bonfius?], Bonn, 13 November 1532, *Epist.*
VII, xiv, and many other letters of 1532 and 1533.

[22] *Epist.* VII, xlii.

and several months later he died at Grenoble.[23] Two later French antiquaries confirm this story and add that he died under honorable circumstances and that he was buried (strange fate indeed for such a foe of the Friars Preachers!) in the Dominican church in that city.[24] This information would place his death in 1535 or, at the latest, 1536. Why he returned to France is not at all certain, but he certainly had many friends still living there; and three of his children survived him and became residents of Saint-Antoine in Viennois, a town where his friends the family of Laurencin had certain connections.[25]

This puzzle of his motive in returning to France is not the only unsolved problem in the man's biography. Most of the period from 1502 to 1507 remains a blank which one can fill only conjecturally. The same is true for much of the years 1510 and 1511. There are also some episodes in his life, and some of his minor writings, which one can date only by guessing. One such episode is his claim that at one time he was in charge of some imperial mines and began writing a special treatise on mining.[26] If there is any truth to this claim, the experiences must have occurred before 1518, when his life becomes more fully documented, and probably before 1512, when he had reached Italy. The real meaning of the Spanish episode is another of the many unsolved biographical problems, and it will probably remain unsolved unless new material comes to light.[27]

[23] The tales go back to Paolo Giovio, *Elogia doctorum virorum* . . . (Basileae, 156?), pp. 236-37, and were frequently repeated. For Wier's refutation of them and his own testimony about Agrippa's remarriage, return to France, and death, see Wier, *Opera omnia* (Amstelodami, 1660), pp. 110-11.

[24] For the testimony of these antiquaries, Allard and Chorier, see Prost, *op. cit.*, II, 403-7.

[25] Luc Maillet-Guy, "Henri Corneil Agrippa, sa famille et ses relations," *Bulletin de la Société d'archéologie et de statistique de la Drôme*, LX (1926), 200-8, suggests that Agrippa may have gone to Saint-Antoine on his release from imprisonment and may have been sheltered there. He thinks that Agrippa's little undated work, *Sermo de inventione reliquiarum Beati Antonii Heremitae, pro quodam venerabili ejus ordinis religioso* may have been written at this time (1535) in thanks for his place of refuge. But Ferguson, *loc. cit.*, 13, shows that the treatise existed by 1532.

[26] *De vanitate*, ch. xxix: "verum quum ego ante aliquot annos a Caesarea maiestate aliquot mineris praefectus essem, omnia quantum potui indagatus, coepi de illis specialem librum scribere, quem adhuc vsque in manibus habeo. . . ."

[27] Another unsolved problem not discussed above is the date of two small treatises, *De vita monastica sermo* and *In geomanticam disciplinam lectura*. The latter did not appear in print until after Agrippa's death but is probably the geomantical work which he recants in *De vanitate*, ch. xiii. It thus would

Nevertheless, the major outlines of the man's life are clear enough. His adventuresome life reflects much of the turmoil and instability of his times. One of the outstanding traits of his career is the way in which he was exposed to the influence of many intellectual traditions: the skepticism (or at least, skeptical tendencies) of late scholasticism, the transrationalism of Nicholas of Cusa, the magic of Trithemius, the rationalism of Ramon Lull, the Platonism and humanism of Italy, the religious humanism of northern Europe, the Cabala of the Jews. He typifies the roving adventurer so common in that age, and the dependence of this type on the favor of great patrons. His career also suggests the financial inability of these great patrons to support the scholars who clamored for their aid. His ability to attract such widespread attention as he did also demonstrates the mixture of interest and horror with which even the highly educated men of the time looked upon one who reputedly had mastery not only of all human learning but also of the magical lore of the ancients as well. In general, his varied career suggests the adventurous and agitated life of the ambitious in his age; and it offers an interesting if brief glimpse of intellectual conditions in each of the several places where he resided. Agrippa's chief significance, however, lies not in the external happenings of his adventurous life but in the even more adventurous development of his mind. This history of Agrippa's thought forms the main subject of the chapters that follow.

---

be earlier than the summer of 1526. It is printed in *Opera*, I, 405-25. *De vita monastica*, which appears in *Opera*, II, 565-72, was added along with the work on the relics of St. Anthony to the 1532 reprint of an Agrippan miscellany of 1529. See Ferguson, *loc. cit.*, 13-14. There is no proof, however, that it was written between 1529 and 1532.

CHAPTER SIX

AGRIPPA'S READINGS

The forces which shaped the thought of Agrippa are not evident merely from the preceding sketch of his biography and of the influences to which he was directly subjected at the various stages of his career. His readings extended his knowledge far beyond the confines of his personal experience. Thus it will be necessary to study the literary sources of his thought. The preceding biographical chapters have already suggested the time and nature of his acquaintance with standard school manuals in logic and with the *Ars brevis* of Ramon Lull, as well as with one or more writings of Albertus Magnus and with the occultist writings of Trithemius of Sponheim, at least the *Steganographia;* and later chapters will show in some detail how Agrippa followed the controversial literature of the Reformation. One must also assume a great deal of reading in law. The present chapter, after certain general remarks about Agrippa's readings, will suggest further sources for the two chief components of his thought, occult philosophy and skepticism.

The problem of the materials on which Agrippa drew for his

writings is difficult because he tells too little about his sources, and at the same time too much. Citations are so plentiful in his writings that long passages are nothing but strings of quotations and paraphrases. But of course Agrippa possessed most of these citations at second hand, drawing heavily on the quotations of those whom he did read. The immediate sources of his thought are very little evident. Relatively few works of his own age and the immediately preceding period appear among the authorities whom he presents; and his correspondence, which one might expect to abound in references to his readings, is singularly barren, especially during his formative years up to his departure from Italy early in 1518. Yet these unfruitful letters often enough make vague references concerning wide-ranging readings, even in these earlier years.[1] Agrippa had a collection of books which he valued highly; and on one occasion, urging a friend to lend him interesting books, he confessed, "for you know what a glutton I am for books, and how I take greater pains to get no other [kind of] property."[2] Throughout his life, Agrippa's habits were those of a learned, studious, and bookish man. If only he had troubled to specify in his letters just which books! Lacking such specific direct references, the historian has to content himself with indirect evidence.

A further problem in the study of the Nettesheimer's sources is that it is hard to integrate his readings with the external events of his life. One might suspect that since he lectured on Reuchlin's *De verbo mirifico* at the University of Dôle in 1509, most of his cabalistic studies occurred early in his life, while his enthusiasm for Hermetic and Neoplatonic writings came during his seven years in northern Italy, where interest in these works was widespread among the intellectual classes. Yet as a matter of fact, the reverse is more nearly true. The original version of *De occulta philosophia*, probably the very copy which Agrippa sent to Trithemius of Sponheim early in 1510, survives and shows no essential differences from the printed version in the kinds of sources that it cites.[3] It abounds in

---

[1] *Epistolarum Liber I*, xxii, xxxi, and xxxix, in Agrippa's *Opera* (2 vols.; Lugduni, n.d.), II, 701, 707, and 710-11. (Henceforth this collection is cited as *Epist.*)

[2] *Epist.* IV, xi: "scis enim, quam sim ego helluo librorum, nec ullam supellectilem mihi magis parare curem aliam."

[3] I have used a microfilm copy of this text, Würzburg, Universitätsbibliothek, MS. M.ch.q.50; but it still awaits publication of a critical text edition with commentary before it can be fully useful. Dr. Paola Zambelli of the Archivio di Stato at Florence has undertaken the task of preparing such an edition.

citations from Neoplatonists, from the Hermetic writings, from the classical encyclopedists, philosophers, and poets, from the Church Fathers and Scripture, and from such medieval authorities on magic as Albertus Magnus. The printed version of 1533 has added many citations, but all of the same general sort as the original ones. The least change appears to have occurred in the numerological portion of Book Two; while perhaps the greatest alteration is the greater frequency and far greater completeness of cabalistic materials in the later recension. The tables of the divine and angelic names of the Schemhamphoras and the details of the sephirotical system are absent from the early manuscript version, while the sephirotical names as given in the printed text show the influence of Reuchlin's later and definitive work on Cabala, *De arte cabalistica*, not published until 1517.[4] Comparison of the two versions of *De occulta philosophia* suggests, in short, that Agrippa's interest in cabalistic, Hermetic, Neoplatonic, and magical authors went back to a very early date and that he gradually increased his command of these materials; further, that the greatest increase was probably in the field of Cabala. Further discussion of just what kinds of citations were added later than 1510 will occur at the conclusion of the present chapter.

There is a third preliminary consideration, the linguistic one. Agrippa had a reputation for speaking "every language" and himself once claimed some acquaintance with eight tongues, six of which he said he could not only read and understand but even speak elegantly.[5] He did not further specify these eight languages, but they included German, French, Italian, and perhaps Spanish and English among modern languages, and Latin, Greek, and Hebrew among the learned ones. German was his native tongue; Italian, that of his first wife, the speech of a land where he spent seven years; French was the speech of his second wife and of lands where he studied and resided for many years and where his children settled and lived as natives after his death;[6] and Latin was the universal

---

[4] *De occulta philosophia libri tres* (Coloniae, 1533), Bk. III, ch. x. Cf. Johann Reuchlin, *De arte cabalistica* (Hagenau, 1517), fols. lxi-lxii[r].

[5] For his linguistic fame in his own time, see Philippe de Vigneulles, *La chronique de la ville de Metz*, ed. Charles Bruneau (4 vols.; Metz, 1927-33), IV, 332. For Agrippa's claim, see his autobiographical letter to Mary of Hungary, written from Bonn in 1532, *Epist.* VII, xxi.

[6] In 1529, Agrippa wrote in French to his wife, a practice which caused his secretary inconvenience since he could not read the letter to her, being ignorant of the tongue. Apparently the wife could not read. See *Epist.* V, lxxvii.

language of scholarship, the one in which he wrote all his extant books and letters. Of Hebrew and Greek, Agrippa had some knowledge; but in 1519 he confessed that it was not thorough and sighed for the leisure to become truly expert in these two great tools of Biblical study.[7] For all practical purposes Agrippa's significant readings were confined to books available in Latin, though he may have been able to draw on Hebrew and Greek texts to a limited extent.

Few ancient Latin authors escape at least a passing reference somewhere in the extensive *corpus* of Agrippa's writings, and there are citations of many Greek authors also (probably in most cases used in Latin translations). Many medieval authorities also appear, both Latin and Arab. Yet these references are often of a most superficial sort; and most of Agrippa's sources serve as mere quarries whence he draws little but (supposedly) factual information. Pliny's *Natural History* is the most important source of this kind. Citations of it abound in Agrippa's works, especially the *De occulta philosophia*, since much of Pliny's material was of use for the student of magic.[8] But the classical poets, Homer, Lucretius, Ovid, Lucan, and above all Vergil, serve the same purpose, as do such ancient men of encyclopedic learning as Ptolemy and Boethius. These authors are sources of Agrippa's thought only in that he drew from them quotations, stories, or facts to support his conclusions. They are sources of illustrations more than sources of ideas. Even these classical references, however, could be put to striking and at times disturbing use. Agrippa's predilection for the shocking element in what he read appears clearly from his use of an Epicurean argument on immortality. In *Dialogus de homine* he sought to quiet the fear of death of one of his interlocutors by the rather facile argument that death poses no danger, since while one lives, it is not with one; and after death arrives, one does not exist. This argument probably reached Agrippa through Diogenes Laertius.[9] Most of his citations from such

[7] *De beatissimae Annae monogamia ac unico puerperio* (n.p., 1534), fol. K7r: "Nam hebraeam linguam aliquando leuiter agnoui, graecam parum attigi, postea fortunarum mearum iniquitate ab ijs literis distractus, multa rursus amisi. . . ."
[8] On the magical element in classical literature, see Lynn Thorndike, *The Place of Magic in the Intellectual History of Europe* (New York, 1905), *passim;* for Pliny, pp. 37-55. Thorndike, *A History of Magic and Experimental Science* (8 vols.; New York, 1923-58), I, 41-99.
[9] *Dialogus de homine*, in Lyons, Bibliothèque Municipale, MS. No. 48, fol. 57r [*sic; recte*, 58r]. This manuscript has recently been edited by Paola Zambelli in *Rivista critica di storia della filosofia*, XIII (1958), 47-71, where the

medieval authorities on natural science and magic as Albertus Magnus, Roger Bacon, Pietro d'Abano, and the Arabs (Algazel, Alkindi, Almadel, Avicenna, and Averroes are among these) are also quite superficial. In the manuscript *De occulta philosophia*, he often cites William of Paris, and the *De fato* of pseudo-Aquinas, but only on points of detail. They did not shape his thought. Indeed, even those authors who furnished him richer fare also served as quarries of facts. Most of the hundreds (perhaps thousands) of references which Agrippa gives are of this insignificant sort. Yet certainly he did not make up his own ideas solely out of his own head. The very number of his citations indicates wide reading; and surely some of what he read must have helped to form his ideas.

Magical treatises were one source of Agrippa's general ideas as well as of the details of his books. Despite his dissatisfaction with these older magical authorities, he could not draw specific information from them in such quantity without also undergoing the influence of the ideas that lay behind them. In particular, his idea that magical knowledge is a way to power and glorification for man was a reflection of the distinctive magical attitude. For example, the Arabic text *Ghâya*, which Agrippa cited under its Latin title *Picatrix*, made it abundantly clear that the goal of magical study was the attainment of a science that gives man power.[10] The goal of power for man was also clearly present in Agrippa's writings, especially in *De occulta philosophia* and in the short treatises of the Italian period. Agrippa's chapters on astral figures and seals in *De occulta philosophia*, as well as his use of magical squares in the numerological chapters of that work, suggest extensive contact with medieval Arabic magic, and particularly with *Picatrix*.[11]

---

original page-numbering, which I cite, is also reproduced. My citation is based on a microfilm copy of the manuscript. Cf. Diogenes Laertius, *Lives of Eminent Philosophers*, ed. and trans. R. D. Hicks (2 vols.; London, 1925), Lib. X, 125 (II, 650, 651) (Loeb Classical Library edition).

[10] Eugenio Garin, *Medioevo e Rinascimento: Studi e ricerche* (Bari, 1954), pp. 173-76, including an apt illustrative quotation from *Picatrix*. On editions of *Picatrix*, see n. 75, below.

[11] Jean Seznec, *La survivance des dieux antiques* (London, 1940), pp. 50-74, discusses *Picatrix* and the influence of this text on Agrippa. Agrippa's magic squares probably came from Arabic sources, but his method of associating these squares with the planets differed from that of the Arabs and became standard in Europe after his time. See the informative articles of I. R. F. Calder, "A Note on Magic Squares in the Philosophy of Agrippa of Nettesheim," *Journal of the Warburg and Courtauld Institutes*, XII (1949), 196-99, and Karl Anton Nowotny, "The Construction of Certain Seals and Characters in the Work of Agrippa of Nettesheim," *ibid.*, XII (1949), 46-57.

Another influence, the obvious source of Agrippa's idea of an animated and closely linked world, must have been the Neoplatonic writings. These are what he means most of the time when he cites the *Platonici*, who are frequent authorities for his most important doctrines, such as the notion that the supernal ideas are the source of the occult properties of things, or belief in God's use of the intermediary deities in the creation of the physical world, or in the illapsion of superior souls into human ones to produce prophetic fury.[12] Those whom he mentions by name include, besides Plato himself, who is cited both at first and at second hand, Philo Judaeus, Ammonius, Plotinus, Porphyry, Iamblichus, and Proclus. Agrippa certainly read some of Plato at first hand,[13] but the character of his Platonism is determined by Neoplatonic commentary.

Whence did Agrippa draw his Neoplatonic doctrines? One would not be justified in assuming that he read every author whom he cited. Ammonius Saccas, for example, left no writings; and his teachings are known only through citations by Plotinus and other pupils;[14] yet Agrippa cites him. This is probably how Agrippa learned most of what he knew about the Hellenistic Neoplatonists: from citations made by more recent authors. Such Neoplatonic citations were not unknown to medieval literature. On the contrary, the works of the Fathers, especially of Augustine, abound in them, while standard medieval authors like Albert, Aquinas, Scotus, and Bacon passed on to later times the knowledge of Neoplatonic theses which they had derived chiefly from patristic writings. Thus much of what Agrippa knew about Neoplatonism could have come and probably did come from these standard medieval texts. Hence his acquaintance with the Neoplatonists could have begun very early. A likely source of many of his citations is Reuchlin's *De verbo mirifico*, which abounds in citations from Neoplatonic and Neo-pythagorean authors and which Agrippa knew certainly as early as 1509. On the other hand, Agrippa also must have known many Neoplatonic sources directly, since humanistic scholars, and above all, Marsilio Ficino, had made many such texts available in Latin translation during the generation or two preceding Agrippa's ma-

---

[12] *De occulta philosophia*, Bk. I, ch. xi, p. xv; Bk. I, ch. lxi, p. lxxx; Bk. III, ch. xlv, p. cccxi.

[13] Citations of the *Timaeus*, the *Phaedrus*, and other dialogues are not infrequent in his works, which include a Neoplatonizing commentary on the *Symposium* (printed as *Oratio I*, in *Opera*, II, 1062-73).

[14] Friedrich Ueberweg, *Grundriss der Geschichte der Philosophie des Altertums*, ed. Karl Praechter (11th ed.; Berlin, 1920), p. 618.

turity. In addition to frequent vague references to the *Platonici*, he at times gave more explicit citations. In *Dialogus de homine*, he quoted directly and explicitly from the *De occasionibus* of Porphyry. In the same treatise, his discussion of the Platonic definition of man as a soul using a body probably came from reading Ficinian translations of either Plotinus or Proclus (or both).[15] Citations of Platonists, either as a group or as individuals, are especially numerous in the passages of *De occulta philosophia* which Agrippa composed between the original draft of 1510 and the appearance of the printed version in 1533. Yet the Platonists were already among his favorite sources when he wrote the early form of his magical treatise; and of the Platonists cited by name in the printed form of the book, only Chalcidius and Philo (both mentioned only twice) did not appear by name in the youthful work. Obviously, he learned much about Neoplatonic writings as a youth, and continued to learn more in his later career, especially during his seven-year residence in Italy.

In reality, however, much of the Neoplatonist element in Agrippa's thought, as well as the closely related interest in applying Neoplatonic principles to man's mastery of the world through magic, came not from these traditional sources whom he cited openly and often, but from three authors of the generation preceding his own, and one more strictly contemporary author whom Agrippa possibly —just possibly, though there is no direct evidence—knew in person. These authors he cited only rarely, but on their writings he drew extensively, often without acknowledgment. Two were famous figures, Marsilio Ficino and Giovanni Pico della Mirandola. The other two were of some importance and notoriety in their own time, but have become rather obscure secondary figures in the opinion of later centuries: the Hermetic enthusiast and fanatical occultist Ludovico Lazzarelli, and the converted Jewish scholar Paolo Ricci, translator of Joseph Gikatilla's *Sha'are Orah*, and

---

[15] For the reference to Porphyry, see *Dialogus de homine*, Lyons, Bibliothèque Municipale, MS. No. 48, fol. 59ʳ [incorrectly numbered 58]. For the Platonic definition of man, *ibid.*, fol. 50ᵛ [incorrectly numbered 49]. Here he cites merely the "Platonici." Cf. Plotinus, *Opera omnia*, trans. Marsilio Ficino (Florentiae, 1492), Ennead VI, Lib. VII, No. 4, fol. rr3ʳ: "An denique homo sit anima tali quodam corpore utens"; and "Excerpta Marsilii Ficini ex Graecis Procli commentarijs in Alcibiadem Platonis primum," in Ficino, *Opera omnia* (2 vols.; Basileae, 1576), II, 1917: "Homo est anima utens corpore, ut instrumento." The original Platonic text is *Alcibiades* I, 129-30.

brother of that Agostino Ricci who was Agrippa's friend and bene-
factor at Casale Monferrato about 1515.

Marsilio Ficino played a twofold role in Renaissance thought as
translator of ancient texts from the Greek, and as a philosopher who
sought by his own works to make the sacred writings of Hermes,
Plato, and the Neoplatonists once again a living factor in western
culture. To Ficino, his work as translator and philosopher was not
merely an employment, but a divinely ordained mission, for he
regarded Platonism as a powerful aid to Christian religion. Indeed,
he regarded it as a special derivative of divine revelation, fore-
ordained by God as an instrument in the divine plan for redeeming
fallen mankind.[16] Agrippa never explicitly cited any work of Ficino
as an authority. The only hint of the degree to which he was in
the debt of the Florentine master was his letter of 1533 to the Senate
of the city of Cologne, a tart defense of his own work *De occulta
philosophia*, in the course of which, in order to discredit his critics
on the Cologne theological faculty, he pointed out that not only
he, but all learned and virtuous men of the present age, had been
subjected to denunciations by the Cologne faculty. Ficino was one
of the recent authors whom Agrippa regarded as being involved by
the slanderous attacks of the theologians on himself.[17] In reality,
Agrippa had made free with both the ideas and even the actual
words of Ficino. His doctrine of the human soul shows marked
resemblance to Ficino's; Ficino was one of the most important
authors whence he drew his belief in that tradition of *prisca theologia* which supposedly stretched from Moses through Hermes,
Zoroaster, Orpheus, and Pythagoras, down to Plato and the Platonists. The other Platonic texts which Agrippa did cite were usually
available to him only in translations by Ficino.[18] The full measure
of his indebtedness, however, appears in *De occulta philosophia*,
which on some points copied Ficino's book *De vita* at length, almost
verbatim, and without acknowledgment, a literary practice almost

[16] Paul Oskar Kristeller, *The Philosophy of Marsilio Ficino*, trans. Virginia
Conant (New York, 1943), pp. 22-29.

[17] Agrippa to Senate of Cologne, Bonn, 11 January 1533, *Epist.* VII, xxvi:
". . . qui cum me accusare et damnare praetendunt, Ioannem Picum Mirandu-
lanum, Marsilium Ficinum Florentinum, Ioannem Capnionem Phorcensem,
Petrum Galatinum Romanum, Paulum Ricium Papiensem, Franciscum de Geor-
giis Venetum et minoritanum, nostra aetate commendatissimae doctrinae viros.
. . ."

[18] His very phrasing shows use of these versions; cf. n. 15, above.

universal among Renaissance authors. What Agrippa did was to take over Ficino's concept of nondemonic, spiritual magic, and use it, rather haphazardly and carelessly, as one part of his own effort to purify magic and restore its good name. Agrippa changed the character of what he took from Ficino, dropping the safeguards which Ficino had erected to keep at least this particular one of his discussions of magic free of the use of demons.[19] But though Agrippa altered, he also took. Ficino was one of his most important sources. Agrippa's acquaintance with Ficino's original writings was not limited to *De triplici vita*. His lecture *Oratio in praelectione convivii Platonis*,[20] for example, shows that not only the original text of the *Symposium* (doubtless in Ficino's translation) but also Ficino's commentary on that dialogue helped to shape, though not absolutely to determine, Agrippa's own treatise.

Just as important for Agrippa as Ficino was that other leading figure of the Florentine circle, Giovanni Pico della Mirandola. Pico, in fact, had the distinction of being one of the few modern authors cited by Agrippa, who gave Pico's attack on judicial astrology high praise in his work of 1526, *De vanitate*. Probably Agrippa knew something of it as early as 1509.[21] Not only doubts about astrology, but also many other key doctrines must have come to him through Pico's writings. Pico's enthusiasm for the Jewish Cabala certainly affected his German admirer, as will appear below in the discussion of cabalistic influences on Agrippa. Agrippa's ability to combine attacks on the science of astrology with a firm belief in the importance of celestial influences was strongly reminiscent of the Italian philosopher-prince. The magical view of man as master of the created world was available to the Nettesheimer in Pico's

[19] Agrippa's use of this text of Ficino is clearly established by D. P. Walker, *Spiritual and Demonic Magic from Ficino to Campanella* (London, 1958), pp. 27, 75, 85-86, and especially 91-96.

[20] Certain portions of Agrippa's *Oratio I* show verbal reminiscences of Ficino's *In convivium Platonis*. Cf. Agrippa, *Opera*, II, 1066-68, with Ficino, *Commentarium*, Oratio Quinta, cap. VIII, printed in his *Opera* (2 vols.; Parisiis, 1641), II, 301, edited more recently in *Commentaire sur le Banquet de Platon*, ed. Raymond Marcel (Paris, 1956), pp. 192-93, for the statement that love is free and cannot be forced, and for the dominance of Venus over Mars. There are other similarities of detail, though the general arguments of the two treatises are not parallel.

[21] *De incertitudine et vanitate scientiarum declamatio inuectiua* (Coloniae, 1531), ch. xxxi, fol. G4r-v. (Henceforth cited by chapter only, as *De vanitate*.) For mention of Pico in 1509, see Theodoricus Wichwael, Bishop of Cyrene, to Agrippa, Cologne, 29 November 1509, *Epist.* I, xxi.

writings on man, as well as in the books of the magicians. Like Ficino and many other Renaissance syncretists, Pico could have passed along to Agrippa the belief in an esoteric tradition of revealed philosophical and religious truth stretching from Moses through the cabalists, Hermes, Zoroaster, Orpheus, and Pythagoras down to Plato and his followers. From Pico he could have gained his idea that the book of nature and the book of God (divine revelation) were both ways to truth, if given the proper spiritual interpretation. In fact, Pico, though he was deeply versed in Platonism, was far more than just a Platonist, being learned in scholasticism, in Jewish thought, and, in fact, in every form of learning he could discover.[22]

The full extent of Agrippa's indebtedness to Pico, however, becomes clear only from a detailed study of some short but significant treatises which Agrippa wrote during and immediately after his residence in Italy. De originali peccato, written at Metz, made explicit use of the Bible and of such Church Fathers as St. Jerome, St. Augustine, and John of Damascus; but it drew more often and more significantly on Pico's Heptaplus. This unacknowledged use of the Heptaplus, only occasional in De originali peccato, was habitual in the earlier Dialogus de homine; and in this treatise Agrippa was not merely making generalized use of a few ideas, but was copying out passages verbatim and at considerable length.[23] The passages used concerned not just peripheral illustrative materials, but also ideas of capital importance, such as the ethereal body, the threefold division of the world, the distinction between the position of man and of God in the world, and the dignity of human nature. There is even one pretty clear piece of evidence that Agrippa was able to use not only Pico's Latin works but also his vernacular Commento alla canzone d'amore.[24] Unlike most northern visitors to Renaissance Italy, Agrippa doubtless had a good command of the Italian language, less on account of his long residence and personal acquaintance with scholars there than because he married an Italian wife while at Pavia.

Another source for Agrippa's broadly Platonic world view, less

[22] Eugenio Garin, Giovanni Pico della Mirandola: Vita e dottrina (Florence, 1937), pp. 74-76.
[23] For detailed evidence, see the notes to this treatise, as published by Paola Zambelli, loc. cit., 56, 59-63, 65, 67.
[24] Cf. Agrippa, Opera, II, 554, with Giovanni Pico della Mirandola, De hominis dignitate, Heptaplus, De ente et uno, e scritti vari, ed. Eugenio Garin (Florence, 1942), p. 494.

respectable than Ficino and Pico, and strongly colored by Hermetic influences, was the poet and heterodox religious enthusiast Ludovico Lazzarelli. The pertinent text here was Lazzarelli's *Crater Hermetis,* which was published at Paris in 1505 as an adjunct to that edition of the Hermetic *Pimander* which Agrippa probably used. Agrippa himself once explicitly quoted the *Crater Hermetis,* in one of the passages added between 1510 and 1531 to *De occulta philosophia.* This one instance, however, was not the only evidence of Lazzarelli's influence. Unacknowledged use of *Crater Hermetis* is apparent in the *Dialogus de homine,* a fact which suggests that the thought of this fantastic millenarian, Lazzarelli, was current in the circles at Casale Monferrato among whom Agrippa was living when he wrote the *Dialogus.* The general influence of Lazzarelli may be traced in the increased emphasis which Agrippa gave to the Hermetic writings during his residence in Italy.[25] While Agrippa's *De occulta philosophia* always stressed a mystical illumination of the soul, his contact with the thought of Lazzarelli may help explain why the theme of spiritual regeneration of the soul received a more thorough treatment in the revised version of his treatise on occult philosophy. Lazzarelli put much stress on the regeneration of the soul under the tutelage of a spiritually illuminated master, and also on the power of the *magus.*[26] There were also more specific influences of Lazzarelli on Agrippa. For example, the discussion in *Dialogus de homine* whether

[25] In fact, Zambelli, in her edition of *Dialogus de homine, loc. cit.,* 54-55, suggests that Agrippa's isolation from his books after his flight from Milan, and his intimate association with his Casale friends, Agostino Ricci and the Carmelite Chrysostom of Vercelli, explain not only the rather "unlearned," or nonbookish, character of the *Dialogus,* but also a marked and henceforward persistent reorientation of his thought. She detects a predominantly classical texture in the manuscript version of *De occulta philosophia,* and insists that even his treatment of Hermes Trismegistus is there less colored by religious themes and the Christian interpretation of Hermes (a reinterpretation effected by such men as Lazzarelli, Lefèvre, and Champier) than is true of works written after the *Dialogus.* Thus she maintains that this whole experience marks a reorientation of his thought toward greater emphasis on religious questions. There may be some truth in her contention. Certainly the earlier form of *De occulta philosophia* gives an impression of relying more on classical authors, and less on Christian ones, than the later, printed version. This, however, is only a difference of degree. It is noteworthy, on the other side of this question, that his lectures on Reuchlin's *De verbo mirifico,* his Scriptural studies (however brief) with John Colet, and his defense of the orthodoxy of his Dôle lectures in his *Expostulatio* against Catilinet, all date from before his Italian experience.

[26] Paul Oskar Kristeller, *Studies in Renaissance Thought and Letters* (Rome, 1956), pp. 221-42, 249-57. Cf. Walker, *Spiritual and Demonic Magic,* pp. 64-72.

man is the image of God shows striking similarity to a passage of the *Crater Hermetis*.[27] Likewise, the notion that Adam before his sin was inherently mortal but was kept from dissolution by the presence of a divine light is similar to assertions by Lazzarelli.[28] Even the problem of Agrippa's citation of the *Zohar*, a cabalistic text that he may never have read, is clarified, for his citation was lifted bodily out of Lazzarelli's book.[29] A habit of his in making Biblical citations in *Dialogus de homine* and in *De originali peccato* may also come from Lazzarelli. A consistent practice of twisting and slightly misquoting Biblical passages in order to make them conform to his own esoteric presuppositions characterizes his *Dialogus*. It also characterices Lazzarelli's *Epistola Enoch*.[30] Perhaps it is a reflection of radical exegetical habits among the circles in which Agrippa moved at Pavia and at Casale.

The general influence of all three Italian authors was broadly Neoplatonic, with the admixture of varying degrees of emphasis on the Hermetic and cabalistic books, and with the admixture also of a greater or lesser tendency to develop the magical and syncretistic religious elements of the Neoplatonic heritage. Yet another influence on the thought of Agrippa pushed him in a Platonic direction: the works of Nicholas of Cusa. But this influence, thanks to the twofold tendency of Platonism, skeptical and mystical, contributed less to Agrippa's magical world view than to the elements that dominated the skeptical stage of his thought.

Almost as important a source of Agrippa's Neoplatonic cos-

[27] Cf. *Dialogus de homine*, Lyons, Bibliothèque Municipale, MS. No. 48, fol. 49 [*sic; recte* 50], with Ludovico Lazzarelli, *Crater Hermetis*, cap. 6, printed in *Testi umanistici su l'Ermetismo*, ed. Eugenio Garin *et al.* (Rome, 1955), p. 61. In her edition of *Dialogus*, Zambelli has also noted these textual similarities.
[28] Cf. *Dialogus de homine, loc. cit.*, fol. 55 [*sic; recte* 56], with Lazzarelli, *loc. cit.*, cap. 3, p. 59, and cap. 5, p. 60. Agrippa's discussion of the *lignum vitae* and the tree of the knowledge of good and evil (*De originali peccato*, in his *Opera*, II, 554) shows similarity of ideas, though not of words, to Lazzarelli, *loc. cit.*, cap. 3, p. 59.
[29] Cf. *Dialogus de homine, loc. cit.*, fol. 56 [*sic; recte* 57], with Lazzarelli, *loc. cit.*, cap. 5, p. 61.
[30] Mirella Brini, Introduction to *Crater Hermetis, loc. cit.*, p. 26. For Agrippa's similar practice, see *De originali peccato*, in Lyons, Bibliothèque Municipale, MS. No. 48, fol. 17v: "salua autem fiet per filiorum generationem, si permanserint in fide, et caritate, et sanctificatione. . . ." The Scriptural text, 1 Timothy 2:14-15, has the singular, *permanserit*, which is less suited to the point which Agrippa is making. Agrippa's *Opera*, II, 560, has adopted the correct Vulgate reading, but MS. probably reflects what he originally wrote.

mology and epistemology as any of these writers was patristic literature, for the sixteenth century, far from breaking away from the Fathers who dominated the medieval mind, was an age of renewed interest in patrology. Erasmus, for instance, made his greatest contribution to scholarship in this field, surpassing even his textual and exegetical work on the Bible. Agrippa drew directly and indirectly from most of the great Church Fathers and apparently did not depend merely on the standard medieval collections of their sentences for his knowledge of these writers. At least he charged that one of his opponents distorted the meaning of Jerome and Augustine on a disputed point because the opponent had read them only in Peter Lombard and not in the original context.[31] On matters of church history and tradition, Agrippa's preferred patristic authorities were Eusebius and Hegesippus because of their greater nearness in time to the events of early ecclesiastical history.[32] His writings also cite St. Jerome and St. Ambrose rather frequently. But the writers whom he cites most frequently and for the most significant doctrines are St. Augustine and, above all, Dionysius the Areopagite. Both authors show strong Neoplatonic influences; and in the pseudo-Dionysius these Neoplatonic elements are so strong that his writings, although basically theistic themselves, have been a constant stimulus to pantheistic heresies.[33] These influences from Dionysius, particularly from *De divinis nominibus*, are particularly frequent in the chief product of Agrippa's years in Italy, *De triplici ratione cognoscendi Deum.* Whereas there was only one citation of Dionysius in the original version (1510) of *De occulta philosophia*, by 1533, the number of references to the Areopagite had increased to nine.[34] Although the Fathers served Agrippa in many respects, their most important use was as sources of his Neoplatonic world view.

[31] *De beatissimae Annae monogamia*, fol. F8v.
[32] *Ibid.*, fol. D4r.
[33] P. Godet, art. "Denys l'Aréopagite," *Dictionnaire de théologie catholique*, IV, col. 434, argues that the apparently pantheistic elements in Dionysius are only superficially so, and that he is an orthodox theist.
[34] Several Latin translations of pseudo-Dionysius were already available, including medieval ones by Johannes Scotus Erigena and Robert Grosseteste, and two Renaissance ones, by Ambrosius Traversarius Camaldulensis and Marsilio Ficino. On medieval knowledge of pseudo-Dionysius, see *Realencyklopädie für protestantische Theologie und Kirche*, IV, 691. The medieval and early modern Latin translations of pseudo-Dionysius are edited in *Dionysiaca: Recueil donnant l'ensemble des traductions des ouvrages attribués au Denys de l'Aréopage* (2 vols.; Paris, 1937).

A special type of influence similar to that of the Platonists was numerological. The doctrines of the special virtues of numbers appear especially in Book Two of *De occulta philosophia*. Ultimately, these doctrines have a twofold source: the numerological astrology of the Babylonians and the number mysticism of the Pythagoreans.[35] Agrippa on occasion cites Pythagoras, but Pythagoras himself left no writings at all.[36] Doubtless much of Agrippa's knowledge of Pythagoras, like our own, came from Neoplatonic lives of him. But most of it came no doubt from patristic and medieval literature, which abounded in numerological symbolism,[37] and from Reuchlin. When Agrippa listed Jerome, Augustine, Origen, Ambrose, Gregorius Nazianzenus, Athanasius, Basil, Hilary, Rabanus, and Bede as authorities for the marvellous powers of numbers,[38] he was not distorting their thought, but rather included authors who really were likely sources for numerological mysticism.

Similar in doctrinal content to these broadly Neoplatonic sources was the Jewish literature on which Agrippa drew. In defense of his lectures at Dôle on Reuchlin's *De verbo mirifico*, Agrippa upheld the use of Jewish writings,[39] while the first version of *De occulta philosophia* itself contained frequent mention of the cabalists even though cabalistic influence was far less prominent and far less detailed than in the printed version. Thus Agrippa's use of cabalistic materials went back to a very early date, and his mastery of those materials (as his very latest surviving correspondence shows) gradually increased through lifelong study. The difficult problem is to determine just what Hebrew cabalistic texts Agrippa knew. His usual practice in citing the Cabala was not very specific. Generally he merely gave a broad reference to the *cabalistae*, or to the *mecubales* of the Hebrews. This was all the citation he gave, for instance, in his chapters expounding the *sephiroth* (or divine numerations) and the names of God.[40]

The greatest of the works of Cabala was *Sepher Zohar*, or *The Book of Splendor*. Agrippa cited it by name, as *sepherzour*, in his

[35] Vincent Foster Hopper, *Medieval Number Symbolism: Its Sources, Meaning, and Influence on Thought and Expression* (New York, 1938), p. 46.
[36] *De occulta philosophia*, Bk. II, ch. v, p. cv. I cite the 1533 edition unless otherwise indicated. Cf. Ueberweg, *op. cit.*, pp. 74-75.
[37] Hopper, *op. cit.*, pp. 86-87.
[38] *De occulta philosophia*, Bk. II, ch. iii, p. cii.
[39] *Expostulatio contra Catilinetum*, in *Opera*, II, 509: "Christianosque doctores omnibus praefero, tamen Iudaeorum rabinos non contemno. . . ."
[40] *De occulta philosophia*, Bk. III, ch. x-xi, xli.

Dialogus de homine, but this citation does not prove that he knew
more than the title, for as the discussion of his use of Lazzarelli's
writings shows, he copied this whole passage, including the citation
of the *Zohar,* from the *Crater Hermetis.* An obstacle to rating his
Zoharic learning very highly is the fact that his command of the
Hebrew language was rather limited, while the *Zohar* did not receive a published Latin translation till later in the sixteenth century.
Quite recently, however, François Secret has warned against exag-
gerating the limitations of knowledge of the *Zohar* by men of the
Renaissance.[41] There were at least two attempts at a translation
before the work finally appeared in print at Mantua and at Cremona
between 1558 and 1560. One of these early versions was by
Guillaume Postel, but the other was by a man fully contemporary
with Agrippa, Egidio, Cardinal of Viterbo. Not only Cardinal
Egidio, but also Pietro Galatino and Francesco Giorgi in that generation knew some Zoharic passages. In fact, Giorgi's *Problemata*
abounded in themes drawn from the *Zohar.* Since Agrippa certainly
was in touch with Jewish or converted scholars, briefly in Spain
and for quite some time at Casale, he may have obtained considerable knowledge about the *Zohar* even if his own Hebrew was too
rudimentary to permit independent reading. In any event, there are
traces of a knowledge that went beyond mere awareness that the
Zohar existed. Certainly Agrippa showed some acquaintance with
the interlocutors of the Zoharic dialogues, such as "rabi Symeon,
ben Ioachim," the central character, and "Rabi Hama," perhaps the
"Rab Hamnuna the Venerable" of the same book.[42] Likewise
Agrippa's mention of the *Zih Luz,* or bone of resurrection, which
survives the dissolution of the body and becomes the nucleus of
the resurrected body, was an allusion to a distinctively Zoharic
doctrine, one also mentioned in the *De harmonia mundi* (1525) of
Francesco Giorgi.[43] Perhaps Agrippa learned of this Zoharic doctrine during his Italian residence, or even from reading *De harmonia
mundi* itself. In any event, the reference to this doctrine represents
one of the later additions to the original text of *De occulta philoso-*

[41] François Secret, *Le Zôhar chez les Kabbalistes chrétiens de la Renaissance*
(Paris, 1958), pp. 20-23, 30-49.
[42] *De occulta philosophia,* Bk. III, ch. xi, pp. ccxxvii-ccxxxii. Cf. *The Zohar,*
trans. Harry Sperling and Maurice Simon (5 vols.; London, 1931-34), I, 9.
[43] *De occulta philosophia,* Bk. I, ch. xx, p. xxvi. This passage is not in the
corresponding chapter of the manuscript version (I, 13). Cf. Secret, *op. cit.,*
pp. 91-92.

phia. There may also be Zoharic influence in Agrippa's remark that the cabalists do not admit transmigration of human souls into animal bodies.[44] Agrippa's doctrine of the fate of the soul, that only the lower and middle portions of the soul can be involved in sin and punishment, is reminiscent of the *Zohar* but, as a later chapter will show, probably reached him more directly through the Florentine Neoplatonists since his terminology is directly taken from Ficino. The most likely conclusion about the extent of Agrippa's knowledge of the *Zohar* is that he did not know the full work with great thoroughness, but that he did gain considerable knowledge about it, perhaps with the aid of Hebrew scholars, and perhaps in part by the use of Latin extracts in manuscript, of the sort known to Egidio of Viterbo and other contemporaries.

Still another cabalistic work which Agrippa cited was the *Sepher Yetzirah,* or *Liber Formationis*—again in a portion of *De occulta philosophia* that did not appear in the 1510 recension. Like the *Zohar,* this cabalistic text received no published Latin translation till later, the work of Guillaume Postel in 1552.[45] But again, Agrippa could have read the treatise, which develops the sephirotical system, with the aid of some more skilled Hebraist like his Italian friend Agostino Ricci, a Jewish convert to Christianity.

Of all of the Hebrew cabalistic texts, however, the one that Agrippa knew best was the *Sha'are Orah* of Joseph Gikatilla, which was also the chief source of Johann Reuchlin's acquaintance with Cabala.[46] This pre-Zoharic work appeared in print almost simultaneously with the composition of the work of Agrippa which cites it, the *Dialogus de homine.* The translator was Paolo Ricci, a learned Jewish convert to Christianity, who was from Pavia and was a brother of one of Agrippa's closest friends at Pavia and at Casale Monferrato, Agostino Ricci. It is far from certain that

[44] *De occulta philosophia,* Bk. III, ch. xli, p. ccxcv. Gershom Gerhard Scholem, *Major Trends in Jewish Mysticism* (New York, 1946), pp. 241-43.

[45] *De occulta philosophia,* Bk. III, ch. xxiv, p. cclvi (not in the manuscript version). On Postel's translation, William J. Bouwsma, "Postel and the Significance of Renaissance Cabalism," *Journal of the History of Ideas,* XV (1954), 220. For Reuchlin's sources, see Ludwig Geiger, *Johann Reuchlin: Sein Leben und seine Werke* (Leipzig, 1871), pp. 172-75.

[46] *Dialogus de homine,* Lyons, Bibliothèque Municipale, MS. No. 48, fols. 51v-52r [*sic; recte* 52v-53r]: "Sed vt rabi Ioseph castiliensis, in libro portarum lucis, quicquid illorum in sacris literis legitur velut manus, pes, oculus, quamuis magnitudinem veritatemque dei insinuant, quid tamen res illa sit, quae manus uel oculus dicitur nulla creatura cognoscere potest." (Printed by Zambelli, *¹oc. cit.,* 63-64.)

Agrippa had a personal acquaintance with Paolo Ricci, since Ricci had left Pavia for Augsburg by 1514, and by 1516 had become physician to the Emperor Maximilian.[47] But it is very certain that Agrippa drew heavily on his translation of the *Sha'are Orah*, under the title *Portae lucis*, while he was writing his *Dialogus de homine* in the company of the translator's brother Agostino at Casale in 1516. And it is quite likely that he knew of Paolo Ricci's other polemical works against Judaism. This Paolo Ricci, incidentally, was well informed about the *Zohar* also; and in *De coelesti agricultura* he cited Rabi Simeon (i.e., the *Zohar*), via the commentary of Menahem ben Benjamin Recanati, as a cabalistic authority upholding belief in the Trinity. His translation *Portae lucis* could have been known to Agrippa even before it was printed, since it circulated in manuscript at least as early as 1513, when Cardinal Egidio of Viterbo wrote out a copy in his own hand.[48]

Agrippa did not, however, learn all he knew about Cabala directly from the original texts. He also learned much—perhaps most—of what he knew from Christian writings on the same subject. His Italian friend Agostino Ricci, for example, shared his brother's enthusiasm for Cabala and wrote an astronomical book, *De motu octave sphere*, which also treated of cabalistic themes.[49] It is remotely possible that Agrippa did not yet have a copy of this book in 1528; but since it was printed in 1513, he quite probably saw it while he was in personal touch with the author in Italy.[50] So Agostino Ricci, brother of the translator of Gikatilla's *Sha'are Orah*, exercised a

[47] Zambelli, *loc. cit.*, 52-53; for the date of Ricci's removal to Germany, see *Opus epistolarum Des. Erasmi Roterodami*, ed. P. S. Allen [and H. M. Allen and H. W. Garrod] (12 vols; Oxonii, 1906-58), II, 500n.

[48] I have seen a photostatic reproduction of this manuscript, MS. Lat. 598 of the Bibliothèque Nationale at Paris, in the rare book room of the University of Illinois Library. Agostino Ricci was a pupil of Zacuto and later became physician to Pope Paul III. On him and his brother, see Secret, *op. cit.*, pp. 11-12, 15, 27-30; Zambelli, *loc. cit.*, 52-53; and Thorndike, *History of Magic and Experimental Science*, V, 264, 284.

[49] The full title of Ricci's book is *Augustini Ritij de motu octaue sphere: opus mathematica atque philosophia plenum, vbi tam antiquorum quam iuniorum errores luce clarius demonstrantur: in quo et quamplurima platonicorum et antique magie (quam cabalam hebrei dicunt) dogmata videre licet intellectu suauissima. Nuper in ciuitate Casalis sancti Euasij sub diuo Gulielmo marchione Montisferrati editum. Item eiusdem epistola de astronomie auctoribus ad magnificum dominum Galeottum de Careto* (Tridini, 1513).

[50] Agrippa to Orentius, Paris, 1 June 1528, *Epist.* V, xliv. The recipient appears to be Oronce Finé (1494-1555), a well-known author on mathematical questions. See also Agrippa's correspondence with Agostino Ricci, in Lyons, Bibliothèque Municipale, MS. No. 48, fols. 39v-42r.

literary as well as a personal influence on Agrippa, although Agrippa's writings do not draw heavily on *De motu octave sphere*. Another Latin cabalistic work which Agrippa possessed no later than early 1532 was the *De arcanis Catholicae veritatis contra obstinatissimam Judaeorum nostra* [*sic*] *tempestatis perfidiam* of Pietro Galatino, first printed in 1518.[51] This is apparently the same book which Agrippa had lent to his friend Augustinus Furnarius "several years" before the date of a letter written on 17 July 1532.[52] At the same period, he was trying, through his friends in Italy, to get hold of a "Cabala Samuelis" and a Hebrew alphabet attributed to Esdras. Late that same year, his friend Bernardus Paltrinus, writing from Bologna, reported that at Pavia he had met Francesco Giorgi of Venice, had spoken with him about Agrippa, and had got permission to read the Hebrew books owned by this man, but not to copy them. The man whom this exciting news concerned was a Franciscan student of the Cabala, author of a philosophical poem, *De harmonia mundi*, printed at Venice in 1525, and an important pupil of Pico della Mirandola. More exciting still, perhaps, was Paltrinus' design to buy the library of the late Cardinal Egidio of Viterbo, an avid collector of cabalistic texts and author of an unpublished Latin adaptation of the *Sha'are Orah*.[53] This hope apparently was not fulfilled, for Paltrinus reported that the Cardinal of Brindisi had already secured the books.[54] Agrippa cited Giorgi's

[51] Agrippa to [Bernardus Paltrinus], Brussels, 6 February 1532, *Epist.* VII, ii. Same to Agrippa, Bologna, 28 December 1532, *Epist.* VII, xxii. On Galatino, see Arduinus Kleinhans, "De vita et operibus Petri Galatini O.F.M.," *Antonianum*, I (1926), 145-79, 327-56; cf. Gershom Gerhard Scholem, *Bibliographia kabbalistica: Verzeichnis der gedruckten die jüdische Mystik (Gnosis, Kabbala, Sabbatianismus, Frankismus, Chassidismus) behandelnden Bücher und Aufsätze von Reuchlin bis zur Gegenwart* (Leipzig, 1927), p. 52 (No. 401).

[52] [Augustinus Furnarius?] to Agrippa, Ratisbon, 17 July 1532, *Epist.* VII, x.

[53] Joseph Leon Blau, *The Christian Interpretation of the Cabala in the Renaissance* (New York, 1944), pp. 31-32, regards Giorgi's poem as syncretistic rather than cabalistic, but with strong cabalistic influence. Secret, *op. cit.*, pp. 11-12, 43-49, is sharply critical of Blau's judgment and establishes that while cabalistic elements were only occasional in *De harmonia mundi*, Giorgi's *Problemata* (1536) was full of themes drawn from the *Zohar*. He also asserts that Giorgi was in touch with Egidio da Viterbo, while Egidio, in turn, knew Galatino at Rome. On Galatino and Egidio, see Secret, *op. cit.*, pp. 30-43. On Giorgi, see also Walker, *Spiritual and Demonic Magic*, pp. 112-19.

[54] This would be the learned Girolamo Aleandro. Not only did he acquire Egidio's books, but he also at one time possessed a copy of Agrippa's *De occulta philosophia*, according to an inventory of books which he presented to the Vatican library on 26 July 1532. See MS. Vat. Lat. 6937, fol. 5r (microfilm belonging to Knights of Columbus Foundation, St. Louis University, Roll No. 857).

eclectic poem in a work written in 1532 in order to defend his own statement that there are errors in the Bible.[55]

Despite the importance of all these lesser Christian cabalists, the earliest and strongest influences of this sort were the works of the two great founders of the fashion for cabalistic studies in Italy and in the north, Giovanni Pico della Mirandola and Johann Reuchlin. Pico was not, it has been recently shown, an isolated and solitary pioneer in the early history of Christian Cabala;[56] but he was the great figure whose work first caught wide attention and fired the imagination of later generations of Hebrew scholars. The precise stages in which Agrippa learned of his writings are not clear. Some he clearly knew before his departure for Italy in 1511. Others he learned about—or learned more about—while circulating among the scholars of Pavia and Casale Monferrato. In any event, sooner or later he came to know Pico's writings rather well, as has already been shown above. His seven years in Italy were doubtless decisive in deepening this cabalistic influence.

As for Reuchlin, the opening paragraphs of the present chapter have already shown that Agrippa was a close reader of both cabalistic works, *De verbo mirifico* and the later and more thorough *De arte cabalistica*. Agrippa made a point of reading carefully every publication from the pen of the scholar of Pforzheim. He did not miss a passing reference to his former disciple at Pavia, Christoph Schylling of Lucerne, in the *De accentibus* of Reuchlin.[57] He had read this book within a year of its publication. While Agrippa's writings did not plunder Reuchlin's two cabalistic works verbatim as they did Pico's, there are strong similarities on points of detail and illustration. For example, although Reuchlin's and Agrippa's treatment of the names of the *sephiroth*, or divine numerations, was by no means identical, the names given by Agrippa show much similarity to those of the *De arte cabalistica*.[58] Agrippa in *De*

[55] *Apologia adversus calumnias, propter declamationem de vanitate scientiarum, et excellentia verbi Dei, sibi per aliquos Lovanienses theologistas intentatas*, in *Opera*, II, 310. Henceforth cited as *Apologia*.

[56] Secret, *op. cit.*, pp. 14-16, and Gershom Gerhard Scholem, "Zur Geschichte der Anfänge der christlichen Kabbala," in *Essays Presented to Leo Baeck* (London, 1954), pp. 158-93.

[57] Agrippa ad Amicum, Metz, n.d. [1518-19], *Epist.* II, xv. Cf. Johann Reuchlin, *De accentibus, et orthographia, linguae hebraicae* (Hagenoae, 1518), fol. XI^r.

[58] *De occulta philosophia*, Bk. III, ch. x, pp. ccxxiiii-ccxxvii; cf. Reuchlin, *De arte cabalistica* (Hagenau, 1517), fols. LXI^v-LXII^r, and *De verbo mirifico* (Tubingae, 1514), fols. 33v-34r.

originali peccato also echoed Reuchlin's accusation that Eve in speaking with the Serpent had twisted the words of God's commandment concerning the forbidden fruit. On the other hand, the antirationalistic interpretation that he gave to this notion was not in Reuchlin's text.[59] Agrippa's belief that Cabala was incomplete until perfected by Christian revelation was common among Christian cabalists; but the further statement that all the power of divine names had devolved on the one name *Jesus* is an obvious reflection of the main point of Reuchlin's *De verbo mirifico*.[60] Agrippa's first important appearance before the learned public of Europe was as a lecturer on *De verbo mirifico*, at Dôle in 1509. Thus the influence of Reuchlin's books began very early, and it persisted throughout the lifetime of the Nettesheimer.

The extent of Agrippa's knowledge of cabalistic materials grew steadily as his studies in this literature continued. Although the youthful version of *De occulta philosophia* already showed cabalistic influences, explicit references to Cabala are fairly uncommon in the surviving manuscript.[61] In the printed version of 1533, however, cabalistic citations have become very common, especially in Book Three. These citations are not only more numerous, but also more explicit. The 1510 version refers only generally to *hebreorum cabalistici*, or to *hebreorum antiqui doctores*. That of 1533, on the other hand, offers many more detailed citations, such as references to the ten divine attributes, to that division of Cabala called *notarikon*, to the ten numerations (*sephiroth*), to the derivation of angelic names from the Schemhamphoras, and to individual spokesmen of the cabalistic and other Hebrew discourses.[62] The increase in Agrippa's command of Cabala probably stems from his studies and associations in Italy; yet there can be little doubt that even up to his latest years, he continued to seek and find new materials in the vast, obscure, still largely unstudied mass of Renaissance Cabala.

The way in which Agrippa used cabalistic materials is at least as significant as the sources from which he drew them. Most of the Christian cabalists regarded Cabala chiefly as an instrument of religious polemic by means of which they could convince the Jews that the essential doctrines of Christianity were already contained

<hr/>

[59] Cf. Agrippa, *Opera*, II, 554, with Reuchlin, *De verbo mirifico*, fol. e6r.

[60] *De triplici ratione cognoscendi Deum*, in *Opera*, II, 488; *De occulta philosophia*, Bk. III, ch. xi-xii, pp. ccxxvii-ccxxxiiii; *De vanitate*, ch. xlvii.

[61] Würzburg, Universitätsbibliothek, MS. M.ch.q.50, Bk. III, ch. 2, 15, 36, 49.

[62] *De occulta philosophia*, Bk. II, ch. xiii, xix; III, ch. x, xi, xxiv, xlviii, li. All of these are portions not found in the earlier manuscript version.

in their own Cabala. This hope was encouraged not only by the fact that the Neoplatonic emanation theory of Cabala offered a possible support for the doctrine of the Trinity but also by a number of actual conversions of leading Jewish cabalistic scholars, among them Paulus Riccius, translator of the *Sha'are Orah*.[63] Agrippa's teaching that the Christian revelation and the coming of Jesus Christ perfected the Jewish Cabala is of this tradition. With great satisfaction he notes that since the Incarnation the Jewish cabalists have been able to accomplish few if any marvelous works from the power of divine names.[64] Yet the missionary significance of Cabala is only incidental in his thought. Nor does he, like Pico, use cabalistic exegetical techniques merely as a device for lending scriptural authority to his teachings.[65] His interest in Cabala is twofold, as a confirmation for his Neoplatonic system of an animated world, all parts of which are united by occult bonds, and above all as a possible means of deriving divine and angelic names which will assist the *magus*, the worker in occult philosophy, to make use of these occult bonds and to accomplish works beyond the ordinary reach of human powers. This is why he added to the final version of *De occulta philosophia* extensive tables of Hebrew and angelic names and why he elaborated the sephirotical system in the later version.[66]

Parallel to the Neoplatonic and cabalistic sources, and deriving, like the latter, from the Neoplatonic ones, was the Hermetic literature. Agrippa traced the cabalistic, Hermetic, and Neoplatonic writings all back to the original Cabala or secret revelation of God to Moses. In Agrippa's mythical history, the writings of Hermes and other Egyptian sages were the link between the Pythagoreans and Platonists on the one hand and the original revelation to Moses on the other hand. Something of the writings of the pseudo-Hermes had long been known to Christian thinkers. Aquinas, for example, cited the Hermetic books, though only indirectly.[67] But the revival of Greek studies in fifteenth-century Italy had aroused new interest

---

[63] Blau, *op. cit.*, pp. 65-77.

[64] *De triplici ratione cognoscendi Deum*, in *Opera*, II, 487-88; *De vanitate*, ch. xlvii.

[65] Garin, *Giovanni Pico della Mirandola*, p. 71, explains Pico's use of cabalistic materials thus.

[66] *De occulta philosophia*, Bk. III, ch. x-xi, pp. ccxxiiii-ccxxxii, and ch. xxv, pp. cclvi-cclxv.

[67] *Summa contra gentiles*, Bk. III, ch. civ (a citation taken from St. Augustine, *De civitate Dei*, VIII, 23).

in these Hellenistic writings, an interest reflected in the translation
of the *Pimander* by Marsilio Ficino. The first draft of *De occulta
philosophia* contains occasional references to this Hermes or Mercurius,[68] while the intellectual climate of Italy in the second decade
of the sixteenth century is suggested by the frequent Hermetic
references in the writings of this period, including *De triplici ratione
cognoscendi Deum* (1516) and the first of Agrippa's lectures at
Pavia on the *Pimander* of Mercurius Trismegistus (1515).[69] The
citations of the *Pimander* in the former treatise in all probability
come from the version of Ficino. For the Hermetic *Asclepius*, available in the ancient translation attributed to Apuleius, Agrippa
probably used the recent edition by Lefèvre d'Étaples.[70] These
Hellenistic apocryphal works are thus a third major source of the
magical world view which Agrippa develops in *De occulta philosophia* and in several of his lesser works.

Comparable to these are the Orphic writings.[71] The Orphic texts
appeared as authorities even as early as the manuscript version of
De occulta philosophia (1510). There Agrippa quoted the most
famous of the Orphic fragments (perhaps indirectly through
Ficino's *Theologia Platonica*, since Ficino never published his Latin
translation of this work), the one which Renaissance syncretists
regularly used to establish the monotheistic nature of the Orphic
religion. This was the famous *Palinode*. Again, in his university lecture on the *Pimander* of Hermes Trismegistus, Agrippa quoted
from Orpheus the striking passage in which he banished from the
lecture hall any who would interpret his words in a profane manner.[72] Like other Renaissance enthusiasts for esoteric wisdom,

[68] Würzburg, Universitätsbibliothek, MS. M.ch.q.50. For example, III, 1-2.
[69] The latter is printed as *Oratio II* in *Opera*, II, 1073-84.
[70] On these Hermetic works in the Renaissance, see Karl H. Dannenfeldt,
"Hermetica Philosophica," in *Catalogus translationum et commentariorum*, ed.
Paul Oskar Kristeller, I (Washington, 1960), 137-56.
[71] On Renaissance interest in the Orphic hymns, see Karl H. Dannenfeldt,
"Oracula Chaldaica," in *Catalogus translationum et commentariorum*, I, 157-64;
D. P. Walker, "Orpheus the Theologian and Renaissance Platonists," *Journal
of the Warburg and Courtauld Institutes*, XVI (1953), 100-20; and Walker,
Spiritual and Demonic Magic, pp. 107-8.
[72] *Oratio in praelectione . . . Trismegisti . . .* printed as *Oratio II* in *Opera*,
II, 1081; cf. *De occulta philosophia*, Bk. III, ch. ii, in both printed and manuscript versions. Paola Zambelli, in an introduction written for *Testi umanistici
su l'ermetismo*, ed. Eugenio Garin *et al.*, pp. 110-11, interprets the passage to
mean that Agrippa and his hearers thought of themselves nearly as a secret
conventicle. Despite a few textual variations, it is clear that Agrippa cited the
translation by Ficino (Walker, "Orpheus the Theologian," *loc. cit.*, 110-11).

Agrippa associated these Orphic texts with various other ancient and occult traditions, such as the *Hermetica*, the Cabala, and the Neoplatonism of such figures as Dionysius the Areopagite. For him, all these texts were sacred expressions of one and the same religious truth.[73]

In addition to the Neoplatonic, patristic, cabalistic, and Hermetic influences on the shaping of Agrippa's view of an animated and sympathetic universe, he certainly had some acquaintance with those earlier writers on magic whom he declared unsatisfactory and whose books he hoped to replace with his own *De occulta philosophia*. These he listed in the revised version of his letter dedicating that work to Trithemius: Roger Bacon, Robert of England (probably Robert Grosseteste, Bishop of Lincoln), Pietro d'Abano, Albert the German (Albertus Magnus), Arnold of Villanova, Giorgio Anselmi of Parma, *Picatrix*, and Cecco d'Ascoli. On occasion he cited most of these, chiefly on factual points; [74] and while surely he did not have great familiarity with all of them, he probably read whatever of their works came within his reach.

Medieval occultists possessed a large if obscure body of anonymous and pseudonymous literature on astrological, alchemical, and magical topics. The Arabic treatise *Picatrix* cited by Agrippa was a part of this literature. How many others of these writings he knew is uncertain. Of the strange and obscure occultist texts of late classical and medieval times, a large and influential group was attributed to the name Hermes Trismegistus. Agrippa certainly knew the philosophical *Hermetica* (as shown above), and it is probable that he knew some of the other texts which tradition ascribed to the

---

It is true that Ficino's translation of Orpheus was never printed as a whole, but the passage quoted by Agrippa in both *Oratio II* and *De occulta philosophia* appears in a letter of Ficino to Martinus Uranius. See Ficino, *Opera omnia* (2 vols. in 4; Turin, 1959 [a photo-reprint of edition Basileae, ex officina Henricpetrina, 1576, which was in two volumes, consecutively paginated]), I², 934.

[73] *De occulta philosophia*, Bk. III, ch. x, pp. ccxxiiii-ccxxv.

[74] *De occulta philosophia*, fol. aa3v. I here cite a photostat of the University of Chicago copy, which supplies materials missing from the copy in the rare book room of the University of Illinois Library, but which represents a second, almost identical edition of the same year (1533). This list of magical authorities does not appear in the original dedicatory epistle as found in the Würzburg manuscript; in fact, of the group, only Albertus Magnus and Pietro d'Abano are cited at all in the manuscript. For variant lists of authorities on magic, see *De vanitate*, ch. xxxi, xlii, xlv. Agrippa's citations are usually on points of detail. For example, he cites Pietro d'Abano on the presence of certain images in the Zodiac (*De occulta philosophia*, Bk. II, ch. xxxvii, p. clxxxii), for a secret alphabet (*ibid.*, Bk. III, ch. xxix, p. cclxxiii), and on other points of information.

same author, texts which were usually late classical in origin and had generally passed through Arabic translations or adaptations. His familiarity with those *Hermetica* which dealt with alchemical topics seems to have been rather slight, despite his own habitual concern with alchemical operations. Certainly his writings show little kinship with Hermetic alchemical texts. The *Hermetica* which dealt with magic, on the other hand, were probably familiar to him. His descriptions of ceremonies, preparations, and materials used for magical amulets and figurines, for inducing dreams, and for invoking spirits suggest some general influence from the magical *Hermetica*, though the present writer can only report a general impression, not a series of detailed correspondences. Finally, the third major type of Hermetic occultist writings, the astrological ones, seems to have a closer relationship to Agrippan occultism than do the other types. The leading modern authority on Hermetic literature has already observed interesting correspondences between the lists of stars in *De occulta philosophia* and the materials in the Hermetic treatise *De quindecim stellis*. While Agrippa introduces some alterations which make it uncertain whether he knew this particular text, the likelihood that he did is great. In any case, his lists of stars and his method of assigning planetary demons and terrestrial substances to various celestial bodies are quite similar to the practice of pseudo-Hermes.[75]

The problem of sources for Agrippa's skeptical tendencies,[76]

[75] André Marie Jean Festugière, *La révélation d'Hermès Trismégiste*, I, *L'astrologie et les sciences occultes* (2nd ed.; Paris, 1950), 160-70, and *passim*. Note also Julius Ruska, *Tabula smaragdina: Ein Beitrag zur Geschichte der hermetischen Literatur* (Heidelberg, 1926), especially p. 206, for brief reference to the fact that Agrippa knew less of the alchemical than of the astrological *Hermetica*. This whole subject of Agrippa's acquaintance with late classical and Arabic magic would benefit from further investigation by someone familiar with the Hermetic literature and equipped with the necessary linguistic training, especially in Greek, Hebrew, and Arabic. The Latin text which Agrippa knew as *Picatrix* has not yet been edited, but it is a translation of the work of pseudo-Majrītī, edited in the Arabic original by Hellmut Ritter under the title *Das Ziel des Weisen* (Leipzig, 1933). The same editor and Martin Plessner have recently brought out a German translation, *"Picatrix": Das Ziel des Weisen von Pseudo-Mağrītī* (London, 1962). My study of this translation suggests that Agrippa's use of *Picatrix* was not extensive, and that *De occulta philosophia* was by no means modeled on it. When the Latin text is made available in print, it may be possible to re-examine this point and to discover verbal similarities between Agrippa and this source.

[76] Whether Agrippa's thought can properly be called skeptical is a question which will be treated in later chapters. Certainly there are elements in his thought that undermine trust in human learning and in reason, and so contrib-

especially for his destructive criticism of all human arts and sciences, is considerably more difficult than the task of discovering the multiple sources from which he drew his knowledge of the occult sciences. Like most of his works, *De vanitate* abounds in citations; yet even less than his other works does *De vanitate* reveal the true sources of its fundamental ideas. In criticizing ancient philosophy or late scholasticism, Agrippa gives many names of philosophers and Schoolmen.[77] The real problem, however, is not to explain these citations, but to explain how he came to reject these famous authorities: how his attitude passed from that of the respectful student of ancient sages to that of the scornful critic of human learning. Agrippa did not draw very extensively from such ancient philosophical skeptics as Sextus Empiricus.[78] Though he was aware of the general lines of the criticism of causation by the Pyrrhonists and the Academics,[79] he rarely mentioned them by name in *De vanitate*. The Academics do not appear at all in the original recension of *De occulta philosophia*, and the citations of them in the sections added later are neither numerous nor very significant.

Yet uncertainty and doubt about traditional human learning abounded in Agrippa's generation. Hence the development of his thought in the direction of a sort of generalized doubt, with hints· of a more thoroughgoing rejection of human reasoning powers, is not impossible to explain. In fact, the general intellectual situation of early sixteenth-century Europe, with the continual clashing of authorities both ancient and modern, and with the unsettling religious crisis that opened the century, was in many ways strikingly similar to the situation which had produced ancient skepticism. The skepticism of certain thinkers of the early Reformation period, Agrippa among them, seems "an almost inevitable result" of the clash of opinions which characterized the age. Perhaps it is the relative rarity, instead of the existence, of skepticism in the sixteenth century that requires explanation.[80] As a later chapter will show

---

ute to the genesis of what Richard H. Popkin, *The History of Scepticism from Erasmus to Descartes* (Assen, 1960), calls a "Pyrrhonist crisis" in Renaissance thought.

[77] *De vanitate*, ch. i, vii, viii.

[78] Popkin, *op. cit.*, pp. 19, 21, notes that Sextus was little known in Agrippa's generation.

[79] *De vanitate*, ch. i.

[80] Thomas Greenwood, "L'éclosion du scepticisme pendant la Renaissance e: les premiers apologistes," *Revue de l'Université d'Ottawa*, XVII (1947), 69-70

more fully, intellectual unrest, a certain spiritual malaise that questioned many, though not all, received authorities, lay very close to
the heart of Renaissance culture. Doubt and questioning were common among leading humanistic thinkers. What sets Agrippa off
from the rest is not that he felt serious doubts, but that he carried
those doubts further than most men, and showed an inclination in
De vanitate to undermine the authority not only of medieval thinkers, but also of the revered ancients.

Among the sources of a generally skeptical tendency in Agrippa's
thought, few past historians would list his interest in magical writings. Yet the usual assumption, that skepticism is incompatible with
an interest in magic, is really quite unfounded; and a few recent
historians have shown that enthusiasm for magic undermined the
medieval belief in an orderly universe amenable to the workings
of human reason.[81] Although Agrippa's magical studies would not
expose him directly to arguments directed against the validity of
human reason, the intellectual foundations of magic would suggest
that the real world far exceeds the scope of rational understanding.
Furthermore, the fact that magical "science" had never produced a
great systematizer, but was still involved in the clash of unreconciled
authorities, must have encouraged Agrippa in *De vanitate* to question many of those authorities, just as it encouraged him to attempt,
in *De occulta philosophia*, the insuperable tasks of unifying and
reconciling the same authorities.

The progress of humanistic classical scholarship in the fifteenth
and sixteenth centuries must have been another general source of
Agrippa's tendency toward doubt. The rapid recovery and publication of lost or little-known texts could easily create a troubled
awareness of the disagreements among ancient authorities. This
awareness, in turn, might easily create an intellectual crisis. Some
such effect was evident in the thirteenth century, when the fairly
sudden recovery of a large mass of ancient writings, especially the
works of Aristotle, disturbed the intellectual climate. St. Thomas
Aquinas personifies the effort of thirteenth-century scholastic think-

---

[81] See especially Garin, *Medioevo e Rinascimento*, pp. 98-99, 153-54, 158-60,
167-69, 173-75, and two articles by Paola Zambelli, "A proposito del 'De vanitate
scientiarum et artium' di Cornelio Agrippa," *Rivista critica di storia della filosofia*, XV (1960), 180; and "Umanesimo magico-astrologico e raggruppamenti
segreti nei platonici della preriforma," in *Umanesimo e esoterismo: Atti del V
convegno internazionale di studi umanistici, Oberhofen, 16-17 settembre 1960*,
ed. Enrico Castelli (Padua, 1960), pp. 142-44.

ers to master these new materials and reconcile them with traditional Christian beliefs. To a considerable extent, this earlier effort
succeeded. But the materials made newly available by Renaissance
scholarship were far more numerous and far more diverse than those
offered by the editors and translators of the thirteenth century.
Furthermore, the early sixteenth century produced no Aquinas.
The clash of opinions was never resolved; and there were, in fact,
conscious efforts to revive each of the chief ancient schools of philosophy, so that men of the sixteenth century were keenly aware
of the disunity of ancient thinkers.

This awareness, which obviously offered materials for the rise
of a new skepticism among those who despaired of the attempts to
harmonize the sources of ancient wisdom, was reinforced by a
growing interest in the ancient skeptics themselves. Although the
principal text of ancient skepticism, the works of Sextus Empiricus,
did not receive their first edition until 1562, references to ancient
skeptical authors, and expositions of their thought, were so numerous that Agrippa could hardly have avoided learning much about
their viewpoints. In fact, De vanitate cites the Pyrrhonists and
Academics by name, though not often.[82] There was among Renaissance thinkers a growing awareness of the disunity of ancient philosophy, and of the standpoint of the ancient skeptics. Ancient texts
that discussed philosophical controversies and set forth the theories
of Pyrrhonists, Academics, and other skeptical schools, were widespread. In fact, the favorite Latin author of the humanists, Cicero,
had described many of the philosophical controversies of his prede-
cessors and had given special attention to the skeptics among the
schools which he discussed. Cicero's Academica has even been
called "the Bible of skepticism" in the Renaissance.[83] Whether
Agrippa knew this particular text well cannot be proved; certainly
he did not explicitly argue from its standpoint. But he must have
known something of the Academics, whom he occasionally mentioned in the passages he added to De occulta philosophia. Early in
the very year when Agrippa wrote De vanitate, 1526, the press of
Froben at Basel brought out the Erasmian translation of Claudius
Galen's De optimo docendi genere, another ancient work which
expounded the views of the Academics and Pyrrhonists in the

[82] De vanitate, ch. i.
[83] Greenwood, loc. cit., 73; but Popkin, op. cit., pp. xii-xiii, 17, contends that
Sextus Empiricus was the crucial ancient influence on the revival of skepticism.

course of refuting them.[84] Again, there is no direct proof that
Agrippa read this book just as he was working on his *De vanitate*
or at any later date; but it appeared from the press of Froben, with
which Agrippa had been indirectly in touch less than two years
earlier;[85] and the place of publication, Basel, was a city in which
Agrippa had had connections ever since his friend Cantiuncula had
been a student and teacher in the university there. Basel was also a
city from which Agrippa had previously ordered books. Furthermore, the very fact that the translator was Erasmus makes it even
more likely that Agrippa would have seen the book, and that very
soon after its publication. Even though neither *De vanitate* nor the
Apologia which Agrippa later wrote in its defense explicitly adopts
the standpoint of the ancient skeptics, there can be no doubt that
such an omnivorous reader as Agrippa knew something, and perhaps very much, of the arguments of his ancient precursors.

Another influence, much more respectable, was the traditional
Christian contempt for pagan learning. Agrippa adopted this standpoint explicitly. In fact, the fundamental constructive message left
by *De vanitate* is that only the Word of God, the Gospel, is worthy
of man's trust, while all human sciences are vitiated by errors and
uncertainties. This was one of the two contradictory attitudes to
worldly learning which had created tension within Christian consciences since ancient times. This potential conflict between Christian and pagan wisdom was still very real in the sixteenth century;
and in *De vanitate*, Agrippa produced an influential expression of
the antirationalistic, antihumanistic current in the thought of his
time. Agrippa clearly was drawing on this Christian tradition, which
was not truly skeptical on strictly epistemological questions, but
which did depreciate the value and even the reliability of worldly
wisdom. The influential St. Augustine, though he could also be
cited by the other side, certainly did have much to say about the
dangers of human learning. Many patristic authors, and among them
Agrippa's favorite, the pseudo-Dionysius, maintained that ultimate
truth, the Godhead, was wholly incomprehensible to human rea-

[84] *Galeni medicorvm principis exhortatio ad bonas arteis, praesertim medicinam, de optimo docendi genere, et qualem opporteat esse medicum. D. Eras.
Roter. interprete* (Basileae, 1526). The colophon dates it May, 1526; Erasmus'
preface is of 28 April. The little treatise *De optimo docendi genere* (on fols.
c4r-d2r) expounds the views of the Academics and Pyrrhonists in the course of
refuting them.
[85] *Epist.* III, lxiv.

son.[86] This Christian antirationalism, though challenged by such medieval authorities as Abélard and Aquinas, was still strong in the Middle Ages. In late scholasticism, this Christian antirationalism became even more pronounced. One student of Agrippa's treatise on Lullian logic, the *In artem brevem Raymundi Lullii commentaria*, has detected the influence of both Duns Scotus and the nominalism of William of Ockham on the philosophical vocabulary of Agrippa's Lullian commentary. This authority attributes this influence to Agrippa's scholastic education at Cologne, and especially at Paris, where Occamist terminism was strong.[87] Scotus and Ockham and their followers were not truly skeptics, but they did deny the power of reason to attain ultimate truth—in particular, Ockham did so with a sweeping radicalism. Although late medieval Occamism failed to develop a truly skeptical critique of human powers,[88] it did adopt positions which were critical of reason and which might have been expanded from a generalized antirationalism into a more thoroughgoing attack on the human understanding.

Agrippa's contact with these antirationalistic tendencies of Christian thought passed beyond a mere general awareness of them. He was in direct touch with contemporary thinkers who carried on this tradition in his own time. The most obvious example is his interest in the writings of Erasmian humanism and of Luther and other leaders of early Protestantism. The works of Erasmus, and still more those of Martin Luther, must have further stimulated his own questioning of human learning and his stress on the Bible, even though neither of those thinkers was a skeptic. Agrippa was also an admirer of the French Biblical humanist, Jacques Lefèvre d'Étaples, whose preface to his Commentaries on St. Paul showed a mystical and fideist insistence on the feebleness of human reason

---

[86] Dionysius, *De divinis nominibus*, ch. I, pgh. 2 (*Patrologia graeca*, ed. J. P. Migne, III, col. 614). In his *Apologia*, in *Opera*, II, 288-89, Agrippa defends himself with the authority of these two favorite Fathers, Augustine and Dionysius, and also cites Philo Judaeus and Nicholas of Cusa in favor of his defense of ignorance. The same passage also refers to several scholastic authors.

[87] Johann Meurer, *Zur Logik des Heinrich Cornelius Agrippa von Nettesheim* (Bonn, 1913), pp. 5-11, 55-58.

[88] Maurice de Wulf, *History of Medieval Philosophy*, trans. P. Coffey (London, 1909), p. 418; cf. Gerhard Ritter, "Romantische und revolutionäre Elemente in der deutschen Theologie am Vorabend der Reformation," *Deutsche Vierteljahrsschrift für Literaturwissenschaft und Geistesgeschichte*, V (1927), 348-49.

unless illumined by divine grace,[89] precisely the position which Agrippa adopted at the conclusion of *De vanitate*. Agrippa was an avowed partisan of Lefèvre's thought by 1518 at the latest; and his Biblical enthusiasm went back at least to his study of the Pauline Epistles under John Colet during his short stay at London in 1510.

A recent student of the Nettesheimer's thought has suggested that he may have felt the influence of a skeptical tendency in the thought of his friend François Lambert of Avignon, a runaway Franciscan friar who later became a Protestant leader at Strasbourg and in Hesse, and whom Agrippa befriended at Geneva in 1522. Lambert maintained contact with Agrippa at least through the period when the latter lived at Lyons.[90] His writings reveal a number of similarities of viewpoint to Agrippa's opinions, including a contention that all knowledge is "vain, curious, lying and pernicious" unless it comes from faith.[91] Scholastic degrees and human philosophy, Lambert insisted, not only are useless in interpreting Scripture or the world of experience, but are even "to be abhorred and detested more than any filthiness that falls from man." [92] Perhaps Agrippa never read Lambert's writings, but the two may have discussed these questions when they met at Geneva.[93]

Another and far more important source of this "edifying skepticism" which influenced Agrippa was the thought of the great fifteenth-century German cardinal, Nicholas of Cusa. The Nettesheimer knew of Cusanus' works. Not only did he cite him (along with Albertus Magnus, Thomas Aquinas, and Scotus) as one of the "more recent" theological authorities,[94] but also he associated him directly with the attack on learning in *De vanitate*. Having been denounced by members of the Louvain faculty on account of *De vanitate*, Agrippa produced an *Apologia* in which he used the authority of Cusanus, along with that of ancient mystics like Diony-

[89] Pierre Imbart de la Tour, *Les origines de la Réforme* (4 vols.; Paris, 1905-35), II, 566-68. Popkin, *op. cit.*, pp. 1-3, 14-15, argues that the Reformation itself, by flatly denying the established criterion of religious truth, led directly to philosophical criticism of the foundations of human knowledge.

[90] Lambert is obviously the author of a letter written to Agrippa from Strasbourg, 31 December 1525, *Epist.* III, lxxxii.

[91] Zambelli, in *Rivista critica*, XV, 175-76.

[92] Roy Lutz Winters, *Francis Lambert of Avignon (1487-1530): A Study in Reformation Origins* (Philadelphia, 1938), p. 114.

[93] Zambelli, in *Rivista critica*, XV, 175-76.

[94] *De occulta philosophia*, Bk. III, ch. xv, p. cxxxix.

sius and medieval ones like Hugh of St. Victor, to justify his preference for ignorance over learning. Agrippa explicitly cited Cusanus' *De pace fidei* and, still more significantly, his principal philosophical work, *De docta ignorantia*. He also referred, more generally, to others of Cusanus' *opuscula*.[95] This interest in Nicholas of Cusa is not surprising in a person educated at Cologne, nor in an admirer of Lefèvre d'Étaples, who edited the German cardinal's works. Agrippa's use of the ass as the symbol of the patient and humble Christian believer is especially reminiscent of Cusanus' use of the term *idiota*; and Agrippa himself uses the Cusan term when he praises the religious insight of the *simplex et rudis idiota*.[96] This ideal of learned ignorance, as Nicholas called it, had affinities not only with traditional Christian suspicion of worldly science, but also with Platonism, which strongly influenced the great German cardinal. The thought of Nicholas of Cusa went further than that of most adherents of Christian antirationalism, and it could have done more for the growth of skepticism in Agrippa's thought than merely accentuate doubts about rational theology already raised by the Fathers and the later scholastics. For Cusanus, human knowledge was mere belief, and awareness of the grave limitations of human reason was the only sure knowledge.[97] Even though Cusanus was no skeptic, his writings must have fed Agrippa's doubts about human reason. At the very least, the *Apologia* shows explicitly that the Nettesheimer was quick to use the authority of this famous mystic and church reformer when he sought to defend his views on reason from charges of heresy and impiety. This may have involved distortion of Cusanus' thought, but it is how Agrippa read him.

All of these Christian critics of human sciences either were explicitly cited by Agrippa or were personally associated with him. Only in the case of François Lambert is the exercise of at least a certain degree of influence purely hypothetical; and even in this case, there is undeniable evidence of personal contact and correspondence between the two men. But two other authors, both important in the genesis of skepticism in sixteenth-century thought, were contemporary with Agrippa and may have been of importance

[95] *Apologia*, in *Opera*, II, 288-89, 323.
[96] *De vanitate*, ch. cii.
[97] Rudolf Stadelmann, *Vom Geist des ausgehenden Mittelalters: Studien zur Geschichte der Weltanschauung von Nicolaus Cusanus bis Sebastian Franck* (Halle, 1929), pp. 53-62.

in shaping his attitudes even though he never referred to either of them. Imbart de la Tour lists both as representatives of an anti-intellectual fideism which appeared in the early sixteenth century as an extreme reaction against the delicate balance of orthodox Christian humanism.

The first of these books, the less dangerous and the more traditional one, was the *De vera philosophia* of Cardinal Adriano Castellesi. Against Ficino and the Platonic Academy, Cardinal Castellesi upheld the existence of a sharp antagonism between natural reason and Christian faith.[98] Castellesi went very far in his depreciation of reason. Like Agrippa a few years later, he even denied that rational philosophy is useful in defending faith against unbelievers or heretics, for the mysteries of religion are believed by faith, not by reason.[99] Heretics are to be confuted not by reason but by authority of Scripture,[100] not only because religion contains many mysteries that are beyond reason and about which human conjectures are not permitted,[101] but also because dialecticians are helpless unless their postulates are granted, and their conclusions are false unless their postulates are correct, no matter how logical the reasoning.[102] Without illumination by divine light, human reason can never behold the true and the divine.[103] Reason itself cannot prove spiritual things, and so heavenly mysteries are not to be disputed upon in the light of merely human understanding.[104] Nor can reason undermine divine miracles, for reason cannot reach conclusions about singulars, and God can do things which fallible human reason calls impossible.[105] Humility is required of the man who wants knowledge of God, for this knowledge depends on grace, not on the wisdom of worldly philosophers.[106] In addition to this attack on natural reason and on philosophy, Cardinal Adriano questions the value of many special arts and sciences, including astrology. Finally, the book ends with a chapter devoted to the praise of the Bible.[107]

The similarity of many of these views to the opinions expressed

[98] Imbart de la Tour, *op. cit.*, II, 566-68.
[99] *De vera philosophia* (Coloniae, 1540), Bk. III, ch. 14, fols. K5v-K6v.
[100] *Ibid.*, Bk. III, ch. 14, fols. K6v-K8v.
[101] *Ibid.*, Bk. III, ch. 1-3, fols. G4v-G7v; cf. Bk. I, ch. 14-15, fols. A6v-A7r; Bk. I, ch. 18-19, fols. A8r-B1v.
[102] *Ibid.*, Bk. IIII, ch. 1, fols. L1r-L3r.
[103] *Ibid.*, Bk. I, ch. 25, fols. B7r-B8v; cf. Bk. II, ch. 4-6, fols. D7r-E4r.
[104] *Ibid.*, Bk. I, ch. 27-28, fols. C1r-C2v.
[105] *Ibid.*, Bk. I, ch. 31, fols. C5v-C7v.
[106] *Ibid.*, Bk. III, ch. 12-13, fols. I6r-K5v.
[107] *Ibid.*, Bk. IIII, ch. 22, fols. R1v-R8r.

by Agrippa in *De vanitate* is striking. Even more striking, however, is the dissimilarity of approach between the two books. Cardinal Adriano argues not by his own composition, but by presenting an anthology of quotations from the four Latin doctors, Augustine, Jerome, Ambrose, and Gregory. There are certainly cases where Agrippa uses the same patristic citations as Castellesi,[108] but it would be useless to contend that Agrippa could have known such commonplaces from the leading Latin Church Fathers only through reading *De vera philosophia*. Perhaps he read the book; perhaps he even took some of his antirationalist patristic quotations from it. But he nowhere appears to have quoted it directly, nor does Cardinal Adriano's name appear among his authorities. It is possible, even probable, that Castellesi's *De vera philosophia* influenced him; but there is no conclusive proof. This book and *De vanitate* are, in any case, two nearly contemporary expressions of a generally hostile attitude to human science, both with overtones of distrust of human reason.

A second contemporary book, far more philosophical in its approach to the problem of human knowledge, was *Examen vanitatis doctrinae gentium, et veritatis christianae disciplinae*, by Giovanni Francesco Pico della Mirandola, nephew of the more famous Giovanni Pico della Mirandola.[109] This book, more than Castellesi's *De vera philosophia*, and even more than Agrippa's *De vanitate*, marks a decisive stage in the introduction of ancient skeptical influence into sixteenth-century discussions. Like the work of Cardinal Adriano, but with a more explicit adoption of philosophical arguments drawn from the skeptics, Pico's book teaches the bankruptcy of all human sciences, both in general and taken one by one. And in the end it, too, turns from bankrupt reason to the certainty of a simple Christian faith based on the Bible. The development of skeptical arguments goes much further than in any other author of that generation, and Pico explicitly adopts a Pyrrhonist attitude. He directly cites the writings of Sextus Empiricus.[110] He recites the skep-

---

[108] Cf. the citation of St. Jerome in *De vera philosophia*, Bk. IIII, ch. 3, fol. L7r, with *De vanitate*, ch. xi. This commonplace passage also appears in Giovanni Francesco Pico della Mirandola, *Examen vanitatis doctrinae gentium, et veritatis christianae disciplinae* (Mirandulae, 1520), Bk. III, ch. 6, fol. XCʳ.

[109] On the younger Pico, see Imbart de la Tour, *op. cit.*, II, 568-72; Fortunat Strowski, *Montaigne* (Paris, 1906), pp. 124-30; and Pierre Villey, *Les sources et l'évolution des Essais de Montaigne* (2nd ed.; 2 vols.; Paris, 1933), II, 154-55.

[110] *Examen vanitatis*, Bk. I, ch. 2, fol. VIIʳ: "Decem et ego sexti sceptici libros perlegi. . . ."

tics' arguments against the validity of the syllogism (and also against inductive reasoning); he attacks both traditional metaphysics and the whole concept of causation.[111] Repeatedly he returns to the destructive analysis of sensory knowledge.[112] He also analyzes the philosophical difficulties of defining terms, of knowing objects, and of making valid demonstrations.[113] Like a true pyrrhonist, the younger Pico accepts neither the affirmations of dogmatism nor the negations of the Academics, but prefers to suspend judgment.[114] The only real value of philosophy, in fact, is that it leads to pyrrhonist doubt and so destroys any philosophical arguments against Christian religion. Philosophy, however, is utterly useless for proving Christian truth, which is based not on human reason but on divine revelation.[115]

The similarity of this argument to viewpoints of Agrippa in *De vanitate* is so striking that a number of scholars regard the *Examen vanitatis* as a source of the slightly later work, and one asserts flatly that the theoretical-metaphysical parts of *De vanitate* were virtually plagiarized from Pico's book.[116] Certainly Agrippa could have known Pico's book, or even the author himself, since Pico had begun to write his attack on human learning before 1510, and brought out a printed edition in 1520. Agrippa certainly knew and even copied from the writings of the elder Pico; and his failure ever to mention the nephew is not decisive, since he rarely made overt reference to contemporary authors. Even Agrippa's title, *De vanitate*, is reminiscent of Pico's.

Nevertheless, although the influence of Giovanni Francesco Pico on Agrippa is possible, even probable, the differences between the two books are as striking as the similarities. It is an exaggeration to say that Agrippa plagiarized his skeptical sections from *Examen vanitatis*, even though this work may well be one of the channels for skeptical influence on him. The similarities between the two books are great. Both present arguments against human reason drawn from ancient skepticism. Both also take up individual sci-

[111] *Ibid.*, Bk. III, ch. 10-11, fols. XCVII^r-C^v.
[112] *Ibid.*, Bk. IV, ch. 12, fols. CXXVIII^r-CXXIX^v; Bk. V, ch. 2, fols. CXXXII^v-CXXXVII^v; Bk. V, ch. 5-6, fols. CXXXV^v-CL^v.
[113] *Ibid.*, Bk. IV, ch. 7-11, fols. CL^v-CLXIIII^r.
[114] Strowski, *op. cit.*, p. 126; cf. *Examen vanitatis*, Bk. II, ch. 20, fols. L^v-LI^r.
[115] *Ibid.*; cf. *ibid.*, Bk. III, ch. 14, fols. CVIII^r-CX^r.
[116] Zambelli, in *Rivista critica*, XV, 178-79; cf. Strowski, *op. cit.*, p. 130. Villey, *op. cit.*, II, 154-55, n. 1, regards Agrippa as the channel for indirect influence from the younger Pico on Montaigne.

ences (grammar, history, poetry, rhetoric, dialectic, geometry, astrology, among others) and subject them to severe criticism. Both turn from bankrupt reason to a trusting faith in Christian revelation, with strong overtones of that veneration of the Bible which was very marked among both Protestants and Christian humanists of their generation. Yet the differences are striking, too. Gianfrancesco presents skeptical arguments directly, explicitly, and at much length. For all its historical importance and wide influence, Agrippa's skepticism is so fragmentary that some critics cannot find it at all and would discount the philosophical significance of *De vanitate* in spite of its great popularity.[117] As far as actual plagiarism of details is concerned, comparison of the two texts does not bear out this contention. On the question of philosophical disagreements about the soul, for instance, the differences are so striking that, granting the same general idea (that philosophers are unable to reach any firm conclusions about the soul, and that their ideas are contrary to Christian belief), granting also that both men proceed by citing the opinions of many of the same standard ancient philosophers, the two chapters could hardly be more unlike. The general structure of the discussions is not the same. Only some questions receive treatment in both texts. Even in these cases, the two authors do not always use the same authorities and do not even in all cases assign the same views to the same ancient authorities.[118] Likewise, the particular chapters in which *De vanitate* and *Examen vanitatis* assail the various branches of human learning show a few general similarities but no close textual relation.[119]

There is rather stronger evidence of influence on a less significant portion of Agrippa's *De vanitate*, the chapter *De medicina in gen-*

[117] Most recently, Zambelli, in *Rivista critica*, XV, 179-80, has renewed this contention; and Popkin, *op. cit.*, pp. 23-25, denies that Agrippa was a skeptic, though admitting that his book stimulated interest in skepticism.

[118] *De vanitate*, ch. lii, and *Examen vanitatis*, Bk. I, ch. 14. For a contrary view, see Zambelli, in *Rivista critica*, XV, 179.

[119] Cf. Pico's discussion of grammar, history, and poetry in *Examen vanitatis*, Bk. III, ch. 3, fols. LXXVIIIʳ-LXXXIIIʳ, with *De vanitate*, ch. iii, iv, and v. Likewise, Pico's ensuing attacks on rhetoric, geometry, music, dialectic, and even astrology bear no evidence that the corresponding portions of *De vanitate* borrowed from them. The discussions of moral philosophy show some similarities and some differences, but no clear proof that Agrippa's text (*De vanitate*, ch. liv) borrowed directly from Pico's (*Examen vanitatis*, Bk. III, ch. 13, fols. CIIIIʳ-CVIIIʳ).

ere.[120] On a number of issues, chiefly involving human generation but also including nutrition and the cause of illness, there are numerous parallel passages. Textually, there is very little similarity; but many of the same authorities are cited on the same points and in similar ways. Each of the two chapters, Pico's and Agrippa's, contains certain topics not discussed in the other. Within each of the topics which both discuss, there are variations in the authorities selected, and on occasion even flat contradictions in the standpoint which the two chapters attribute to the same authority.[121] But there are some cases where authorities are cited not only in the same way but also in the same order; pretty strong evidence either that Agrippa is following Pico's text (perhaps only from memory or from notes), or that both authors are frequently referring to the same handbook of medical opinions. Both Pierre Villey and Paola Zambelli draw the inference that Agrippa used Pico as a source; and this pair of chapters, far more than those dealing with metaphysics, does point strongly, if not quite unequivocally, to such a conclusion. It is hard to explain how Agrippa's mordant wit could have missed some of the telling instances of medical absurdity that the younger Pico wrote down: for instance, the pointless debates about which part of the foetus is formed first, and the opinion attributed to some that the big toe is the first organ to take shape in the womb.[122] Nevertheless, the parallels remain striking; and either the use of one text by the other, or the use of a common source by both, is an almost inescapable conclusion.

But even if one concludes from the similarities in the medical chapters that Agrippa knew the younger Pico's work, there is no question of utter and abject dependence on it. His key philosophical chapters contain sections that may well have been influenced by Pico; but the similarities are not so striking that they justify any dogmatic assertions. If he knew the *Examen vanitatis*, he felt its influence only in a general way. Possibly—even probably—he had

[120] Cf. *De vanitate*, ch. lxxxii, with *Examen vanitatis*, Bk. I, ch. 16. Zambelli, in *Rivista critica*, XV, 179, has apparently discovered this parallelism, but mistakenly gives the Agrippan reference as ch. liii.
[121] *De vanitate*, ch. lxxxii: "Porro Aristoteles et Democritus nil dicunt mulieres semen ad generationem conferre. . . ." *Examen vanitatis*, Bk. I, ch. 16, fol. XXVIII[r]: "Pythagoras, Democritus, hippocrates, Epicurus, et foeminam quoque semen proiicere sanxerunt." Pico couples the name of Zeno with that of Aristotle as authority for the view given by Agrippa.
[122] *Examen vanitatis*, Bk. I, ch. 16, fol. XXXVIII[v].

at some time read it. He may even have had some of its ideas consciously in his mind when he wrote his own *De vanitate*. But he
did not extract whole passages verbatim from it as he did in his
other books from the *Heptaplus* of the elder and more famous Pico.
Nor did its treatment of philosophical problems dominate his own
treatment of the same topics. Gianfrancesco's work may have influenced *De vanitate*, just as Erasmus' *Praise of Folly* very likely did.
The relation of Agrippa's book to Pico's may be closer and more
specific than that to the work of Erasmus; but this relation remains
only highly probable, not certain.

In addition to the influence of the various representatives of
Christian mistrust of natural reason and worldly learning, Agrippa's
development of the antirational and fideistic standpoint of *De vanitate* may have received nourishment from Platonism. Although
Platonism had in the past given rise to skepticism, Florentine Neoplatonism did not show any properly skeptical tendencies. But its
chief representative, Ficino, did make the power of human reason
to comprehend truth depend ultimately on the assistance of divine
grace.[123] Such a view was not skepticism. But it did contribute to
Agrippa's resolution of the problem of knowledge through an
appeal to mystical illuminism and Biblical revelation.

What Agrippa had to do in creating his skepticism out of such
materials was to extend intellectual pessimism from the fideistic
standpoint of the later Schoolmen along lines already suggested by
Cusanus, and to link his thought with that of the ancient skeptics.
Some of the materials for this latter step were at hand in excerpts
given in medieval literature which he probably knew. Ancient and
contemporary discussions of philosophical problems and of skepticism helped him complete his task.

Agrippa also kept abreast of the contemporary controversial
literature of his time. Although this point will receive further
treatment in a later chapter, it is worth noting here that the writings
of Erasmus and still more of Martin Luther must have further
stimulated him to question human learning and to stress the sole
value of the Bible. His interest in the Bible did not, however, begin
with reading Erasmus or Luther or their contemporary, Jacques
Lefèvre d'Étaples, nor with his trip to Italy. Agrippa laid great
stress on his study of the Epistles of Paul under John Colet during
his short stay in London in 1510. Citations from Scripture abound

[123] Kristeller, *Philosophy of Marsilio Ficino*, p. 248.

in his writings; and he exalted the Bible almost (but not quite) in the same way as did the Protestant Reformers.

The writings of the Reformers and the Biblical humanists were not the only sort of current literature which Agrippa read. Doubtless because of his years in Italy, his books contain references, though not always specific ones, to the writings of humanists and literary figures like Dante, Petrarch, Boccaccio, Poggio, Leon Battista Alberti, Aeneas Sylvius Piccolomini, Lorenzo Valla, and Antonio Mancinello; to the astronomer Paolo Toscanelli; to the medieval religious prophet Joachim of Flora; and even once to Machiavelli (though only as a writer on military affairs). He also refers to Greek refugees of the fifteenth century, especially George of Trebizond.[124] He had contact with the works of Ficino, Pico, Galatino, and Paolo and Agostino Ricci. His writings do not contain enough extended and specific citations from these authors to make a reader well acquainted with these Italians; but they certainly suggest the spread of interest in Italian literature north of the Alps. Even his tendency to interpret Aristotle in Averroistic terms may be the product of his years in Italy, although he could also have learned of the heterodox Aristotle at Paris when he studied there. In either case, the heterodox Aristotle, teacher of the political necessity of religion, of the eternity of the world, and of the unity of the human intellect, was yet another of the influences (although chiefly a negative one) on the formation of the Nettesheimer's thought.

The existence of two distinct forms of De occulta philosophia, one completed by 1510 and the other probably not finished until shortly before the appearance of the first partial edition in 1531, makes possible a closer understanding of the chronological development of Agrippa's knowledge of his sources. The preceding discussion has already shown how his familiarity with certain sources increased. The Neoplatonic authorities, already prominent in 1510, became even more numerous during the following two decades. The ancient Hermetic materials continued to grow in number, and were supplemented by the increasing influence of modern enthusiasts for Hermes and the other prisci theologi, notably Ludovico

[124] On Poggio and Boccaccio, see Apologia, in Opera, II, 306-7, and De occulta philosophia, Bk. I, ch. lviii. For George of Trebizond, Valla, and Mancinello, De vanitate, ch. iii. Petrarch is cited rather often, for example as a critic of the Schoolmen, ibid., ch. viii. For Toscanelli as an authority on astronomy, see ibid., ch. xxx. For the other Italians, ibid., ch. lxiv. For Machiavelli, ibid., ch. lxxix.

Lazzarelli. A similar increase in the number of Orphic citations occurred. The command of cabalistic materials, furthermore, became very noticeably greater—not only were there more citations, but those citations became more detailed and more prominent in the development of the argument.

Certain other developments in Agrippa's readings become obvious from a comparison of the early and late forms of *De occulta philosophia*. One modern student of Agrippa's thought contrasts the original prominence of purely classical sources (Vergil, Ovid, Pliny, for example) with the far greater number of Platonic, magical, and Biblical citations apparent in the portions that were written after 1510.[125] There can be no doubt that such materials were more common in the later form. Yet Dr. Zambelli herself observes that the later version sought to present its materials in a broader philosophical context, and this desire itself would explain many of the added citations. Biblical citations were already numerous in Book Three of the manuscript. They became even more numerous in the revised text; but many of these citations came along with the increased use of cabalistic materials. It would be an error to conclude that Agrippa in 1510 was little but a humanistic student of the classics, and that his Biblical interests and the esoteric influences which he associated with Christian revelation were almost wholly the result of his residence first in Italy and then in the spiritually upset North of Europe during the Reformation crisis. On the other hand, there can be no doubt that his interest in religious readings was stimulated by his Italian experience and then, in a somewhat different direction, by the intellectual ferment of the early Reformation.

Comparison of the manuscript with the printed *De occulta philosophia* also suggests certain other directions which Agrippa's reading followed in the second and third decades of the century. While even the manuscript contains citations of Plato himself and of the Platonists, it completely lacks mention of the Academics. Yet these *Academici* appear four times as authorities in the first complete printed edition, that of 1533. Aristotle is cited in the Würzburg manuscript, but only rather infrequently. The number of Aristotelian and pseudo-Aristotelian citations has greatly increased in the printed form, which refers not only to Aristotle generally, but also to his *Meteorologica*, his *Ethica*, his *Liber de*

125 Zambelli, in *Rivista critica*, XV, 171-73.

temporibus, his *De divinatione*, his *De coelo*, his sixth book of *Mystica philosophia*, and his *Secreta dogmata*. The manuscript of 1510 had already cited a pseudo-Aristotelian treatise on a fire that burns water and the pseudo-Aristotelian *Problemata*, and had given a very few unspecified general references to Aristotle and to the *Peripatetici*. In addition to its expansion of the list of Aristotelian works, the printed *De occulta philosophia* introduced references to two influential commentators on Aristotle, Alexander of Aphrodisias and Averroes.[126] Of more recent authors, Agrippa added references to Martianus Capella, Saxo Grammaticus, the visionary Joachim of Flora, Peter Lombard's *Book of Sentences*, Duns Scotus' commentary on the *Sentences*, Nicholas of Cusa, the mathematician Luca Pacioli of San Sepolchro, and the humanistic and astrological writer Giovanni Pontano. He included many new citations of the Church Fathers, and new references to Jewish rabbinical opinion. Finally, the number of citations of medical and astrological authors increased markedly between 1510 and 1531, both in number and in accuracy. New medical authorities included Ruffus Ephesius medicus, Isaac Judaeus (whose *Opera omnia* were printed at Lyons in 1515), Celsus, Galen, the medical poet Serenus Sammonicus, Dioscorides, Alpharus,[127] and Hippocrates. New authorities on as-

[126] For Alexander, *De occulta philosophia*, Bk. I, ch. xiii; for Averroes, *ibid.*, Bk. I, ch. lxi, and Bk. II, ch. ii. For mention of the pseudo-Aristotelian work on Greek fire, *De occulta philosophia* (Würzburg, Universitätsbibliothek, MS. M.ch.q.50), Bk. I, ch. 3. The references to the *Meteorologica*, *Ethica*, and *De coelo* are to genuine Aristotelian works. If Agrippa's *De divinatione* means *De divinatione per somnum*, then this is also a genuine Aristotelian source. Aristotle produced *Problemata*, but the writings which survive under that title are not genuine, though of ancient origin (*Paulys Real-Encyclopädie der classischen Altertumswissenschaft*, 2nd ed., ed. Georg Wissowa, II, col. 1049). The reference to *Liber de temporibus* may mean the treatise *De tempore* of the Aristotelian commentator Alexander of Aphrodisias. This work is mentioned by S. D. Wingate, *The Mediaeval Latin Versions of the Aristotelian Scientific Corpus, With Special Reference to the Biological Works* (London, 1931), p. 123. Perhaps, as Professor Kristeller suggests, Agrippa meant the pseudo-Aristotelian *Theologia Aristotelis* when he cited *Liber sextus mysticae philosophiae*, though this possible source has nothing Aristotelian about it except the false attribution, and is really Neoplatonic in origin (see Pauly-Wissowa, II, col. 1043). The title *Secreta dogmata* suggests that Agrippa meant to refer to another pseudo-Aristotelian book, the *Secreta secretorum*, which Wingate, *op. cit.*, p. 33, ascribes to Philip of Tripoli. On it, cf. Valentinus Rose, *Aristotles pseudepigraphus* (Lipsiae, 1863), p. 583. I have found no other trace of a pseudo-Aristotelian treatise on Greek fire.

[127] Assuming that this is the eleventh-century Salernitan medical writer Alphanus, and not the famous tenth-century Arabic writer on philosophy, music, and science, Al-farabi.

trology and other occult sciences included Orus Apollo, Apollonius Rhodius, Michael Scotus, Almadel, Alchandrinus, Nicomachus, Hyginus, Aratus, Maternus, Xystus the Pythagorean, Geber the alchemist, Roger Bacon, Avicebron, and Lycophron, in addition to the authorities listed in the revised letter of dedication to Trithemius and mentioned above. Last, Trithemius himself is cited, and so is the mysterious Marcus Damascenus whose works Agrippa secured while living at Metz. The addition of such sources as these suggests study not only of occultism in general, but also of medicine, a profession which Agrippa certainly practiced at Geneva and Fribourg, and in both France and the Low Countries. Wherever he lived, and whatever he read, Agrippa hunted unceasingly for new sources of wisdom in the writings of ancient men.

CHAPTER SEVEN

AGRIPPA AND THE RELIGIOUS CRISIS

Also, about this time, a man named Master Martin Luther, a German, a doctor and a heretic, a religious of the order of Augustinian friars, made and composed several large and remarkable writings printed and published throughout Christendom, touching certain articles of our faith and of the holy sacraments, and also the governors and agents of Holy Church. Whom several great clerks and doctors followed, and others did not. . . . Among those who followed him was a young man from Cologne, a marvelously great clerk, and small of body, named Master Agrippa, who all his life had wandered about the world, and spoke all languages, and had studied in every science.[1]

Thus does Philippe de Vigneulles, a contemporary of Agrippa at Metz, describe Agrippa von Nettesheim's relation to the great religious crisis which after 1517 coalesced around Martin Luther. This view that Agrippa supported the Reformation likewise appears in contemporary attacks on his writings, as for example the Sorbonne's condemnation of *De vanitate*, "which much favors Lutheran

---

[1] Philippe de Vigneulles, *La chronique de la ville de Metz*, ed. Charles Bruneau (4 vols.; Metz, 1927-33), IV, 332.

doctrine, having many things against the worship of images, temples, feasts, and ceremonies of the church, and is also blasphemous against the writers of the holy canon; and so must be publicly burned. . . ." [2] Agrippa's reputation for a concealed, but ill-concealed, adherence to Protestantism lived on into the later sixteenth century. John Calvin regarded Agrippa as one of those whose early interest in the new faith was transformed into open impiety and unbelief, a judgment seconded (but of course with different implications) by Paolo Giovio, Martin Del Rio, and other Roman Catholic writers.[3] Crypto-Protestantism and even (provided the accuser saw any difference) disbelief: this was the charge which his enemies in both camps made against Cornelius Agrippa.

More recent biographers of Agrippa also regard him either as a Protestant by conviction who lacked the force of character to risk open adherence to the Reformation, or as a one-time adherent of the Reformation who later returned to the fold of the old confession. His biographers Morley and Prost, though they disagree on many other points, are essentially at one in holding the first point of view. Prost, to be sure, presents a more subtle concept: Agrippa was more a Protestant than he himself realized. Yet for all that, a Protestant he was, although (like Erasmus, suggests Prost) he was too timid to avow his real belief. More recently, Henri Naef, recognizing the obvious fact that Agrippa died in the Roman Catholic faith, supposes that he adhered to the Reformation during his stay at Geneva and Fribourg in the early 1520's but later fell away from the new faith. Indeed, Naef regards Agrippa as the very center, the inspirer, of those Genevan humanists who were favorably inclined to the Reformation in the early 1520's and who a decade later were the first leaders in the Reformation at Geneva.[4]

---

[2] Act of 2 March 1530 (1531, n.s.), printed in Auguste Prost, *Les sciences et les arts occultes au XVI siècle: Corneille Agrippa, sa vie et ses oeuvres* (2 vols.; Paris, 1881-82), II, 464 (Appendix X).

[3] Josef Bohatec, *Budé und Calvin: Studien zur Gedankenwelt des französischen Frühhumanismus* (Graz, 1950), p. 149. Martinus Antonius Del Rio, *Disquistionum magicarum libri sex* (Coloniae, 1679), p. 283 (Bk. II, Sect. XVI). Paolo Giovio, *Elogia doctorvm virorvm* . . . (Basileae, 156?), pp. 236-37. I use the term *Protestant* because of its convenience, although strictly speaking it is anachronistic until after the Diet of Speyer in 1529.

[4] Henry Morley, *The Life of Henry Cornelius Agrippa von Nettesheim, Doctor and Knight, Commonly Known as a Magician* (2 vols.; London, 1856), II, 85-86. Prost, *op. cit.*, I, 90-92, regards anticlerical satire as the disguised aim of the whole of *De vanitate*. Cf. *ibid.*, I, 297-99, for the comparison with Erasmus and the conclusion that prudential reasons kept both of them from openly

The problem of Agrippa's relation to the Reformation really has two parts. The first, essentially biographical, has to do with his own relation to and opinion of the movement which we have come to call the Protestant Reformation. The second involves a study of Agrippa's own religious views as expressed in his published writings and his private letters.

I

Certainly there are many pieces of evidence to support one or both of the theories which hold that at one time or another Agrippa was a supporter of the Reformers. Agrippa's friendships, for one thing, were suspect. Jean Rogier, called Brennonius, to whom Agrippa was as close as to any friend, was himself of doubtful orthodoxy and in 1525 was briefly imprisoned at Metz as a suspected heretic. He supported Agrippa's attack on the procedures of the Dominican inquisitor at Metz and in his own right as a parish priest engaged in litigation over the exorbitant claims of the regular clergy. Yet a certain boldness and a readiness to defend his own rights against the regular clergy do not prove any firm adherence to Protestantism. His letters show satisfaction with the discomfiture of the Schoolmen and a tendency to blame the pope's negligence for many schisms and heresies, but they also show certain reservations about Ulrich von Hutten's violent attacks on the papacy.[5] Brennonius' attitude would perhaps not please the strictly orthodox, but it is no proof that he was a follower of Luther. Another close associate of Agrippa was Claudius Cantiuncula, who showed Erasmian tendencies and some sympathy for the Reformers but was never an adherent of the new faith.[6] Hilarius Bertulph of Lede,

embracing Protestantism. *Ibid.*, II, 306-7, for the view that Agrippa was more heretical than he himself realized. Cf. *ibid.*, II, 390-91, 412-18. In Appendix X, *ibid.*, II, 462-65, Prost makes greater reservations but still stresses Protestant sympathies. Henri Naef, *Les origines de la Réforme à Genève* . . . (Geneva, 1936), pp. 309-51, especially pp. 331-42.

[5] Brennonius to Agrippa, Metz, 17 June 1520, *Epistolarum Liber II*, lv, in Agrippa's *Opera* (2 vols.; Lugduni, n.d.), II, 773. (Henceforth this correspondence is cited as *Epist.*)

[6] Rivier, "Claudius Cantiuncula," *Allgemeine deutsche Biographie*, II, 767. In fact, Chansonnette was a determined opponent of the extreme Protestant Farel, who used his personal contacts with friends in the entourage of Marguerite d'Alençon to prevent a warm welcome for Chansonnette's translation of Erasmus' *Exomologesis sive modus confitendi*, which the translator had dedicated to Marguerite. See the co-operative biography *Guillaume Farel, 1489-1565* (Neuchâtel, 1930), pp. 122-26.

another friend of Agrippa, eventually became a servant of Margaret of Alençon (later of Navarre), sister of Francis I and a princess who was to show strong inclinations to Calvinism; but his primary associations were not with Protestant Reformers but with Erasmus, to whom he was secretary from 1522 to 1524. Similarly, Agrippa's association with Jacques Lefèvre d'Étaples, though perhaps more questionable than that with these Erasmians, involved a man who never openly left the Roman Catholic faith.

It is true that other friends of Agrippa did leave the old institutional church and adhere to the Reformation. One such was Wolfgang Fabricius Capito, who was Bucer's co-worker in the Reformation at Strasbourg. Yet it is worth noting that his acquaintance with Agrippa began at a time when Capito was still within the pale of Catholicism, suspicious of the sincerity of Luther and, judging from his letter of 23 April 1522 to Agrippa, still felt strong reservations about what Luther's partisans had been doing at Wittenberg during their leader's absence at the Wartburg. This letter is worth analysis because Agrippa's reply, written from Geneva on 17 June 1522, expressed agreement with its views on Luther. Although a chance acquaintance had informed Capito that Agrippa, being a forerunner of Luther, could hardly be expected to oppose him, the still unconverted Capito described in most critical terms what had been going on in Germany during Luther's temporary disappearance from public life:

First, whatever they conjectured out of the Gospel truth, they commanded with loose words to be observed. I shall add a few [examples]: Whoever, they say, does not eat meat and eggs and such things on Fridays, let him not be a Christian. Let him who does not take into his hands and touch the sacrament of the Eucharist not be held a Christian. Let him who confesses in Lent not be a sharer in the mercy of God. He who thinks that works of piety are anything loses for himself the way of salvation; and many things of this sort.[7]

The result of such preaching, Capito said, was to stir up the masses to violence, although Luther had returned to Wittenberg and was busy calming the common people and attacking his own radical

---

[7] *Epist*, III, xv: "Primum, quicquid ex veritate evangelica suspicabantur, observandum liberis verbis praeceperunt. Pauca inseram. Quicunque, ajunt, non vescitur carnibus et ovis et id genus, diebus Veneris, Christianus non esto. Qui sacramentum eucharistiae suis manibus non sumit et contrectat, ne Christianus habeatur. Qui confitetur in quadragesima, non esto particeps clementiae Dei. Qui pietatis opera esse aliquid putat, sibi viam salutis praecludit: et id genus multa." Agrippa's approving reply is *Epist*. III, xviii. On Capito, cf. Herzog, "Wolfgang Fabricius Capito," *Allgemeine deutsche Biographie*, III, 772-75.

followers. Capito granted the existence of abuses but felt that no pope would hinder the growing number of men who were preaching the pure Gospel. He did not at all feel that Luther was right in calling the pope Antichrist. He was a Reformer in the making but certainly was not yet committed to what he still called "the German heresy." And Agrippa agreed with Capito at this time.

There were other friendships with Protestants. Claude Dieudonné, for example, a man with whom Agrippa was in touch at Metz and who was almost certainly the anonymous correspondent from Annecy during Agrippa's Genevan period, later became a Reformed pastor in Switzerland. As in the case of Capito, however, this was later. In this instance Agrippa may have contributed to the later development, for Dieudonné, writing from Annecy on 2 October 1521, asked "what you now think of the Lutheran doctrines. You will not forget, I think, how at Metz you deigned to communicate to me some Lutheran things and extolled them with remarkable praise." [8] But not all persons who read, discussed, and even praised Luther's books in 1518 and 1519, a time when few people foresaw the Reformer's later course, were Lutherans.

Futhermore, even if Naef is right in his argument that Agrippa knew the future Protestant François Bonivard during his Genevan period, even if his friend "Ulrich" from Fribourg was the sometime Protestant Uli Techtermann, even though he certainly knew Louis Beljaquet, a Genevan schoolmaster and physician much esteemed by Calvin in later years, and Hans Wannenmacher of Fribourg, all this is no real justification for making Agrippa appear to be the nucleus around which gathered those persons who later led the early Reformation at Geneva and tried unsuccessfully to do the same at Fribourg. Another friend of the years in Switzerland was Claude Blancherose, who opposed Guillaume Farel and Calvin in the Lausanne disputation of 1536, while Guillaume Furbity, the relative of Agrippa's Genevan wife who cared for her during her illness at Paris, was apparently the same Dominican Guillaume Furbity who in 1534 was imprisoned at Geneva for his opposition to the Reformation. [9]

<hr/>

[8] *Epist*. III, x: ". . . quid nunc sentiat de Lutheranis lucubrationibus. Non te praeterit, arbitror, qualiter apud Metenses mihi nonnulla Lutherana communicare dignatus sis, eaque mira laude extulisse."

[9] Furbity appears in Agrippa's correspondence as early as the fall of 1522 (*Epist*. II, xxxii), and is apparently the relative who cared for Agrippa's wife during her illness at Paris in 1528: *Epist*. V, lv, lx, lxi, lxxxi, lxxxii, lxxxiv, lxxxv; VI, xxxiv. In 1535 Guillaume Furbity became suffragan Bishop of Belley

The same generalization holds true for Agrippa's other associations and friendships in the city of Metz, where he first met Dieudonné. Even more in the Metz years (1518-20) than in the Swiss period of his life, the whole movement for church reform was amorphous and showed no clear distinction between fundamentally Catholic critics of church abuses and individuals who displayed significant deviations on matters of doctrine and discipline. So while Agrippa's friendships in Metz definitely were with the reform-minded faction, there is no reason to attribute particular significance to the fact that some of his friends, such as the aristocrat Nicole d'Esch or the bookseller Jacques, later became directly associated with extreme Protestant activities. As already shown in an earlier chapter, Agrippa at Metz was closer to moderate reformers like his friends Brennonius and Chansonnette than to Esch, the later chief of the Lutheran faction among the governing aristocracy, or to the bookseller Jacques, the associate of the iconoclastic immigrant wool-carder Jean Leclerc.

Precisely the same rule holds for Agrippa's "evangelical" friendships while he lived in France. His closest friends, such as the physician Chapelain or the Bishop of Bazas, Symphorien Bullioud, sympathized with reform and Biblical humanism, but retained their loyalty to the old church. Some of the Laurencins became Protestant, but this event occurred later and in any case involved a younger generation: those who befriended Agrippa were holders of important offices in the old institution. Other friends, such as the Lyonese woman, Claudine Dumas, who later testified concerning the parentage of Agrippa's sons, were also Protestant at a later date, but this fact does not prove the heterodoxy of their German friend.[10] It is essential to realize that the religious situation in France

---

under Claude d'Estavayer (the chancellor of Savoy whose favor Agrippa sought while at Geneva): Conradus Eubel *et al., Hierarchia catholica medii et recentioris aevi* (2nd ed.; 4 vols.; Monasterii, 1913-35), III, 342. Prost, *op. cit.*, II, 485-86, identifies him as a Dominican rather than a Carmelite, the term used in *Epist.* III, xxxii, and also refers to him as a doctor of the Sorbonne. Charles Borgeaud, in the co-operative *Guillaume Farel*, p. 316, gives the Christian name of this Furbity as Guy rather than Guillaume, and says that he was called to Geneva from Chambéry to preach Advent in the Church of Saint-Pierre. Both Borgeaud and Prost describe his opposition to Farel during this residence at Geneva in 1533. For the religious views of Blancherose, Furbity, and other friends of the Swiss period, see Léon Charvet, "Correspondance d'Eustache Chapuys et d'Henri-Cornélius Agrippa de Nettesheim," *Revue savoisienne*, XV (1874), 25-30, 33-39, 45-50, 53-58, 93-95.

[10] For more complete treatment of these Lyonese connections of Agrippa, see Chapter Four above.

was so confused during the 1520's that it is difficult for historians to sort out the real Protestants from the reform-minded Catholics. It is still debated whether Marguerite d'Alençon, or even Jacques Lefèvre d'Étaples, was really heterodox, at least heterodox in the direction of Lutheranism. Furthermore, this uncertainty rests less on lack of knowledge about such figures than on inability to establish valid criteria for judging the position of individuals on the broad spectrum of early sixteenth-century religious belief. The religious situation in France was confused; the figures involved, contradictory and vague themselves.[11] The sharp and precise categories of later French religious history simply are not applicable to the generation of the 1520's. Even in the case of such a "Prottestant" as Michel d'Arande, almoner to Marguerite d'Alençon, the issues are debatable. It may be true that he contributed much to the conversion of the Protestant extremist Guillaume Farel by turning him against veneration of saints [12] (a view which Agrippa would not approve, since he opposed excessive and superstitious practices but admitted that saints and images must be retained).[13] It is certainly true that Arande was one of the most notorious of the "evangelical" preachers of the early 1520's. But Agrippa's only letter to him (and it does not suggest great intimacy) was written after he had become Bishop of St. Paul-Trois-Chateaux in 1526. From that date on, Arande seems to have acted the role of moderate reforming bishop, quite like the ideal supported by his early patron, Lefèvre, and personified by another patron, Guillaume Briçonnet, the famous reforming Bishop of Meaux.[14] So Agrippa's acquaintance with Arande, with Arande's patroness Marguerite d'Alençon, and with Lefèvre, proves no more than a general sympathy with a vaguely "evangelical" reform. His acquaintance with a more radical "evangelical" leader, Antoine Papilion, does not appear to have been particularly close: he merely sent greetings through Papilion (whom he would have met at court) to the exiled French Protestant François Lambert. Although Herminjard may be right in saying

---

[11] *Guillaume Farel*, pp. 11-12.   [12] *Ibid.*, pp. 108-10.

[13] Although he traces the introduction of images to pagan influence and denounces their abuse, Agrippa, *De incertitudine et vanitate scientiarum declamatio inuectiua* (Coloniae, 1531), ch. lvii, concludes against their abolition: "quod quemadmodum imaginum exuperans cultus idololatria est, ita illarum pertinax detestatio haeresis est." In the same chapter, he regards the Reformers' attacks on images as a revival of the iconoclastic heresy.

[14] Roman d'Amat, art. "Arande, Michel d'," in *Dictionnaire de biographie française*, III, col. 227-30.

that Agrippa was in touch with Protestant sympathizers at the French court,[15] most of these were just sympathizers and never made a full break with the old church. The same general rule applies to all these cases: Agrippa definitely sympathized with reform and cultivated the friendship of like-minded persons. Like the great majority of those with whom he associated, he felt sharp antipathy to the ultraconservatives and tended to feel that the excesses of the more extreme reformers could be at least partly excused by the stupidity, brutality, and downright wickedness of these obscurantists. But also like the great majority of his reform-minded friends, he felt that the Lutherans and Sacramentarians had gone too far, and he refused to abandon the traditional doctrines and the traditional hierarchy completely.

In the latest period of his life, Agrippa enjoyed the patronage of the prince-archbishop of Cologne, Hermann von Wied, the same who later openly summoned Bucer and Melanchthon to help him reform his archdiocese, and was eventually forced to resign his see and retire to his hereditary principality of Wied on account of Lutheran beliefs. But all these events occurred ten and more years after Agrippa knew him. In the early 1530's, Archbishop Hermann was merely a princely bishop with a taste for scholarship and for church reform. His support of Agrippa proves that the Nettesheimer had a great reputation for learning and favored the idea of church reform, but it does not prove that Agrippa was a follower of Luther.

In short, Agrippa's friendships at Metz, in Switzerland, and elsewhere were with persons of Erasmian or humanistic reform inclinations. They all followed the outbreak of the Lutheran Reformation with considerable interest and some sympathy. They all felt that grave abuses existed in the church and ought to be reformed. Some of them later became open adherents of Protestantism. Some did not. These associations, while they certainly would exclude Agrippa from the ranks of the narrowly orthodox, the

[15] A.-L. Herminjard, ed., *Correspondance des Réformateurs dans les pays de langue française* (3 vols.; Geneva, 1866-70), I, 316, n. 2 (No. 133). For the Protestant leanings of Antoine Papilion, a member of the Great Council, and of Arande, cf. letter of Pierre de Sébiville to Anémond de Coct, Grenoble, 28 December 1524, printed *ibid.*, I, 313-16 (No. 132). Agrippa addressed a defense of his *De sacramento matrimonii* to Arande; but if this protégé of Marguerite d'Alençon was as thoroughly committed to Protestantism as Sébiville's letter implies, Agrippa must not have known it, for his letter exalts ecclesiastical authority in general and papal power in particular: *Epist.* IV, vii.

viri obscuri, as Hutten and his friends were calling them even before 1517, would not necessarily make Agrippa an open or secret adherent of the Reformation.

There are also certain direct statements of Agrippa concerning Luther and the Protestants; and his enemies made use of some of these in accusing him of heresy. The most frequently repeated was his description of Martin Luther as an "unconquered heretic." This apparently dangerous phrase appears not only in Agrippa's one letter of greeting to Melanchthon but also in a published work, *De vanitate*. One might make a fair case out of the letter to Melanchthon, for besides the fact that Agrippa wrote it all, he describes Luther in it as one "who, as Paul says in Acts, serves God according to the sect which they call heresy." [16] Yet Luther is still, after all, a heretic, unconquered though he be. The fact that Agrippa wrote the letter at the insistence of a friend, apparently the bearer, lessens its significance. And it was a time (1532) when, involved in strife with the religious conservatives over both of his major works, Agrippa naturally felt an affinity for other foes of the religious orders. Except for the salutation explaining that he writes at the behest of a friend and for his greetings to Luther and to Spalatin, whom he calls "my old friend," the only content of the letter is to inform Melanchthon that he has declared eternal war on the monks. The other usage of the term "unconquered heretic" was not even so favorable to Luther as this. Speaking of women who take lovers and then try to convince their husbands of the legitimacy of their children, he adds that this "unconquered heretic," Martin Luther, has asserted that the laws of Lycurgus and Solon, allowing the wife of an impotent man to conceive children by a lover, are permissible even in the church: "which I want you to know lest you think even theologians are not bawds." [17]

Still, one of the charges which the Louvain articles against *De vanitate* made was that Agrippa had called Luther an unconquered heretic. In his *Apologia* he rebutted the charge vigorously, by admitting it, explaining himself, and then turning the discussion into an attack on his opponents: "But I am not unaware that Luther has been condemned of heresy, but I do not see that he has been

[16] Agrippa to Melanchthon, Frankfurt-am-Main, 17 September 1532, *Epist.* VII, xiii. Cf. *De vanitate*, ch. lxiv.

[17] *De vanitate*, ch. lxiv: "quod vos ideo scire volo ne putetis non etiam theologos esse lenones."

conquered, since to this day he still progresses in the fight and rules in the hearts of the people, among whom the improbity, ignorance, malice, and lying of very many of our priests, monks, and masters has procured for him so much trust and authority. . . ." [18] Agrippa adds that he is speaking of the results, not of dogma. Then he continues by counterattacking: All efforts to overcome Luther have failed; and princes, bishops, scholars, theologians, and whole universities have gone over to him. If he is conquered, why are his foes talking of a general council? Prierias, Hochstraten, and even the learned Eck opposed him unsuccessfully. Then the monks preached against him among the masses, forcing him to reply in the Saxon tongue and so to infect the common people with his heresy. The condemnations of the universities of Louvain, Cologne, and Paris merely made his books sell faster. Papal bulls and imperial rescripts were of no effect. Was Arius defeated when Arian churches outnumbered orthodox ones? Is Mohammed conquered, whose sect today is more widespread than Christianity? Furthermore, who overcame the Anabaptists and sacramentarians? Not the orthodox doctors! Luther alone fought for the church; alone he freed it of these dangerous errors. Finally, Agrippa warned the Louvain doctors not to appeal to fire and sword lest they suffer fire and sword.

Now it is true that such an impassioned defense must have been offensive to the strictly orthodox. But it is hardly the work of a crypto-Protestant. It shows a certain sympathy, to be sure; and it is violently anticlerical. But then it is a response to an attack on Agrippa by a clerical group. Luther remains a heretic and an example of how those who were lionized as eloquent rhetoricians and skilled linguists have within a few years become leaders of heresy, so that almost every city has its own religious sect.[19]

Having analyzed those statements by Agrippa which gave greatest offense to the orthodox in his own time, one ought next to trace the development of his attitude toward Luther and his followers. One must not be surprised to see a certain alteration in the way in

[18] *Apologia adversus calumnias, propter declamationem de vanitate scientiarum, et excellentia verbi Dei, sibi per aliquos Lovanienses theologistas intentatas,* in *Opera,* II, 294: "At ego Lutherum haereseos damnatum non nescio, sed victum non video, quum ille in hunc diem adhuc proficiat in pugna, regnetque in animis populorum, quos penes tantam fidem authoritatemque conciliavit illi plurimorum Sacerdotum et Monachorum et Magistrorum nostrorum improbitas, inscitia, malitia, mendacia. . . ." (Henceforth cited as *Apologia.*)

[19] *De vanitate,* ch. vi. Despite its emphasis on the pure and unadulterated Gospel, this passage could have hardly been pleasing to either humanists or Protestants.

which Agrippa regarded the great Reformer. Once, cataloguing victims of monkish calumnies in modern times, he included Giovanni Pico della Mirandola, Peter of Ravenna, Johann Reuchlin, Sebastian Brant, Martin Luther, Andreas Carlstadt, Erasmus of Rotterdam, Jacques Lefèvre d'Étaples, and, of course, himself. All appeared on an equal footing. But this was in a work composed in 1519. In a similar catalogue of 1531, he listed by name only Pico, Reuchlin, Erasmus, and Lefèvre, none of whom was an avowed Lutheran.[20] In the interim, it had become clear that Luther, whatever one might say in his defense, was a heretic, albeit an unconquered one. This awareness that Luther was not just a reformer in the Erasmian sense (and that Erasmus was not a Reformer in the Lutheran sense) dawned only very slowly and painfully except in the consciousness of the two principals. Strong doubts about the Lutherans were present in Agrippa's mind by June of 1520, during his stay at Cologne. On 16 June he wrote a letter to Brennonius, exulting over the success of Reuchlin and Franz von Sickingen in putting to confusion Hochstraten, the Cologne faculty, and the Dominicans of all Germany. But then Agrippa added news "not so happy," reporting "how far the bold temerity of some bold men is going." Hutten and several other adherents of the Lutheran faction had been in Cologne; and their violence in attacking the Roman see made Agrippa fear "great seditions, unless God prevents." Apparently their appeals to throw off the Roman yoke and to be ruled solely by German prelates had shocked Agrippa. He saw that certain princes and states were inclining to such notions. Perhaps the newly elected emperor, Charles V, could check the movement, but Agrippa had serious doubts: "What the authority of Caesar will avail, I do not know; indeed I, having contemplated the wholly saturnine man, have no good hope reposed in him; the times that follow will teach what sort of emperor we have chosen for ourselves." [21]

---

[20] The earlier list is in *De beatissimae Annae monogamia ac unico puerperio* (n.p., 1534), fols. M5r-M6v. The later one is in *Querela super calumnia, ob editam declamationem de vanitate scientiarum, atque excellentia verbi Dei, sibi per aliquos sceleratissimos sycophantas, apud Caesaream majestatem nefarie ac proditorie intentata,* in *Opera,* II, 453-54. (Henceforth cited as *Querela.*)

[21] Agrippa to Brennonius, Cologne, 16 June 1520, *Epist.* II, liv. The quoted passages read thus: "non tam laeta, et quorsum audacium aliquot hominum pregrediatur audax temeritas." "magnas seditiones, ni Deus provideat. . . ." "Quid Caesaris valitura sit autoritas, nescio: ego certe contemplatus hominem totum saturnium, nihil in illo bonae spei repositum habeo: ipsa, quae sequuntur, tempora docebunt, qualem nobis elegimus Caesarem."

Thus, Agrippa by 1520 saw the radical danger posed by the Lutheran movement; and one may doubt whether this awareness ever left him. Yet the stupid conservative theologians, he felt, were greatly to blame. By their eagerness to distort the teachings of learned persons on account of envy of their learning, they in the past expelled from the church many persons who were Catholic and orthodox. ". . . Because of the same arts, today the Lutheran evil has grown from a little spark into a most vast conflagration, an evil which from the beginning could have been calmed easily if Luther had been treated somewhat more civilly when he did not yet oppose the Roman church but was opposing certain indulgence-hawking monks' intolerable improbity and the tyranny of certain prelates. . . ." [22]

This is really Agrippa's final judgment of Luther: unconquered still, but still a heretic. Before, however, turning to the broader question of Agrippa's own religious views, many of them well developed before Lutheranism even became a factor in religious history, one should continue to trace the development of his position regarding the whole Reformation movement by introducing certain modifications of this general conclusion.

First, it is a fact that Agrippa's interest in the writings of the Reformers (and of their opponents), an interest which began very early, continued to be very lively despite his growing reservations about what Luther and his followers were doing. In its origin, this following of the literature of the German Reformation was merely an outgrowth of his interest in the "advanced" humanistic literature of the day, the writings of men like Erasmus, Reuchlin, and Lefèvre.[23] As has been shown above, Agrippa communicated Lutheran works to Dieudonné at Metz; but he also lent the Celestine friar

[22] *Apologia*, in *Opera*, II, 279: ". . . Eisdem artibus hodie Lutheranum malum, ex modica scintilla in vastissimum incendium excrevit, quod ab initio facile sedari potuisset, si Lutherus tractatus fuisset aliquanto civilius, quando non adhuc repugnaret Romanae Ecclesiae, sed quorundam monachorum indulgentiariorum intolerabili improbitati, atque quorundam praelatorum tyrannidi sese opponeret. . . ."

[23] For example, Amicus [Dieudonné] ad Agrippam, Annecy, 26 June 1521, *Epist.* III, vii: "Cupio etiam per te certiorfieri, an secunda recognitio Erasmi super novum Testamentum sit typis excusa. . . . Item quid de Luthero agitur: et an interpretatio sua super psalterium sit expressa: hanc profecto vehementer cupio." Erasmus' clash with Luther is well known. Ludwig Geiger, *Johann Reuchlin: Sein Leben und seine Werke* (Leipzig, 1871), pp. 150-56, notes that before his death, Reuchlin had become gravely suspicious of Luther. Lefèvre's position is complex, but at least he never openly left the old church.

works of Erasmus and Lefèvre as well as his own.[24] His friend Cantiuncula, living at Basel in touch not only with the university where he taught law but also with the city's publishers, was Agrippa's chief source for news and for books of the Reformers and the humanists.[25] After Agrippa left Metz, Brennonius also exchanged news of the Reformation with him. This interest in Protestant writings was still active in 1525. On 12 May of that year, an anonymous friend, writing from Vic-sur-Seille in Lorraine, warned Agrippa that "under the pretext of evangelical liberty the fury and inconstancy of the insane people is increased," and especially deplored the radicals' attacks on elevation of the sacrament of the altar. The writer added: "I do not know whether you have read their ravings and blasphemies. But if you have read them, I think that you will do nothing but regret that you have given one or another hour to reading fruitlessly these seditious insanities."[26] On 25 May, Agrippa wrote a reply which shows some of what he had read. He possessed in German a copy of Carlstadt's radical work on the eucharist but did not even know the title of anything by Zwingli on that topic, unless it were *De vera ac falsa religione*, a work published that very year and one which Agrippa had not seen. He had a copy of Luther's German work against Carlstadt, obviously the book *Wider die himmlischen Propheten*, which had appeared in two parts in December, 1524, and January, 1525. This book, he reported, discusses the mass but not specifically the meaning of the eucharist. That Luther had written a special book on the eucharist he had only heard. Agrippa expressed a desire to see this treatise of Luther's, as well as that of "anyone else besides him who is not a sophist."[27] This phrase suggests that Agrippa was

[24] Dieudonné to Agrippa, n.p., n.d., printed in appendix to *De beatissimae Annae monogamia*, fol. N5r-v, and also as *Epist.* II, xxiv.

[25] Amicus [Cantiuncula] ad Agrippam, [Basel], 23 May 1519, *Epist.* II, xxxii. Even after leaving Metz, Agrippa continued to rely on Cantiuncula for news and books. For example, his letter of 6 January 1523, *Epist.* III, xxxv, where he asks: ". . . quid Erasmus agat, ac quomodo ille cum Luthero consentiat, dissentiatve."

[26] *Epist.* III, lxix: ". . . sub praetextu libertatis evangelicae insani populi furor et inconstantia grassetur." "Nescio, an illorum delimarenta [*sic*; should be deliramenta] et blasphemias legeris. Sed si legeris, arbitror te nihil aliud facturum, nisi quod dolebis unam vel alteram horam te hisce factiosis insaniis legendis nequicquam tribuisse."

[27] Agrippa ad Amicum, Lyons, 27 May 1522, *Epist.* III, lxxi: "et si quis praeter illum alius non sophista responderit." Although the printed text is dated 1522, this letter must be of 1525. It is printed with the letters for that

more opposed to the sacramentarians than to the largely conservative Luther, and that he had no respect for any defense of orthodox doctrine that came from the sophists (his common synonym for scholastic theologians).

There is yet one further problem to discuss before leaving the subject of Agrippa's relation to the Reformation movement and turning to a study of his own doctrinal positions. Is there evidence, as Herminjard claims, that Agrippa played an active part in promoting the spread of the Reformation, especially in Switzerland? [28] There is indeed a little such evidence. On 5 June 1522, an anonymous friend wrote to Agrippa from Aix-les-Bains in Savoy, recommending the bearer of his letter as learned and as "a preacher of evangelical truth," [29] and asking Agrippa to listen to the man and help him. The bearer was a priest and was passing through Geneva. On 17 June, Agrippa wrote from Geneva a letter to a friend at Basel, beyond all doubt Cantiuncula, recommending the same man to his friend: "Now indeed since this good father of the Franciscan family, a singular friend, going thither, earnestly asked me to recommend him to some one of my friends, I did not want him to go empty-handed to you, knowing how much you can benefit him with advice and assistance." [30] On the same date, Agrippa wrote to Capito, asking him to write further letters of introduction for "this good father," whom he described as a virtuous man and "a diligent minister of the Word of God." [31] These were dangerous phrases to use in the third decade of the sixteenth century.

Herminjard identified this unnamed Franciscan "preacher of evangelical truth" as François Lambert, an Observant friar of

---

year and is written from Lyons, where Agrippa was in 1525 but not in 1522. Furthermore, the open break between Carlstadt and Luther and the latter's first polemic against his former supporter, referred to in the letter, did not occur until 1524-25. See Preserved Smith, *The Life and Letters of Martin Luther* (Boston, 1911), pp. 153-56.

[28] Herminjard, *op. cit.*, I, 99-102. Printing Capito's letter of 23 April 1522 to Agrippa, Herminjard completely omits (though indicating an ellipsis) the central portion of the letter, wherein Capito criticizes the excesses of the radical followers of Luther and attacks the Lutheran claim that the pope is Antichrist. And Agrippa explicitly expressed agreement with Capito!

[29] *Epist.* III, xvi.

[30] *Epist.* III, xvii: "Nunc vero cum bonus iste pater Franciscanae familiae amicus singularis istuc iturus, me obnixe rogaret, ut sese apud aliquem amicorum meorum commendatum facerem, nolui illum ad te venire inanem: sciens, quantum tu illi prodesse potes et consilio et auxilio. . . ."

[31] *Epist.* III, xviii.

Avignon who deserted his order and became a Protestant. Like Martin Luther, Lambert had entered a friary at an early age but had found the religious discipline unable to solve his personal religious problems. Having been refused permission to enter the stricter Carthusians, he at length came upon Luther's writings in the early 1520's and apparently resolved to leave his order. His opportunity came early in 1522, when his superiors sent him to carry letters into Germany, whence he never returned. He passed through Geneva (where Agrippa was living) and Lausanne and turned up in Zürich in July of 1522. A letter written to Agrippa from Strasbourg on 31 December 1525 strongly supports Herminjard's identification. Internal evidence proves beyond a doubt that it is the work of Lambert.[32] This letter shows that Agrippa and Lambert were friends. Lambert's letter of 1525 greets Agrippa in the name of "the whole church of the saints" at Strasbourg, especially Capito, and rejoices at word from a mutual friend, the French Protestant leader Antoine Papilion, of "the progress of the Word among the courtiers, and likewise in almost all France." Finally he asks for news from Geneva, "whether, that is, they love the Word." And he expresses satisfaction "that you are always the same, that is, a lover of the truth," [33] a phrase so vague that although it tells much about Lambert's beliefs, it tells little about Agrippa's.

This exchange of letters appears to indicate more than just another case of friendship for a reform-minded man who later became an avowed Protestant. It looks as though Agrippa welcomed to Geneva a man who was teaching Protestantism and helped that man with letters of recommendation to Cantiuncula and Capito. There is evidence of other instances of the same sort. In November, 1522, a friend writing to Agrippa from Lyons recommended the bearer,

[32] Agrippa ad Amicum, Strasbourg, 31 December 1525, *Epist.* III, lxxxii. This is an obvious misprint for "Amicus ad Agrippam," as almost all the biographers recognize. Morley, *op. cit.*, II, 122, conjectures that this letter was from Zwingli; but there is no evidence for this conclusion, while internal evidence in the letter clearly points to Lambert (e.g., his residence in Strasbourg, his interest in news from France, his authorship of a book on marriage, his poverty, his intimacy with Capito). On Lambert, see Carl Mirbt, "Franz Lambert," *Realencyklopädie für protestantische Theologie und Kirche*, XI, 220-23, and Roy Lutz Winters, *Francis Lambert of Avignon (1487-1530): A Study in Reformation Origins* (Philadelphia, 1938).

[33] The quoted passages come from the same letter quoted in the preceding note: "tota ecclesia sanctorum." ". . . fructum verbi apud aulicos, itidem apud Galliam fere omnem." ". . . an scilicet verbum ament." ". . . quod semper idem es, nempe, veritatis amator."

who was going to Geneva "for the sake of evangelizing." In January, 1524, Agrippa wrote from Fribourg a letter commending to Cantiuncula a man "who is leaving here for the sake of the Gospel, which has been given for the destruction and the resurrection of many." The exiled bearer of this ambiguous letter was Thomas Gyrfalk, who not long after was openly a Protestant.[34] Actually, however, the letters concerning Lambert and these two other men prove nothing more than what was established at the outset of this chapter: that Agrippa had many friends who like himself were interested in church reform, and that some of these friends eventually wound up in the Protestant camp. Even Lambert, although already under the influence of Lutheran writings and probably determined never to return to his friary from his mission in Germany, had by no means completed his evolution in the direction of Protestantism when Agrippa knew him, as appears clearly from his disputation with Zwingli in July, 1522 (hence after Agrippa helped him), when he defended invocation of the saints.

This chapter so far has shown that Agrippa displayed much sympathy for the general idea of church reform, and a lively interest in the efforts of Luther and the other Reformers to achieve that end. He read much of the controversial literature on both sides. In 1519, he regarded Luther as merely a fellow-worker with Erasmus, Reuchlin, and Lefèvre d'Étaples, like them exposed to the slander and threats of ignorant monks who were hostile to all good letters. By 1520, however, a realization was dawning that Luther was aiming at something else than had the earlier agitators for reform, and also that some of his followers were even more radical than Luther himself. As the early 1520's went by, Agrippa observed the radical disorders during Luther's absence from Wittenberg and the growth of all sorts of radical sacramentarian and Anabaptist groups which pleased him even less than the Lutherans did. Nevertheless, his dissatisfaction with the old order in the church continued; and he inclined to look with favor on all who merely claimed to be preaching the pure Gospel (even in the mid-1520's, for example, François Lambert did not call himself a Lutheran). Perhaps like the Capito of very early 1522, Agrippa still was confident that the

---

[34] Amicus ad Agrippam, Lyons, 11 November 1522, *Epist.* III, xxxiv. Agrippa ad Amicum [Cantiuncula], Fribourg, 5 January 1524, *Epist.* III, lii: ". . . recedit abhinc evangelii causa, quod datum est in ruinam et resurrectionem multorum." On Gyrfalk, see Alexandre Daguet, "Agrippa chez les Suisses," *Archives de la Société d'histoire du canton de Fribourg*, II (1858), 152.

old institutional church would be able to assimilate the ferment of reform and would throw off those whom he regarded as sophists and obscurantists, the anti-Erasmian and ultraconservative group of Schoolmen, especially the Dominicans. His final position was that Luther was a heretic, but a less objectionable one than the radicals, and a theologian far more capable of checking the radicals than were slow-witted sophists like Hochstraten; furthermore, that if Luther had been handled by able and skillful men rather than by the reactionary fools who conducted his case, he would never have left the church at all. Nowhere do Agrippa's letters show any intention of breaking with the existing ecclesiastical institution. Reform was necessary, but reform without schism. Agrippa sometimes mouthed phrases commonly used by the Lutherans, such as "evangelical preacher" and even "Christian Liberty." [35] But one can hardly attribute any emotional commitment to the cause of the Protestants to a man who could write to one of his most intimate friends the following remark about a bookseller who had been mutilated and exiled from Metz on account of his Lutheran sympathies: "Greet for me Tilmannus, and Carboneius, and our Tyrius, and all our other friends; and the ears of Jacques the bookseller, for (as I hear) he for his Lutheranism left only them at Metz, the rest of him being quite absent; still on account of our old familiarity, I wanted him to be greeted, even minus his ears. . . ." [36] Finally, one must not forget that on every possible occasion Agrippa declared his allegiance to the Catholic faith. Err he might, but in such cases he would (he always insisted) submit to the judgment of the church; and, as he argued persuasively, error is not heresy unless one persists in it stubbornly against a clear pronouncement of the universal church.[37]

[35] Agrippa ad Amicum, n.p. [Geneva], 1521, *Epist.* III, xii. That despite such statements Agrippa found schism abhorrent appears clearly from *De vanitate*, ch. lxii: "Quicunque autem in ecclesiam dei sectas introducunt . . . aut fictae sanctitatis gloria secedunt a principe Romana ecclesia, ij tanquam Nadab et Abiu alienum ignem offerentes ad altare dei, ab eo comburentur," etc.

[36] Agrippa to Brennonius, Lyons, 23 June 1526, *Epist.* IV, xx: ". . . Salutabis mihi Tilmannum, et Carbonejum, et Tyrium nostrum, caeterosque amicos omnes: atque auriculas Iacobi librarii. nam (quod audio) ipse pro Lutheranismo illas solas Metis reliquit, reliquus totus absens: attamen ob veterem consuetudinem, vel inauriculatum, salutari volo. . . ."

[37] Examples of Agrippa's insistence on his loyalty to the Catholic church and willingness to submit to its judgment are numerous: *De occulta philosophia libri tres* (Coloniae, 1533), Bk. I, ch. i, p. i; *Apologia,* in *Opera,* II, 260, 275; *Epist.* VI, xxxvi (his first letter to Erasmus, written from Brussels, 16 Decem-

II

Agrippa's statements about the Reformers prove beyond reason-able doubt that he never consciously broke with the old faith. Yet Prost and others suggest that Agrippa may have been more of a Protestant than he realized. Granted an intention to remain ortho-dox, to be loyal to the old church and to its teachings, there is the further question whether his beliefs really were compatible with those of the church or whether, in spite of his intentions, his beliefs aligned him with the Reformers. Only a survey of his position on the controversial theological issues of the age can throw light on this further problem.

The most immediately apparent characteristic of most of Agrippa's pronouncements on religious questions is their violently anticlerical tone. Although he sometimes fails to distinguish clearly, he directs most of his venom not against the secular clergy but against the scholastic theologians, whom he virtually identifies with the regular clergy. The specific charges against the monks are several, and most of the accusations have a clear connection with efforts of Agrippa to defend himself against conservative attacks on him as a heretic. Why are there abuses of images and pilgrimages? Why do simple folk suffer from the tyranny of confessors? It is, Agrippa answers, because the clergy, especially the mendicant orders, profit from such abuses and hence not only perpetuate them but also denounce as a heretic anyone who wants to introduce reforms. A second general line of attack is that the clergymen themselves are immoral hypocrites, quick to criticize the failings of others because they want to cover up their own misdeeds by a show of righteous-ness. A third type of charge connects the monks with scholastic theologians who have obscured the pure and simple word of God by their sophistical subtleties, bending the teachings of Christ to the opinions of pagan philosophers. A closely related accusation is

---

ber 1531). His *Expostulatio contra Catilinetum* as early as 1510 followed the same general line. It is true that there are few statements for the early 1520's but then Agrippa wrote few if any books during these years. In his lecture on the *Pimander*, delivered at the University of Pavia in 1515, he made an especially full proclamation of submission to the church (*Oratio II*, in *Opera*, II, 1081): "His nolo quenquam plus assentiri, quod et ego ipse facio, quam ab ecclesia catholica fideliumque choro, ac sacro episcoporum collegio, ejusque capite summo Pontifice comprobatur: quibus omnia dicta mea et dicenda scripta ac scribenda subijcio . . . paratissimus semper ab illis et a quovis melius sentiente, fraterna Christianaque charitate erudiri et corrigi. . . ." All these passages suggest at least a lifelong *intention* to be loyal to the old church.

that the monks denounce to the vulgar masses any person who tries to return to the pure and simple teachings of Christ. A fifth line of attack, one not often repeated, is that the clergy throughout the hierarchy lacks the prophetic gifts which originally distinguished the leaders of the Christian church.[38] A sixth charge grows out of the conservatives' opposition to humane letters, especially the study of Greek and Hebrew.

This bitter anticlericalism of the Nettesheimer steadily increased. The causes are probably two. One, the product of his own development, is the accumulation of griefs against the monks and Schoolmen because of their attacks on Agrippa personally and on his writings. The other is the result of historical circumstances. Increasingly in the second decade of the sixteenth century and in particular after the beginning of the Lutheran movement, the intellectual atmosphere of Agrippa's *milieu* was conducive to anticlericalism in extreme form. Even before the appearance of Luther, however, Agrippa's attack on the monks was well under way.[39]

This catalogue of the lines of Agrippa's attack on the clergy does not sufficiently characterize his attitude. Some examples of the bitterness of his denunciation and the sharpness of his satire are necessary. Examples abound alike in his private letters and in his published works. There is his satirical tale of the origin of the cowl, published in *De vanitate*. After criticizing the abuse of plastic arts to depict lewd scenes, Agrippa, tongue in cheek, admits one type of usefulness. While he was in Italy, he relates, the papal curia settled litigation over the color of Augustinian habits by referring to ancient paintings and statues. So when Agrippa was investigating the origin of the monks' cowl, he likewise inspected paintings. None of the Old Testament priests and prophets was depicted wearing a cowl. Nor could he find any painting that depicted Christ or John

[38] *De triplici ratione cognoscendi Deum*, in *Opera*, II, 494.
[39] For example, *ibid.*, p. 500. For the increasingly aggressive anticlericalism of the German humanists in the second decade of the sixteenth century, Henri Hauser and Augustin Renaudet, *Les débuts de l'âge moderne* (3rd ed.; Paris, 1946), pp. 142-43; Willy Andreas, *Deutschland vor der Reformation: Eine Zeitenwende* (2nd ed.; Berlin, 1934), p. 502; and Gerhard Ritter, *Die Neugestaltung Europas im 16. Jahrhundert: Die kirchlichen und staatlichen Wandlungen im Zeitalter der Reformation und der Glaubenskämpfe* (Berlin, 1950), pp. 70-71. Not all of these humanists were radically anticlerical, but most of the leading figures, especially those who reached intellectual maturity in the immediate pre-Reformation decades, were. See Lewis W. Spitz, *The Religious Renaissance of the German Humanists* (Cambridge, Massachusetts, 1963), p. 274, and *passim*.

the Baptist or the apostles or the scribes and pharisees wearing a cowl. Finally, however, he found a painting of the temptation of Christ in the desert; and there, sure enough, the Devil was wearing a cowl. "I rejoiced very much that I had found in pictures what I had not up to then been able to find in writings, that is, that the Devil was the first author of the cowl, from whom then, I think, the other monks and friars borrowed it under various colors, or perchance received it left to them as if by hereditary right." [40] Another example, directed this time against the hierarchy, is less mordant: Formerly priests and prelates were appointed because of their holiness: "But since the ancient constitutions of the fathers have little by little fallen from their majesty and since the more recent papal law has with blameworthy custom come into use, very many such pontiffs and apostles have ascended the seat of Christ as formerly on the seat of Moses sat the scribes and pharisees, who speak and do not do, binding heavy burdens onto the shoulders of the people, while they are unwilling to lift a finger." [41] Monastic orders are of recent origin (though not the ideal of monastic life), Agrippa goes on, although they seek to dignify themselves with the names of holy men like Augustine, Basil, and Francis. Few of the present-day monks are of sound and holy life. Most of them are ignorant and vicious.[42] ". . . Openly we see that wherever there are those great churches and colleges of priests and monks, there are very close by houses of prostitution; nay more, many houses of nuns and virgins and beguines are certain private brothels of prostitutes, whom also we know that monks and religious (lest their chastity be maligned) sometimes maintained in monasteries under a monk's cowl and a man's clothing." [43] Then there is the way in which

[40] De vanitate, ch. xxv: "Gauisus sum plurimum reperisse me in picturis quod hactenus nequiui in literis, diabolum scilicet primum cucullae autorem, a quo deinceps puto caeteri monachi et fratres hanc sub diuersis coloribus mutuarunt, aut forte velut haereditario iure sibi relictam acceperunt."
[41] Ibid., ch. lxi: "sed antiquis patrum constitutionibus paulatim a sua maiestate cadentibus, ac recentiore pontificio iure cum damnabili consuetudine inualescente, tales plaerique super sedem Christi conscendunt pontifices et apostoli, quales olim super sedem Moysi sedebant scribae et pharisaei, qui dicunt et non faciunt, alligantes onera grauia in humeris populi, ipsi autem nolunt digito mouere."
[42] Ibid., ch. lxii.
[43] Ibid., ch. lxiii: "palamque videmus vbicunque sunt magnifica ista templa, et sacerdotum monachorumque collegia, vt plurimum in proximo esse lupanaria, quin et plurimae monalium et vestalium ac beguinarum domus priuatae quaedam meretricularum fornices sunt, quas etiam monachos et religiosos (ne

monkish preachers hypocritically use absurd gestures and deep guile to hoodwink the masses. A private letter from the same summer (1526) in which Agrippa produced *De vanitate* contains a description of "the monkish art." He asks concerning a friend, a lawyer, who had become a monk:

Whether, as he formerly was especially skilled in the art of opinions, knowing how to use the laws at will and how to feign and pretend, bend and flee them with invented glosses . . . so now he is skilled in the monkish, or cowled, that is, sycophantical, art, and knows how to flit about everywhere with simulated sanctimoniousness and impudent mendicity; and, rubbing his forehead and with importunate hypocrisy, how to scrape together money, as long as he doesn't touch it with his bare fingers; how to be ashamed of no gain in the marketplace, in the choir, in churches, in schools, in courts, in palaces, in councils, in banquets, taverns, barber shops, in public and private discussions, in confessions . . . how impudently by their arts to scatter among the masses the dirges of indulgences, how to sell his benefits, to measure out ceremonies, and how to squeeze ill-gotten gains out of usurious merchants and noble plunderers, and how to cheat coins out of fat townsmen and the unlearned people and superstitious old women; and, like the Serpent, how first to enchant stupid little women and through them to prepare his way to deceive their husbands; finally, how to involve himself in the business of all, to compose marriages sticking together poorly, to upset wills, to stir up quarrels, to reform holy virgins: but all these not except to his own advantage.[44]

One further example shows how Agrippa resented the monks' objection to being criticized. In 1531 he wrote a friend that if

---

diffametur eorum castitas) nonnunquam sub monachali cuculla ac virili veste in monasterijs aluisse scimus." In the following chapter, Agrippa attacks prelates who by imposing regular fines on unchaste priests, in effect licensed concubinage and derived considerable income therefrom.

[44] Agrippa ad Amicum, Lyons, 11 August 1526, *Epist.* IV, xxxii: "an, sicut olim, egregie percalluit artem placitatoriam, sciens ad omne arbitrium uti legibus, easque adinventis glossis fingere, refingere, flectere, subterfugere . . . itane nunc calleat artem fratricam, sive cucullonicam, hoc est, sycophanticam: sciatque personata sanctimonia, ac impudendi [sic] mendicitate quocunque pervolare: et perfricata fronte, importuna hypocrisi undique pecunias corradere, modo non tangat nudis digitis: nullius quaestus pudere in foro, in choro, in templis, in scholis, in aulis, in palatiis, in conciliis, in conviviis, tabernis, tonstrinis, in publicis et privatis colloquiis, in confessionibus . . . impudenter illorum artibus spargere in vulgus indulgentiarum nenias, vendere sua benefacta, emetiri caeremonias, et a mercatoribus usurariis et a nobilibus praedonibus male partorum praedam extorquere, et a crassis civibus et indocta plebecula superstitiosisque aniculis emungere nummos: et, serpentis exemplo, stultas mulierculas primum allicere, et per illas sibi aditum parare ad fallendos viros: denique omnium negotiis se miscere, compingere matrimonia male cohaerentia, intervertere testamenta, componere lites, reformare sacras virgines: sed omnia haec non, nisi suo compendio."

Margaret of Austria had not died, "now I would have been about to perish as impious against the Christian religion, guilty of [offense against] the sacred cowl, which is the greatest crime."[45] Agrippa bitterly resented the inquisitorial techniques of monks, especially the inquisitors' way of presenting the accused with a list of articles and then demanding that he forthwith retract these articles or face punishment as a heretic.[46] In *De occulta philosophia*, Agrippa records as a common belief the idea that it is an ill omen to see a monk, especially in the morning, "because that class of men feeds very much on death-fees as vultures on the dead."[47] It was this quality of emotional and unreasoned denunciation that made Erasmus suspicious of Agrippa, since he could see no expectation of success in such attacks.[48] Agrippa's war on the monks, as he called it, was indeed an impassioned one.

Yet anyone who looks beyond the fury of Agrippa's invective will find qualifications which make it clear that he attacks not the institution of monasticism but only those who in his opinion were abusing that institution. Even in his most bitter work, *De vanitate*, he introduced the qualification that he did not mean to attack all monks, for there were many good ones, although most were bad. He did, however, argue that the primitive church knew no distinctions of dress and that the contemporary orders were unworthy successors of the saints whom they claimed as their patrons.[49] On the other hand, although he taught in *De sacramento matrimonii* that all men must marry to be saved, and defended marriage even for the clergy, arguing that the institution of clerical chastity was not *de jure divino* but was a human law and could be dispensed with by the papacy, he exempted two classes from this general requirement to marry: those who were eunuchs by nature and those who for the love of God vowed perpetual chastity.[50] So far

---

[45] Agrippa ad Amicum, Malines, 19 January 1531, *Epist.* VI, xv: "jam ego, quod maximum crimen est, monachalis Majestatis sacraeque cucullae reus, tanquam in religionem Christianam impius, periturus fuissem."

[46] *De vanitate*, ch. xcvi.

[47] *De occulta philosophia*, Bk. I, ch. liv., p. lxviii: "quia id hominum genus plurimum e mortuario ueluti uultures ex morticiniis uictitat."

[48] See Erasmus' letter of 25 April 1532 to Abel Closter, in *Opus epistolarum Des. Erasmi Roterodami*, ed. P. S. Allen [and H. M. Allen and H. W. Garrod] (12 vols.; Oxonii, 1906-58), X, 209-11 (No. 2800).

[49] *De vanitate*, ch. lxii.

[50] *De sacramento matrimonii*, in *Opera*, II, 548-49. He further justified these statements in a letter to Michel d'Arande, Lyons, 7 May 1526, *Epist.* IV, vii. For his views on clerical marriage, see *Apologia*, in *Opera*, II, 292-94, 299.

was he from attacking the institution of monasticism that in a work of uncertain date written for the abbot of Brauweiler, true monastic life appears as the highest form of Christian life, a combination of the penitential life of the ordinary believer and the contemplative life which "rests in the light of divine wisdom." [51] Agrippa traces the origins of this true and spontaneous monastic life back to apostolic times. Only the cooling of religious ardor in later eras made necessary the introduction of the various existing monastic rules, all of which contain the three essential points once practiced by the whole Christian community: poverty, chastity, and obedience.

The same general pattern of attacking abuses but making reservations in favor of the basic ecclesiastical institutions appears in Agrippa's attitude to many other questions. He is critical of the papacy, for example, on account of the way in which unworthy men have been able to abuse its powers: the monks, for instance, allege papal immunities against efforts of the secular clergy to resist their exorbitant claims and reform their vices. The papal curia is worldly and immoral. Popes and other prelates encourage secular rulers to engage in war. Some popes (he mentions Sixtus IV, Alexander VI, and Julius II by name) were themselves wicked men.[52] Pope and emperor alike receive criticism for their haughty claims to plenitude of power in law. Agrippa expresses horror at papal audacity in presuming to release souls from purgatory, regarding this doctrine as "erroneous and intolerable temerity, not to say almost heresy." [53] Popes claim excessive powers over bishops, over temporal rulers, over all the faithful, using the canon law as their instrument. His insinuation that popes can err becomes explicit elsewhere, when Agrippa argues that the power of savage inquisitors is based not on theological traditions and Scriptures but on canon law and papal decretals, "as if it were impossible for a pope to err." [54] He even gives an example of a pope who erred, John XXII, who taught that the souls of the blessed will not see the face of God until the Last Judgment.[55] The unwisdom of popes, he

---

[51] *Sermo de vita monastica*, in *Opera*, II, 567: "in divinae sapientiae lumine quiescit."

[52] *De vanitate*, ch. lxi.

[53] *Ibid.*, ch. xcii: "erroneam intolerabilemque temeritatem, ne dicam prope haeresim. . . ."

[54] *Ibid.*, ch. xcvi: "ac si papam errare impossibile sit. . . ."

[55] *Ibid.*, ch. liii. Actually, John XXII held this doctrine only as a private belief and never gave it dogmatic status.

complains, has been responsible for the Greek and Bohemian schisms, for if only the pope had been willing to tolerate diversity in ceremonies, these schisms would never have occurred.[56]

Even though these antipapal assertions greatly restrict the powers normally claimed by the papacy, there is another side to them. True, for example, Agrippa blames unwise popes for the Greek and Bohemian schisms. Yet at the same time it is clear that at heart he still grants to the popes control over such external matters: unwise though their action may have been, the popes had a right to waive (or not to waive) the usual ceremonial requirements. Similarly with clerical marriage. Like many another of his contemporaries who desired to be loyal to the traditional ecclesiastical institution, Agrippa felt that it would be prudent to permit priests to marry. Clerical chastity, he argued, was not a requirement of divine law but was a human ordinance "which by the pope or council, for reason of times, places, persons, or any other serious or reasonable cause, can be remitted, changed, or altogether removed." Agrippa further shows that there were married priests in the primitive church, a situation which the pontiffs would not have tolerated if Christ and the apostles had forbidden it, "since the evangelical law can neither be rejected nor relaxed. . . ." [57] Nevertheless, Agrippa warns, this does not mean that priests may marry in spite of the canons, for as long as the pope continues to require clerical chastity, all good Christians must submit. Thus Agrippa still recognizes papal jurisdiction except where the exercise of that jurisdiction clashes directly with Scripture.

What appears to be Agrippa's final view on the papacy finds expression in the chapter "De magistratibus ecclesiae" of De vanitate. The chapter opens with a devastating catalogue of abuses of papal power. It is dangerous and unwise to oppose the popes unless one is prepared to undergo martyrdom as a heretic, "just as Jerome Savonarola, theologian of the Order of Preachers, and also a prophetic man, was formerly burned at Florence." [58] The only path

---

[56] Ibid., ch. lx.

[57] Apologia, in Opera, II, 293: "qui per Pontificem, vel concilium, pro ratione temporum, locorum, personarum, seu alia quavis gravi, seu rationabili caussa, potest remitti, mutari, vel omnino tolli." "quum lex Evangelica, nec rejici possit, nec relaxari. . . ."

[58] De vanitate, ch. lxi: "quemadmodum Hieronymus Sauonarola praedicatorij ordinis theologus, simul ac propheticus vir olim apud Florentiam exustus est."

to follow is that of passive obedience. If there are wicked and unworthy prelates, they are sent by God as a judgment on the wickedness of His people. The basic power and authority still is good, for it comes from God.

Whoever therefore is constituted by the Lord a bishop in the church, it is worthy and just to obey him and to contradict him in nothing, for whoever scorns to obey a bishop and a priest scorns not him but God. . . . It is unfaithful not to believe in the sacred scriptures, it is impious to spurn priests; priests are good, a bishop is better, holiest of all is the supreme pontiff and prince of priests, to whom are entrusted the keys of the kingdom of heaven, and [to whom] are committed the secrets of God, verily a prince according to God, a priest according to Christ; whoever honors him will be honored by God; whoever dishonors him, God will dishonor that man, and he will not be able to escape retribution.[59]

Agrippa argued vigorously that a good Christian is not saved because of assiduous participation in the external acts of worship: ". . . Those carnal and external ceremonies are unable to profit men with God, to whom nothing is acceptable except faith in Jesus Christ, with ardent imitation of Him in charity, and firm hope of salvation and reward. . . ."[60] God observes not external acts but the hearts of men. This doctrine, despite a superficial similarity, is not Lutheran justification by faith alone, but rather the stress on inwardness in religion that characterized lay piety in northern Europe for a century or more before the Reformation.

No more truly Protestant in its real import is the thoroughgoing criticism which Agrippa directs against current practices in the church on the basis of this belief in the primacy of internal religion. As he sees it, perfect Christians require little or no externality in religion. But the church has long since included Christians who have not attained this perfection. For their sake there began a

[59] *Ibid.*: "Quicunque igitur a domino constitutus est episcopus in ecclesia, dignum et iustum est obedire illi, et in nullo contradicere, qui enim episcopo et sacerdoti obedire contemnit, non illum sed deum contemnit. . . . Infidele est scripturis sacris non credere, impium est sacerdotes spernere, boni sunt sacerdotes, melior episcopus, super omnes sanctissimus summus pontifex et princeps sacerdotum, cui creditae sunt claues regni coelorum, et commissa sunt secreta dei, princeps quidem secundum deum, pontifex secundum Christum, quem qui honorat, honorabitur a deo, qui inhonorauerit, inhouorabit [*sic*] illum deus et vltionem euadere non poterit."

[60] *Ibid.*, ch. lx: ". . . Carnales illae et externae ceremoniae nequeunt homines promouere ad deum, apud quem nihil est acceptum, praeter fidem in Iesum Christum, cum ardenti imitatione illius in charitate, ac firma spe salutis et praemij. . . ."

cumulative process of adding external acts of various sorts; and this process has reached the point where the essentials of religion are obscured by the external husk. What is worse, clergymen, especially monks, finding such abuses profitable, encourage them and cry heretic against anyone who criticizes them.

Even in his outspoken and bitter book *De vanitate*, Agrippa is careful to qualify his denunciations, although he does make the general complaint that while Christ freed men from the ceremonial burdens of the old law, the canons today impose upon Christians a burden far heavier than that of the Jews.[61] With regard to images, for example, Agrippa feels that they are essentially an intrusion of paganism into Christian worship. Pope Gregory I had defended them as books for the humble; but, the Nettesheimer argues, the preaching of the Bible would instruct the people better. Similarly the relics of the saints often receive excessive veneration: "It is safer not to attach our faith to visible things but to worship the saints in spirit and truth through our lord Jesus Christ, imploring their assistance. And so we have no relics more certain and more worthy than the sacrament of Christ's body, which single holy of holies is kept in all the churches of us who venerate and adore Christ, who is present [and] who although He is present everywhere, still there is corporeally present." [62] But immediately Agrippa qualifies this statement. Christ has performed many miracles through saints; and although excessive devotion to images and relics is idolatry, persistent detestation of them is heresy, for which the iconoclasts Philip and Leo were condemned, a heresy which "in recent years has begun to recur among the Germans." [63] Likewise the early church was able to get along without temples; but since the number of Christians has greatly increased, it has seemed advisable to set aside certain places for divine worship. Even so, such temples are too numerous and often consume in their magnificence money that would better go to relieve the poor, "the true temples

[61] *Ibid.*, ch. xcii.

[62] *Ibid.*, ch. lvii: ". . . Tutius est fidem rebus visibilibus non affigere, sed colere sanctos in spiritu et veritate per dominum nostrum Iesum Christum, illorum opem implorantes. Certiores itaque reliquias et digniores non habemus sacramento corporis Christi, quod vnicum sanctum sanctorum in omnibus templis nostris seruatur, qui coram Christum veneramur et adoramus praesentem, qui licet ubique praesens sit ibi tamen etiam corporaliter praesens est."

[63] *Ibid.*: "a proximis annis apud Germanos repullulascere coepit." On relics, cf. his *De inventione reliquiarum beati Antonii eremitae*, in *Opera*, II, 573-77.

and images of God." [64] Again, for perfect Christians all days are the same; but for the sake of the weak, it proved necessary to set aside certain days to be free from all activities except worship. Now, however, the vulgar do not use such days for worship but abuse them for riot and dissipation.[65] Fasting, too, has become subject to abuse, for there are some who act as if God had detested the eating of certain foods and who therefore, while abstaining from meat, glut themselves on fish and wine.[66] The use of secular music in the church also comes in for critical mention.

There is nothing to prove that Agrippa was any more unfavorable to the veneration of saints than he was to other external acts of worship. He specifically taught that the study of saints' lives was good. He interpreted his support of Lefèvre d'Étaples on the question of the monogamy of St. Anne as being an effort to purify the cult of St. Anne and of the Virgin from unauthorized and untrue fables which cast dishonor on those saints. Certainly he did not regard his views as an attack on the cult of those saints. He was perfectly capable of arguing that a traditional belief ought to be maintained if conducive to piety; but he argued emphatically that the legend of St. Anne's three marriages was not conducive to piety: rather, it discouraged the ideal of chaste widowhood and, in general, of continence. He charged that this erroneous teaching tended to undermine the doctrine of the immaculate conception and noted with consternation that it was promoted by the very group, the Dominican order, which had only recently been in serious trouble because some of its members denied the immaculate conception. It is worth noting that the Roman church has not in fact accepted the legend of the three Marys and the three marriages of St. Anne, but rather has followed the teaching which Agrippa and Lefèvre set forth. It is also worth noting, in view of Agrippa's usual stress on the Bible, that he nowhere rejects the legend of St. Anne and Joachim because it does not appear in the New Testament. Nor is there anything particularly suspicious about Agrippa's rejection of the breviary as evidence concerning the conception of the Virgin by St. Anne. He does not attack this authority on the ground that the story is not in Scripture; rather, he argues that the breviary contains many legends which the church

[64] *De vanitate*, ch. lviii.   [65] *Ibid.*, ch. lix.
[66] *Ibid.*, ch. lxxxix.

has never approved, legends which are even sometimes contrary to church doctrine. Again, the church is the decisive factor.[67]

In his *Apologia*, Agrippa tried further to safeguard his orthodoxy by arguing that the ceremonies and legends which he condemned lacked the authorization of the church. He was quite critical of popular religious processions in Ghent and other parts of the Low Countries. But so far was he from condemning external rites as such, that he would not even object to circumcision, a practice which would be tolerated in certain Christian sects if only they did not insist that it was necessary for salvation. He defended himself on this point with the authority of Nicholas of Cusa, whose *De pace fidei* had offered to accept this rite in the interests of church unity.[68] Furthermore, Agrippa's system of occultism attributed a positive—though perhaps not an orthodox—valuation to religious ceremonial. Penitence, confession, and almsgiving are forms of expiation which purify the soul and so greatly enhance its mystical powers. Likewise things which are consecrated in religious ceremonies have great powers and uses in magical operations.[69]

Finally, Agrippa in his own private life appears never to have rejected the external side of Catholic religion. After the death of his first wife, he arranged carefully for the saying of masses on the anniversary of her death—this in the midst of what Henri Naef regards as Agrippa's Protestant period. When his second wife died in 1529, he begged all his intimate correspondents to pray for her, and charged her relative, Guillaume Furbity, with the duty of fulfilling a vow she had made to go on pilgrimage to a Swiss shrine.[70]

[67] *De beatissimae Annae monogamia*, especially fols. A7v-A8r and I8v-K3v. Cf. *Epist.* VII, xxxvi. On the breviary, *Epist.* III, xiii-xiv.

[68] *Apologia*, in *Opera*, II, 323.

[69] *De occulta philosophia*, Bk. III, ch. lvi, pp. cccxxvii-cccxxviii, and Bk. III, ch. lxiii, pp. cccxxxviii-cccxli. Of course Agrippa's belief that religious consecrations could be applied to magical works may be regarded as a profanation of the sacred; but within certain limits, many of his contemporaries would have approved such practices. The heresy, if any, was not Protestant.

[70] For the first wife, Agrippa to Brennonius, Lyons, 23 June 1526, *Epist.* IV, xx: "Commendo tibi funeralia charae quondam conjugis in ecclesia tua sepultae, ne quid circa illa omittatur: quin, ut disposuimus et fundavimus, sic omnia executa sint et exequantur." Cf. Brennonius to Agrippa, Metz, 23 July 1526, *Epist.* IV, xxvii: "Vxoris tuae annua obsequia in die obitus ejus, prout voluisti, celebramus: videlicet pridie Mortuorum vigilias, postridie vero missam solemnem facientes, dominica quoque die praecedenti, quam hoc faciamus, e suggesto nos id facturos in ea septimana, publicamus." One must recall that Brennonius was an intimate friend who knew Agrippa's innermost thoughts as

This evidence from his life indicates that Agrippa was sincere when he claimed to be opposing not all external acts of worship but only abuses. Hence when he accuses the priests of vividly depicting the horrors of purgatory in order to get money out of simple folk, or denounces the way in which they use confession to tyrannize over the laity, one must not jump to the conclusion that Agrippa is attacking the Catholic doctrines of purgatory and penance.

Agrippa's stress on the inwardness of religion involved a radical rejection of the use of human reason in religion and of the scholastic theology which had sought to use reason in the elaboration of its systems. Like Nicholas of Cusa three-quarters of a century earlier, Agrippa did not see any contradiction between a universal theism which gave a positive valuation to all religious experience and activity, even non-Christian, on one the hand, and denial of the ability of the human mind to attain God, the ultimate reality, on the other hand. Unlike Cusanus, however, he did not develop universal theism to any significant extent, although both *De occulta philosophia* and *De vanitate* contain traces of the attitude, the former in a far more positive way than the latter. Even in the former, however, Agrippa taught that imperfect religions were largely superstitious and that they were only relatively acceptable to God, who at least preferred them to total unbelief.[71] Agrippa's stress on the weakness of man when unaided by grace also led him to vacillate on the question of the human will. In *De occulta philosophia*, he maintained that although each planet governed certain activities of the soul, yet the intellect guided the will, which was mistress of its own operation and so was called free. The will could err and lead to evil. Grace or infused love was present in the will as a prime mover; this being absent, the harmony of the soul fell into dissonance. In *De vanitate*, he denounced the fatalism caused by belief in astrology, upholding the freedom of the will; yet in a later chapter of the same work, he argued that belief in free will and the dictates of right reason led to Pelagianism.[72] Clearly, he was trying, none too suc-

---

well as any other person. For the death of the second wife and the request to fulfill her promised pilgrimage, Agrippa to Guillaume Furbity, Antwerp, n.d. [shortly after 17 August 1529], *Epist.* V, lxxxi.

[71] *De occulta philosophia*, Bk. III, ch. iiii, pp. ccxvi-ccxvii. *De vanitate*, ch. lvi.

[72] *De occulta philosophia*, Bk. II, ch. xxviii, pp. clxx-clxxi. *De vanitate*, ch. xxxi, liv.

cessfully, to strike a balance between the dangers of fatalism on the one hand, and human self-sufficiency on the other.

Agrippa roundly denounced those modern (that is, scholastic) theologians who in trying to elaborate a rational theology were, he felt, bending Christian truths to the imaginings of pagan philosophers. He charged them with trying to take heaven by storm. Although there were times when he did feel that some non-Christian philosophers might throw light on Christianity and on the Bible, his chief ground for believing so was that they were sharers in an occult tradition that went back through Plato, Pythagoras, and Hermes Trismegistus ultimately to God's revelation to Moses. By the mid-1520's, he appears to have abandoned even this gnostic tradition, arguing that the unadorned Word of God is sufficient without reference to any gentile theology. The human mind is unable to grasp ultimate reality by its own powers: what man must do is believe, not understand. This, of course, is fideism. The only theology which Agrippa could praise was that of the Church Fathers.[73]

The skepticism which underlay Agrippa's fideism is the subject of a later chapter of this work; but it is worth noting here that the theoretical justification for his distrust of the powers of the human mind was a religious doctrine. The reason for the inability of man to know God, the ultimate truth, by his unaided reason is original sin. Although Agrippa interprets the actual act of sin as sexual intercourse between Adam and Eve, he also advances what he calls a moral interpretation. According to this view, Adam typifies faith, led astray by reason (Eve), which in turn has been deceived by sensual desires (the Serpent).[74] The result of this sin is that the divine light, which dwelt in man to maintain incorrupt his compounded (and hence *in se* corruptible) body, has departed, leaving

[73] See *De vanitate, passim*, for attacks on scholastic theologians; in particular, see ch. xcvii ff. For the occult tradition, see an early (1515) treatise, *Oratio in praelectione . . . Trismegisti*, in *Opera*, II, 1077-79. For rejection of even the Hermetic tradition, see *Dehortatio gentilis theologiae*, in *Opera*, II, 502-7, a work no later than early 1526. For a good short statement of Agrippa's condemnation of rational theology, see, in addition to the chapters of *De vanitate* already mentioned, *De triplici ratione cognoscendi Deum*, in *Opera*, II, 480-501. The Hermes myth was common among Italian Neoplatonists like Ficino and Pico, as shown in the preceding chapter.

[74] *De originali peccato*, Lyons, Bibliothèque Municipale, MS. No. 48, fols. 4v-5r. Also printed in *Opera*, II, 553-64.

man subject to death and illness.[75] Nor is this the only effect. The human mind formerly had great powers because the ideas of all things were innate in it; but now all these ideas are veiled; and only illumination by the Holy Spirit can remove this veil of sin so that man can know. Man without this Spirit is sunk in the senses, tortured by his desires, and ignorant of God. All his sciences, which arise from sense perceptions, are of no avail in securing knowledge of God, the ultimate good for which man was created.[76]

How is man to know God if not by rational theology? Agrippa envisioned two ways to God, neither of them putting the primacy in the unaided effort of man. Indeed, the ultimate good of man is not knowledge of any sort: "For true beatitude consists not in the knowledge of good but in a good life. . . ." Elsewhere, Agrippa called it man's highest felicity to know and to love God. His general stress on love rather than on cognition of God as the highest beatitude is reminiscent of Scotist doctrines which he may have come to know at Paris or another of his universities. Scotism, however, is not the only likely source of this emphasis on love over intellect. The same view appears in the thought of several humanists, and especially in Ficino.[77]

The first way to God is a mysticism which in Agrippa's view aims at the deification of man,[78] using ritual aids for purification of the soul (including the sacraments of the church), and applying the secret religious knowledge contained in various gnostic traditions. These traditions, chiefly the Cabala of the Jews and the Hermetic literature, Agrippa regarded (at least in his youth) as divine in origin. The mystical life is contemplative, but in its most perfect form it unites the active with the contemplative life. This is the true monastic life, the true imitation of Christ; its prerequisites

[75] *Dialogus de homine*, Lyons, Bibliothèque Municipale, MS. No. 48, fol. 55r-v [*sic;* should be 56r-v]. This work, which exists only in this fragment, has recently been edited by Paola Zambelli in *Rivista critica di storia della filosofia*, XIII (1958), 47-71.

[76] *De vanitate*, "Peroratio," fols. a5v-a6r. Cf. *De triplici ratione cognoscendi Deum*, in *Opera*, II, 480-86.

[77] *De vanitate*, ch. i: "Vera enim beatitudo non consistit in bonorum cognitione, sed in vita bona. . . ." *De triplici ratione cognoscendi Deum*, in *Opera*, II, 482. For Ficino's emphasis on love over intellect as the way to God, especially in his later works, see Paul Oskar Kristeller, *The Philosophy of Marsilio Ficino*, trans. Virginia Conant (New York, 1943), pp. 256-57, 270-76.

[78] *Oratio in praelectione convivii Platonis*, in *Opera*, II, 1073: "et haec est summa hominum foelicitas, Deum scilicet fieri."

are poverty, chastity, and obedience. Its only real essential is to love God and one's fellow man; and its only doctrinal implication is a statement of Agrippa's which is a paraphrase of the Apostles' Creed.[79] Mystical experience underlies the statements of the true prophets whom Christians honor. This experience is of several kinds. First there is vision of God face to face. The second type is a vision of the hinder parts of God (creatures) and may take the form of seeing the creatures in God or of seeing God in the creatures. A third type of prophetic vision is that which is granted in dreams. A fourth type is to hear God speaking words. A final type is possession by the Holy Ghost. To this latter kind of vision certain ceremonies are conducive; and Agrippa notes that the Jewish Cabalists have even dared to elaborate a prophetical technique, the thirty-two paths of wisdom. Only persons enlightened by the Holy Ghost have full knowledge of the concealed essentials of the Gospel. Ideally, these persons should be identical with the ecclesiastical hierarchy; and it is a clear proof of the decadence of the clergy that they lack these prophetic gifts.[80]

How can lesser souls, souls which have never experienced such sublime prophetic gifts, find the truth? This was a question which concerned Agrippa himself, for he laid no claim to exalted spiritual powers on his own behalf.[81] Like Nicholas of Cusa, he was a non-mystical mystic, a man who valued mystical experience highly but did not claim to share it personally. This second way to find the truth, the way of the humble nonmystic, is study of Scripture:

But you who are unable to see these things by clear and revealed understanding with the prophets and apostles and those holy men, you may get understanding from those who have seen them with true intuition: this way remains to be sought out (as Jerome says to Rufinus), that what the spirit suggested to the prophets and apostles, you must seek by the study of letters, I mean those letters which are handed down in divine oracles and received by the church with unanimous consent, not those that are thought up by human minds, because these do not enlighten the mind, but make it grow dark.[82]

[79] De vita monastica, in Opera, II, 568-72. De triplici ratione cognoscendi Deum, in Opera, II, 501.

[80] De vanitate, ch. xcix.

[81] Agrippa Amico suo, Dôle, 1509, Epist. I, xvii, where he warns a friend not to claim that he has any divine gifts, "sed ut humanitatis nostrae mediocritatem plane agnoscatis." He develops this idea even further in a letter of 19 November 1527, printed in De occulta philosophia, p. cccxlviii, and also, with a few textual variations, in Epist. V, xix.

[82] De vanitate, "Peroratio," fol. a6r-v: "Qui autem non potestis cum prophetis et apostolis et sanctis illis viris claro et reuelato intellectu ea intueri, procuretis

This stress on the Bible as the source of religious truth for the common man, together with the accompanying denunciation of scholastic theology as the perversion of the pure and simple Gospel by blind human reason, has doubtless done more than any other trait except his violent anticlericalism to make Agrippa appear Protestant, although the attitude was a commonplace in Erasmian circles, even those which never adhered to the Reformation. Contemporaries were often deceived themselves. Agrippa was confident that the Bible was so clear that it needed no commentary or glosses. Although he accepted the four scholastic modes of interpretation (literal, moral, tropological, and anagogical), and added two of his own, the typical and the cabalistic, he felt that the literal sense was the most important.[83] He also believed that illumination by the Holy Spirit is necessary for interpretation of the Bible, but his dominant thought was the simplicity and clearness of Scripture. He drew the natural conclusion that the Scriptures ought to be open to all Christians, citing Hebrew practice and the Apostles' eagerness that all believers should hear the Word. The theologians, he argued, err greatly in concealing the Bible from the people: "Know therefore that there is nothing in sacred letters so arduous, so profound, so difficult, so secret, so holy that does not pertain to all believers in Christ; or which is so entrusted to these puffed-up masters of ours that they ought to or can hide it from the Christian people: nay rather, all this theology ought to be common to all the faithful, to each one, however, according to his capacity and the measure of the gift of the Holy Spirit." [84] Quite in the Erasmian tradition, Agrippa also freely cited the Greek Scriptures against the Vulgate, which in any case he denied either to have the sole and authoritative

---

intellectum ab his qui vero intuitu ea conspexerunt: haec via quaerenda superest (sicut ait Hieronymus ad Ruffinum) vt quod prophetis et apostolis spiritus suggessit, vobis studio literarum quaerendum sit, earum inquam literarum, quae diuinis oraculis traditae, et ab ecclesia vnanimi consensu receptae sunt, non quae humanis ingenijs excogitatae sunt, quia hae non illustrant intellectum, sed obtenebrescere faciunt."

[83] At least he felt so by 1526, when he wrote *De vanitate*. Earlier, in *De occulta philosophia* and *De triplici ratione cognoscendi Deum*, he laid stress rather on a secret revelation concealed behind the apparent literal meaning, a revelation expressed in Hebrew cabalism.

[84] *De vanitate*, ch. c: "Scitote ergo nunc nihil esse in sacris literis tam arduum, tam profundum, tam difficile, tam absconditum, tam sanctum, quod ad omnes Christi fideles non pertineat: quodve sic concreditum sit istis sesquipedalibus magistris nostris, vt id Christianum populum debeant possintve celare: quin tota ipsa theologia omnibus fidelibus communis esse debet, vnicuique autem secundum capacitatem et mensuram donationis spiritus sancti."

approval of the universal church or even to be the work of St. Jerome.[85]

Far from restricting knowledge of the Bible to the theologians, Agrippa attacked them sharply. At its best, in the days of its founders, Thomas Aquinas and Albertus Magnus, and the more contentious Duns Scotus, scholasticism was a monstrous mixture of Scripture and philosophical reasons (and all human science, Agrippa insists repeatedly, comes from the Serpent). But it at least had some usefulness against heretics. In this decadent age, however, it has degenerated into mere contentious sophistry, calling into question all beliefs, undermining faith, leading to heresy. Yet the theologians are so strong that anyone who dares to criticize them may perish. True Christianity flourished best in ages when men were most ignorant, Agrippa observed, using words that might be directed against religion itself but which in this context certainly are not.[86]

In placing the Bible above all human learning and in opening it to all, Agrippa came close to locating the ultimate source of authority in it. But he did not quite do so. In one place, it is true, he argued that any science that does not have authority from the Bible can be as easily disproved as proved. And the authority of canonical Scripture depends solely on the authority of God, the Revealer.[87] Though he honors the authority of the church fathers, he says, he honors Scripture more. But Agrippa does not appear to regard the authority of Scripture as standing in opposition to the authority of the ecclesiastical hierarchy.

Whenever therefore there is strife about the sense of Scripture, one must not on that account attribute its interpretation to the human mind, but to the gift of the Spirit, and prophecy . . . which gift of prophecy never leaves the church, but always remains, not in our contentious masters, or in doctors howsoever learned, but in those who have succeeded to the place of the apostles, even if they have nothing of human learning. . . . Hence the canonists in agreement with the theologians say that the pope has this right of prophesying, that is (as they say), the power of interpreting Scripture; and although there were many wicked popes, still it has been found that none of them ever committed any offense against the Scripture.[88]

[85] De beatissimae Annae monogamia, fols. K3v-L2r.

[86] De vanitate, ch. xcvii, ci.   [87] Ibid., ch. c.

[88] Apologia, in Opera, II, 312-13: "Quoties ergo de sensu scripturae pugna est, non propterea humano ingenio tribuenda est ejus interpretatio, sed dono spiritus, et prophetiae . . . quod prophetiae donum, nunquam relinquit ecclesiam, sed continuo manet, non in contentiosis magistris nostris, neque in quantumcunque eruditis doctoribus, sed in his qui successerunt in locum Apos-

Debate on points of scriptural interpretation is free, but only if those questions have not been authoritatively determined by the church. One is not obliged to follow the doctors of the church, nor even the church itself except on the essentials of faith, although Agrippa fails to make any clear distinction between what is essential and what is not. He claims to give due obedience to papal decretals, more to general councils, but absolute submission only to Scripture and the essential beliefs of the church universal.[89] Agrippa does not very clearly state who determines what these essentials are. The real source of scriptural authority, then, remains vague, although the ultimate interpretation of the Scriptures is clearly the prerogative of the church. At times Agrippa seems to insist that no one may add to or take from the Bible. At other times he feels that the church is free to alter the counsels of the Bible on many points, as in dissolving marriages for causes other than adultery. But his eventual conclusion appears to favor church authority. The only sure way of telling which Gospels are canonical and inspired is by the judgment of the universal church, not by the authority of the apostles who wrote the books.[90] The true cause of the unclearness of Agrippa on this point is that he does not really conceive the possibility that the authoritative teaching of the church could ever clash with the Bible. The church and the papacy, he felt, could and did err on many peripheral questions (hence his liberty in attacking them), but never on the essentials of faith.

If this aspect of Agrippa's teachings on scriptural authority put him at odds with Protestant doctrines despite certain superficial tendencies toward those teachings, yet there was another aspect of his teaching about the Bible that made him seem hateful to the self-styled orthodox of both camps and aligned him rather with a party-less man like Sebastian Franck. For Agrippa taught that even the Scriptures, the one source of truth which remains to him, contain many errors. The Holy Ghost itself, of course, did not err. Human frailty is the source of error in Scripture. The inspired writers erred not intentionally but because of human weakness or because of some

---

tolorum, etiamsi nihil habeant humanae eruditionis. . . . Hinc canonistae cum theologis, communi sensu dicunt: Papam habere hoc jus prophetandi, hoc est, (ut ipsi ajunt) potestatem interpretandi scripturam, et licet multi extiterint pravi pontifices, nullum tamen illorum unquam aliquam falstitatem in scripturam commisisse compertum est."
[89] *Ibid.*, ch. xxv, in *Opera*, II, 300-03.   [90] *Ibid.*, ch. xxxii, in *Opera*, II, 315.

alteration made in their text by others. Even great prophets like Moses lost the spirit of prophecy at times. Furthermore, there are inspired books in Scripture which have been lost, such as the canonical Book of Enoch cited by Jude. Some of the examples of error which Agrippa gives are these: Moses promised to lead the Israelites out of Egypt and into the promised land; but though he did the former, he did not live to take them into the promised land. Isaiah predicted the death of Hezekiah for the morrow, yet it did not occur for fifteen years. The apostles also erred, as when Peter had to be reproved by Paul.[91] Only Jesus Christ never erred and never lost the spirit of prophecy. In his *Apologia*, having been taken to task for these teachings, Agrippa argued that the church had the right to correct such errors in Scripture and had done so at the Council of Vienne in the case of an error of chronology in Matthew.[92] In addition to the judgment of the church, Agrippa could reintroduce certainty only by teaching that prophetic utterances were to be tested by their general harmony with the rest of the Scriptures accepted by the church.[93] It was Agrippa's raising of these doubts and his ultimate resolution of them by the authority of the church which, more than anything else, made John Calvin catalogue Agrippa among those who scorned the Gospel.[94]

Certainly Agrippa's religious views were not wholly orthodox. His tendency to stress religion as an internal experience and to discount (though not reject) external forms, the great weight he gave to faith (though a faith expressed in works), his unclearness about free will (though his usual position is the orthodox one), his emphasis on the literal sense of the pure and simple Gospel (though in a sense undermined by his critique of the Bible and the position which in the last resort he gave to the judgment of the church), his violently anticlerical statements (though qualified by a distinction between the office and its incumbent): all these teachings were close to heterodoxy, though perhaps still short of it. Yet his professed submission to the church recurs everywhere; and it would be foolish to see in it nothing more than practical prudence. He did not deny that some of his teachings might be erroneous; but he did insist strenuously that error is not the same as heresy. To err, especially on a question not yet defined by the church, is not heretical unless one does so pertinaciously and consciously in opposition to the

[91] *De vanitate*, ch. xcix.   [92] *Apologia*, ch. xxxii, in *Opera*, II, 315.
[93] *De vanitate*, ch. xcix.   [94] Bohatec, *op. cit.*, pp. 162-65.

known pronouncements of ecclesiastical authority. Thus Agrippa's doctrinal position ran parallel to his attitude toward the Reformation itself. He was friendly to many elements that were contrary to the usual teaching of the church, but he never regarded himself as opposed to the church itself. What heresy there was in him, furthermore, was largely independent of the Lutheran movement. His early works, above all his *De triplici ratione cognoscendi Deum*, show that before 1517 he had already reached many of his questionable beliefs, for example his anticlericalism and his stress on faith and on internal religious experience. The historian Rudolf Stadelmann realized some of this when he discussed Agrippa in relation to a group of northern Europeans, all (like Agrippa himself) showing signs of the influence of Nicholas of Cusa, and culminating not so much in Martin Luther as in the religious anarchy of scattered, partyless individuals like Sebastian Franck.[95]

[95] Rudolf Stadelmann, *Vom Geist des ausgehenden Mittelalters: Studien zur Geschichte der Weltanschauung von Nicolaus Cusanus bis Sebastian Franck* (Halle, 1929), pp. 79-97. For other studies of the lay piety of the fifteenth century and its possible contribution to the spread of Protestantism, see Albert Hyma, *The Christian Renaissance* (Grand Rapids, Michigan, 1924), and Gerhard Ritter, "Romantische und revolutionäre Elemente in der deutschen Theologie am Vorabend der Reformation," *Deutsche Vierteljahrsschrift für Literaturwissenschaft und Geistesgeschichte*, V (1927), 342-80, especially Part II.

CHAPTER EIGHT

THE ODYSSEY OF AGRIPPA'S MIND

From his own age down to the present, Agrippa von Nettesheim has received widely varying evaluations from students of his thought. Some have dismissed him cursorily as an intellectual lightweight or as a wicked familiar of demons. Even those who have valued him highly have often done so for most contradictory reasons. Much of this disagreement results from uncertainty about which Agrippa to believe: Agrippa the credulous magician, author of a widely used magical compilation, *De occulta philosophia*, or Agrippa the skeptical doubter, writer of *De incertitudine et vanitate scientiarum*. This dual personality as magician and skeptic is evident not only in Agrippa's numerous writings but also in the reaction of others to these writings. To some, such as Giordano Bruno in the sixteenth century and Thomas Vaughan in the seventeenth, the exposition of a magical world, the parts of which are intimately connected by occult bonds, was the fruitful element in his thought. Bruno found in *De occulta philosophia* much of the detail of his own *De monade;*

and his world view was little different from Agrippa's except that it was more consistently worked out.[1] To others, however, the stimulating element in Agrippa's writings was the universal doubt which in *De vanitate* he cast on all human learning. One late sixteenth-century French writer complained of the existence of a whole school of "atheists" or doubters who called themselves Agrippans, while there is no doubt that *De vanitate* furnished both ideas and illustrative material for the skeptical thought of Michel de Montaigne.[2] Some of the themes of *De vanitate* also show similarity to the thought of the libertines of seventeenth-century Italy.

The presence of these two apparently contradictory elements, magic and skepticism, in the thought of the same man made his writings disturbing to many readers. The clash between his credulity and the anguished doubts of *De vanitate* helped to mold the legend which symbolizes the intellectual malaise of the sixteenth century, that of Faust. Christopher Marlowe's Doctor Faustus explicitly takes Agrippa as his ideal when he renounces human sciences in favor of magic. Much later, Agrippa contributed to the concept of Faust in the mind of Goethe, who admitted that as a youth he passed through an intellectual crisis after reading the pessimistic *De vanitate*.[3] Thus the juxtaposition of magic and skepticism in

[1] For the relation between Agrippa and Bruno, see J. Lewis McIntyre, *Giordano Bruno* (London, 1903), pp. 131, 148-49. Ernst Cassirer, *Das Erkenntnisproblem in der Philosophie und Wissenschaft der neueren Zeit* (3 vols.; Berlin, 1906-20), I, 344-45, notes the similarity between the two world views. Among more recent authors, Dorothea Waley Singer, *Giordano Bruno, His Life and Thought* (New York, 1950), pp. 69, 141, mentions Bruno's familiarity with Agrippa, but her discussion (pp. 120-25) of his *Cabala del cavallo Pegaseo con l'aggiunta dell'Asino Cilenico* does not point out the obvious similarity between Bruno's use of the ass as a symbol of the humble Christian believer and Agrippa's use of the same symbol at the end of *De vanitate*. Cf. John Charles Nelson, *Renaissance Theory of Love: The Context of Giordano Bruno's Eroici Furori* (New York, 1958), p. 250, which also fails to note the possible source of Bruno's use of the ass. For Agrippa's influence on Thomas Vaughan and his twin brother Henry, the poet, see Alexander C. Judson, "Cornelius Agrippa and Henry Vaughan," *Modern Language Notes*, XLI (1926), 178-81; cf. Thomas Vaughan, *Anthroposophia theomagica* (London, 1650), p. 50.

[2] The complaint about "Agrippans" is in André Thevet, *Les vrais povrtraits et vies des hommes illustres* (Paris, 1584), p. 544. Pierre Villey, *Les sources et l'évolution des Essais de Montaigne* (2nd ed.; 2 vols.; Paris, 1933), II, 166-70, notes close textual relationship between *De vanitate* and parts of Montaigne's great "Apology."

[3] Marlowe's Doctor Faustus takes Agrippa as his ideal in Scene II, lines 104-16. Goethe confesses in *Dichtung und Wahrheit*, Part I, ch. 4, that *De vanitate* upset his youthful optimism. On Agrippa's contribution to his *Faust*, Anton

Agrippa's thought has been fruitful in the artistic world; but no modern student of his writings has satisfactorily analyzed the relations between these elements and the way in which they developed within the mind of Agrippa.

Most recent students of Agrippa's thought have attained a resolution of this problem by largely discounting one or the other of these two major elements. For some, Lynn Thorndike among them, the important part of Agrippa's thought appears in his magical treatise; and *De vanitate* is either a mere rhetorical exercise or else the product of a passing mood evoked by the depressed state of Agrippa's fortunes in the summer of 1526, when it was written.[4] A superficial inspection of the *Apologia* which Agrippa wrote to protect the book from the attacks of the Louvain theological faculty seems to bear out this point of view. At every turn, Agrippa excused himself by saying, "I was only declaiming," and by charging that his accusers were so slow-witted that they took all his statements seriously. Certainly *De vanitate* contains many tales that are not presented as serious fact. The story that the Devil invented the monks' cowl, for example, is a mere joke. Who, Agrippa asks, would not laugh at the monks if they took offense at everything said about them in Boccaccio's *Decameron* or Poggio's *Facetiae* as they did at similar tales in *De vanitate?* [5] But the fact that Agrippa said many things with tongue in cheek does not vitiate the importance of the whole work. In the first place, Agrippa did write the book, even the joking parts; and even the jokes reflect his own state of mind. In the second place, more careful reading of the *Apologia*

Reichl, "Goethes Faust und Agrippa von Nettesheim," *Euphorion: Zeitschrift für Literaturgeschichte,* IV (1897), 287-301, and Gerhard Ritter, "Ein historisches Urbild zu Goethes Faust (Agrippa von Nettesheym)," *Preussische Jahrbücher,* CXLI (1910), 300-5. More recently, Harold S. Jantz, *Goethe's Faust as a Renaissance Man: Parallels and Prototypes* (Princeton, 1951), p. 55, recognized the similarities between Agrippa and Faust, but was more concerned with the general influence of a dominant Renaissance *Weltanschauung* on the thought of Goethe (see pp. 58, 124-27).

[4] Lynn Thorndike, *A History of Magic and Experimental Science* (8 vols.; New York, 1923-58), V, 129-31. Even Thorndike appears uncertain which Agrippa to believe in. He does not take either one very seriously. An example of a credulity-disbelief-credulity explanation of Agrippa's writings is Joseph Leon Blau, *The Christian Interpretation of the Cabala in the Renaissance* (New York, 1944), p. 85.

[5] *Apologia adversus calumnias, propter declamationem de vanitate scientiarum, et excellentia verbi Dei, sibi per aliquos Lovanienses theologistas intentatas,* in Agrippa's *Opera* (2 vols.; Lugduni, n.d.), I, 273-75, 306-7. (Henceforth cited as *Apologia.*)

shows that Agrippa, far from recanting, sharply reasserts the ideas found in *De vanitate* and at times develops them even further. A good example is the way in which, after excusing his motto, "Nihil scire foelicissima vita," as mere jest, he proceeds to defend it, with the aid of citations from Augustine, Dionysius, Philo Judaeus, and Nicholas of Cusa.[6] Certainly Agrippa's *Apologia* is trying to work both sides of the street at once: to shrug off daring statements as mere jest and also to defend what the original treatise said. It is possible, as Follet has suggested, that to later generations, the book may have seemed merely a rhetorical exercise, a collection of paradoxical sayings, and a manual for witty conversation at court, as the title page of the French translation of 1582 suggests; but far more than that is available in this often-printed and much translated book.[7] It contains the fullest development of a corrosive, anarchical, and skeptical strain in Agrippa's thought. It contributed much more to Montaigne's "Apology for Raymond Sebond" than mere anecdote and paradox.

Those critics who have refused to discount *De vanitate* have generally undervalued *De occulta philosophia*. To them, the latter book is a product of Agrippa's early youth (as, indeed, the first version of it, dated 1510, really was). They then have to determine when Agrippa ceased to believe in the magical nonsense which he heaped up in his early book. Any preoccupation with magic after 1526 is to them mere charlatanry; and one of them, Prost, argues that Agrippa's credulity was probably at an end by the time he reached Metz in 1518.[8] This point of view explains Agrippa's publication of

[6] *Ibid.*, II, 288.

[7] H. Follet, "Un médecin astrologue au temps de la Renaissance, Henri Cornelius Agrippa," *Nouvelle revue*, XCVIII (1896), 330. The title page of the French translation by Louis de Mayerne-Turquet (1582) has the subtitle: "Oeuvre qui peut proffiter et qui apporte merveilleux contentement à ceux qui fréquentent les cours des grands seigneurs, et qui veulent apprendre à discourir d'une infinité de choses contre la commune opinion." This translation and another in the same tongue were reprinted several times. The six Latin editions which I have seen, dated between 1531 and 1714, represent only a tiny handful of all the editions. For an incomplete but helpful bibliographical study of Agrippan editions, see John Ferguson's posthumous fragment in *Proceedings of the Edinburgh Bibliographical Society*, XII (1924), 1-23. I have seen English editions of 1569, 1575, 1676, 1684, and 1694, representing two independent translations. A Dutch translation (1651, 1661), an Italian (1547, 1549, 1552), and a German one (1713), are listed by Auguste Prost, *Les sciences et les arts occultes au XVI siècle: Corneille Agrippa, sa vie et ses oeuvres* (2 vols.; Paris, 1881-82), II, 507-10.

[8] Prost, *op. cit.*, II, 288.

De occulta philosophia late in his life by claiming that mere desire for gain motivated his printing a book in which he no longer believed.[9]

The problem of Agrippa's credulity and his skepticism deserves close study. First, however, it will be necessary to explore this charge that his attitude toward the occult sciences, at least late in his life, was that of a charlatan. He certainly was not entirely free from desire to profit by the credulity of others. This he himself admitted when he wrote concerning astrology: ". . . And I should wish to be rid of every memory and use of it, and I have long since cast it out of my mind; nor would I ever have taken it up again, if the violent prayers of the powerful (who are accustomed sometimes to misuse even great and honest minds for unworthy employments) had not often forced me to touch on it again, and economic utility had not at times forced me to profit by their stupidity and to serve with nonsense those who so greatly desire nonsense. . . ." [10] Yet the alleged charlatan who wrote this did so not only in a private letter but also as part of the chapter in *De vanitate,* a published work, where he denounced astrology as wicked and inane. One of the causes of his disgrace at the French court in 1526 was that he refused to cast the horoscope of King Francis I, since he regarded such things as both sinful and vain. He expressed this belief frequently to courtiers; and one such letter fell into the hands of the Queen Mother, Louise of Savoy, who had asked for a prognostication for her son. When, under great pressure, Agrippa did cast the King's horoscope, he did not, as a charlatan doubtless would, draw up a favorable but safely vague prognostication. Rather, he plainly reported that the stars, if one could put any faith in them, were unfavorable to King Francis.[11] It is quite true that Agrippa continued in later years to make occasional astrological predictions,

---

[9] G[iuseppe]. Rossi, *Agrippa di Nettesheym e la direzione scettica della filosofia nel Rinascimento* (Turin, 1906), p. 72.

[10] *De incertitudine et vanitate scientiarum declamatio inuectiua* (Coloniae, 1531), ch. xxx: ". . . Cuperemque omnem illius memoriam vsumque expoliare, abiecique iamdudum ex animo: nec reassumerem vnquam, nisi me potentum violentae preces (qui solent nonnunquam ad indigna artificia etiam magnis probisque ingenijs abuti) saepe rursus impingere compellerent, suaderetque domestica vtilitas me aliquando illorum frui debere stultitia et nugas tantopere cupientibus nugis obsequi. . . ." (Henceforth cited as *De vanitate.*) Cf. Agrippa ad Amicum, n.p., n.d. [Lyons, 1526], *Epistolarum Liber IV,* viii, in *Opera,* II, 837-38. (This collection of letters is henceforth cited as *Epist.*)

[11] Agrippa to Chapelain, Lyons, 30 September 1526, *Epist.* IV, li.

but this is not necessarily charlatanry. Despite his denunciation of astrology, he still felt that there might be something to it and that if one were to practice it, one must follow its rules faithfully. He strongly doubted, but he did not quite so strongly deny. He continued to study the pseudo-science throughout his career, and he sought the resolution of its contradictions and uncertainties from many of his correspondents.[12]

Agrippa's more frequent and less equivocal statements about interpretation of terrestrial and astral prodigies (comets, for instance) do not run counter to these grave doubts concerning astrology.[13] It was quite possible for one to deny the possibility of an exact science of astrology without denying that the Almighty might use strange celestial phenomena, such as comets, as portents of great happenings. Martin Luther, for example, chided Philip Melanchthon for his trust in astrology but still believed strongly in astral and other portents.[14]

As with astrology, so with other occult sciences. Agrippa followed all of them closely throughout his life. He had doubts about the certainty of all of them, but to the end of his days he remained sincerely eager to read new books and learn of new experiments in them. His doubts began early and grew considerably, but he was incapable of utterly abandoning occultism. The explanation that Agrippa continued to practice occult sciences and published *De occulta philosophia* after writing *De vanitate* only because he was a charlatan is insufficient. The true account of Agrippa's intellectual odyssey is much more complex than either of the views just explored. More careful study of his shorter writings would perhaps have prevented these oversimplifications, which do not in any case really resolve even the problems arising out of the two major books.

In his brilliant though much-criticized book, *The Counter-*

---

[12] As early as 1509, a friend complained that Agrippa's expressions about astrology were equivocal: Theodoricus Wichwael, Bishop of Cyrene, to Agrippa, Cologne, 29 November 1509, *Epist.* I, xxi, where he complains thus: "Interseras rogo, quid tibi in astrologia judiciaria placeat displiceatve. Quantus ad illam disputator fuerit Picus Mirandula, certe nosti. et quid quasi exsufflando omnes ejus rationes et explodendo Lucius Balancius egerit, ut arbitror, vidisti. Qualis vero tuus sit in eam animus, vellem scire: cum, quando apud nos causas ageres, ambiguus nobis visus fueras. . . ."

[13] *De beatissimae Annae monogamia ac unico puerperio* . . . (n.p., 1534), fols. Q4v-Q5r, Q6r-v; *Epist.* IV, lv.; *Epist.* VI, xi. For the meaning of the comet of August 1531, *Epist.* VI, xxviii.

[14] Aby Warburg, "Heidnisch-antike Weissagung in Wort und Bild zu Luthers Zeiten," *Gesammelte Schriften* (2 vols.; Leipzig, 1932), II, 512.

Renaissance, Hiram Haydn has suggested a dialectical interpretation of the development of European thought in the sixteenth century. In opposition to the orderly world view which the Thomists and humanists shared, there arose a general skepticism concerning the power of the human mind to gain truth. This skepticism in turn produced two results, sometimes at odds but often found in the same person: unsystematic empiricism, which granted truth only to sensory knowledge, and occultism, which appealed rather to gnostic traditions of revealed truth, especially the Hermetic and the cabalistic. Finally, these two tendencies, especially the empirical, contributed in some measure to the birth of modern scientific methodology, which restored faith in the power of the human mind, but on a different level from that of medieval rationalism.[15] Haydn's most perceptive critic has acknowledged that this is a fruitful pattern if one does not apply it too rigidly and does not insist too strongly on the chronological element in the process. Christoph Sigwart in the last century foreshadowed this view, while Ernst Cassirer has stated the skeptical basis of magic quite clearly, with specific reference to Agrippa, and has insisted that this skepticism was a necessary preliminary to the philosophical reconstruction of the seventeenth century.[16] More recently, Eugenio Garin has clearly shown that belief in magic was far from being incompatible with a skeptically inclined assault on the traditional learning, and that both the occultist and the skeptical elements were intimately related to the central intellectual problems of Renaissance civilization. Indeed, he suggests that belief in magic and corrosive doubt about the validity of human reason and about contemporary civilization were merely two aspects of the same mentality.[17]

This dialectical pattern is particularly fruitful in interpreting the thought of Agrippa. In particular, it hints at quite another pattern of development than the credulity-incredulity-charlatanry one

[15] Hiram Haydn, *The Counter-Renaissance* (New York, 1950), xi-xvii, and *passim.* To Haydn, Agrippa is a key figure in the development of this tendency, which he labels "Counter-Renaissance."
[16] Paul Oskar Kristeller, Review of *The Counter-Renaissance, Journal of the History of Ideas,* XII (1951), 468-72. To Sigwart, it is not so much a general skepticism as a disillusionment with medieval thought which underlies Agrippa's flight to the occult. See his essay on Agrippa in *Kleine Schriften* (2nd ed.; 2 vols.; Freiburg-i-B., 1889), especially I, 1-5. Cassirer, *op. cit.,* I, 162, 181.
[17] Eugenio Garin, *Medioevo e Rinascimento: Studi e ricerche* (Bari, 1954), pp. 90-99, 151-69, 170-91.

which has been most common, for distrust in the powers of the human mind to attain truth becomes the basic presupposition of occultism rather than the product of disillusionment with it. It is not true that Agrippa represents the full course of this dialectical movement, nor is it true that his mind proceeds steadily from step to step without contradiction and without backtracking. But it is true that even *De occulta philosophia* is not the product of a man with confidence in the powers of the human mind; rather, it is an appeal from bankrupt reason to an occult tradition believed to be based ultimately on a divine revelation.

De occulta philosophia is highly complex. In large part it is just a compilation of facts and alleged facts from earlier writers, and as such it reveals an astounding degree of erudition (and of credulity) on the part of its author. The vast wealth of medieval literature and the rediscovered treasures of Antiquity have been laid under contribution. Authority of the past, not human powers in the present, receives the author's emphasis. Agrippa's underlying intention, although he does not adhere to it consistently, is to rediscover the truths known to wise men of the past, and to restore the good name of magic by stripping away the errors and superstitions which have obscured its holy teachings.[18] The truths found in magical writings stem not from human reasoning but from divine revelations which in the last analysis go all the way back to the one given to Moses. These revelations supposedly included an esoteric interpretation of Scripture which passed into the Cabala of the Jews and into the Hermetic literature of the Egyptians, and from the latter into the philosophical mysticism of the Pythagoreans and the Platonists. This myth of a continuous esoteric tradition was a commonplace of the fifteenth-century Italian Neoplatonists, and found expression in the writings of men like Gemistos Plethon, Marsilio Ficino, and Pico della Mirandola.[19]

[18] Dedicatory epistle to Trithemius of Sponheim, *De occulta philosophia libri tres* (Coloniae, 1533), fol. aa3r-v; cf. Würzburg, Universitätsbibliothek, MS. M.ch.q.50, dedicatory epistle and Bk. I, ch. 1 (the unprinted manuscript version of *De occulta philosophia*).
[19] Agrippa best states this myth in *Oratio in praelectione . . . Trismegisti,* in *Opera,* II, 1077-74 [*sic;* should be 1077-78]. Cf. *De occulta philosophia,* Bk. III, ch. ii, pp. ccxi-ccxii. For Ficino's statement of this Neoplatonic myth, Eugenio Garin, *Giovanni Pico della Mirandola: Vita e dottrina* (Florence, 1937), pp. 75-76; Nesca Adeline Robb, *Neoplatonism of the Italian Renaissance* (London, 1935), p. 48; and Paul Oskar Kristeller, *The Philosophy of Marsilio Ficino,* trans. Virginia Conant (New York, 1943), pp. 15, 25-27.

Although *De occulta philosophia* contains no explicit statement of skeptical ideas, human reason clearly is not primary to the work. Agrippa admits, to be sure, that man can accomplish great works, seeming miracles, not through the aid of demons but by natural powers. These natural powers, however, are not synonymous with reason. When Agrippa writes "natural," he sometimes means merely "terrestrial." Generally, however, he uses the term to describe anything or any event which exists or occurs without the direct action of some divine or angelic power. Thus the use of celestial influences to accomplish mighty works is "natural," in Agrippa's terminology. But man does not by his rational powers learn to use such natural forces; he depends, Agrippa argues, on divine inspiration for his control over them. Hence the *magus* may construct images which will accomplish great things; but such images are useless "unless they be so brought to life that either a natural, or celestial, or heroic, or animastic, or demonic, or angelic power is present in them or with them." [20] The soul of the magician who employs these images draws its ability to use them not from reason but from a mystical ascent aided by ceremonial preparation and dependent for its consummation on divine illumination.[21] More than twenty years later, writing a dedication for Book Three of *De occulta philosophia*, Agrippa repeated this assertion that the mind is unable to make its ascent to God, the ultimate truth, if it trusts in merely worldly things rather than in divine things.[22]

Clearer proof that Agrippa saw no inconsistency between belief in the truth of the esoteric tradition and a thoroughgoing denial of the power of the human mind to grasp ultimate reality appears in a somewhat later work, *De triplici ratione cognoscendi Deum*. This book is a product of Agrippa's years in Italy and is dedicated to Guglielmo Paleologo, Marquis of Monferrato. Dated in 1516, it bears strong traces of the influence of Hermetic literature, on which Agrippa had lectured at Pavia the preceding year, and also of Cabala, on which he had lectured at Dôle in 1509. Original sin, he teaches in this work, has so beclouded man's mind that he cannot know God by his own powers. Three ways of knowing God never-

---

[20] *De occulta philosophia*, Bk. II, ch. 1, pp. cxciii-cxciiii: "nisi uiuificentur ita quod ipsis aut naturalis aut coelestis aut heroica, aut animastica, aut daemoniaca uel angelica uirtus insit, aut adsistat. . . ."

[21] *Ibid.*, Bk. III, ch. xliii, pp. cccvi-cccix; Bk. III, ch. li, pp. cccxvii-cccxx; Bk. III, ch. liii-lvii, pp. cccxxii-cccxxix.

[22] *Ibid.*, pp. ccix-ccx.

theless remain open to him. The first, the Book of Nature, depends on the power of his mind to know God as His creatures reflect Him. But this way cannot lead to knowledge of God in Himself; and even the limited knowledge that can come in this way is distorted by the passions of the soul. The second way to know God is the Book of the Law, the revelation of God to Moses and the secret, revealed interpretation of revelation found in the Cabala. But this book, even interpreted by Cabala, reaches its perfection only with the coming of the Messiah, Jesus Christ, who fulfilled the Old Law and gave mankind the third way to know God, the Gospel. This Gospel, like the Old Testament, is divided into an open revelation contained in the words of Scripture and a secret revelation which interprets the published words in gnostic fashion. These last two ways, the Law and the Gospel, can truly lead man to God, the ultimate truth, but only through faith and grace, not through the unaided powers of human reason.[23]

The first two stages in Agrippa's development, then, were a fundamental doubt concerning the powers of the human mind, and an effort to escape this doubt by an appeal to the authority of the past, especially Antiquity. The Antiquity to which he turned was not primarily the aesthetic and reasonable Antiquity of Cicero but the mystical Antiquity of Neoplatonism, an Antiquity which included the Hermetic and cabalistic writings. Ultimately this ancient wisdom depended on an esoteric tradition supposedly based on divine revelation.

An obvious next step in Agrippa's development was the growth of doubts concerning the validity of the authorities on which his occult system was founded. The germ of this process was present even in De occulta philosophia, for Agrippa felt that the usual authorities in the various occult sciences, Albertus Magnus, Robert of Lincoln, Roger Bacon, Arnold of Villanova, Picatrix, Pietro d'Abano, and Cecco d'Ascoli, had mixed much nonsense with their writings and so were largely responsible for the ill repute in which magic (which, to Agrippa, was the generic term for all the occult sciences) was generally held.[24] Agrippa throughout his life appears

[23] De triplici ratione cognoscendi Deum, in Opera, II, 480-503, especially pp. 483, 489, 491, 493-94.
[24] Dedicatory epistle to Trithemius, De occulta philosophia, fol. aa3r-v. Würzburg, Universitätsbibliothek, MS. M.ch.q.50, Bk. I, ch. 1 (fol. 2r-v) makes the same point but lacks the list of names appearing in the later recension.

to have searched avidly for more knowledge about occult subjects. Perhaps he never felt completely satisfied with what he knew, but continued to hope that just round the next corner, just on the next page he read, he might find satisfaction. His lecture on the *Pimander* in 1515 and his lecture on the *Symposium* of Plato, undated but probably of the same period, show no weakening of his trust in ancient occult traditions. His *Dialogus de homine*, a work about contemporary with *De triplici ratione cognoscendi Deum*, exalts man's powers almost beyond the confines of the occultist tradition.[25] Yet even it offers no real contradiction to the viewpoint of *De triplici ratione*, for the great powers there ascribed to man are his only if he remains free from sin. In reality, man's powers as set forth in *Dialogus de homine* could be his only before original sin, or perhaps after an act of divine illumination which has restored the divine light which illuminated man's mind before the fall of Adam.

On the other hand, Agrippa's *De originali peccato*, completed between 1516 and early 1519, shows considerable doubt about the various arts of prognostication, especially astrology, a pseudo-science about which Agrippa may have felt doubtful as early as 1509.[26] It appears that astrology was the first of the occult sciences to suffer from the growth of doubts in the Nettesheimer's mind. It was perhaps the weak link in his whole occult system, for Agrippa, like nearly all men of his age, gave celestial influences a central position in his occultism. One must distinguish, however, between a form of occultism which used celestial influences to control nature and one which attempted to predict the future from the stars. Attack on astrological prophecy might well lead him to a more general renunciation of belief in occult forces coming from the stars, but this result did not necessarily follow.

An unusually frank letter of early 1519 shows both the extensiveness and the limitations of Agrippa's doubts about not only human learning but also occult sciences. Dialectic and philosophy are "diabolical and seductive artifices and errors." After studying dialectic, natural science, and astrology, Agrippa feels that he has

[25] This work survives in the fragment preserved in Lyons, Bibliothèque Municipale, MS. No. 48, fols. 44r-59v [*sic;* should be 45r-60v]. This text has been edited by Paola Zambelli in *Rivista critica di storia della filosofia*, XIII (1958), 47-71.

[26] *Ibid.*, fol. 6r-v. Cf. *Epist.* I, xxi. In the other hand, see *Opera*, I, 405-25, for an undated work which seems fully astrological, *In geomanticam disciplinam lectura*.

wasted his time, effort, and substance and has got nothing in return but sin, "for all these are not from faith." Finally, "by the grace of God at length realizing how great [is] the vanity of human sciences," and after taking doctorates in medicine and both laws, Agrippa has turned to sacred letters.[27] This letter contains no trace of the epistemological critique found in the early chapters of his later work De vanitate (1526), no extended demonstration of the vanity of arts and sciences, and no reference to the thought of ancient skepticism. It also fails to strike very clearly at any of the occult sciences but astrology, the most vulnerable one in Agrippa's estimation. In particular, it makes no attack on the gnostic myth of an esoteric revelation which justified study of Hermetic and cabalistic writings. Nevertheless, this letter does show two important facts. One is that by 1519 Agrippa had progressed far toward the rejection of human learning and had begun to question natural philosophy and astrology as well. The other is the intimate connection between his interest in the Bible and his depreciation of human learning. His thought since at least 1516 had assumed an increasing tendency to stress simple, Biblical religion;[28] and this religious coloration of his thought was working to the detriment of human reason and of at least some of the occult sciences.

From mid-1519 to early 1526, Agrippa wrote no books at all, though he did produce an astrological calendar for the year 1523

[27] Agrippa to Theodoricus Wichwael, Bishop of Cyrene, Metz, 6 February 1518 (1519, n.s.), in Lyons, Bibliothèque Municipale, MS. No. 48, fols. 31v-32v (printed as Epist. II, xix, with a few variant readings): "Porro laudas, quia secularibus vtcumque abiectis: me sacris literis mancipauerim, consulisque vt oblatis deo castis orationibus; diabolicas [et] seductrices machinas erroresque (dialecticam arbitror te dicere, et philosophiam) precaueam. En tute in parte nosti, quemadmodum post dialecticam; naturaliumque rerum peruestigationem, insuper totam celorum militiam perlustrarim: ducibus duabus illis magnis magni alberti sapientiis; quas in speculo suo; opusculo non admodum laudato: describit. Tamdem (vt verum fatear) consumpto multo tenpore [sic]; ac laboribus: cum anime, corporis, fortunaeque bonorum iactura: nichil superlucratus sum ex his omnibus; praeter peccatum, omnia siquidem hec ex fide non sunt, sed gratia dei; tantas humanarum scientiarum vanitates aliquando recognosce[n]s; post vtriusque iuris ac medicine (vt meorum desiderio satisfacerem: qui me doctorem malunt quam doctum) acceptis scolastico more tiaris et annulis; ad sacras literas, quamuis sero toto me studio contuli; easque (sed procul contentionibus, rixosisque syllogismis) totus amplector, nec effari possim, quam in his oblectatur simul et quiessit [sic] animus."
[28] Ritter, in Preussische Jahrbücher, CXLI, 309, observes this increase in religious interest and traces it back to 1510 or even 1509.

toward the end of his residence in Geneva.[29] Then in 1526 came an apparently sudden proliferation of works, especially *De vanitate*, which call in question not only the fruits of human reason but occult sciences as well, and which go far beyond the doubts expressed in any earlier works. Agrippa's doubts, already expressed in 1519, must have matured gradually during the intervening years.

When, however, lacking any books from this period, one turns to Agrippa's numerous letters, one finds few evidences for this growth of doubt, and no hint at all of the emotional and explosive rejection of learning that was to follow. Most of the letters show Agrippa following with interest (though also with a bit of amusement) the alchemical enthusiasms of his friend Tyrius at Metz; interpreting prodigies on the model of similar instances in Roman history; studying the writings of Trithemius, Ptolemy, and the unidentified Marcus Damascenus; and giving and taking opinions on occult matters. Perhaps he shows a certain reluctance to commit himself decisively on occult questions during this period, but mention of such subjects is as frequent as ever. A letter of early 1524 shows Agrippa painfully aware of the contradictory doctrines and procedures of various astrological texts, but still eager to find from one of his correspondents an explanation which would resolve these difficulties.[30]

One may conjecture that one source of the crisis of 1526 was his study of the great religious controversy which was unfolding. From the time he went to Metz early in 1518, Agrippa had been reading avidly the works of Erasmus, Lefèvre d'Étaples, and Martin Luther. This reading would have stimulated the antirational element already present in his thought, for all three writers stressed the Bible and deprecated what they regarded as the excessive and contentious rationalism of the Schoolmen. Erasmus' ideal of *philosophia Christi* was that of a reasonable faith, but not of a rationalistic one. Luther, of course, would impel his reader to an even more extreme depreciation of all human learning, for although many have exaggerated his irrationalism, his own unbridled and intemperate statements are much to blame.[31] This influence was not the only root of Agrippa's

[29] Published at Geneva by Jacques Vivain, according to *Registres du Conseil de Genève* (12 vols.; Geneva, 1900-36), IX, 93n, and Henri Naef, *Les origines de la Réforme à Genève* (Geneva, 1936), p. 342.

[30] *Epist.* III, lvi.

[31] For Erasmus' position, see Roland H. Bainton, *Here I Stand: A Life of Martin Luther* (New York, 1950), p. 127. On Luther's rejection of human reason, *ibid.*, pp. 219-24, where his debt to late medieval thought (Occamism)

skeptical development, and in any case it was directed against rational theology rather than against the occult tradition of Hermes and the cabalists; but its general effect was adverse to any knowledge except that gained from the Bible.

Another source of the growth of skepticism in Agrippa's thought was some acquaintance, probably at second hand and perhaps in part through Erasmus' translation of Galen's *De optimo docendi genere*, with the ancient skeptical schools.[32] Skeptical viewpoints, based in part on knowledge of the ancient skeptics, were not unprecedented in Agrippa's generation. Although there does not appear to be any textual relationship to *De vanitate*, an important treatise by Giovanni Francesco Pico della Mirandola appeared not long before Agrippa's work and set forth a well-developed system of skeptical criticism that goes much further than Agrippa's treatise. This book, *Examen vanitatis doctrinae gentium, et veritatis christianae disciplinae*, shows first-hand knowledge of Sextus Empiricus, the principal text on ancient Pyrrhonist skepticism.[33] Like Agrippa, the younger Pico cast doubt on all merely human learning and by contrast praised the excellence of a Christian religion that rests on faith rather than on human reason.[34] Another contemporary publication which attacked human learning, not from an explicitly skeptical standpoint but from the standpoint of Christian antirationalism, was the *De vera philosophia* of Adriano, Cardinal Castellesi.[35]

---

is brought out, and pp. 253-56, 334. Note, however, that Gerhard Ritter has placed great limits on the importance of skeptical elements in Occamism; see his article, "Romantische und revolutionäre Elemente in der deutschen Theologie am Vorabend der Reformation," *Deutsche Vierteljahrsschrift für Literaturwissenschaft und Geistesgeschichte*, V (1927), 348-49. For a recent work which attributes the "Pyrrhonist crisis" of sixteenth-century thought largely to the unsettling effects of the Reformation, and which discusses Agrippa, see Richard H. Popkin, *The History of Scepticism from Erasmus to Descartes* (Assen, 1960).

[32] The early chapters of *De vanitate* contain references to the Pyrrhonists and Academics. For a full discussion of Agrippa's acquaintance with ancient skepticism, see Chapter Six above.

[33] Giovanni Francesco Pico della Mirandola, *Examen vanitatis doctrinae gentium, et veritatis Christianae disciplinae* (Mirandulae, 1520), Bk. I, ch. 2 (fol. VIIʳ).

[34] *Ibid.*, Bk. II, ch. 20 (fol. Lᵛ-LIʳ).

[35] *De vera philosophia libri IIII* (Coloniae, 1540), Bk. I, ch. 25 (fol. B7r-B8v); Bk. II, ch. 4-6 (fol. D7r-D8v). Castellesi stresses the need of reason for divine light and attributes the darkness of the human mind to sin; but textually, the argument is not like that of *De vanitate*.

Perhaps Agrippa knew one or both of these books; perhaps he knew neither. In any case, antirationalistic attacks on human learning, inspired in part by acquaintance with ancient skepticism, were being produced by others of the Nettesheimer's contemporaries.

Unhappy personal experience was yet another influence on Agrippa's development. The inability of all his learning to relieve the want of himself and his family from early 1526 onward must have created a feeling that his studies had been futile, as well as a bitterness against court life, both elements which are very pronounced in De vanitate.[36]

The year 1526 saw the full development of Agrippa's doubts concerning occultism, the maturation of his earlier depreciation of the powers of human reason, and the introduction of specific reference to the ancient skeptical schools. It was the year which produced not only two letters denouncing astrology but also two treatises which called the whole occult system into question. The first of these, Dehortatio gentilis theologiae, existed by 10 June 1526 and may date back to an earlier year. The composition of De vanitate took place in the summer of 1526 and was completed by 16 September, when Agrippa mentioned it in a letter to his friend Chapelain.[37] The tone of the little treatise and of the much larger book is quite consistent. Both of them elaborate Agrippa's earlier skepticism about the power of human reason. What is more, both of them indicate disillusionment with the occult sources to which he had once turned for refuge from intellectual anarchy; and both contain an appeal to simple faith in the words of the Bible.

There is nothing surprising about the denunciation of pagan philosophy in the Dehortatio. The idea that pagan philosophers were pernicious or at best superfluous in the study of Christian theology is a commonplace in almost all of Agrippa's earlier works and is the real basis of his denunciation of scholastic philosophy in both his published works and his private letters. But now the distinction which he once made between profane and sacred authors in Antiquity has disappeared. The little treatise opens by reproving certain friends for urging him to expound Hermes' Pimander, as he had earlier done at Pavia, rather than the Epistles of St. Paul, as he had proposed:

[36] Ritter, in Preussische Jahrbücher, CXLI, 312-14, regards this personal disappointment as a cause of his skepticism.
[37] For the Dehortatio, Epist. IV, xv; for the date of De vanitate, Epist. IV, xliv.

I marvel greatly and am astounded and angered that you, who have been baptized in the Gospel of Christ, who fulfill the priesthood in the church of Christ, after sacred baptism, after the sacred chrism, are seeking knowledge of God from the heathen, as if the Gospel were imperfect and it were pardonable to sin against the Holy Ghost; for whoever think they can get knowledge of God elsewhere than from the Gospel, they truly are those who attack the Holy Ghost, a blasphemy which is pardoned neither in this nor in the next world.[38]

All truth is in the Gospel, and pagan letters are at best superfluous and usually lead to destruction. Agrippa flatly denies any special value to the doctrines of Hermes or the Sibyls; and with them fall Plato, Plotinus, and Proclus, and all those who had benefited by the Neoplatonic myth of esoteric revelation.[39]

De vanitate goes much further. This treatise, the pungent invective and sometimes startling argumentation of which make it the one work of Agrippa which can still be read with enjoyment, contains four chief elements. The first is a full elaboration of his denial of the power of human reason to achieve truth. This denial, of course, is not wholly new, though its elaboration and development are. The second element is an attack on the occult sciences and their authorities. The third ingredient of Agrippa's declamation is a denunciation of abuses in contemporary society, both secular and ecclesiastical. The final element, which contains his effort to resolve the problems he has raised, is his appeal to the Bible and the grace of God as the only real source of truth. In itself, this element is no innovation, for it strongly marks works produced as early as his Italian period and in a sense is presupposed by his interest in the cabalistic interpretation of Scripture. But the statement has become much more complete than in his earlier writings.

The declamation certainly seems to mark the end of Agrippa's belief in the occult sciences. He directly recants the errors of *De occulta philosophia*, and this recantation even appears as an appendix to the printed edition of the latter work which he brought out in 1533: "But I while yet a youth wrote in a quite large volume three books of magical things, which I called *De occulta philosophia*, in

[38] *Dehortatio gentilis theologiae*, in *Opera*, II, 502: "miror admodum et stupeo, irascorque, vos qui in Evangelio Christi baptisati estis, qui in Ecclesia Christi sacerdotio fungimini, post sanctum baptismum, post sacrum chrisma, Dei cognitionem ab Ethnicis quaerere, quasi Evangelium mancum sit, et in Spiritum sanctum peccare sit venia: quicunque enim Dei notitiam aliunde quam ab Evangelio parandam putant, ii vere sunt qui Spiritum sanctum incessunt, quae blasphemia neque in hoc neque in futuro seculo remittitur."
[39] *Ibid.*, p. 505.

which whatever was then erroneous because of my curious youth, now, more cautious, I wish to retract by this recantation, for formerly I spent much time and goods on these vanities. At length I have gained this, that I know by what arguments one must dissuade others from this destruction." [40] Elsewhere in the same book he retracts his little treatise *In geomanticam disciplinam lectura*: "I also wrote a certain geomancy quite different from the others, but not less superstitious and fallacious, or, if you want me to say it, even mendacious." [41]

Agrippa then proceeds to destroy the authorities to which he once had appealed to escape the feebleness of human reason. Medieval writers on magical subjects had already come under attack in *De occulta philosophia* itself. *Dehortatio gentilis theologiae* had abolished the esoteric myth of Neoplatonism, and with it the special authority of the Hermetic writings and the Platonists and Neoplatonists. Now, in *De vanitate*, the authority of the Jewish Cabala also falls. After a careful study of Cabala, Agrippa says, he found it to be "nothing but a mere rhapsody of superstition." [42] If it had had any real merit, he felt, God would not so long have concealed it from His church, for the Holy Ghost had abandoned the synagogue and had come to teach Christians all truth. Agrippa notes with satisfaction that since the Incarnation of Christ, the Jews have been able to accomplish few if any miraculous works with divine names. He concludes:

And so this Cabala of the Jews is nothing but a certain most pernicious superstition, by which according to their own will they gather, divide, and transfer words and names, and letters placed here and there in Scripture . . . constructing from this [practice] words, conclusions, and parables from their own imaginings; they want to fit the words of God to them, defaming the Scriptures and saying that their imaginings arise from them; they calumniate the law of God and by impudently twisted computations of words, syllables, letters, and numbers, try to infer violent and blasphemous proofs of their perfidy.[43]

---

[40] *De vanitate*, ch. xlviii: "Verum de magicis scripsi ego iuuenis adhuc libros tres amplo satis volumine, quos de occulta philosophia nuncupaui, in quibus quicquid tunc per curiosam adolescentiam erratum est, nunc cautior hac palinodia recantatum volo, permultum enim temporis et rerum in his vanitatibus olim contriui. Tandem hoc profeci quod sciam quibus rationibus oporteat alios ab hac pernicie dehortari."

[41] *Ibid.*, ch. xiii: "scripsi et ego quandam Geomantiam ab alijs longe diuersam, sed non minus superstitiosam, fallacemque, aut si vultis dicam etiam mendacem."

[42] *Ibid.*, ch. xlvii: "non nisi meram superstitionis rapsodiam."

[43] *Ibid.*: "Est itaque nihil aliud haec Iudaeorum cabala, quam pernitiosissima quaedam superstitio, qua verba et nomina, et literas sparsim in scriptura positas

Having thus renounced the occult authorities, Agrippa felt no com-
punction in denouncing one by one the occult sciences as vain and
superstitious: geomancy, dicing, Pythagorean lots, astronomy and
astrology, physiognomy, metoposcopy, chiromancy, auspices, interpretation of dreams, prophetic madness, the various branches of
magic. The several arts of divination and prognostication suffer
particularly heavily. Surely, one would think, any later activity by
this man in the field of occult sciences must be the work of a charlatan and swindler.

Yet the break with the occult sciences was neither so sudden
nor so complete as a superficial comparison of the two major books
suggests. Agrippa's position on astrological prognostication had
long been wavering, even unfavorable. It is worth noting that Giovanni Pico della Mirandola, like Agrippa, had directed his attack
against astrology and divinatory arts, especially because they undermined the freedom of the human will. But Pico did not thus attack
those parts of the occult system which presented themselves as
means for the human mind to use in controlling the universe.[44]
Agrippa, who cites Pico's attack on astrology in his own chapter
on the subject, does not really go so far as Pico, who reduced the
influence of the heavens on the earth to a merely physical one.
Agrippa points to the conflicts among authorities, the lack of objective existence of astrological and astronomical constructions, the
ambiguity and subterfuges of those who practice astrology, and
the impiety of seeking to read in the stars a future which is determined not by celestial influences but by God. This latter idea, that
"in truth, neither do the stars govern a wise man, nor a wise man
the stars, but God governs both," [45] is as close as Agrippa comes to
a frontal assault on the doctrine that the stars influence terrestrial
events. His main line of argument is rather that even if such influences do exist, there is no certain science of them and probably
never can be one, and that anyway a desire to know the future
betokens an impious lack of trust in divine providence.

---

pro arbitrio suo colligunt, diuidunt, transferunt . . . sermones, inductiones, et
parabolas hinc inde ex proprijs fictionibus construentes, aptare illis volunt
eloquia dei, infamantes scripturas, et dicentes sua figmenta ex illis constare,
calumniantur legem dei, et per impudenter extortas supputationes dictionum,
syllabarum, literarum, numerorum tentant violentas et blasphemas perfidiae
suae inferre probationes."
    [44] Garin, *Giovanni Pico della Mirandola*, pp. 174-93.
    [45] *De vanitate*, ch. xxxi: ". . . Re vera nec astra sapienti nec sapiens astris,
sed vtrisque dominatur deus."

Even in the case of Cabala, Agrippa's break with his earlier views is neither so sudden nor so complete as one might think. He had long taught that Jewish Cabala was imperfect until the coming of Jesus Christ. And he still did not deny that God gave to Moses a secret and divinely revealed interpretation of the external teachings of the Old Testament.[46] He merely denied that the currently circulating Jewish writings were a true cabala. His efforts as late as 1532 to learn of new cabalistic discoveries of his friends in Italy [47] are not inconsistent with his dissatisfaction with what he already knew of Cabala. He had serious doubts, but he still did not exclude the possibility of a true cabala.

One more example of the persistence of his old views will be illuminating, especially as it leads out of the realms of prognostication and mystical exegesis and into the relations of man with the natural world. Agrippa's chapter on natural magic in De vanitate leaves that field of endeavor almost unscathed. Just like De occulta philosophia, the later work defines natural magic as "the highest peak of natural philosophy and its most absolute consummation." [48] It was professed not only by the Brahmans, Gymnosophists, and Zoroastrians, but also by the three Magi of the New Testament. It produces works seemingly marvellous but actually natural, though the ignorant masses think that they are miracles. Examples of its works are the growing of plants out of season, the causation of thunder, and transmutations of things. Of course Agrippa has reservations about natural magic, for all its authorities have mixed superstition with it; and its works are often impious and subject to serious misuse. The most serious abuses, however, occur in the other major subdivision of magic, the ceremonial, which consists of goetia (necromancy and witchcraft) and theurgy. These arts depend on the summoning of spirits, a most dangerous practice even if one calls on good spirits, for good angels rarely appear because they are obedient to God, while evil spirits often disguise their true nature and lure the rash conjurer to his destruction.[49] Already

[46] De triplici ratione cognoscendi Deum, in Opera, II, 488; De vanitate, ch. xlvii.
[47] Agrippa to Bernardus Paltrinus, Bonn, 13 November 1532, Epist. VII, xv.
[48] De vanitate, ch. xlii: "summum philosophiae naturalis apicem eiusque absolutissimam consummationem." Cf. De occulta philosophia, Bk. I, ch. ii, p. ii: "Haec perfectissima summaque scientia, haec altior sanctiorque philosophia, haec denique totius nobilissimae philosophiae absoluta consummatio."
[49] De vanitate, ch. xlv-xlvi.

in the 1510 version of *De occulta philosophia*, the one he sent to Trithemius, Agrippa showed keen awareness of the admixture of superstition in the occult arts. Indeed, his avowed aim in writing the book was to purify magic by turning away from its present depraved and impure state, and leading it back to correct and holy principles.[50] Thus even in this case, the roots of Agrippa's doubts extend back to his earliest years, while on the other hand, his great declamation does not utterly destroy (in this case, it hardly does more than mildly criticize) his earlier teaching. Perhaps something could yet be salvaged from occult arts, though even if it could, it would be relatively unimportant, since no science, occult or not, can make any significant contribution to man's beatitude, which depends not on a rich intellect but on a virtuous will.[51]

Agrippa's subsequent work in the occult arts (and one must never forget that his studies and researches continued through every period of his life) was nevertheless an effort at such a salvage operation. A letter written about a year after the completion of *De vanitate* suggests that mere rejection of occult sciences did not satisfy Agrippa, that he shrank back from the destruction which his critical thought had accomplished. He warned his correspondent not to be misled as others had been:

Oh, how many writings are read about the insuperable power of the magical art, about the prodigious images of the astrologers . . . which are all found to be vain, fictitious, and false as often as they are practiced to the letter. And yet they are related and written by great and weighty philosophers and holy men. . . . Indeed it would be impious to believe that, having taken pains, they wrote lies. Therefore there is another sense than what is given in the words, a sense concealed by various mysteries, but up to now expounded openly by none of the masters, which sense I doubt whether anyone can attain solely by the mere reading of books without a skilled and trusty master, unless he be illuminated by a divine spirit, a thing which is granted to very few; and so, many strive in vain who pursue these most recondite secrets of nature, applying their mind to a mere course of reading.[52]

[50] See Würzburg, Universitätsbibliothek, MS. M.ch.q.50, fols. 1ʳ-2ᵛ, comprising the dedication to Trithemius of Sponheim and Bk. I, ch. 1 of the text. In the printed editions, many of these materials appear in an expanded dedicatory epistle: fol. aa3r-v.

[51] *De vanitate*, ch. i.

[52] Agrippa to Aurelius ab Aquapendente, Lyons, 24 September 1527, printed in *De occulta philosophia*, p. cccxlvi, and with minor textual variants in *Epist.* V, xiv: "O quanta leguntur scripta de inexpugnabili magicae artis potentia, de prodigiosis astrologorum imaginibus . . . quae omnia comperiuntur uana, ficta et falsa quoties ad literam practicantur. Atque tamen traduntur ista, scribun-

A key exists to these secrets, Agrippa adds; it is the human soul. But how the spirit in man can unlock these secrets is a matter not to be committed to a letter, he darkly concludes, but only to be revealed by word of mouth. A letter written later in 1527 further explains that the key to the occult sciences is the intellect, which can achieve the deification of man, but only if it is freed from the bonds of the flesh by a mystical ascent, a death to the world and to the flesh which Agrippa can only indicate to others, since he has never achieved it himself.[53] His final refuge, then, is mysticism, as is also clear from the later chapters of De vanitate. Like Nicholas of Cusa, he turned to a mystical experience which he himself had never personally known.[54]

Yet the restless mind of Cornelius Agrippa did not stop with mysticism. The real philosophical justification of his continued alchemical experiments, of his unceasing search for new books of Cabala and natural magic, was not just a confidence that there must be in the works of such distinguished authors a deeper truth visible only to the mind illumined by mystical experience. Even in the midst of his most critical passages, there are materials for an attempt at reconstruction on an intellectual plane. Agrippa had really never denied the validity of sensory knowledge in theory, although he felt that the passions of the soul and man's liability to err made it unreliable in practice. His real skepticism concerned rather the jump from sensory knowledge of singulars to the higher levels of ratiocination.[55] Thus in attacking the various occult arts of prognostication, he does not deny that there may be some factual truth in their predictions. Rather, his favorite charge against such arts as chiromancy (or palmistry) is that their defenders can allege no solid reasons but only fortuitous experiences to uphold their claims.[56]

---

turque a magnis grauissimisque philosophis et sanctis uiris. . . . Quin imo credere impium esset, illos data opera scripsisse mendacia: Alius est ergo sensus quam literis traditur, isque uariis obductus mysteriis, sed hactenus a nullo magistrorum palam explicatus, quem nescio si quis sine perito fidoque magistro sola librorum lectione possit adsequi, nisi fuerit diuino numine illustratus quod datur paucissimis: ideoque in uacuum currunt multi qui haec secretissima naturae arcana prosequuntur, ad nudam lectionis seriem referentes animum."

[53] Agrippa to Aurelius ab Aquapendente, Lyons, 19 November 1527, printed in De occulta philosophia, pp. cccxlvii-cccxlviii, and as Epist. V, xix.

[54] Rudolf Stadelmann, Vom Geist des ausgehenden Mittelalters: Studien zur Geschichte der Weltanschauung von Nicolaus Cusanus bis Sebastian Franck (Halle, 1929), p. 102.

[55] De vanitate, ch. vii.   [56] Ibid., ch. xxxv.

Agrippa had been equally aware of this fact when he wrote *De occulta philosophia* in 1510, for his discussion of the occult properties of things stated flatly that knowledge of such properties depended on experience rather than on reason. Such statements were not really unusual or contradictory in a writer on occult subjects. Many important writers on magic had taken precisely the same position. Indeed, magic broke most sharply with the medieval scientific tradition precisely in this respect, that it ascribed discovery of truth to experience rather than to *a priori* reasoning from general principles.[57] By the time he wrote *De vanitate*, Agrippa argued that any higher patterns of explanation, in the occult arts or in any science, are merely arbitrary constructs of the human mind without any objective existence. This is true of the various astronomical cycles, epicycles, signs, and houses; it is also true of metaphysical concepts.[58] Real but possibly erroneous sensory knowledge and arbitrary intellectual patterns: after all has been said, these still survive the general intellectual wreckage produced by *De vanitate*.

How, then, could Agrippa have excused his continued practice of the occult arts? One way, shown above, was the vague claim that a mystically illumined mind could see the real truth under the apparent inconsistencies. Another way was empiricism or authoritarianism, for they could be much alike: passive acceptance of brute fact as discovered by his alchemical experiments and daily observations, or passive acceptance of the reports of others concerning their discoveries. That he accepted many ridiculous tales in his final recension of *De occulta philosophia* is not surprising, for simple empiricism and skepticism do not offer an adequate basis for criticism of fact. Michel de Montaigne, a far greater skeptic than Agrippa, used many of the same anecdotes (and probably believed or half-believed many of them) that appear in the Nettesheimer's writings. A third way of justifying his occult practices, even in their theoretical aspects, could have been Agrippa's own doctrine of the arbitrariness of mental constructs. All patterns of interpreta-

---

[57] *De occulta philosophia*, Bk. I, ch. x, p. xiiii: "longa experientia, plus quam rationis indagine. . . ." This passage is also in the Würzburg MS., Bk. I, ch. 4 (fol. 5v). For medieval examples, Lynn Thorndike, *A History of Magic and Experimental Science* (8 vols.; New York, 1923-58), II, 535-48 (Albertus Magnus); II, 854-55 (Arnald of Villanova); II, 906 (Pietro d'Abano); V, 104-5 (Pietro Pomponazzi). Garin, *Medioevo e Rinascimento*, makes this point repeatedly: pp. 158-60, 164-65, 185-86, 188-90.

[58] *De vanitate*, ch. xxx, liii.

tion, he teaches, are artificial and arbitrary, the magical ones no more so than any others. So one may adopt them provisionally as long as they are useful.

It is precisely on this utilitarian basis that Agrippa defends magical arts in a letter of 13 February 1528 to a friend at the French court, probably the royal physician Chapelain. Natural sciences, metaphysical arts, and occult devices do exist, he says, whereby one can licitly defend kingdoms, increase wealth, and cure sickness. Similarly in his dedication of Book One of *De occulta philosophia* to Hermann von Wied, dated January 1531, after admitting that even in its revised form the book contains much that is not true, he adds that it nevertheless contains many useful and necessary things. His preface to the reader justifies its publication partly by fears of an offensive and imperfect pirated edition but also because many of the things that it contains are useful for overcoming magical spells and for the conservation of health, honor, and fortune. He urges his readers to accept what they find useful and reject the rest, for he himself merely relates the opinions of others and does not approve all that the book contains.[59] What Agrippa is really approaching with his pragmatic attitude toward conjectures and empirical facts is an adumbration of the idea of hypothesis and its subjection to the test of facts, a procedure that characterizes the methodology of modern science. He has, of course, no clear awareness of this principle, and there is no hint of either controlled experimentation or quantitative expression; but his mind is tending in this direction. He will accept the data and the general principles of the magical arts so long as he finds them useful and consonant with his own experience.

This attempt to trace the movement of Agrippa's mind would not be complete without some mention of the restlessness of his thought. No path seemed too much out of the way to be explored, even though Agrippa might on another occasion develop its opposite just as fully. For instance, he could extol the excellences of women in *De sacramento matrimonii* and especially in *De nobilitate et praecellentia foeminei sexus*, and yet could cry out against the fickleness and gullibility of the sex during his troubles with Louise of Savoy

[59] Agrippa to Chapelain, Paris, 12 February 1528, printed in *De occulta philosophia*, pp. cccxlviii-ccclii, and as *Epist.* V, xxvi. See especially *De occulta philosophia*, p. cccl. The dedication to Archbishop Hermann von Wied is on fols. a4v-aa5r [*sic;* should be aa4v-aa5r] of *De occulta philosophia* and also in *Epist.* VI, xiii; the preface, on fol. aa2r-v and also in *Epist.* VI, xii.

at Lyons from 1526 to 1528, and again when he fell from the favor of Margaret of Austria in 1530.

The most striking example of the flexibility of his mind, however, appears in what one might call his minority report on the powers of the human mind. Most of the statements where he seems to exalt the power of human reason are not really rationalistic, for he is referring to the power of the divinely illuminated mind, not to native reason. But in one work, his *In artem brevem Raymundi Lullii commentaria*, he seems to grant almost unlimited powers to the mind of man. By the use of the Lullian art, he claims, man can easily and quickly master all sciences. This art judges all sciences and can attain all knowledge, even without the aid of Scripture.[60] In illustrating its powers, Agrippa undertakes logical proof of even the most abstruse dogmas of religion, for example, that God contains a coeternal spirit.[61] The mind, he argues, is perfectly justified in holding a given proposition because it seems more pleasant and reasonable than its opposite.[62]

If taken as a purely rationalistic treatise, this Lullian commentary appears to represent the earliest stage of Agrippa's intellectual development, before growing doubt had driven him first to occult traditions and then to the near-despair which his works of 1526 show. Logically, this commentary would then antedate even *De occulta philosophia* or the cabalistic lectures at Dôle. Unfortunately, there is no sure way of dating the Lullian treatise very closely. Its dedication to Jean de Laurencin probably occurred about 1517 and certainly no later than 1523. But the book itself could be considerably older than the dedication; and Agrippa's contact with that Andreas Canterius whom in the preface he calls his teacher in the Lullian art occurred early in his life, probably while he was still an undergraduate in the University of Cologne.[63]

[60] Dedication of *In artem brevem Raymundi Lullii commentaria* to Jean de Laurencin, n.p., n.d., in *Opera*, II, 332.

[61] *In artem brevem Raymundi Lullii commentaria*, printed in Raymundus Lullius, *Opera* (Argentinae, 1598), p. 913.

[62] *Ibid.*, p. 839.

[63] For the presence of Andreas Canterius or Canter at Cologne during Agrippa's undergraduate years in that university, see *Opus epistolarum Des. Erasmi Roterodami*, ed. P. S. Allen [and H. M. Allen and H. W. Garrod] (12 vols.; 1906-58), I, 125-26 (No. 32). Cf. the anonymous *Die Cronica van der hilliger stat van Coellen 1499*, in *Die Chroniken der deutschen Städte*, ed. C. Hegel (Leipzig, 1877), XIV, 876-77, and also Karl Krafft and Wilhelm Crecelius, eds., "Mittheilungen über Alexander Hegius und seine Schüler,

Yet an extremely early date for the commentary may not, after all, be very important even if it could be established by more than conjecture. From a very early age, from the very opening of his surviving correspondence in 1507, Agrippa was already deeply involved in the study of magic; and Renaissance magic, as the present chapter has already shown, was antithetical to rationalism in its intellectual tendencies. Recent studies have suggested that the Lullian *ars* was far more than merely a system of logic and mnemonics to be applied in a rationalistic way. To Lull himself, it was a personal gift from divine revelation. And it applied to all fields of study.[64] Although Agrippa's discussion of the Lullian art may seem to be an excursion into a rationalism quite foreign to his usual standpoint, Lullism was not purely rationalistic. It claimed to be founded on a divinely revealed insight into the fundamental structure of nature.[65] And in a way not fully clear to modern scholarship, Lullism was intimately associated with astrology, medicine, and even alchemy.[66] Hence although Lullism was indeed a rationalistic system of thought, it also served as a possible route to mastery of the basically nonrationalistic occult sciences; and no matter whether Agrippa really did write his commentary in earliest youth or as late as the early 1520's, his lifelong interest in Lull's thought was probably the product of his lifelong interest in magic. The contrast between the rationalistic tone of his commentary and his more usual postion on the powers of reason is not quite so sharp as it seems. Lull claimed to offer a key to the mastery of all learning, especially astrology and medicine. Agrippa's excursion into the intricacies of this system is further illustration of his effort to turn away from the dominant forms of science and to explore alternative forms in order to restore his dwindling trust in human

sowie andere gleichzeitige Gelehrte, aus den Werken des Johannes Butzbach, Priors des Benedictiner-Klosters am Laacher See," *Zeitschrift des bergischen Geschichtsvereins*, VII (1871), 273-75.

[64] Frances A. Yates, "The Art of Ramon Lull: An Approach to It Through Lull's Theory of the Elements," *Journal of the Warburg and Courtauld Institutes*, XVII (1954), 117; and two works by Paolo Rossi, *Clavis universalis: Arti mnemoniche e logica combinatoria da Lullo a Leibniz* (Milan, 1960), pp. 41-45, and "The Legacy of Ramon Lull in Sixteenth-Century Thought," *Medieval and Renaissance Studies*, V (1961), 182-213. Rossi also notes (*Clavis universalis*, pp. 27-30) that Peter of Ravenna, whom Agrippa probably heard lecture at Cologne, was an important figure in Renaissance study of mnemonics, though more in the "Ciceronian" than the Lullian tradition.

[65] Yates, *loc. cit.*, 155-58.   [66] *Ibid.*, pp. 118-32.

learning. Just as his interest in occult arts survived the pessimistic mood of 1526, so also his interest in Lull did not disappear despite his warnings against the *ars* in *De vanitate*,[67] for he preserved the Lullian commentary and in 1533 published it.

Finally, one must not forget that Agrippa lived in the age of humanism, of enthusiasm for ancient literature, and that he spent some seven years in Italy, the center of humanistic activities. He avowed to Erasmus that he was a loyal follower of Erasmian learning. Some of the optimistic trust of the age in the value of ancient literature (*bonae literae*) is reflected in his writings. On two occasions, he urged students to study classical letters and to return to the sources of Roman law, disregarding modern (that is, medieval) legal commentaries. In 1518, sending advice to the young Claudius Cantiuncula, he sounded very optimistic, urging his friend not to confine himself to one field of study but, trusting in the powers of the mind, to master the whole of human learning. But in a second letter to the same friend, Agrippa made it clear that while law and humane letters were praiseworthy studies, they also had their dangers and were in the last analysis vain and perishable in comparison with the study of sacred letters, to which he strongly urged his young acquaintance.[68] Thus even in this exchange of 1518, his optimism concerning humane letters was subservient to a stress on sacred letters.

Like so many of the northern humanists, Agrippa found the best of the *bonae literae* in the Bible. Perhaps the highest recommendation of literary endeavor which he could make was that a good mastery of the three languages, Latin, Greek, and Hebrew, was necessary for a thorough mastery of the Bible and so for the education of a theologian.[69] Grammar alone among human sciences, he said, is useful for understanding of Scripture; and even in this one science of grammar, the danger of pride and of willful misinterpretation of the Bible is great. Even it can be praised only when

---

[67] *De vanitate*, ch. ix.

[68] Agrippa to Ioannes ———, Antwerp, 28 January 1529, *Epist.* V, lxv. The exchange with Cantiuncula occurred in 1518. See *Epist.* II, xii-xiv. Another instance of such advice to a student occurred when in 1522 Agrippa urged a youth to study languages, especially Greek, to read good authors, especially Pliny and Plutarch, but above all to study Scripture ("sacras literas tibi consulo omnibus anteponendas, sine quibus omne reliquum studium tuum vanum erit, et forte etiam noxium"): Agrippa ad Amicum, Geneva, 7 October 1522, *Epist.* III, xxxi.

[69] *De beatissimae Annae monogamia*, fols. K5r-K6v.

it is confined to its most elementary stage, the understanding of a text. If one passes on to a study of elegance of diction and a critique of the language, grammar becomes like all the other human sciences: vain, uncertain, leading to perdition.[70]

The general development of Agrippa's mind, then, proceeded not by a sudden intellectual revolution in the mid-1520's but in three stages. His early position, as represented especially by *De occulta philosophia*, already doubted the power of unaided human reason to grasp reality but found refuge from intellectual anarchy by an appeal to the wisdom of an occult Antiquity, a wisdom that came ultimately from divine revelation. The second stage in his intellectual odyssey was the growth of doubts about the validity of those occultist writings in which he had first acknowledged ancient wisdom. Parallel to this growth was the further maturation of his early doubts about the validity of human reason. These two movements of his thought found their chief expression in his works of 1526, especially *De vanitate*. But Agrippa recoiled from the glimpse he had had of utter intellectual anarchy. So the third stage, an attempt at reconstruction, is evident even in *De vanitate* and also in some of his later writings. His attempt at reconstruction followed three lines. Most prominent of these was his fideistic appeal to the pure and unadulterated Gospel as the only source of truth. This use of religion to solve intellectual problems was a consistent practice of his. Religion—that is, the invocation of the one supreme God and of lesser deities or *numina*—formed the concluding and climactic portion of *De occulta philosophia*.[71] Religion, now more strictly limited to the Christian Scriptures, continued to provide his chief solution to the search for truth. The second way of escape from skepticism likewise made a religious factor the key. This second way was the doctrine that magical writings contained a deeper meaning open only to the initiate or to the man whose mind has been illumined by an act of God's grace. The third way was an attitude of which Agrippa himself surely did not see the full implications. By continuing to uphold the reality of sense perception of singulars, by teaching that all intellectual abstractions are equally

---

[70] *De vanitate*, ch. iii. For the admission that grammar does have some value, see *Apologia*, in *Opera*, II, 287.

[71] This is true of the manuscript version of 1510 as well as of the printed form, despite the reshuffling and rearrangement of many other elements during the revision of the text.

arbitrary, and by hinting that one might in practice follow any abstract system as long as it met the pragmatic test of experience and utility, Agrippa was unconsciously moving toward the epistemological doctrines underlying modern science: scientific hypothesis and its subjection to the test of facts. Only the single treatise on Lull's *ars* fails to fit into this pattern of development; and it is almost certainly an annex to his probing of the occult sciences.

As far as Agrippa himself was concerned, the only fixed point of certainty in his insecure intellectual world was his constant recurrence to the action of divine grace as the means of restoring the powers which man had lost through the sin of Adam. Different though they are on a thousand points, both *De occulta philosophia* and *De vanitate* end on the same theme: man's need for illumination through grace, either by direct experience of mystical ecstasy or (in the later treatise) by simple faith in the unadulterated Word of God.

CHAPTER NINE

AGRIPPAN MAGIC AND
RENAISSANCE CULTURE

To the men of his own generation, Agrippa's chief title to fame
lay in his reputation for deep learning in the occult sciences—that is,
in all those many fields of pseudo-science to which he and his contemporaries applied the term *magia*, or magic. Doubtless this very
fact explains why the thought of Agrippa has been so little studied,
despite his fame in his own and the succeeding century, and despite
the wide dispersion of his books, both in the Latin original and in
translations into all of the major western European languages. To
engage seriously in the study of a magician might almost seem to
take seriously the absurd pseudo-sciences in which he specialized.
Historians, who ought to know better, have been unable to rid
themselves of a sense of embarrassment when faced with magical
phenomena. Even those of them who have been intellectually honest enough to acknowledge the importance of magic in ancient,
medieval, and Renaissance culture [1] have often salved their modern

[1] Notably Lynn Thorndike, *The Place of Magic in the Intellectual History
of Europe* (New York, 1905), pp. 11-36, and throughout his vast *History of
Magic and Experimental Science* (8 vols.; New York, 1923-58).

consciences by hastening to show the undeniably intimate relationship between magic and those more respectable pursuits which eventually led toward modern science.

Yet this attitude is the result of judging past ages by modern criteria. Magic was important in medieval culture, and even more important in Renaissance culture. That fact in itself necessitates careful, unblushing study of magic as a historical phenomenon in its own right, whether or not it led western mankind toward the great scientific advances of the seventeenth and later centuries. Forgetting that medieval and Renaissance magic involved not just witchcraft and sorcerers' pacts with devils but also a whole concept of the world and of the relation of man to the world, those historians of thought who have not judged magic solely as the threshold of modern science have engaged in a virtual conspiracy of silence about its existence. It is as if the religious taboos which frightened most medieval and Renaissance men away from open consideration of magic still weighed on the consciences of present-day historians.[2] Agrippa the Doubter, the destructive critic of his age, has found a deservedly important place in the works of modern intellectual historians,[3] for the categories of modern intellectual history offer a respectable, established, even dignified position to those who carped at the remnants of medieval culture. But Agrippa the Credulous, whom Jean Bodin dubbed the "master Sorcerer," and the hostile Jesuit, Martin Del Rio, called the "Arch-Magician," [4] what honorable place does the history of modern European thought have for him?

And yet, the belief in magic was omnipresent in the intellectual world of the Middle Ages and the Renaissance. As Lynn Thorndike capably demonstrated a half-century ago, the magical element was already extremely prominent in the Greco-Roman heritage on which modern civilization was built. The elder Pliny, despite his avowed intent of being critical of magic, also despite that enthusiasm for direct personal observation that cost him his life, pro-

[2] Eugenio Garin, *Medioevo e Rinascimento: Studi e ricerche* (Bari, 1954), pp. 172-73.

[3] Notably in Rudolf Stadelmann, *Vom Geist des ausgehenden Mittelalters: Studien zur Geschichte der Weltanschauung von Nicolaus Cusanus bis Sebastian Franck* (Halle, 1929); Hiram Haydn, *The Counter-Renaissance* (New York, 1950); and Ernst Cassirer, *Das Erkenntnisproblem in der Philosophie und Wissenschaft der neueren Zeit* (2nd ed.; 3 vols.; Berlin, 1911-23).

[4] D. P. Walker, *Spiritual and Demonic Magic from Ficino to Campanella* (London, 1958), pp. 174, 183.

duced in his *Natural History* a work which was not only "the best single example of the science of the classical world," [5] but also a rich mine of attitudes and information (and misinformation) from which writers on magical topics throughout the Middle Ages (none more often than Agrippa) drew much of their knowledge. The best minds of the Middle Ages continued to accept the ideas and practices of the various magical sciences without serious question. They sometimes, perhaps even usually, wagged their heads in disapproval over certain magical practices that seemed to endanger religion or morality; but they did not deny the reality, the effectiveness, the importance of magic. This was true not only of uninspired compilers of encyclopedias who heaped up uncriticized ancient materials for use by barbarous centuries, but also of men of high talent. Even the most creative minds of the flourishing, sophisticated, urbanized culture of the High Middle Ages, men as great as Albertus Magnus, St. Thomas Aquinas, and Dante, believed fully in the sympathetic bonds linking all reality, the hierarchy of being, the existence of occult qualities, the astral influences, the action of good and bad demons, as described in books of magic. Albertus Magnus, in fact, was a prolific writer on all sorts of magical questions.[6] His writings, both the genuine ones and the numerous forgeries that passed under his name, were one of the most important of medieval magical sources. Agrippa, himself brought up in Albert's own Uni-

[5] Thorndike, *Place of Magic*, p. 38.

[6] Thorndike, *History of Magic*, II, 578-92, 692-706. On Aquinas, *ibid.*, II, 607-9. As Walker, *Spiritual and Demonic Magic*, pp. 43-44, 137, 214-15, shows clearly, Aquinas in his genuine works disapproved strongly of certain magical practices, such as belief in astrological determinism and the use of talismans and incantations that might be directed to demons. But his writings upheld belief in the influence of the stars on man, saving only man's freedom of will. And Aquinas, while strictly forbidding worship (*latria*) of planetary angels, in at least one place authorized veneration of them, on the order of the cult of saints (*dulia*). Thus when later writers like Ficino and Campanella cited Aquinas in defense of their magical writings, they were not wholly distorting his thought. Furthermore, in the Renaissance the authorship of *De fato*, which submits even the mind of man to astral determinism, was regularly attributed to Aquinas. Agrippa, *De occulta philosophia libri tres* (Coloniae, 1533), Bk. III, ch. xv, defends belief in astral intelligences on the authority of Aquinas, Albert, and Scotus, as well as on the authority of Augustine, Jerome, Origen, Eusebius, and Nicholas of Cusa, among others. He also cited *De fato* as a work of Aquinas. See *De occulta philosophia*, Bk. II, ch. xxxv (a citation also made in the earlier manuscript version of *De occulta philosophia*: Würzburg, Universitätsbibliothek, MS. M.ch.q.50, Bk. II, ch. 4). On Aquinas see also Charles Edward Hopkin, *The Share of Thomas Aquinas in the Growth of the Witchcraft Delusion* (Philadelphia, 1940), especially pp. 174-84.

versity of Cologne, not only cited Albert repeatedly but also explicitly stated that he had studied Albert's works from an early age.[7] The Renaissance continued unbroken this traditional belief in the occult sciences. Despite all the humanistic brag of rediscovering ancient sources of wisdom, despite also the humanists' "conspiracy of silence" about their continued dependence on medieval sources,[8] the traditions of medieval magic lived on with "nothing else than a continuous growth." [9] The same medieval magical authorities continued to furnish the details for the magicians' books.[10] Agrippa, for example, still had to draw heavily from authors like Alkindi, Avicenna, Peter of Abano, and that greatest of all medieval manuals of magic, *Picatrix*, as well as from more respectable medieval sources like Roger Bacon and Albertus Magnus. Even Marsilio Ficino, whose cautious treatises on magic made a serious attempt to avoid the old, demon-invoking type of occultism, and whose humanistic activities, especially as translator of most of the corpus of Hermetic and Neoplatonic writings, did contribute really significant new sources, still took many details from the same old authors.[11] There was a direct continuity of traditions in magic throughout the medieval and Renaissance periods, right on down into the seventeenth century.

Indeed, so far was medieval magic from perishing in the Renaissance, that some intellectual historians have concluded that magic became more important, not less so, in the later epoch. From being an unspoken and often unacknowledged element in the mental world of European men, magic during the Renaissance stepped forth into the light of day as a central element of culture; and the Renaissance

[7] Agrippa to Theodoricus Wichwael, Bishop of Cyrene, Metz, 6 February 1519, in Lyons, Bibliothèque Municipale, MS. No. 48, fol. 32r (printed as *Epistolarum Liber II*, xix, in Agrippa's *Opera* [2 vols.; Lugduni, n.d.], II, 736-39. Henceforth this correspondence is cited as *Epist.*).

[8] Thorndike, *History of Magic*, V, 3-4, makes such a charge.

[9] Will-Erich Peuckert, *Pansophie: Ein Versuch zur Geschichte der weissen und schwarzen Magie* (Stuttgart, 1936), p. vi; cf. p. 52, where the magical traditions of Hellenism are said to extend "in einer niemals unterbrochenen Kette bis in das 16. Jahrhundert."

[10] Garin, *Medioevo e Rinascimento*, pp. 170-72.

[11] Walker, *Spiritual and Demonic Magic*, pp. 36-37. Peuckert, *op. cit.*, pp. 54-69, demonstrates that *Picatrix* and other medieval magical works mentioned in 1456 by Dr. Johann Hartlieb, court physician of Bavaria, were still the sources used by Trithemius a half-century later, and by Agrippa yet another quarter-century after Trithemius. Peuckert (pp. 69-77) also shows that Albertus Magnus as far back as the thirteenth century had also used the same sources, recipes, and practices, which were ultimately Hellenistic in origin and were transmitted by Hebrew and Arabic authors.

marks not a stage in the abandonment of the occult in favor of pure reason, but a re-emphasis of the magical world view.[12] Thorndike has observed with some puzzlement that in the sixteenth century "there was less objection to the word magic and more approving use of it than in the preceding centuries." [13] This is undeniably true. The only danger for a historian of culture is that he may misinterpret the fact simply as evidence of retrogression and decadence, whereas in reality the world view promoted by study of magic marked an important step forward in the growth of late medieval civilization.[14]

The truth is that the occult sciences—that is, magic—formed a nearly omnipresent, often a dominant, part of the intellectual baggage of Agrippa's century. Belief in astrology, witchcraft, divination, alchemy, Cabala, and a host of other "special sciences" within the general field of magic was well-nigh universal. It was the Renaissance, not earlier or later ages, which gave rise to the legend of the arch-magician, Faust. Nearly all of the culturally significant figures of the late fifteenth and sixteenth centuries showed interest in one or more of the occult sciences. Marsilio Ficino, leader of the Florentine Neoplatonists, wrote voluminously on magic. In fact, his book *De vita*, especially the portion entitled *De vita coelitus comparanda*, constitutes an attempt to reform magic along lines that would make it less distasteful to pious souls like the author himself, chiefly by presenting a system of magic that did not overtly depend on demonic forces for its effects.[15] One of the most significant early attacks on astrology, a treatise probably known to Agrippa as early as 1509, was the *Adversus astrologiam* of Giovanni

---

[12] Garin, *Medioevo e Rinascimento*, pp. 151-52, 167-69, 171-73, 190-91.

[13] Thorndike, *History of Magic*, V, 13.

[14] *Ibid.*, V, 3-14, lays much stress on the decadent, uncreative character of the Renaissance (or, as he prefers to call it, "the classical reaction"). Certainly there were decadent elements in the culture of the fourteenth, fifteenth, and sixteenth centuries; but the whole concept of decadence needs to be more satisfactorily related to the concept of Renaissance. In any case, Eugenio Garin in three brilliant essays has shown that the "decadence" of the Renaissance points ahead to the brilliant future of post-Renaissance culture, and that the growth of magic is intimately related to the general intellectual movement of the age. See his "Interpretazioni del Rinascimento," "Magia ed astrologia nella cultura del Rinascimento," and "Considerazioni sulla magia," in *Medioevo e Rinascimento*, pp. 90-107, 150-69, and 170-91, respectively.

[15] Walker, *Spiritual and Demonic Magic*, Part I, *passim*, especially pp. 30-35, 40-43, 53; but in reality, Ficino surreptitiously continued use of a magic involving good planetary demons: *ibid.*, pp. 48-53.

Pico della Mirandola.[16] But even this author, for all his sharp and telling criticism of the pseudo-science of astrology, did not deny all celestial influence on man. Nor did Pico deny the magical powers of man. Far from it! He regarded the magical powers of the soul using incantations and other methods as the very confirmation of his belief in man's dignity. Perhaps the capital error of judicial astrology, in his eyes, was that it made the lower (the material celestial bodies) rule over the higher being (the nonmaterial soul). Pico's writings are rich in magical themes, extending far beyond his use of cabalism as a method of achieving free exegesis of the Bible.[17]

But the Florentine leaders, Ficino and Pico, are only two of the many examples who could be cited to show the prominence of the magical world view, and even magical practices, in the culture of Agrippa's lifetime. In the circle of Protestant Reformers, while Martin Luther was most dubious about astrology and would accept no element of astral influence except the idea that God sometimes gives portents of catastrophe through signs in the heavens, Philip Melanchthon was notoriously credulous, and Georg Spalatin (whom Agrippa later called "my old friend" [18]) was active in hunting up prophetic utterances and portents for use in polemical Reformation treatises.[19] The popes of the Renaissance, even as late as the pontificate of Urban VIII in 1628,[20] frequently employed astrologers. Other important Renaissance figures who shared the fascination of the age with occult subjects included, to name but a few, the medical reformer, Paracelsus;[21] the miscreant philosopher, Pietro Pomponazzi;[22] and, to take just one later figure, the political philosopher, Jean Bodin.[23] Among the contemporary figures who influenced Agrippa's thought, magical elements are prominent in the

---

[16] Theodoricus Wichwael to Agrippa, Cologne, 29 November 1509, *Epist.* I, xxi.

[17] Walker, *Spiritual and Demonic Magic*, pp. 54-56; Eugenio Garin, *Giovanni Pico della Mirandola: Vita e dottrina* (Florence, 1937), pp. 167-204; Cassirer, *op. cit.*, I, 541.

[18] *Epist.* VII, xiii.

[19] Aby Warburg, "Heidnisch-antike Weissagung in Wort und Bild zu Luthers Zeiten," *Gesammelte Schriften* (2 vols.; Leipzig, 1932), II, 490-535.

[20] Walker, *Spiritual and Demonic Magic*, pp. 203-7.

[21] Walter Pagel, *Paracelsus: An Introduction to Philosophical Medicine in the Era of the Renaissance* (Basel, 1958), pp. 37-39, 62-65, 111.

[22] Walker, *Spiritual and Demonic Magic*, pp. 107-11; Thorndike, *History of Magic*, V, 98-110.

[23] This despite Bodin's bitter attacks on magic: Walker, *Spiritual and Demonic Magic*, pp. 171-77.

thought of Trithemius of Sponheim, Johann Reuchlin, Agostino and Paolo Ricci, Francesco Giorgi of Venice, Cardinal Egidio di Viterbo, Pietro Galatino, Symphorien Champier, Ludovico Lazzarelli, and even, for all his caution, Jacques Lefèvre d'Étaples, who sharply attacked the folly and impiety of certain magical writers, but who had himself committed the indiscretion of writing (but not publishing) a treatise *De magia naturali* in the early 1490's.[24] Erasmus stood almost alone among the influential men of Agrippa's lifetime in his doubting attitude toward the occult sciences. Although in 1531 he did refer a priest named Andreas to Agrippa for information about occult sciences, his own attitude, according to this same priest, was to belittle natural magic as "smoke, or mere words." Erasmus was not quite so skeptical about alchemy, though he regarded it as ambiguous and difficult to master.[25] But his reserved attitude was far from typical of the age. Leaving aside even the "purified" or philosophized magic of respectable authors, there was by mid-sixteenth century a whole subterranean literature of hard-boiled, demon-conjuring magic, much of it centered round the pseudo-Agrippan *Fourth Book of Occult Philosophy*.[26]

Not all of these individuals practiced magic or even wrote directly and at length on the occult arts. But for all of them, magical themes and magical sources constituted "at least the rank underbrush of the better-known philosophical and theological literature: they are themes and texts used or rejected, combatted and execrated to be sure, sometimes surrounded by a deliberate silence, but never ignored." [27]

[24] According to Lewis W. Spitz, "Reuchlin's Philosophy: Pythagoras and Cabala for Christ," *Archiv für Reformationsgeschichte*, XLVII (1956), 12-13, Reuchlin, despite his acceptance of Neoplatonic cosmology and his interest in Cabala, was hostile to astrology and to all magic; but even he "had his playful moments." For this whole group of individuals, there is useful material in Walker, *Spiritual and Demonic Magic*, Thorndike, *History of Magic*, and François Secret, *Le Zôhar chez les Kabbalistes chrétiens de la Renaissance* (Paris, 1958). On Lefèvre, see Walker, pp. 169-70; Thorndike, IV, 513-16; and Augustin Renaudet, *Préréforme et humanisme à Paris pendant les premières guerres d'Italie (1494-1517)* (2nd ed.; Paris, 1953), pp. 150-51, who dates the work 1493.

[25] Andreas to Agrippa, n.p., 1531, *Epist.* VI, xxxii: "sed quasi fumum, aut verba sola parvi fecit praefatam magiam. . . ." For Erasmus' polite but reserved letter of recommendation to Agrippa, see his letter from Freiburg-im-Breisgau, 19 September 1531, printed in *Epist.* VI, xxxi, and in *Opus epistolarum Des. Erasmi Roterodami*, ed. P. S. Allen [and H. M. Allen and H. W. Garrod] (12 vols.; Oxonii, 1906-58), IX, 350-52 (No. 2544).

[26] Peuckert, *op. cit.*, pp. 136-201.

[27] Garin, *Medioevo e Rinascimento*, p. 171.

In this vigorous survival of the magical traditions of the Middle Ages and the Renaissance, Agrippa himself played a role of great importance, a role only partly suggested by the fact that his own *De occulta philosophia* became and long remained the most comprehensive, the most widely used and respected of all books on the magical arts. What really makes Agrippa important in this history of Renaissance occultism is that he represents the conjunction of the older medieval traditions with the new magical sources added by Renaissance scholarship. To put it differently, *De occulta philosophia* represents the decisive moment—and the foredoomed failure —of the Renaissance attempt to purge the older magic of its demonic, unorthodox, and fatalistic character by the introduction of a broader, more thoroughly Neoplatonic philosophical outlook. The basic magical world view, that of a hierarchically ordered world in which all parts are joined together by infinitely complex interrelationships and harmonies, had always been Neoplatonic in character. But Florentine Neoplatonism, especially in the thought of Ficino and Pico, sought to reorient the Neoplatonic heritage in a way that would de-emphasize those practices that involved the invocation of demons and other overtly anti-Christian practices. Instead, they stressed those elements of Neoplatonic thought which allowed man to make use of natural forces (including, however, occult connections, celestial influences, and the subtle but still physical action of the human spirit) in his magical operations. Trithemius of Sponheim, the chief figure of northern European magic prior to Agrippa, knew in a general way of the work of the Florentines; but his chief magical work, *Steganographia*, remained essentially untouched by this Neoplatonic reform. His magic was still that of the unaltered medieval heritage.[28] Agrippa, on the other hand, avowedly and directly sought to purify magic and to restore its good repute.[29] In his effort to do so, he quoted Ficino extensively though without acknowledgment. Magic for him was not a series of diabolical rites and incantations, but a high and holy philosophy stemming from ancient wisdom. He thus took up Ficino's work of reform and transported it north of the Alps.

If Agrippa is important for his amalgamation of the Florentine heritage with the flourishing traditions of medieval occultism, and

[28] Peuckert, *op. cit.*, pp. 107-8.
[29] *De occulta philosophia*, dedicatory epistle and "Ad Lectorem," fols. aa3r-v, aa2r.

for the introduction of the ideas of Ficinian magic into the far different cultural milieu of Northern Europe, he is also important because his attempt at purification of magic failed. Magic continued to elicit almost universal belief, but it remained in ill repute. Although Agrippa did indeed present many occult effects which could be explained in natural, nondemonic terms,[30] he also presented innumerable instances of works that could not be achieved without demonic aid. There is plenty of information in De occulta philosophia about the summoning and use of good demons, and more than a few suggestions that similar rites, invocations, and figures, slightly altered, can be used in the risky business of black magic: that is, in the conjuration of evil demons.[31]

The reason for the failure of Agrippa's attempt to purify occult philosophy may have been partly the lesser cultural sophistication of his North European milieu, and of himself, when contrasted with the cultural world of Renaissance Florence.[32] Yet there was a more far-reaching cause. The demons were present even in those ancient and Florentine texts from which he drew his new materials. Even the pious and cautious Ficino himself did not really achieve a purely nondemonic magic. If one recent student of his thought is right, Ficino did not really object to the practice of demonic magic, so long as only good demons were invoked, and also so long as the whole affair was veiled from the eyes of the vulgar masses, who might easily relapse into paganism and idolatry if they tried to engage in the invocation of demons.[33] In any event, Agrippa's treatise on occultism was both widely influential and broadly significant because it brought together the Florentine and the medieval strands of magic. And one reason why Ficino's proclaimed reform of magic did not have better success in restoring the good name of that pseudo-science was that the works of successors like

[30] De occulta philosophia, Bk. I, ch. vi. p. viii, for attempts to explain mass panic by the occult effects of air on the human spirit, and for a still less unorthodox-sounding description of the camera obscura (a passage not found in the earlier manuscript version of the work). For a good example of miscellaneous occult effects, some (e.g., the magnet) quite rational, others fantastic, but all clearly "innocent" and nondemonic, De occulta philosophia, Bk. I, ch. xiii, pp. xvii-xviii; Bk. I, ch. xv, pp. xx-xxi.

[31] De occulta philosophia, Bk. I, ch. xxxix, p. xlv, for one of many examples. For discussion of this point, see the treatment of the dangers of demonic magic later in the present chapter.

[32] Peuckert, op. cit., pp. 196-201.

[33] Walker, Spiritual and Demonic Magic, p. 51. For this whole discussion of Ficino's views on magic, ibid., Part I, passim.

Agrippa made obvious a fact that Ficino probably never quite admitted, even to himself: that his own nondemonic magic was little more than a mask for a pseudo-science which remained largely the domain of good and evil spiritual beings.[34]

Granted, then, that the occult sciences exercised a hold on Agrippa's contemporaries, the further question arises, why did they have such a hold, and in particular, why was this hold even increasing over what it had been throughout the Middle Ages? The easiest answer to this question is that there was an obvious affinity between the Renaissance hunger for the ancient and the claim of magical texts to represent the deepest wisdom of Antiquity. Whatever modern scholars may eventually make of the Renaissance period, there can be no missing of its enthusiasm for ancient learning. This enthusiasm went so far that at times men wrote and spoke as if the solution of all their intellectual, religious, and scientific problems depended on nothing more than the relatively easy process of rediscovering the original texts and getting rid of the allegedly obscuring layer of medieval commentaries.[35] To this rather childish overconfidence in the superior wisdom of Antiquity, the occult sciences owed much of their vogue. Agrippa, one of the best possible examples, heaped his works, especially *De occulta philosophia*, full of references to ancient writers, while usually remaining discreetly silent about the more recent authors, such as Pico, Ficino, Lazzarelli, or Paolo Ricci, from whom he took many of his general doctrines and specific points of detail. Medieval magic itself had already claimed to stem from the ancient Persian Magi, the sages of Egypt, and the Hebrew elders, and its authorities were regularly ancient as well as exotic. But humanistic scholarship added "new" sources of even greater antiquity. Ficino himself, the man who began the attempt to recast and purify magic, was the great translator of the works of Plato and the ancient Neoplatonists, and still more important, of the hitherto largely unknown Hermetic literature, which was most useful for magic, and which was among the earliest and most influential of his translations.[36] Alongside the venerable

[34] *Ibid.*, pp. 85-86, 90-96.   [35] Thorndike, *History of Magic*, V, 3.

[36] Ficino regarded his lifework, the restoration of Platonism, as perhaps the most important aspect of a general rebirth of the arts and sciences that was occurring in his time; and he attributed to it vast and even providential significance for the growth of true religion. See Paul Oskar Kristeller, *The Philosophy of Marsilio Ficino*, trans. Virginia Conant (New York, 1943), pp. 13, 22-29.

Hermes stood the even more sacred writings of the Cabala, which the sixteenth century generally regarded as genuine documents representing a secret revelation given by God to Moses. Seen in this light, cabalism offered profound religious insights; and on account of the magical power of the divine and angelic names which could be derived through its use, it provided an equally valuable aid for all kinds of magical practices. Although in one sense this cabalistic interest may be labeled a mere transitory fashion, it excited the interest of men of high ability from the time of Pico della Mirandola or before down until the seventeenth century.[37] Cabala was not itself a set of magical practices. To most of its Christian students, it was primarily a tool of anti-Jewish religious polemic which actually won a number of converts from among Jewish cabalists. It was also a method of Biblical exegesis which freed independent-minded individuals like Pico from the restraints of traditional exegesis.[38] But its metaphysical assumptions were fully Neoplatonic and hence consonant with the magical idea of a world of hierarchies, harmonies, and mysterious correspondences. And its methods of deriving divine and angelic names, its doctrines of a mystical ascent which could confer power as well as bliss on the soul, and its assumptions about the marvellous power of language (especially Hebrew) made Cabala yet another ancient source for the study of occult wisdom.

A second reason for Renaissance enthusiasm for the occult grew out of the general cultural tone of the age. Just as prominent among the traits of that period as enthusiasm for Antiquity was a tendency to exalt the powers and significance of man. Though this trait is less tangible than enthusiasm for ancient literature, and is even more open to misinterpretation, the dignity and powers of man were frequent themes of Renaissance authors. Man is, as the writers of Agrippa's time (and Agrippa himself) repeated almost *ad nauseam*, the microcosm, the central and most important figure of the created world, linking together the material and the spiritual worlds, joined to God by his soul and to the earth by his body.[39] The famous

[37] Joseph Leon Blau, *The Christian Interpretation of the Cabala in the Renaissance* (New York, 1944), p. vii, regards this enthusiasm as a mere fad; but Secret, *op. cit.*, pp. 12-13, 103, is highly critical of this conclusion, and of the thoroughness of the research on which it rests.

[38] Garin, *Giovanni Pico della Mirandola*, pp. 71, 150, argues that this was the chief attraction of Cabala for Pico.

[39] One of the most influential Renaissance statements of these views is in the

passage of the Hermetic *Asclepius*, "A great miracle is man, worthy of honor and veneration," struck one of the main themes of the Renaissance mentality, and was repeatedly cited by the Nettesheimer.[40]

At first glance, it might appear that enthusiasm for magic, which seems to press down upon the human spirit the enslaving bonds of demonic power and astrological determinism, would be profoundly contrary to this tendency to glorify man. Yet the reverse was true. Even those individuals who were most hostile to judicial astrology because it subjugated man to the stars might accept magical beliefs and practices. Pico della Mirandola was one such.[41] The reason was that to the Renaissance mentality, magic and astrology might not seem to be forces working against human freedom, but rather powerful instruments whereby man might liberate himself from subjection to the usual order of nature. Magic became still more prominent in a culture that exalted the dignity of man, because magic expressed the divine power in man. It was—or claimed to be—"the new way which will open to man the rule over nature." [42] The Neoplatonic world view, of a universe of close interrelationships, a world-animal pervaded by occult links among its parts, was the theoretical basis of all magic. Furthermore, the exalted position of man as the link joining spiritual and material reality, the "knot of the universe," as Ficino and Agrippa both called him, was especially appealing to magicians. Since man stood between the

works of Marsilio Ficino. For Ficino's exposition of the position of man and its significance, see Kristeller, *Philosophy of Marsilio Ficino*, pp. 99-105, 397-99. The original Latin texts which Kristeller cites are given in the Italian translation of his book, *Il pensiero filosofico di Marsilio Ficino* (Florence, 1953), pp. 433-34. For discussion of Pico's similar but distinct view of man, Garin, *Giovanni Pico della Mirandola*, pp. 183-204, and Kristeller, *Philosophy of Marsilio Ficino*, pp. 407-10. Cf. Agrippa, *Dialogus de homine*, Lyons, Bibliothèque Municipale, MS. No. 48, fol. 45v [*sic; recte* 46v]: "Mundus enim ab ornatu et pulchritudine dictus est grecis cosmos, homo autem microcosmos, hoc est minor mundus, quia maioris mundi pulchritudinem ornatissimumque exemplum." His ensuing discussion of man's dignity and power bears traces of the ideological and even textual influence of Ficino, Pico, and Ludovico Lazzarelli, as shown by Paola Zambelli in her edition of *Dialogus de homine, Rivista critica di storia della filosofia*, XIII (1958), 47-71.

[40] *De triplici ratione cognoscendi Deum*, in *Opera*, II, 492; *De occulta philosophia*, Bk. III, ch. xlix, p. cccxvi (also appears in Würzburg, Universitätsbibliothek, MS. M.ch.q.50, Bk. III, ch. 36, fol. 109r).

[41] Garin, *Giovanni Pico della Mirandola*, pp. 167, 180-83.

[42] Garin, *Medioevo e Rinascimento*, p. 153.

upper and nether worlds, he could reach out into either world, and could apply the powers of each to his own purposes.[43]

The important thing was that the astral, demonic, occult, and even natural forces which man as magician applied were not conceived from the viewpoint of outside forces impinging on the freedom of man, but from the viewpoint of man's power. Nowhere did the essentially aristocratic coloration of Renaissance mentality [44] stand out more clearly. From the viewpoint of ordinary men, astrology and magic might signify outside forces enslaving the individual. But writers on magic and astrology regarded the *magus* not as an ordinary man, but as one of a small elite of wise men, able to become (as Francis Bacon later wrote of the scientist) "masters and possessors of Nature." Thus these writers habitually regarded magic not from the viewpoint of the masses who were subject to it, but from the viewpoint of the *magus* who employed it.[45] Since the learned man could influence celestial bodies (and even demons) by properly conducted rites, incantations, talismans, and application of physical objects having celestial affinities, he was not really subject to celestial and demonic and natural forces, but rather could use them, could persuade them, could even rule over them. Magic was not a force hemming man's freedom in, but a tool used to win dominion over the world. Subjection to the rules and practices of magic seemed no more destructive of man's freedom than does the obedience of the modern man of science to the laws and processes of nature. The much-quoted dictum of astrology, that the wise man was not subject to the stars but dominated them, meant not

[43] For Ficino, see quotations in Kristeller, *Il pensiero filosofico di Marsilio Ficino*, pp. 433-34. Agrippa, *Dialogus de homine*, Lyons, Bibliothèque Municipale, MS. No. 48, fol. 47v [*sic; recte* 48v]: "Hinc homo minor mundus dictus est, quia maioris mundi vinculum est, et nodus, absolutaque consummatio."

[44] Observed by Peuckert, *op. cit.*, pp. 1-10, and by Alfred von Martin, *Sociology of the Renaissance*, trans. W. L. Luetkens (New York, 1944), pp. 61-65, 70-76.

[45] E.g., Agrippa's stress on the secrecy of his learning, and the need to keep it from the masses: *Oratio in praelectione . . . Trismegisti*, in *Opera*, II, 1081. Still more plain is *De occulta philosophia*, Bk. III, ch. ii, pp. ccxi-ccxii (a passage also appearing in Würzburg, Universitätsbibliothek, MS. M.ch.q.50, Bk. III, ch. 2, fol. 84v). Cf. the remarks of Paola Zambelli in Eugenio Garin *et al.*, eds., *Testi umanistici su l'Ermetismo* (Rome, 1955), pp. 110-11. This gnostic scorn for the masses and desire to keep the secret truth in the hands of the few was especially significant because it foreshadowed the attitude of seventeenth-century libertinism. See Giorgio Spini, *Ricerca dei libertini: La teoria dell'impostura delle religioni nel Seicento italiano* (Rome, 1950), pp. 40-41.

only that the sage was free from astral determinism, but also that by knowing the influences of the heavens, he would be able to employ the correct prayers, rites, and talismans, pitting force against force so that the stars performed *his* will. Astrology and magic seemed not only profound and noble, but also useful.[46] Even the science of astrological prediction, which so shocked medieval Christian defenders of free will, was not entirely a question of fatal necessity, but rather a means for gaining awareness of all aspects of a situation in order to affect it successfully.[47] The magician who inspected the constellations and other occult influences was merely seeking to understand all the forces at work. The determining properties of climates, seasons, and regions were studied not to weep and pray over them, but to use them.[48] The man who consulted an astrologer might well expect not merely to learn the decisions of blind fate, but rather to learn whether, within the general limits imposed by the position of the constellations, a proposed course of action could be fruitful. Perhaps he would also inquire whether certain types of magical amulets or ceremonies would make a planned action more likely to succeed.[49] Such practices were especially common in medicine, but they might occur regarding any human act.

This quest for power through magic was a major factor in the attractiveness of the occult arts. It was not wholly new. *Picatrix*, the greatest of the medieval manuals of magic, described the *magus* in terms of the most exalted power: "And also man himself comprehends by his sense all the intelligences and compositions of the things of the world, and they do not comprehend him; and all things serve him, and he serves none of them. . . ."[50] The greatest northern European occultist authority of Agrippa's youth, Trithemius, likewise promised power and knowledge of all things through

[46] Garin, *Medioevo e Rinascimento*, pp. 183-85.

[47] *Ibid.*, pp. 186-87.

[48] *Ibid.*, p. 187. No text could demonstrate this point more fully than *De occulta philosophia*, Bk. II, ch. 1 (equivalent to Würzburg, Universitätsbibliothek, MS. M.ch.q.50, Bk. II, ch. 16), which describes in detail how to construct celestial images in order to confer good or evil fortune, to expel certain animals from a place, to gain wealth, to incite love, to get petitions granted, to cause dreams. Another good example, containing an explicit statement that such practices allow man to free himself from blind fate, is *De occulta philosophia*, Bk. III, ch. lix (MS., Bk. III, ch. 47).

[49] Garin, *Medioevo e Rinascimento*, pp. 162-64.

[50] Quoted *ibid.*, p. 175, n. 5.

magic.[51] Practical astrologers were far from thinking that events were controlled by blind fate. For example, in 1509 the astrologer Pellegrino de'Prisciani advised Isabella d'Este that her husband's imprisonment might be terminated if she practiced certain rites and prayers designed to attract favorable celestial influences.[52] The same idea of mastery over nature through astral magic is evident in the conjurations which Tommaso Campanella conducted for Pope Urban VIII in 1628. The rites were aimed to overpower the malevolent "natural" forces from the stars which threatened the Pope's life. If their most recent investigator is correct in interpreting these practices, Campanella carried his magical assault on nature so far that he even constructed in a sealed room a miniature replica of the heavens, with lamps representing the planets, so that the influence of his carefully arranged artificial heaven would outweigh the perilous exhalations coming from the diseased natural skies.[53]

This exaltation of man above the forces of nature (including occult, celestial, and even demonic forces) by virtue of his magical knowledge was deeply appealing to Renaissance intellectuals, and profoundly hostile to the more orderly, more rational scientific habits of medieval scholasticism. Both the medieval and the magical pictures of the world assumed that the world is orderly and hierarchical. But the Schoolman wanted to stick to his rational, orderly categories, while the distinctive trait of the magician was that he wanted to break through the usual series of orderly natural relationships. Magic seemed wicked not just because it might involve invocation of demons, nor even because it might subordinate human free will to the stars. At least as important in arousing the suspicions of cautious Schoolmen was the fact that magic was "unnatural." It taught how the *magus* could subvert the order of nature and bend the world to his own will. The *magus* defied reason and based his activities on "long experience rather than on rational investigation." [54] Reason could not investigate occult effects. It could not do so, the magicians believed, because the world itself was not an inert thing easily contained within the categories of a

[51] Walker, *Spiritual and Demonic Magic*, pp. 87-89, quoting from Trithemius' *Steganographia*.
[52] Garin, *Medioevo e Rinascimento*, pp. 165-66.
[53] Walker, *Spiritual and Demonic Magic*, pp. 206-7, 221-22.
[54] *De occulta philosophia*, Bk. I, ch. x, p. xiiii: "longa experientia, plus quam rationis indagine. . . ." (In Würzburg MS, Bk. I, ch. 4, fol. 5v.) For the importance of "experience" to astrologers, cf. Garin, *Medioevo e Rinascimento*, pp. 188-90.

logical apriorism. Rather, the world was a living, moving, growing thing, where the brute fact might exist, no matter how irreconcilable its existence might seem with the demands of reason. Only long experience could teach man what were the real forces working in the universe, and how they could be controlled. Hence there was a natural association between a skeptical attitude toward rational knowledge and a lively interest in the occult arts. The preceding chapter has already illustrated this close relation in the thought of Agrippa, and in reality, such a relation was not extraordinary among magicians. Magic and skepticism were often the obverse and reverse sides of the same world view. But the scholastic thinker could not help regarding that which broke through the rational orderliness of God's creation as part of the realm of evil. The maverick fact which did not harmonize with reason must be a product of the subrational, Satanic world, the world of dark and frightening forces which man approaches only at his own peril. The occult was the realm of "the diabolical sciences of experiments." [55]

By its detestation of rational apriorism, by its picture of a world beyond the grasp of reason, by its belief that man can overmaster natural forces and bend them to his will, and by its view that knowledge is power, magic pointed sharply away from medieval scientific habits. In many respects, medieval rationalism had produced noteworthy results in natural science. In a sense, it may be very true that fifteenth-century humanistic occultism represents decadence when compared to the scholastic science of the fourteenth century, and that the pretentious quackery of fakirs who looked back to the turgid theurgical literature of Alexandria was a poor substitute for the careful scientific procedures of medieval scholasticism.[56] But this condemnation of Renaissance occultism by Thorndike and others is also misleading to a great degree. Modern science began with a sense of profound alienation from its medieval precursors. For all its great indebtedness to late medieval Schoolmen, its mental habits were very different from theirs. This difference appears very clearly in the thought of Francis Bacon, who may not have been a great scientist himself, but who caught and expressed the mood of the individuals whose thought was creating the seventeenth-century scientific world view. Despite his own distaste for traditional magic, Bacon's views on some points are strikingly

[55] Garin, *Medioevo e Rinascimento*, pp. 159-60, 177, 185-87.
[56] Thorndike, *History of Magic*, V, 4-11.

similar to those of the magicians: the stress on experience rather than reason, the emphasis on the power and practical benefits which man can derive from knowledge, the trust that man can master nature, the hostility to *a priori* determination of practical questions.[57] In many respects, Renaissance magic approached nature in childish terms that in no wise pointed the way to modern science. Its tendency to conceive of natural forces in human terms (they were to be persuaded, conjured, even browbeaten and threatened) rather than in a naturalistic way was primitive, an atavistic survival from the infancy of mankind.[58] Medieval science was far more effective in approaching natural forces in a naturalistic way. But in their questioning of man's ability to know, and in their trust that knowledge confers power upon man, the occultists of the Renaissance did indeed point to the future.

The struggle between the scholastic and the occultist viewpoints, then, was a contest between one mentality which attributed primacy to general principles, discounting irreconcilable, discrete, single phenomena as mere illusions, preferring to determine questions of fact on the basis of abstract considerations, and another mentality which was willing to disregard all generalizations and to uphold the truth of the single, irreconcilable fact drawn from experience, no matter how "impossible" and irrational it might seem. The mental world of modern science is far different from that of Renaissance magic; and modern science is not, and never was, wholly empirical. But like the modern scientist, the astrologer or magician claimed in the last resort to submit his statements to the test of experience, and to modify or cast away any generalization not confirmed by what he observed.[59] The exaltation of man the *magus*, through

---

[57] Garin, *Medioevo e Rinascimento*, p. 152, and especially pp. 176-77, where he argues that the search for Bacon's sources has led inescapably toward the "diabolical" science of experiments, i.e., toward magic. For the persistence of many magical attitudes in Bacon, despite his distaste for traditional magical and astrological practices, see Walker, *Spiritual and Demonic Magic*, pp. 199-202.

[58] Garin, *Medioevo e Rinascimento*, pp. 182-83.

[59] *Ibid.*, pp. 188-90. Of course, not all the "facts" accepted by the occultists were true. Much of the "experience" appealed to by writers like Agrippa was lifted in great heaps from literary sources, and was subjected to very little critical evaluation. But Garin's point is not to contend that the Renaissance magicians worked out a set of satisfactory scientific procedures. They did not. His point is rather that they regarded a supposedly established and attested fact as more important than any general metaphysical principle, and would abandon the latter rather than the former. In this regard, he maintains, Renaissance magic and modern science were akin in spirit.

knowledge based on experience and rediscovered ancient wisdom, was in a real sense the preliminary to the exaltation of man the natural philosopher, through knowledge based also on experience, but with keen desire for new knowledge replacing the old confidence in the ancient heritage.

The preceding discussion has in effect already turned from the exaltation of man by magic to a third factor which made the occult sciences attractive to Renaissance men. The antirationalistic, backward-directed mentality of the *magus* represented a sharp break with medieval patterns of thought, a break which was particularly sharp in the case of a would-be reformer of magic like Agrippa. This desire to break with the "modern"—that is, medieval—world was one of the primary cultural forces in the Renaissance, at least as important as the "rebirth of classical antiquity," or the theme of human dignity. In fact, this sharp sense of discontent with the medieval past, this feeling that traditional beliefs, practices, and institutions were diseased, were "barbaric," was perhaps the most pervasive single element in the Renaissance frame of mind. It would be easy enough to show that in reality an Agrippa, a Ficino, a Petrarch depended heavily on the achievements of the medieval world that they affected to despise. The practice of citing one's ancient authorities explicitly but at second-hand, while discreetly failing to mention the medieval sources from which one had really drawn information, was a standard practice of Renaissance authors. Agrippa was a flagrant offender in this respect. Modern historians are well aware that no one should take at face value a Renaissance author's remarks about his contempt for medieval authorities.[60] But while true enough, such scholarly discoveries miss the main point, which is that the Renaissance man felt a passionate disdain for the medieval scholastics, and that he wanted to be, or to appear, critical, different, original, above all, "ancient." Whether this mood of rebellion was good or justified or even fruitful is not the main point to be considered.[61] It was actual.

This goal of rebirth, of rediscovering treasures from the lost

[60] The neatest example, concerning Giovanni Boccaccio, is that given by Jean Seznec, *La survivance des dieux antiques: Essai sur le rôle de la tradition mythologique dans l'humanisme et dans l'art de la Renaissance* (London, 1940), pp. 186 *et. seq.*

[61] Thorndike, *History of Magic*, V, 9, notes the presence of controversial passion in the Renaissance approach to intellectual questions; but he notes it only to deplore it and to contrast it to the orderly, balanced, decent habits of medieval scholarship.

wisdom of Antiquity, of regenerating Christianity, gave comfort and a sense of importance to these carping humanistic critics of medieval traditions. But their repudiation of the immediate past also meant "the end of a security," [62] a sense of personal loss and intellectual drift and uncertainty. A gnawing sense of lost horizons, cutting doubts about the validity of human knowledge and about the moral order of human society, even crises of religious belief, can be amply illustrated in the thought of such influential and talented figures as Ficino, Pico, and Leon Battista Alberti.[63] If the old concept of a sharp break between medieval and Renaissance culture means that one takes the humanists at their own valuation and treats the Middle Ages as a period of degenerate barbarism, then of course this old concept is indefensible. But the concept of a sharp break was no invention of nineteenth-century scholars. This hatred of things medieval was often passionate, ill-considered, unjust. But it was present in the age itself; and the myth of renaissance and cultural renewal, implying also an agonizing and unsettling spiritual separation from the "modern" (i.e., medieval) ways, was the invention of Renaissance men themselves. Eugenio Garin, in an essay of penetrating insight, has shown that this general spirit of cultural revolt, rather than specific differences of content (such as knowledge of classical literature, or "individualism," or human self-sufficiency, or sensitivity to nature), is the important fact that modern scholarship has generally forgotten about the Renaissance.[64]

Renaissance magic and Renaissance skepticism—and the figure of Agrippa von Nettesheim, who in his own person united these central concerns of the age—were therefore attractive to contemporaries for a third general reason: they were intimately involved in the cultural revolt, the spiritual malaise, of the times. Even the popularity of Antiquity really depends on this mood of rebellion. Things ancient were popular because the Antique provided a handy weapon, a standard of invidious comparison, for belaboring "modern" barbarity. They were also popular because a race of men who were trying to cast off from traditional intellectual moorings found a good measure of reassurance through admiration and imita-

[62] Garin, *Medioevo e Rinascimento*, p. 91.   [63] *Ibid.*, pp. 92-97.
[64] *Ibid.*, pp. 104-5; cf. p. 91, and also the illuminating discussions to the same effect in Kristeller, *Philosophy of Marsilio Ficino*, pp. 20-22, and in Theodore E. Mommsen, "Petrarch's Conception of the Dark Ages," in his *Medieval and Renaissance Studies*, ed. Eugene F. Rice, Jr. (Ithaca, N.Y., 1959), especially p. 129.

tion of the honorable ancients. As shown above, magic itself was popular partly because it, too, was ancient and claimed to be growing more so as scholarship revealed long-forgotten sources from the ancient past. Magic was still more enticing, however, because it fed on the frame of mind which felt spiritually alienated from medieval culture. It represented "a radical change in the view of man, and hence of his relations to reality. . . ."[65] Occultists like Agrippa knowingly rejected the strict, unbreakable hierarchy of medieval Aristotelianism, and the whole set of assumptions about human knowledge associated with the traditional world view. Of course they were credulous, grossly credulous. Yet they were also doubters and, as doubters, were willing to explore provisionally any approach to reality, more particularly if the approach possessed an aura of the ancient and the mysterious. The work of Agrippa, as well as of Ficino, Pico, Paracelsus, Bruno, and hosts of others, combined credulity with doubting incredulity, a peculiar mixture of doubt about rational knowledge and absurd gullibility where the irrational and fantastic were concerned. Hence this work was a reflex of the intellectual anarchy which lay close to the heart of Renaissance culture.[66] Magic was no mere playground for eccentrics in Renaissance culture. It was an expression of the spirit of the times: hence its expanded prominence in the thought of Renaissance men.

Yet although magic was in many ways appealing to Renaissance thinkers, it raised serious problems for its followers. Even though the occult arts played a part in the intellectual rebellion against contemporary society and culture, each practitioner of those arts had to reach some kind of *modus vivendi* with his times. Magical practices, and even magical beliefs, clashed so sharply with what society regarded as acceptable that serious tensions arose between the *magus* and the world in which he had to live. To reach a *modus vivendi* was not just a matter of prudential caution designed to

[65] Garin, *Medioevo e Rinascimento*, p. 153.
[66] For an interpretation somewhat similar concerning the relation between intellectual dissatisfaction and interest in magic, see Peuckert, *op. cit.*, pp. 1-10; cf. Christoph Sigwart, *Kleine Schriften* (2nd ed.; 2 vols.; Freiburg-i-B., 1889, I, 1-5. According to Cassirer, *op. cit.*, I, 88, the problem of knowledge is the unifying factor within the multiplicity and variety of Renaissance culture. He also realizes (I, 181) that magic, specifically in the case of Agrippa, was an attempt to solve these intellectual problems, though an abortive one. But he does not clearly see the broader, more general, and more persistent relation between magic and doubt.

escape the vigilance of the authorities of church and state, though of course there was a good chance that even a pious and discreet student of magic, such as Ficino,[67] might experience personal danger because of his doctrines. No man can live without making some sort of accommodation between his own beliefs and acts, on the one hand, and on the other hand, the standards of decency and propriety commonly accepted by his fellows. Certainly magic, no matter how purified or how defended, created problems of decency and propriety which Ficino, Pico, Agrippa, and all other students of the occult had to resolve in their own consciences.

The most acute of these problems concerned what forces in the world might be lawfully used by man. Obviously, there was nothing inherently evil about the use of natural forces, such as heat, for cooking food or for liquefying metal. Nor was the use of certain occult forces open to objection. The particular force that caused magnetism was indefinable, beyond rational understanding. The magnet, in fact, was a commonly cited example of an occult force. To use it in lifting iron, or to float a sliver of it on alcohol and let it become a magnet pointing mysteriously to the north, was an act perfectly allowable, even though the force involved was occult. Likewise, to expose unfinished cloth to the action of the celestials, particularly of the sun, for purposes of bleaching it, could hardly be construed as mortal sin. But the world as conceived by medieval and Renaissance men was crammed full of forces of many kinds, acting, reacting, and interacting in infinitely complex associations. There were certain forces which no one regarded as allowable for human use. Others were obviously innocent. Still others were borderline cases: forces which some people felt to be innocent and available to man, but which other individuals regarded as dangerous to the soul of man and to society.

The undeniably or potentially dangerous forces were those which involved spiritual beings. No one could publicly defend the thesis that God, the Supreme Being, might lawfully be overmastered and constrained by puny man through theurgic rites. Perhaps some popular superstitions might go almost so far in practice, but there could be no serious defense of theurgy. There were, however, many ranks of spiritual beings ranged beneath the Creator, and supposedly endowed with great powers which perhaps could be placed at the disposal of the man who approached them rightly.

[67] Walker, *Spiritual and Demonic Magic*, pp. 52-53.

Could man use the power of angels for his own ends? Perhaps not, since angels were mightier than man, higher in the order of creation. And yet, perhaps they could be used. After all, was not man the image of God, and hence endowed with the powers of all created beings? [68] If control of angelic powers were possible, the further question then arose whether man sinned if he captured and used such angelic powers for his own ends.

Lurking behind this question was the far more frightening problem of those other angels, the fallen ones. Could man get in touch with the powers of darkness, with devils? Few men in that age would deny it, not even brave men like Agrippa or his pupil Johann Wier, both of whom dared to defend innocent persons against unjust accusations of witchcraft. The further question, whether invocation of devils and use of their power in magic was licit, hardly even needed to be posed. This was black magic, the diabolical art, witchcraft, worship of the Devil—the ultimate and unpardonable crime. Writers like Agrippa were constantly exercised to demonstrate that their own books had nothing to do with such dark practices. Agrippa's avowed aim in writing *De occulta philosophia* was to distinguish the good and holy science of magic from scandalous and impious practices of black magic, and to restore its good name.[69]

The difficulty, however, was that many practices not avowedly demonic might be interpreted as being directed to evil demons. The danger was most evident in ceremonial rites designed to attract good demons (angels) but not bad ones. Since the Devil was a liar and deceiver, how was the *magus* ever to be sure that the spirits he

[68] *Dialogus de homine*, Lyons, Bibliothèque Municipale, MS. No. 48, fol. 47r [*sic;* should read fol. 48r]: ". . . nam omnia que creata sunt, suum aliquid et se tota suaque omnia, in homine agnoscunt, cui etiam deus ipse (vt ait hermes) soli congreditur. vnde solus homo pre ceteris creaturis imaginem dei ferre dicitur, merito ergo omnia illum amant, omnia illi obediunt. . . ." *Ibid.,* fol. 47v [*sic;* should read fol. 48v]: "Et quamuis homo minor mundus dicatur, totus tamen maior mundus omnesque mundi particulares illi seruire compelluntur." Actually, this power of man over creation was lost through the sin of Adam, but it might be restored if the soul were properly purified: *De occulta philosophia*, Bk. III, ch. xl, pp. ccxciii-ccxciiii (a chapter lacking in the manuscript version of 1510).
[69] See Agrippa's dedication of *De occulta philosophia* to Trithemius, in *De occulta philosophia*, fol. aa3r-v. Textually similar but not quite identical passages occur in Würzburg, Universitätsbibliothek, MS. M.ch.q.50, fols. 1r-2v (dedicatory epistle to Trithemius and Bk. I, ch. 1). Cf. his epistle "Ad Lectorem," printed in *De occulta philosophia*, fol. aa2r (not in Würzburg MS.).

tried to conjure up would not prove to be wicked? Good demons were obedient to the will of God, and hence were difficult, perhaps almost impossible, for man to control.[70] Evil ones might appear in their place and might lure the magician to his eternal ruin. The danger was not just that the *magus* might be carried off bodily by a leering demon. The more subtle danger was connected with the rites of conjuration themselves. Rites to invoke spiritual beings partook of the nature of worship. Even if the *magus* could be sure that only good demons were involved, the objection was not entirely removed that such rites and imprecations were incompatible with his obligation to worship only the one true God. In its remote Hermetic and Neoplatonic origins, magic had been a type of theurgy associated with polytheism. Was not any invocation of spiritual forces a kind of non-Christian religious act, a form of devil-worship?

The easy way out of this problem was the narrowly orthodox one: no rites invoking any demons, good or bad, could be tolerated, unless such rites had the sanction of church tradition and authority. In other words, no magical rites at all, properly so called. This viewpoint regarded all forms of magic as inseparably bound up with demon-worship.[71] Such charges could be most easily sustained where the acts of the magician were such that they could not be explained in purely physical terms, but must be directed, consciously or unconsciously, to some intelligent agent. Any magical rite that involved the uttering of words, or the engraving of words, letters, and symbols on talismans, or the sacrifice of any physical object by fire or other means, was *vehementer suspectus*. Even acts which might be defended as using only celestial powers, such as attracting favor for some proposed action through use of objects capable of summoning favorable celestial influences, could be assailed as demonic rather than purely celestial magic, since all things in the world, and especially the planets, were believed to have souls. Every planet, every star, every region, even every man, had his own presiding spirit. Hence every act except the most commonplace might involve use of demonic influences.

[70] Agrippa concedes this point but counts on divine aid to make the spirits obey: *De occulta philosophia*, Bk. III, ch. xxxii, p. cclxxviii. In the Würzburg MS. of 1510, Bk. III, ch. 54, fol. 126r-v, which represents the ensuing discussion of how to overcome this difficulty, also stresses the importance of divine aid, but does not so fully develop the idea that certain rites help overcome the good demons' reluctance.

[71] Walker, *Spiritual and Demonic Magic*, p. 83.

This cautious attitude involved complete renunciation of all occult sciences, not on account of their nullity (for they were believed to be real), but on account of their wickedness. Faced with such a viewpoint, the *magus* had to try, though with indifferent success, to deny and refute these accusations. Furthermore, he had to explain his acts in terms that eliminated the use of demons, or at very least offered safeguards to ensure that only good demons were involved. The most significant and most determined attempt to have done with the demons and to elaborate an occult system based on purely nondemonic principles was the *De vita* of Marsilio Ficino. D. P. Walker has demonstrated that the key to magical power in Ficino's system was the concept of *spiritus,* that extremely subtle but still material substance that joins the material and non-material natures of man.[72] *De vita* was an effort to show how man could make this *spiritus* more celestial, by various natural methods, including use of talismans and astrologically constructed songs, as well as proper diet and bodily regimen, all of which would strengthen the *spiritus* and attract the particular astral influence desired.[73] But despite Ficino's cautious warnings that celestial music should involve not worship of the stars but imitation of them and capture of their natural emanations and influences,[74] his use of engraved seals, his stress on the words (and hence the meaning) of his celestial hymns, suggested that not just the material *spiritus* but also some intelligent being was involved. Ficino did not really succeed in explaining magical effects in purely natural and clearly nondemonic terms, because his use of means that seemed to be directed at an order of reality higher than the material *spiritus* tacitly reopened the door that led to demonic magic. In truth, Ficino probably did not personally object to invocation of good demons, provided such practices were kept from knowledge of the masses, who would surely distort them into devil-worship and idolatry.[75]

Agrippa was even less concerned than Ficino to exclude all demonic agents from occult practices, despite his own goal of purifying magic. Books One and Two of *De occulta philosophia* did claim to set forth systems of natural and celestial magic, though the looseness of the book's organization actually permitted demonic elements to intrude even into these portions of his work. Book Three, which explicitly dealt with religious or ceremonial magic,

---

[72] *Ibid.,* pp. 3-4.   [73] *Ibid.,* pp. 12-18.
[74] *Ibid.,* pp. 16-17.   [75] *Ibid.,* p. 51.

could hardly escape being demonic in any case, since divine and angelic forces were the objects of the ceremonies. Agrippa devoted many of his chapters to discussing how to enhance the powers of the human soul by acts of purification, sacrifice, and prayer. Doubtless he thought that he was employing demons as mere auxiliaries in a magic that rested on the God-given powers of the human soul. Nevertheless, Book Three was irretrievably demonic by its very nature.

Most of Book One, devoted to natural magic, is reasonably cautious regarding demons, and is intent on showing that many magical effects, such as instantaneous transfer of messages across great distances, are possible "naturally, and far from all superstition, with no other spirit taking part." [76] In this connection, Agrippa tries to adopt Ficino's concept of *spiritus* and to attribute magical effects to changes in it, often through transmission of celestial and other forces through the air. But he is careless about confining such occult works to the realm of the material, and easily passes on to show how power from the world of ideas is also transmitted. [77] Still worse, even in Book One he asserts not only that angels can be summoned to help the *magus* "by good works, pure mind, mystical prayers, devout sacrifices, and the like," but also that "evil demons can be bound by evil and profane arts." [78] Any pretence that Book One eliminated the use of intelligent agents is impossible, for there are chapters involving the powers of words, which at least in part must pass from the sphere of natural objects to the realm of intelligences. The presence of demons becomes explicit when Agrippa turns to describe the composition of "songs and prayers to attract the power of any star or divinity." [79] This is true

[76] *De occulta philosophia*, Bk. I, ch. vi, p. ix: "naturaliter, et procul omni superstitione, nullo alio spiritu mediante. . . ." (This passage is not in Würzburg MS.)

[77] *Ibid.*, Bk. I, ch. xxxiv, pp. xl-xli.

[78] *Ibid.*, Bk. I, ch. xxxix, p. xlv: "bonis operibus, pura mente, mysticis orationibus, deuotis suppliciis, et similibus. . . ." ". . . malos daemones malis ac prophanis artibus allici posse." Würzburg MS., Bk. I, ch. 31, fol. 24r. This chapter contains the famous passage from the Hermetic *Asclepius* on pagan rites which attract certain celestial spirits into the statues of the gods. On this point, see Walker, *Spiritual and Demonic Magic*, pp. 40-43, 93, who notes that Ficino also knew this passage.

[79] *De occulta philosophia*, Bk. I, ch. lxxi, p. xci: "carminibus et orationibus pro attrahenda stellae aut numinis alicuius uirtute. . . ." On the power of words, *ibid.*, Bk. I, ch. lxix, p. xc. Neither chapter appears in Würzburg MS.; but MS. does have other chapters, some not included in the later printed version, which also deal with incantations and demonic names: Bk. II, ch. 34-48.

even though Agrippa drags in the Ficinian concept of human *spiritus* as the instrument which effects such works, for he makes no effort to confine the effects to this *spiritus;* instead, he involves "all the power of the soul." [80]

Book Two of *De occulta philosophia* contains still more tendencies toward demonic magic. Some of the references to demons are merely peripheral, as when he writes that musical harmony is helpful in driving away evil demons.[81] Certain practices, Agrippa maintains, are not demonic even though they seem so, in particular the apparently ridiculous gesticulations recommended in magical books, which are not signals to lurking demons, as popularly believed, but rather are graphic representations of symbols for certain numbers whose powers are helpful in a given magical work.[82] But the spirits return when Agrippa describes the power of geometrical figures like the circle, the pentagon, and the cross, to overmaster evil spirits. Not even his attempt to explain the power of such inscribed figures in terms of natural similarities really obviates this danger.[83] The chapters devoted to magical images no doubt intend mainly to show the relation between the power of these images and the influence of celestials; but again, the demons re-enter his magic when he writes: "Images of this sort effect nothing unless they are brought to life in such a way that either a natural, or celestial, or heroic, or animastic, or demonic, or angelic power is in them or present with them. . . ." [84] In any case, it was almost impossible to explain transitive effects exerted on external objects without involving demons as the active agents of the work. Agrippa deepens the heterodox appearance of his discussion of celestial images when he explicitly describes not only images designed to bring good fortune, but also images specifically designed to cause calamity through use of malevolent stellar forces.[85] Likewise, when he turns to the casting of lots in divination, he involves not only celestial forces and the soul of the diviner, but also outside spirits.[86] He could not really

[80] *Ibid.,* Bk. I, ch. lxxi, p. xcii: "tota animae uirtus." (Not in MS.)
[81] *Ibid.,* Bk. II, ch. xxviii, p. clxxi. (Not in MS.)
[82] *Ibid.,* Bk. II, ch. xvi, p. cxxxviii. (Not in MS.)
[83] *Ibid.,* Bk. II, ch. xxiii, pp. cliiii-clv (MS. Bk. II, ch. 30, fols. 65v-66v).
[84] *Ibid.,* Bk. II, ch. l, pp. cxciii-cxciiii: ". . . nihil operari imagines eiusmodi, nisi uiuificentur ita quod ipsis aut naturalis aut coelestis aut heroica, aut animastica, aut daemoniaca uel angelica uirtus insit, aut adsistat. . . ." This passage is lacking in the corresponding chapter of MS., Bk. II, ch. 16.
[85] *Ibid.*
[86] *Ibid.,* Bk. II, ch. liv, pp. cxcix-cc. (Not in MS.)

exclude these spirits even in explaining purely celestial works, since he attributes life and a soul to the world and to all celestial bodies, so that no action by them is purely corporeal.[87] Agrippa himself was not entirely blind to the implications of this repeated demonic intrusion into his discussion of celestial magic; and though he did try to be cautious by showing that imprecations directed to celestials affect the sensual rather than the rational soul, and that works of astral magic are not supernatural, he did not deny that demonic agents are involved. He merely wished to establish two points in this regard. First, he vehemently denied that these were evil demons, insisting that they were natural and divine powers sent by God to aid and minister unto man. Second, he flatly denied that use of these good celestial powers or deities was impious or contrary to religion.[88]

The third book of *De occulta philosophia*, since it deals with religious rites and ceremonial magic involving intelligent agents, is even more dangerous to the good name of Agrippa and of all occult science. In fact, the clarity with which this discussion of ceremonial magic lays bare the demonic affinities of Ficino's more cautious natural and celestial magic may help explain why the Florentine philosopher's magical viewpoints had only a limited influence on later philosophers.[89] This is true even though in an early chapter Agrippa tries to make a distinction between truly religious (hence innocent) ceremonies and superstitious practices. He attempts to defend invocation of demons so long as the demons are good and so long as the ceremonies give only a lesser veneration to them as created servants of God, while reserving full divine honors for God alone.[90] In fact, he tries to turn the force of orthodox attacks by warning that whoever neglects religious invocations and trusts solely in natural powers is likely to be deceived by evil demons.[91] No matter how he might argue, however, use of demonic powers, even good ones, was certain to seem dangerous. And there certainly is use of demonic powers in the third book of *De occulta*

[87] *Ibid.*, Bk. II, ch. lv, pp. cc-cci. (MS., Bk. III, ch. 18, fol. 96r-v.)

[88] *Ibid.*, Bk. II, ch. lviii, pp. cciii-cciiii. This apologetic passage is lacking from the corresponding portion of MS., Bk. II, ch. 17.

[89] Walker, *Spiritual and Demonic Magic*, pp. 95-96.

[90] *De occulta philosophia*, Bk. III, ch. lviii-lix, pp. cccxxix-cccxxxiiii (MS., Bk. III, ch. 45-46). Cf. *ibid.*, Bk. III, ch. iv, pp. ccxv-ccxvii (MS., Bk. III, ch. 4), and ch. vii, pp. ccxix-ccxxi. The latter chapter does not appear in MS. as a separate chapter, but the concluding portion of it is MS., Bk. III, ch. 4.

[91] *Ibid.*, Bk. III, ch. i, p. ccxi. (MS., Bk. III, ch. 1, fol. 84r.)

philosophia! A whole series of chapters discusses demons, not only good but evil.[92] He even describes the use of demonic names to arouse rainstorms, an example of transitive demonic magic which could hardly be reconciled with orthodoxy. Likewise he openly discusses methods for compelling the assistance of evil spirits in magical operations.[93]

Clearly, if demonic magic was dangerous, Agrippa's occult system must have sent a thrill of horror down the spine of many a reader, despite his attempts to vindicate himself by referring all effects ultimately to God, by emphasizing religious preparation and mystical ascent of the soul as the key to magical power, and by warning against the impostures of evil demons.

Although the attempt of Ficino to limit magic to acts attributable to the material *spiritus* (or at least to acts attributable to good demons) failed, and although Agrippa's effort to incorporate Ficino's reforms within his own writings failed even more completely, there was another possible way out of the dangerous realm of demonic magic. This was to argue that any acts that were undeniably directed to an intelligent agent were intended to affect only the intellect of the magician himself. In order to avoid the danger of turning magic into a heterodox theurgy directed at demonic agents, Ficino tended to turn it into a kind of psychology, a set of operations which, if they affected the intellectual realm at all, involved only the intellect of the *magus*. Occultist practices thus became a sort of subjective psychotherapy, conducted by the *magus* and for the *magus*. But this solution of the problem of justifying magic raised still further difficulties, in particular two.

An immediately obvious difficulty was that magic was simply not interested in mere psychotherapy, that is, in mere alterations of the subjective consciousness of the magician. Magical knowledge was power, and this meant power over the world of external objects. Magic was not purely subjective, but transitive, interested in having

[92] *Ibid.*, ch. III, ch. xvi-xxxiv. Much of this material on demons is lacking in the earlier MS. version. But MS. still has considerable material on good and evil demons, a little of which has been dropped in the printed versions (e.g., MS., Bk. III, ch. 7, fol. 90r, has been omitted except for the first two sentences), but most of which has been carried over into the later revision (e.g., MS., Bk. III, ch. 8-11, much of which appears, with some additions and some excisions, as Bk. III, ch. xvi, of the Cologne edition of 1533). MS., Bk. III, ch. 7-15, is fully demonic in subject, and so are later chapters of the work.
[93] *De occulta philosophia*, Bk. III, ch. xxxii-xxxiii, pp. cclxxviii-cclxxxi. (MS., Bk. III, ch. 54-55, fols. 126r-127v.)

effects on objects and persons external to the *magus* and his assistants. Not even Ficino had really succeeded in confining all
external effects to the level of what could be done by the material
spiritus, nor all intellectual effects to the soul of the operator. But
Ficino had less difficulty than most magicians, for he did not
himself wish to become a wonder-working *magus*.[94] He was essentially a philosopher, not a magician. His whole ideal of knowledge
and of human ends strongly emphasized contemplative virtues,
leading ultimately to the soul's contemplation of God, rather than
the active virtues and mastery over the external world.[95] The older
medieval tradition of magic, as in *Picatrix* or even in the *Steganographia* of Trithemius, concentrated on action on outside objects.
The term *magus* for them implied much more than mystical contemplation, though that also might be involved, at least as a preparatory step.[96] To become a *magus* implied the acquisition of power,
lordship, mastery. In other words, it implied effects reaching far
beyond subjective changes in the soul of the operator himself. The
gravity of this problem appears clearly from a passage of Agrippa:
"I have seen and known a certain man inscribing the name and sign
of a certain spirit on virgin paper in the hour of the moon. When
afterwards he had given this to a river frog to devour, and had
murmured a certain song, having replaced the frog in the water,
soon showers and storms rose up." [97] This is a clear example of
transitive magic. The "certain man" of Agrippa's acquaintance was
not improving his soul, or elevating his spirit to attract celestial
power. He was performing an act designed to have a specific external effect. He was making rain. And what about those names
and signs inscribed on paper? What was the significance of using
a frog? To whom—or what—was the murmured song addressed?

---

[94] Even he claimed to possess prophetic powers, and he did exorcise evil
spirits with the aid of astral forces. See Walker, *Spiritual and Demonic Magic*,
pp. 45-46, and Kristeller, *Philosophy of Marsilio Ficino*, pp. 309-14.
[95] Kristeller, *Philosophy of Marsilio Ficino*, pp. 226-27.
[96] Cf. Agrippa, *De occulta philosophia*, Bk. III, ch. li-lxiv, for a whole series
of chapters on mystical preparation for magical works. MS., Bk. III, ch. 38-48,
51-53, 56, has much of the same material, but most chapters have been length-
ened in the later version, and some wholly new ones (Bk. III, ch. lii, lxi-lxii)
have been added.
[97] *Ibid.*, Bk. III, ch. xxiv, p. ccliiii: "Vidi ego et noui quendam inscribentem
in charta uirginea nomen et signaculum spiritus cuiusdam in hora lunae: quam
cum dedisset postea ad deuorandum ranae fluuiali, et carmen quoddam obmur-
murasset, remissa rana in aquam, mox pluuiae et imbres oborti sunt." (Not in
MS.) This is but one of many similar instances in Agrippa's book.

Perhaps the selection of a lunar hour was not directed at the presiding intelligence of the moon, but only at attracting the impersonal natural forces associated with the moon. But all the other parts of the ceremony strongly indicate rites designed to attract demonic assistance; and one could only hope that the demons involved were not evil ones. Without assuming the presence of a supernatural agent, it was extremely difficult to explain any such action on external objects.[98]

This same emphasis on power over external objects appeared in generalized form as well as in such concrete examples. After showing that the purified human mind can attain knowledge of all things and all sciences by a sudden flash of insight, Agrippa at once goes on to show that the mind gains not only science but also miraculous power over the external world. He continues: "Hence it results that [though] placed in nature, we sometimes attain power above nature, and perform operations so marvellous, so sudden, so difficult, by reason of which shades obey, the stars are disturbed, deities are compelled, the elements are made to serve. Thus men devoted to God, and lifted up by those theological virtues, command the elements, drive away fogs, call up winds, compel clouds to rain, cure diseases, and raise the dead." [99] There is nothing purely internal or subjective about this kind of magic. The mind is lifted up and purified, true; but the results are universal knowledge and through that, wonder-working power. Agrippan magic confers not only natural and celestial benefits, but also intellectual and divine. And it affects external objects at all levels of being. His magic is thoroughly transitive and hence, inevitably, also thoroughly demonic, even though he might convince himself that he approved only of good demons.[100] So all real magic inescapably involved external action; and apologetic efforts to explain the pseudo-science and justify it on the grounds that it affected only the soul of the *magus* could never have much success.

There was a second, less obvious reason why magic could not

[98] Walker, *Spiritual and Demonic Magic*, pp. 80-81.

[99] *De occulta philosophia*, Bk. III, ch. vi, p. ccxviii: "Hinc prouenit nos in natura constitutos, aliquando supra naturam dominari: operationesque tam mirificas, tam subitas, tam arduas efficere, quibus obediant manes, turbentur sydera, cogantur numina, seruiant elementa: sic homines deo deuoti, ac theologicis istis uirtutibus eleuati, imperant elementis, pellunt nebulas, citant uentos, cogunt nubes in pluuias, curant morbos, suscitant mortuos." (MS., Bk. III, ch. xxix, fol. 103v.)

[100] Cf. Walker, *Spiritual and Demonic Magic*, pp. 91-93.

be made to look safe by confining its action to subjective effects on the soul of the *magus*. In fact, this objection was valid against any magical apologia which sought to avoid demonic practices by attributing magic to purely natural causes. In the long run, natural magic of all kinds, including subjective magic, was even more dangerous to religion than was demonic magic, though it looked more innocent and was widely so regarded. ". . . Natural, subjective, purely psychological magic could explain all the effects of a subjective, psychological religion without assuming God." [101] The danger, not only of psychological but of every sort of natural magic, was that it would offer a wholly naturalistic explanation of both demonic conjurations and all religion, so that it would not only explain all mysteries, all prayers, all ceremonies, but would even explain them quite away. To reduce prayers, invocations, and all ceremonies to mere internal psychological forces explained the effects well enough, perhaps, but it also explained away the action of God, which was the presumed ultimate cause of all effects.

The clearest single example of the dangers latent in a purely naturalistic approach to magic is the *De incantationibus* of Agrippa's contemporary, Pietro Pomponazzi. His system of magic could hardly be demonic, since one of his aims in writing on magic was to deny altogether the existence of demons. He offered safely natural explanations of such magical actions as prayers. Prayer (he meant both Christian and polytheistic prayer, including magical incantations) could have two possible effects: to obtain some external benefit, and to make oneself more pious. The first of these aims might be frustrated; the second, never. Thus while upholding an extreme and quite heterodox fatalism, Pomponazzi could still recommend prayer, but only on the ground that the second aim of prayer, the natural and subjective one, would always be achieved. All the astral rites and ceremonies which Pomponazzi discussed "are aimed less at altering the planet, than at making the operator more receptive to its influence." [102] Thus all prayer and magical incantation had been reduced to a mere psychological process. Though safely natural, Pomponazzi's naturalistic explanations were far from safely orthodox.

Despite his avowed aim of purifying magic and of devoting at least two of the three books of *De occulta philosophia* to natural

---

[101] *Ibid.*, p. 83.   [102] *Ibid.*, p. 108.

magic, Agrippa's thought never showed so radical a naturalism as did Pomponazzi's. But the same danger of eroding away the religious and the specifically Christian element in the universe was present, though in less extreme form. This tendency appears occasionally in the first two books of Agrippa's magical treatise. While discussing the ability of passions of the soul to alter the body through the agency of the imagination, he suggests that three examples all have this same, purely natural cause: one from classical antiquity, one from Frankish history, and one from Christian religion. The classical example is the story of King Cyppus, who awoke wearing horns because he fell asleep while thinking of a bullfight, so that in sleep his imagination drove the horn-bearing humors to his head. The scars of King Dagobert were a physical result of his anticipation of punishment for his crimes. And the stigmata of St. Francis may have been a physical result of the saint's meditation on the Crucifixion. Agrippa did not assert this, but merely reported it as the opinion of others.[103] Nevertheless, he had raised the possibility that a Christian miracle could have a purely natural explanation. A second naturalistic explanation occurred shortly after, when he used the speckling of Laban's flocks by Jacob's rods as an illustration of how the passions of the human soul can affect external bodies. In this case, he then proceeds to explain that harmful enchantment of persons by sorcerers can be caused in precisely the same way.[104] In this instance, he has indeed avoided the danger of attributing enchantments to demons. But he has fallen into the less obvious but equally great danger of treating miracles of religion, even of the Bible, as purely physical and natural occurrences.

This tendency to naturalize religion and so to explain it away became even more obvious when Agrippa turned directly to the ceremonial aspect of magic in Book Three of *De occulta philosophia*. Repeatedly, religious phenomena receive a thoroughly non-

---

[103] *De occulta philosophia*, Bk. I, ch. lxiv, pp. lxxxv-lxxxvi. These examples, however, do not appear in the corresponding chapter of MS., Bk. I, ch. 40.

[104] *Ibid.*, Bk. I, ch. lxv, p. lxxxvi. MS., Bk. I, ch. 41, lacks this Biblical illustration. Again in *De occulta philosophia*, Bk. II, ch. lx, pp. ccvi-ccvii, Agrippa insists that the use of verbal imprecations to affect external objects, though involving astral influences, is purely natural: "Hinc Magus . . utitur inuocatione astuta superiorum, uerbis mysteriosis et locutione quadam ingeniosa, trahens unum ad aliud, *ui tamen naturali* per quandam conuenientiam inter illas mutuam, qua res sponte sequuntur, siue quandoque trahuntur inuite." (My italics.) This chapter does not appear in MS.

religious explanation, and are treated on a level of flat equality with natural events and magical works. For example, having established that each man has a ruling genius, or guardian angel, he asserts that a change of name sometimes is conducive to good fortune. His examples come from the Bible: Abram and Jacob changed their names to Abraham and Israel.[105] Names of spirits, useful in magical works, come indifferently from the Bible, from the stars, or from the objects which the spirits govern.[106] Though he does label it a superstition, Agrippa demonstrates that certain rites of religion, such as excommunication or burial, may be transferred to magical uses for the curing of diseases or the extermination of serpents, mice, or worms.[107] The manner in which he shifts back and forth from the religious to the profane is often remarkable. In his chapter on necromancy, he passes unflinchingly from a discussion of how the shades of the dead and infernal demons linger about corpses, to a discussion of saints' relics, which owe their efficacy to the continued love of holy souls for their bodies.[108] Or again, he attributes frenzy (*furor*) to the influence of gods or demons on the soul, and then uses frenzy as an explanation for miraculous human acts surpassing the powers of nature.[109] This intermixture of religious, demonic, and purely natural effects becomes still more obvious when, near the end of his book, he devotes a series of chapters to various ways in which man may purify body and soul, and so prepare to receive the divine power which will give him full mastery over the world. Pagan and Christian, natural and demonic, magical and religious are here intermixed in a most casual way. The most extreme example is the chapter on sacrifices, where the Crucifixion and the eucharist are singled out as the only true sacrifice, but where the sixty-six classes of Egyptian sacrifices, the

[105] *Ibid.,* Bk. III, ch. xxi, p. ccli. (Not in MS.)
[106] *Ibid., Bk.* III, ch. xxv-xxvi, xxviii. These chapters do not appear in MS., though it does have plenty of material on demonic names: e.g., MS., Bk. III, ch. 17, which corresponds to Bk. II, ch. lviii, of the printed text; or MS., Bk. III, ch. 50, a list of divine and angelic names which I have not been able to locate in the printed text.
[107] *De occulta philosophia,* Bk. III, ch. xxxiii, p. cclxxxi. (Not in MS.)
[108] *Ibid., Bk.* III, ch. xlii, pp. ccciiii-cccvi. The brief chapter on necromancy in MS., Bk. II, ch. 57, does not contain the reference to the saints.
[109] *Ibid.,* Bk. III, ch. xlix. (MS., Bk. III, ch. 36). For more examples of the tendency to intermix Christian miracles, even those of the Prophets and Apostles, with works of transitive magic, see the discussion of the powers which firm faith bestows on the human soul, *ibid.,* Bk. III, ch. vi, p. ccxviii. (MS., Bk. III, ch. 29, fol. 103r-v).

rites of the Magi, and many other types of sacrifice, however false and pagan, still can open the gates of divine and celestial and natural power to men.[110] A similar failure to make careful distinctions between true Christian worship and acts of magical theurgy is evident when Agrippa compares the effects of credulity in superstitious acts to the effect of faith in religious acts, and regards the results as about the same.[111] In prayers and purifications also, he says that though these should be ultimately directed to the one true God, it is helpful to employ astrologically favorable hours and to know what heavens, stars, guardian spirits, and celestial souls are involved as instruments of God.[112]

This tendency to offer naturalistic or partly naturalistic explanations of both magical and religious phenomena found expression also in several portions of various works when Agrippa discussed the relation between true and false religion. In dealing with this question, he reveals an intellectual connection with an attitude which modern German intellectual historians have labeled "universal theism." [113] The basic trait of universal theism is to recognize some—perhaps even much—religious truth in non-Christian religions. Universal theists generally depict the gradual growth from less true religions toward the one true religion; and the latter is usually a somewhat attenuated and nondogmatic version of Christianity. Agrippa's own *De triplici ratione cognoscendi Deum* is a good example of this idea of gradual religious evolution; and even though it stresses the limitations of gentile and Hebrew religion more than universal theists usually did, it also reduces religion to personal piety and justice toward one's fellow men, two ideals which can be approached even outside the Christian faith.[114] Universal theism also often taught that there is a pure, undefiled faith

[110] *Ibid.*, Bk. III, ch. lix, especially p. cccxxxiiii: "Atque hae sunt (quas uocat Orpheus) claues quae aperiunt portas elementorum atque coelorum, ut per illas penetret homo ad supercoelestia, et ad illum descendant intelligentiae coelorum et daemones elementorum." Nearly the same idea, but not all of the same words, appears in the corresponding chapter of MS., Bk. III, ch. 47, fol. 119r, where, however, the reservation in favor of Christian sacrifice does not appear. Cf. MS., Bk. III, ch. 46.
[111] *Ibid.*, Bk. III, ch. iv, pp. ccxv-ccxvii. (MS., Bk. III, ch. 57.) Cf. *ibid.*, Bk. I, ch. lxvi, pp. lxxxvii-lxxxviii. (MS., Bk. I, ch. 42, where the effect of firm belief is mentioned but not developed so fully as in the later text.)
[112] *Ibid.*, Bk. III, ch. lviii, pp. cccxxix-cccxxxi. (MS., Bk. III, ch. 45, the corresponding chapter, lacks some of the most pertinent passages.)
[113] A good discussion of this late medieval attitude is in Stadelmann, *op. cit.*, pp. 146-87.
[114] *De triplici ratione cognoscendi Deum*, ch. 3, in *Opera*, II, 486.

shared by the wise men of all ages, while the concrete historical expressions of religion (perhaps even Christianity) are mere shadows of this faith of the wise, each one having an admixture of superstition that caters to the superstitions of the vulgar. Agrippa also shows traces of this tendency, tacitly in his repeated insistence on the need to keep the pure truth out of the defiled hands of the masses, and more directly in his acceptance of the Neoplatonic myth of a long series of sages or *prisci theologi*, who, having received an esoteric revelation from God, passed it on from generation to generation.[115]

The origin of these expressions of universal theism lay partly in the general mood of the late Middle Ages, and partly in the humanistic effort to rediscover more and more of the wisdom of ancient times. Ficino and the Florentine Academy of the fifteenth century were especially influential in this attempt to uncover ancient truth.[116] Agrippa drew on both medieval and humanistic traditions. He knew the most important text of late medieval universal theism, the dialogue *De pace fidei* of the Cardinal Nicholas of Cusa.[117] He also drew similar notions from the Florentines; and his remark that religion "is so instilled in us by nature that we are distinguished from other living things more by it than by rationality," parallels a similar statement by Ficino.[118]

Agrippa's relation to this tradition, which in different ways also numbered Erasmus and Sebastian Franck among its followers,[119] is pertinent to the problem of the dilution of religion by attempts to offer naturalistic explanations of both magic and religion, for *De occulta philosophia* contains a passage, taken from a general discussion of magical ceremonies, which tends to rob religion of its mystery by explaining it as a universal human reaction to a uni-

[115] Agrippa, *Opera*, II, 1077-79. On this tradition in France, D. P. Walker, "The *Prisca Theologia* in France," *Journal of the Warburg and Courtauld Institutes*, XVII (1954), 204-59.

[116] Kristeller, *Philosophy of Marsilio Ficino*, pp. 15, 25-27.

[117] See Agrippa's *Apologia*, in *Opera*, II, 323.

[118] *De occulta philosophia*, Bk. III, ch. iv, p. ccxv: "[Religio] . . . ita nobis a natura insita est, ut plus illa, quam rationabilitate, a caeteris animantibus discernamur." Cf. Nesca A. Robb, *Neoplatonism of the Italian Renaissance* (London, 1935), p. 63, for Ficino's attitude. Agrippa's statement, quoted in n. 120 below, that all religions have some measure of truth, is reminiscent of Ficino. Cf. Kristeller, *Philosophy of Marsilio Ficino*, pp. 316-20.

[119] Stadelmann, *op. cit.*, pp. 146-87. Cf. Hans Baron, "Erasmus-Probleme im Spiegel des Colloquium 'Inquisitio de fide,'" *Archiv für Reformationsgeschichte*, XLIII (1952), 254-63.

versal human need. In this passage, Agrippa, quite like the universal theists, in effect robs Christianity of its absolute superiority over other faiths and grants it at most a relative superiority:

The rites and ceremonies of religion, however, are different on account of difference of times and regions; and each religion has something good, which is directed toward God Himself the Creator; and although God approves of only the Christian religion alone, yet he does not entirely reject other cults practiced for his sake; and he does not leave them wholly unrewarded, if not with an eternal, then with a temporal reward; or at least he punishes them less. Indeed, he hates, strikes, and extirpates the impious and wholly irreligious as enemies; for their impiety is greater than that of those who have followed a false and erroneous religion. For no religion (as Lactantius says) is so erroneous that it does not contain some wisdom, whence they can have pardon who have fulfilled the highest duty of man, if not in actuality then at least in intention.[120]

This universal theism, with its tendency to minimize the distinctive elements of Christian religion, and with its usual concomitant of a depreciation of the ceremonies and dogmatic formularies of the church,[121] was probably in itself a danger to orthodoxy even though many of its principal adherents were deeply pious and wished to be orthodox. But occurring as it does in a treatise on magic that involved all sorts of rites and ceremonies, and mixed together Christian prayer, pagan invocation, and even demonic conjuration, this

[120] *De occulta philosophia*, Bk. III, ch. iiii, p. ccxvi: "Religionis autem ritus, ceremoniaeque, pro temporum regionumque uarietate, diuersi sunt: et unaquaeque religio boni aliquid habet, quod ad deum ipsum creatorem dirigitur: et licet unam solam Christianam religionem deus approbet, caeteros tamen eius gratia susceptos cultus, non penitus reprobat: et si non eterno, temporaneo tamen praemio irremuneratos non relinquit: uel saltem minus punit: impios uero et penitus irreligiosos, tanquam hostes odit, fulminat, et exterminat: maior enim est illorum impietas, quam eorum qui falsam et erroneam religionem secuti sunt. Nulla enim religio (teste Lactantio) tam erronea, quae non aliquid sapientiae contineat: qua ueniam illi habere possunt, qui summum hominis officium, si non re ipsa, tamen proposito tenuerunt." (This passage is lacking from MS., Bk. III, ch. 3.)

[121] A tendency not lacking in Agrippa. See *De incertitudine et vanitate scientiarum declamatio inuectiua* (Coloniae, 1531), ch. lx: "Verum deus ipse, quem non delectant caro et corpus, et sensibilia signa, has exteriores carnalesque ceremonias despicit. . . . Ipse enim spectator fidei est, considerans intimum spiritum. . . ." This stress on the "intimum spiritum," this internalization of religion, was common among humanists, especially those of northern Europe. It was quite commonly formulated, as in this chapter by Agrippa, in the form of salvation by faith alone. But this was not quite the same as Luther's *sola fide* and was held by many who refused to break with Rome. For a discussion of the difference between the two concepts of justification by faith, see Stadelmann, *op. cit.*, p. 164, in a discussion of Nicholas of Cusa.

passage provides yet another illustration of the danger to orthodoxy that accompanied any handling of magical materials. What
had begun as an attempt to purify magic and reduce if not destroy
its demonic character had ended by making Christianity seem very
closely akin to pagan worship and demonic ceremonies.

All this does not mean that Agrippa or other men with the same
interests, such as Trithemius and Ficino, were wicked and irreligious, though his enemies made such accusations. The main point
is rather that the very nature of magical texts, and of the problems
that this pseudo-science attempted to treat, created difficulties which
no one, not even a cautious "purifier" of magic like Ficino, could
entirely escape. Of course Agrippa and the others never realized
how incompatible their books were with orthodoxy. As D. P.
Walker has well said, "We must remember . . . that, as with astrology, my magic is always good and pious—only other people's is
ever bad and diabolic. . . ." [122] Magical writers like Agrippa were
always sure that they had guarded against use of evil demons.
Toward the end of Book Three of De occulta philosophia, Agrippa
devoted several chapters to outlining methods for the elevation of
the soul, to prepare it for receiving divine and angelic aid in magical
works. The aim of such magical mysticism was not just to secure
more power but also a precaution against the magician's being deceived by demons. Agrippa explicitly warned that true piety was
necessary for these ceremonies, and that if it were lacking, the
magus might find himself being misled by evil spirits.[123] Likewise
Agrippa's tendency to explain much of his occultism in purely
naturalistic terms, and to attribute many magical effects to natural
forces, was another honest but unsuccessful effort to show that
much magic could be entirely free of demonic influence. There was
no conscious aim of weakening all supernatural beliefs by explaining them away. His expression of religious universalism was not
intended to suggest that all religions are purely natural responses
to certain human needs, nor that pagan theurgy was just as good as

[122] Walker, Spiritual and Demonic Magic, p. 89.
[123] De occulta philosophia, Bk. III, ch. vi, p. ccxix: "Quicunque autem non
purificatus accesserit, superinducit sibi iudicium et traditur ad deuorandum
spiritui nequam." (This passage is not in the corresponding chapter of MS.,
Bk. III, ch. 29.) Cf. De occulta philosophia, Bk. III, ch. i, p. ccxi (MS., Bk. I,
ch. 1, which lacks the most apt phrase but still makes the general point), and
Bk. III, ch. liiii, pp. cccxxiiii-cccxxv (lacking in the corresponding chapter of
MS., Bk. III, ch. 41).

Christian worship. Far from thinking his magical work to be incompatible with his faith, he believed that the cabalistic, Hermetic, and other supposedly ancient sources would restore knowledge of God's original revelation, and so would assist the work of religious regeneration.

Even though his attempt to make magic respectable was foredoomed to fail, Agrippa von Nettesheim lived in a world which believed in magic. More than most men of his time, he dared, perhaps unwisely, to plunge enthusiastically into the dark, nebulous, sometimes frightening, but always enticing world of magic. By so doing, he gave expression to an aspect of sixteenth-century culture which lay very near to the center of the Renaissance view of the world, an aspect far too commonly neglected by later historians of the age. He failed to make either himself or his studies respectable in the eyes of his contemporaries. But for all of that, he still expressed in his writings on magic a complex group of ideas that reflected much of the troubled spirit of Renaissance thought.

CHAPTER TEN

THE MAGICAL WORLD

The universe as it presented itself to the mind of Agrippa, especially the young Agrippa up to his departure from Italy in 1518, was an orderly thing.[1] Its parts stood in intimate relations with one another. The dominant strain in his thought did not make him confident that the human mind by its own powers could comprehend this orderly universe and the relations of its parts, but perhaps there were other ways than reason to attain this end. In his quest for such ways, the Nettesheimer turned to magic. One work,

[1] Eugenio Garin, *Medioevo e Rinascimento: Studi e ricerche* (Bari, 1954), pp. 158-60, 185-88, would prefer to describe the world view of magic as one of disorder, in contrast to the rationally ordered universe of medieval scholastic science. In a sense, this is true. Man as the *magus*, often with demonic assistance, breaks through, masters, and uses the natural world order. He refuses to be bound by it. Yet the magical world itself is still one of harmonic interrelationships, which, indeed, form the basis of most magical practices. Garin himself fully emphasizes this fact (pp. 154, 165). Hence I have chosen to label the magical *world* as orderly. Where the disorder enters is with the appearance of the *magus*. It was his action in defying the natural world-order, often through the summoning of demons (good or evil) as assistants, that made his actions seem so evil to defenders of the world view of scholastic science: Garin, pp. 158-60, 187.

260

begun early in life but enlarged repeatedly until its publication in 1531 and 1533, was the chief expression of these attempts to construct a magical world view. This was *De occulta philosophia,* which Agrippa confessed he would have called *De magia* except for the ill repute into which the term *magic* had fallen.[2] This book is the chief but not the only expression of his view of what the world is like. Many shorter tracts, and even *De vanitate,* contain elements of his opinions on the universe.

Anyone who attempts to present a somewhat orderly exposition of the world view of *De occulta philosophia* must note that in the last resort Agrippa himself failed to give unity and order to his own development of that view. *De occulta philosophia* set out to become a synthesis; and it has been called the *summa* of medieval magic, the magical counterpart to the *Summa theologica* of Aquinas. But it was not a *summa.* It was more like a book of sentences, for the collection of the opinions of authorities has almost smothered the attempt to create a synthesis.[3] Its chapters tend to become not orderly expositions but mere chains of alleged facts, all having some connection, however slight, with the topic announced in the chapter title.

Even this drowning of his general ideas in a sea of facts is not the only internal weakness of Agrippa's magical world view. He is really incapable of deciding what he is about. Although his magical writings never quite degenerate into formulae for enchantments, the danger is always present. It is this tendency to slide off into mere practical operations and to lose sight of the theory he is expounding which causes his thought to be almost smothered by supposedly factual information.[4] He also wavers on specific points.

---

[2] *De occulta philosophia libri tres* (Coloniae, 1533), dedicatory epistle to Trithemius, fol. aa3v. References to the earlier (1510) text represented by Würzburg, Universitätsbibliothek, MS. M.ch.q.50, will be indicated thus: Würzburg MS; to the printed version, simply *De occulta philosophia.* The statement about his preference for the title *De magia* does not appear in the dedication of MS., but this text freely uses the term *magia.*

[3] Auguste Prost, *Les sciences et les arts occultes au XVI siècle: Corneille Agrippa, sa vie et ses oeuvres* (2 vols.; Paris, 1881-82), I, 66-67, calls it a magical *summa.* More accurate perhaps is the phrase "historia potius philosophica de arte magiae" used by Johann Jakob Brucker, *Historia critica philosophiae a mundi incunabilis ad nostram usque aetatem deducta* (4 vols. in 5; Lipsiae, 1742-44), IV¹, 406. *Historia* is used in a sense similar to that found in the writings of Francis Bacon.

[4] For a parallel danger in the "practical" side of Jewish cabalism, see Gershom Gerhard Scholem, *Major Trends in Jewish Mysticism* (New York, 1946), pp. 98-99, 144-45, 273-79.

Generally he regards astral influences as the servants, not the masters, of the magician. Yet both in *De occulta philosophia* and in his treatise on geomancy he also appears at times to teach the opposite. Divine, demonic, and celestial names are capable of reducing superior forces to the service of man. But Agrippa hesitates. It seems that in the last resort they are rather paths for the ascent of the soul to higher realms. He also wavers on the question of the need for illumination. His general message is that the soul must receive divine light before it can excel in magic. Yet he also teaches that even profane and wicked men can summon spirits and do many magical works. Obviously he has been unable to bring himself to a clear choice and then to stick to that choice in the elaboration of his occult world. This world in itself, one, interconnected, and animated, is little different from that of Giordano Bruno at the end of the century.[5] But Bruno was able as Agrippa was not to create a largely consistent system and stick to it. He was also able to solve the problem of knowledge and order in the world in a way for which Agrippa was merely groping. Despite the hints of the modern idea of scientific hypothesis in the Nettesheimer's thought, despite his appeal to mysticism and blind faith for the resolution of his intellectual struggles, despite his effort to purify magic by associating it with an orderly world view, Agrippa's mind drifted uncertainly between intellectual despair on the one hand and a sort of omnivorous, generalized credulity on the other.

This looseness of thought development was also due at least in part to the origin of *De occulta philosophia* itself. Most of the chapters which Agrippa sent to Trithemius in 1510 still survived in the full printed edition of 1533.[6] He could not bear to throw out something once written. But during the ensuing two decades of revision, most of these chapters underwent the addition of all sorts of illustrative materials, sometimes having only the loosest connection with

[5] Ernst Cassirer, *Das Erkenntnisproblem in der Philosophie und Wissenschaft der neueren Zeit* (2nd ed.; 3 vols.; Berlin, 1911-23), I, 344-45.

[6] Careful comparison of the two texts has shown me only a small group of chapters which were not taken over from Würzburg MS. into the later text, namely Bk. II, ch. 45 (of which a few elements appear in Bk. II, ch. lix, of the printed form); Bk. II, ch. 50 (from which one quotation survives in Bk. I, ch. lvii, of the printed form); Bk. III, ch. 15 (of which one short passage was printed in Bk. III, ch. xxvi); Bk. III, ch. 50 (even in this case, some of the divine names were printed in Bk. III, ch. xi). In addition, Bk. II, ch. 28, of Würzburg MS. has disappeared; but its materials have been used for Bk. II, ch. xiv-xv, of the revised form.

the original text. Thus the work, never particularly tightly organized, became more and more of a loose conglomeration as the years went by. The final revision before publication made only a few half-hearted attempts to correct this structural weakness.[7]

Even beyond these reasons, however, the main cause of Agrippa's failure to present his magical world view consistently was his aim in studying magic. His purpose was not to use human reason to elaborate a new science. Rather, he intended to restore the original purity of an old science. Magic, he maintains, has fallen into disrepute because of the admixture of superstition in the works of its modern authorities. But it was not always in ill repute. Once it was the highest wisdom. Indeed, three Eastern Magi were the first to adore the Christ Child; and the Sibyls foretold the Incarnation.[8] His self-imposed task was to recover the secret wisdom of these ancient traditions; and it was especially difficult, he believed, because the old magicians, not wishing their sacred wisdom to fall into the hands of the vulgar masses, used secret forms of writing which only the initiated could understand, so that their real meaning was not apparent merely from the published words of their books.[9] He drew his explanation of the origin of this concealed wisdom from Neoplatonic and cabalistic mythology. Divine revelation, he believed, was the ultimate source of magical truth. This revelation included not only the accepted canon of the Old Testament but also an esoteric interpretation of the deeper meaning of the sacred text. He acknowledged such revealed truth not only in the Jewish Cabala but also in the Hermetic literature and in the Neoplatonic and Neopythagorean writings.[10] With such a belief in the divine

[7] For example, in Bk. I, ch. i, Agrippa has added materials which try to broaden the philosophical setting of his work and to introduce a consistent world view based on the doctrine of the threefold nature of the world, elemental, celestial, and intellectual. This doctrine does not appear, at least not explicitly, in Würzburg MS.

[8] De occulta philosophia, "Ad Lectorem," fol. aa2r. This preface was not a part of the original text of 1510 and does not appear in Würzburg MS.

[9] De occulta philosophia, Bk. III, ch. xxx, pp. cclxxiii-cclxxvi. (Chapter not in Würzburg MS.) This fear of the masses, which Paola Zambelli stresses greatly in her preface to a recent edition of some Agrippan texts, in Eugenio Garin et al., eds., Testi umanistici su l'Ermetismo: Testi di Ludovico Lazzarelli, F. Giorgio Veneto, Cornelio Agrippa di Nettesheim (Rome, 1955), pp. 110-11, was also emphasized by other Renaissance writers on magic: e.g., Marsilio Ficino. See D. P. Walker, Spiritual and Demonic Magic from Ficino to Campanella (London, 1958), p. 51. If not kept from the masses, it was believed, this science would be distorted into evil idolatry and polytheism.

[10] Oratio in praelectione . . . Trismegisti, in Agrippa's Opera (2 vols.; Lug-

origin of the concealed wisdom of all the sages of Antiquity, Agrippa could logically do little but uncritically record their opinions. Even his occasional appeal to personal experience assumed the same authoritarian tone. His mind did not control and interpret facts gained by reading or by personal observation, nor did it make a consistent and sustained effort to create a new synthesis from these materials. As he saw matters, the truth was already present in the authorities, and his sole task was to recognize it and bring it together.

Nevertheless, perhaps as much because of the homogeneity of his sources as because of any achievement of his own, Agrippa does elaborate a fairly systematic world view in De occulta philosophia. He is thinking of this system when he defines magic. According to him, magic is the highest and holiest philosophy, full of the loftiest mysteries, including, uniting, and actualizing the three chief divisions of philosophy, namely physics, mathematics, and theology. Just as these three divisions of philosophy deal respectively with the terrestrial, celestial, and divine worlds, so magic has three parts, natural, celestial, and ceremonial or religious.[11] The division of De occulta philosophia into three books is supposed to correspond to the tripartite nature of magic, but Agrippa does not follow this pattern closely. Elsewhere, he uses a twofold division into natural magic, which studies the highest relationships of natural philosophy and accomplishes works seemingly miraculous but actually natural, and ceremonial magic, which uses certain rites to attract spirits, either good or evil.[12] Apparently on this occasion he associates the celestial with the natural, although he is unclear and seems somewhat inclined to assign the attraction of certain celestial powers to ceremonial magic. The effort to follow his threefold classification keeps Agrippa from expounding the magical pseudo-sciences one by one in orderly fashion. Thus De occulta philosophia gives no extensive exposition of astrology, geomancy, Cabala, necromancy,

---

duni, n.d.), II, 1077-79. The idea of a concealed meaning in the wise men of Antiquity also appears in De occulta philosophia, Bk. III, ch. ii, pp. ccxi-ccxiii (Würzburg MS., Bk. II, ch. 2).

[11] De occulta philosophia, Bk. I, ch. i-ii, pp. i-iii. Würzburg MS. lacks the threefold division of the world; but Bk. II, ch. 2, advances a division of magic into three parts: physics, mathematics, and theology, a division which goes back to Aristotle.

[12] De incertitudine et vanitate scientiarum declamatio inuectiua (Coloniae, 1531), ch. xli-xlvi. Henceforth cited as De vanitate.

theurgy, or any other single magical science as such. In a sense, *De vanitate*, although negative and destructive in approach, does a better job of explaining what each special branch of magic is like. His sole elaboration of a single occult science is *In geomanticam disciplinam lectura*.

The world view of Agrippa is that of Hellenistic and medieval times. All parts of the universe are closely connected, for the superior rules its immediate inferior and is ruled by its own superior; and at the top of this hierarchy, the Archetype, God, reigns supreme, transmitting His power down through the entire system. The human soul may ascend through this hierarchy and so attain the power of the superior ranks, even the power of God. This doctrine of mystical ascent through a hierarchy of being is one basis for magic. The other basis is the belief that all being is so closely linked that whatever affects one part affects all the others. The world may thus be compared to a great living animal, all of which is affected when any member is affected. Or, to use a simile which Agrippa himself employs, the sympathy among its parts is like that between two harps tuned to the same pitch. If one harp is struck, the strings of the other will also vibrate.

The whole universe, Agrippa continues, is orderly and harmonic. Thus for example, the intervals between the planets are in integral proportions corresponding to the proportions between tones on the musical scale. Likewise there are harmonious proportions between the various elements and between the parts of the human body. Symbols such as letters, words, numbers, and geometrical figures can be used to express these relationships. These harmonious relations exist not only within each of the three realms of being, the elementary, celestial, and intellectual worlds, but also among various things in different realms, for example between the sun and animals of solar virtue, such as the lion and the cock. Among the various worlds, the lower is ruled by the middle, and the middle by the highest. Within this harmonious whole, which God created for His own glory, every creature has its proper place and its limits which it is forbidden to transgress. To break this prohibition, to attack this order, to seek to abandon one's proper place is sin, the sin of Adam and of Satan. Agrippa's picture of an orderly, tripartite world, intellectual, celestial, and elementary, doubtless is a borrowing from the Florentine Neoplatonists, probably from Pico della Mirandola, who in turn depends on Jewish (not necessarily cabalistic) sources.[13]

The world is also divided among the traditional four elements of ancient natural science, earth, air, fire, and water; nor, Agrippa believes, are these elements restricted to the elementary or terrestrial world, for they exist also in the upper reaches of being, where they are more perfect, more spiritual, less gross, less material. The elements exist in the celestial world, for some of the planets are predominantly linked to one or another of them. Even angels contain the elements in a still purer state, for some (seraphim, for example) are igneous, some (thrones) are aqueous, and so on. Elements exist even in the Archetype, God, as the ideas of the things produced.[14] Each element, furthermore, has certain characteristic properties (air, for instance, is hot and moist); and these properties are the basis for many operations in natural magic. All individual things in the created universe are subsumed under one of these four elements and so themselves have certain characteristic properties.

Not all the properties of things, however, arise from the elements which compose them. There are properties the cause of which human reason cannot investigate. What philosophers know of these occult properties comes not from reasoning about causes but only

---

[13] De occulta philosophia, Bk. I, ch. i, p. i; Bk. II, ch. xxiii, pp. cliiii-clv (Würzburg MS., Bk. II, ch. 30); Bk. II, ch. xxvi, pp. clviii-clx; De triplici ratione cognoscendi Deum, in Agrippa's Opera, II, 480-82. For the threefold world of the Florentine Neoplatonists, see Nesca Adeline Robb, Neoplatonism of the Italian Renaissance (London, 1935), p. 65. Professor Paul Oskar Kristeller in a letter to the author has raised the question of the precise source of Agrippa's doctrine of the threefold world, elementalis, coelestis, and intellectualis. This was probably Giovanni Pico della Mirandola, Heptaplus, "Aliud prooemium," ed. Eugenio Garin (Florence, 1942), p. 184. A cabalistic writer contemporary to Agrippa, Pietro Galatino, presented a similar but not identical threefold division of the world which Rudolf Rocholl, "Der Platonismus der Renaissancezeit," Zeitschrift für Kirchengeschichte, XIII (1892), 65-72, regards as Zoharic in origin: informis (divinus), formalis (mentalis, intelligibilis), and materialis. Whatever Agrippa's precise source, the 1510 version of De occulta philosophia lacks the chapter (Bk. I, ch. i) which presents the threefold world, while in a work of 1515, Dialogus de homine, Lyons, Bibliothèque Municipale, MS. No. 48, fol. 48r [sic; recte 49r], the doctrine is clearly present (text now edited by Paola Zambelli, Rivista critica di storia della filosofia, XIII [1958], 47-71). Since the doctrine of the threefold world first appears in a work of the Italian period, and since Agrippa's other works of that period show frequent use of Pico's Heptaplus, it is probably justifiable to attribute the doctrine to his studies while in Italy, including his reading of Pico and perhaps of some Hebrew text not yet identified.

[14] De occulta philosophia, Bk. I, ch. viii, p. xiii (not in MS.).

from long experience.[15] This view Agrippa developed in a different sense in his *De vanitate*, where, as Chapter Eight shows, one of the charges against the occult sciences is precisely that no one can give satisfactory reasons for their operations; one can allege only experience. Examples of occult properties come from daily experience and from the authority of ancient writers: the power of the magnet to attract iron, the power of the stomach to transform food into flesh and blood, the power of the Phoenix to regenerate itself, the power of the tiny fish echina to hold fast any ship which it touches. Agrippa attributes such occult properties to the forms of the individual things. He explains these forms in turn by a multiple causation: from the ideas of the things in the mind of the Archetype, from ruling intelligences, from the aspects of the heavens, and from the influence of the heavens on the arrangement of the elements. But it is typical of Agrippa that he does not adhere even to this extremely complicated pattern. Many inexplicable effects are the result rather of a *spiritus mundi*, or quintessence, a fifth element subsisting outside and above the four elements, and permeating all being. Because all generative and seminal power is in the quintessence, alchemists seek to refine it and use it to transform base metal into gold. Agrippa reports that he himself knows how to do this but candidly admits that the substance will not produce a weight of gold greater than the gold from which he originally extracted the quintessence.[16] The world must also have an *anima*, or soul, as well as this *spiritus* or quintessence; and the *anima mundi* is yet another source of occult effects. Agrippa is quite determined to prove the existence of this world soul, on the authority of ancient poets and wise men, and of the Church Fathers and later Christian theologians, as well as by reason, because only in this way can he depict an active world, alive, characterized by force and influence, rather than a dead and passive universe. Thus his occult world is completely the analogue of man, having material body, intermediate *spiritus*, and intellectual soul. The world-soul

[15] *Ibid.*, Bk. I, ch. x, pp. xiii-xv (MS., Bk. I, ch. 4); cf. Bk. I, ch. xx, p. xxvi (MS., Bk. I, ch. 13).

[16] *Ibid.*, Bk. I, ch. xiii-xiv, pp. xvii-xix. Würzburg MS. lacks this specific example of transmutation, but Bk. I, ch. 7, discusses the *spiritus mundi* or quintessence and regards transmutation as one of its effects. Ficino also discussed *spiritus mundi*, but characteristically he was interested in it not as an instrument for causing effects on external objects, but as an aid in making the soul more celestial. See Walker, *Spiritual and Demonic Magic*, pp. 12-13.

is also useful as the medium through which God transmits power to the various individual objects in the world.[17] Occult properties, therefore, result less from any particular portion of the universe than from the fact that this whole world is a living, active thing, a thing of power and activity.

These occult properties are useful for operations of natural magic according to the principle that like begets like. Thus sterile things (the urine of a mule, for instance) cause sterility; the sex organs of passionate animals can be used for making love potions. Occult properties can even be transferred from one thing to another. Thus the magnet transfers its power to iron; thus, too, a woman who uses a prostitute's mirror becomes wanton.[18] There are likewise natural but occult relations of amity and enmity between certain things; and these relations, too, may be used for antidotes and cures.

Another major element in the occult world of Agrippa is the influence of heavenly bodies over terrestrial things, that is, of the higher over the lower. Agrippa's world is one of absolute qualities: up is up and down is down, *per se* and not merely by relation. The aesthetic value judgments which Copernicus could not shake off, for instance the superiority of circular motion, are present in the Nettesheimer's world, too, as is trust in the incorruptibility of the heavens and in the greater dignity of the more elevated and less material.[19]

Since Agrippa's doubts about judicial astrology were probably well developed by the time he left Italy and perhaps even as early as 1509, the question naturally arises whether these doubts do not completely vitiate the importance which he attributes to astral influences in his magical system. How can he continue to insist so strongly that one must observe celestial influences in every magical work? Eugenio Garin has solved a similar problem in the thought of Pico della

---

[17] *De occulta philosophia*, Bk. I, ch. xii, p. xvi (Würzburg MS., Bk. I, ch. 6, which lacks one of the chapter's two references to *anima mundi*); Bk. II, ch. lv-lvii, pp. cc-cciii (an extended discussion of *anima mundi*, based on MS., Bk. III, ch. 18-21); Bk. III, ch. xv, pp. ccxxxviii-ccxxxix (not in MS.).

[18] *Ibid.*, Bk. I, ch. xv-xvi, pp. xx-xxii (MS., Bk. I, ch. 8-9). This juxtaposition of the rational and the fantastic is typical of Agrippa's attempts to make his points by heaping up illustrative "facts" of the most varied sort and most uneven quality.

[19] *In artem brevem Raymundi Lullii commentaria*, printed in Raymundus Lullius, *Opera* (Argentinae, 1598), pp. 812, 814. This work also appears in Agrippa's *Opera*, II, 334-436. Belief in the incorruptibility of the heavens was a commonplace of ancient and medieval science.

Mirandola. For it is one thing to subject the fate of man to the direction of the stars, a thing which neither Pico nor Agrippa wanted to do; and quite another thing to make the assumed connection between celestial and terrestrial things an instrument which man uses to perform works seemingly miraculous but actually natural. This is the way in which Agrippa generally looks at astral influences in *De occulta philosophia*. He does not conceive these influences as governing man but rather as enabling man to do things which he could not accomplish by merely terrestrial powers. In his *In geomanticam disciplinam lectura*, he does seem inclined to subject man's lot to astral influences; but even there he vaguely adds that the purer sort of geomantical divination depends on the power of the soul of the person who casts the lots.[20] Man is not the passive subject of astral influences but rather the active employer of them: he is the *magus*. Agrippa's elaborate enumeration of objects pertaining to each planet and sign of the zodiac and his elaboration of the seals and magic squares of each planet are guides for the magician to use in his operations.[21]

One further characteristic of the universe which Agrippa presents in *De occulta philosophia* and presupposes elsewhere is its permeation by spiritual beings, both good and evil. Not only the heavens, stars, and elements, but also the whole world itself have rational souls. Man can by careful preparation and correct ritual summon these spirits and souls and induce them to do his bidding.

[20] *De occulta philosophia*, Bk. II, ch. xxix, pp. clxxi-clxxii (Würzburg MS., Bk. II, ch. 1), on celestial influences. On Pico, see Eugenio Garin, *Giovanni Pico della Mirandola: Vita e dottrina* (Florence, 1937), pp. 179-82. For Agrippa's geomancy, see his *Opera*, I, 405-25.
[21] *De occulta philosophia*, Bk. II, *passim*, especially ch. xxii, pp. cxlv-cliii. That the strange symbols which accompany this chapter are not mere occultist mystifications but serve as mnemonic aids for the construction of magic squares appears from E. Cazalas, "Les sceaux planétaires de C. Agrippa," *Revue de l'histoire des religions*, CX (1934), 66-82, and "Le sceau de la lune de C. Agrippa," *ibid.*, CXIV (1936), 93-98. See also I. R. F. Calder, "A Note on Magic Squares in the Philosophy of Agrippa of Nettesheim," *Journal of the Warburg and Courtauld Institutes*, XII (1949), 196-99, and Karl Anton Nowotny, "The Construction of Certain Seals and Characters in the Work of Agrippa of Nettesheim," *ibid.*, XII (1949), 46-47. Würzburg MS. lacks Bk. II, ch. xxii, and many of the other tables printed in Book Two; but it still contains ample material on celestial images: MS., Bk. II, ch. 4-16. This material appears in the printed version, with some additions, as Bk. II, ch. xxxv-xlv, xlvii, xlix-l. Cf. MS., Bk. II, ch. 31, which is similar to the printed Bk. II, ch. li, except for the tables of characters of signs and stars, which are constructed on a different plan.

The use of such intelligences and their names in magic, he argues, is quite lawful, not at all impious.[22] He then proceeds to describe in considerable detail the hierarchy of good and bad demons. Good demons are of three main ranks: the supercelestial, which have no relation to any bodies but transmit divine light to the lower orders; the celestial intelligences, which rule the various planets; and ministering demons, which watch over men. There are corresponding orders of dark or rebellious demons. Citing Dionysius and Proclus, he distinguishes nine orders of angels, divided into three groups of three, and nine orders of evil spirits. These good and bad demons struggle for the soul, which Agrippa regards, however, as free to give the victory to either side. Each man has three guardian spirits, a sacred one subject not to the planets but only to God; a spirit of his nativity; and a spirit of profession, which changes as one changes occupations. These spirits, he thinks, give a man certain capabilities and make him suited to prosper in certain places or occupations and not in others.

But the chief importance of this angelology is that one who knows the names of the demons can invoke them to assist in magical operations. The true names of angels, Agrippa declares, are known only to God; but man can derive names from their duties and effects, or by cabalistic interpretation of certain passages of Scripture which describe the divine essence, or from the disposition of the heavens, or from the things over which they preside. Every name having magical power, he thinks, derives that power ultimately from a name of God. He gives lists and tables of names and symbols of good and evil spirits. He points out that it is hard to get good spirits to assist in human works, but that even profane men can bind evil spirits by certain rites, although he who uses these without binding them through good spirits is in danger of damnation.[23] With the aid of spirits, necromancers even succeed in raising dead bodies, though Agrippa feels that many such cases have involved the ending of a state of suspended animation rather than

---

[22] De occulta philosophia, Bk. II, ch. lviii, pp. cciii-cciiii. The corresponding passage of MS. (Bk. III, ch. 17) lacks the apologetic passage justifying use of these names. Cf. De occulta philosophia, Bk. III, ch. xv, pp. ccxxxviii-ccxxxix (not in MS.).

[23] Ibid., Bk. III, ch. xvi-xxxiii, pp. ccxxxix-cclxxx, for Agrippa's treatment of demons. Much, but not most, of this material on demons also appears in MS., Bk. III, ch. 8-14, 54-55. Cf. De vanitate, ch. xlvi, and, for the complaint about the abuse of the names Cabala and magic to mean commerce with evil spirits, his De triplici ratione cognoscendi Deum, in Opera, II, 488-89.

real restoration of life.[24] He claims to have witnessed the following example of the power of demonic names over nature: A man in the hour of the moon inscribed the name and sign of a certain spirit on a piece of virgin paper and then fed it to a frog and murmured a certain song. Shortly after he had returned the frog to the water, a rainstorm began.[25] What is important about such tales (and they abound in De occulta philosophia) is that they show that Agrippa's interest in angelology, like his interest in astral influences and in elementary and occult properties, concerns primarily not the control of these powers over man, but man's use of these powers to control his surroundings.

If it is possible to regard elementary and occult qualities, celestial influences, and good and evil spirits as mere tools of the magus, the same is not true of the Being who underlies all of these others, God. It is not merely that God is the creator of the magus as well as of all other creatures, nor even that the magus is subject to divine providence. The different position of God is chiefly the result of man's inability to become a true magus without aid and illumination from God. Now it is true that Agrippa fails to carry through this idea consistently in all parts of De occulta philosophia. He teaches that even the profane man can summon evil spirits, though at his own risk. Clearly Agrippa regards some elementary, occult, celestial, and angelic influences as amenable to control by any person clever enough to learn something about the sympathetic bonds which connect all parts of the universe. Nevertheless, his usual attitude is to insist on the mind's need for aid from God before it can attain power over the universe. In this respect, it is significant that the concluding chapters of De occulta philosophia contain descriptions of rituals and preparations intended to free the mind from its earthly chains and prepare it to receive divine influences. The final expository chapter of the work in its printed form concludes with the following advice: "Finally, in all things have God before your eyes. . . . Also the assiduous prayer of a just man is of great weight." This same message survives in De vanitate, where illumination by God is held to be necessary for one who wants to comprehend the deeper meaning of Scripture.[26] Divine and angelic names do have

[24] De occulta philosophia, Bk. III, ch. xlii, pp. ccciiii-ccovi. MS., Bk. II, ch. 57, is much less detailed on the subject of necromancy, and also much less cautious.
[25] Ibid., Bk. III, ch. xxiv, p. ccliiii (not in MS.).
[26] Ibid., Bk. III, ch. lxiiii, pp. cccxliiii-cccxlv: "In omnibus denique deum prae oculis habe. . . . Multum quoque ualet oratio iusti assidua." Cf. De vanitate, ch. xcviii.

great power, Agrippa says in one of his treatises; but they are not so much tools of man as paths for the ascent of the soul to God.[27] Since the Nettesheimer believes that ignorance of God after the sin of Adam is the source of all of man's weakness, he is confident that the purified and illuminated soul can perform miracles. This power, however, is the result not of any strength of the soul itself, but of knowledge of and contact with God gained through grace and faith. Even though Agrippa fails to follow this idea consistently, it is one of the chief themes of his magical world view.[28]

Like any good Neoplatonist, Agrippa has difficulty in keeping God distinct from the created world,[29] but he makes the attempt to do so by the device of intermediary deities. God created man's body, and apparently all the material universe, by means of these lesser deities, for had He created the body directly, it would not have been mortal.[30] Agrippa tries to reconcile this hierarchy of deities with Christian orthodoxy. Hence he not only insists on the orthodox belief about the Trinity and the two natures of Christ, but is also sure that the Platonists and all the wisest of the ancients had a trinitarian concept of God.[31] But although his God is of one nature and three persons, a doctrine which he finds reflected in the meaning of the Hebrew term *En-soph* and in the *nox* of the Orphic hymns, there are also in God many divinities (*numina*), emanating from Him like rays.[32] The gentiles, Agrippa says, called these emanations gods; the Hebrews, numerations or *sephiroth*; the Christians (Dionysius, for example), attributes. Although there are ten *sephiroth*, the first three being attributed each to one of the persons

---

[27] *De triplici ratione cognoscendi Deum*, in *Opera*, II, 487-88.

[28] *Ibid.*, II, 491-93. Cf. *Dialogus de homine*, Lyons, Bibliothèque Municipale, MS. No. 48, fol. 52v [*sic;* should be 53v].

[29] *De occulta philosophia*, Bk. III, ch. vii, p. ccxx (Würzburg MS., Bk. III, ch. 4); Bk. III, ch. xii, p. ccxxxiii (not in MS.). Agrippa qualifies these statements by drawing an orthodox distinction between Creator and Creation: Bk. III, ch. xxxvi, p. cclxxxiiii (the qualifying phrase is not in the corresponding chapter of MS., Bk. III, ch. 22).

[30] *Ibid.*, Bk. I, ch. lxi, p. lxxx (not in MS.).

[31] *Ibid.*, Bk. III, ch. viii, pp. ccxxi-ccxxiii. The corresponding chapter of Würzburg MS., Bk. III, ch. 5, has many of the same materials, drawn from ancient Neoplatonists and sustaining a trinitarian concept of God, but it lacks the flat statement that the Platonists "tres in deo personas posuisse." In both versions, the chapter next following presents an orthodox trinitarian confession of faith.

[32] *Ibid.*, Bk. III, ch. x, pp. ccxxiiii-ccxxvii. MS. lacks this chapter, which lists the ten *sephiroth* or divine emanations of the Hebrew cabalists and also insists that the same beliefs are suggested in the Orphic hymns.

of the Trinity, he feels that God has far more manifestations (or names, for each name represents a manifestation) than these ten, or the forty-five listed by Dionysius, or even the seventy-two which the cabalists derive from a certain passage in Exodus. He shows how the cabalists by various ways of moving and exchanging letters can derive innumerable angelic and divine names. Yet he tries to avoid conflict between these teachings and the supremacy of the one true God over these lesser divinities. The true name of God, he teaches, is known neither to men nor to angels, but only to God Himself. All the divine names known to cabalists express merely some work of God, except only the Tetragrammaton, *JHVH*. What is more, all the power of divine names has devolved on the one name *Jesus* since the Incarnation, so that the cabalists no longer can use divine names to work miracles as they once did. Through the name *Jesus*, God rules the entire hierarchy of being. His power descends through all His ministers and angels down even to the lowest realm of being.[33]

This use of divine names and other symbols merits study in its own right. One of the chief ways in which Agrippa pulls together his doctrine of the sympathetic universe is by the place which he assigns to symbols, especially letters, words, and numbers. It is by understanding the numerical and literal relationships of things, he teaches, that man can most effectively perform magical works. Suffumigations, aspersions, magical rings, observation of the phases of heavenly bodies, are all of importance; but the *magus* performs his greatest works by incantations and by use of verbal and numerical relationships.

Agrippa's philosophical realism makes him regard the divine ideas in the mind of God as not only the source of all particular being but also the cause of all power in particulars.[34] Even physical beings are in a sense only symbols of the divine ideas, a notion which clearly shows the influence of Neoplatonism, from Florentine and

[33] *Ibid.*, Bk. III, ch. xi-xii, pp. ccxxvii-ccxxxiiii. This argument forms the main point of Johann Reuchlin's *De verbo mirifico*, on which Agrippa lectured at Dôle in 1509. See Ludwig Geiger, *Johann Reuchlin: Sein Leben und seine Werke* (Leipzig, 1871), p. 183. Although Würzburg MS., Bk. III, ch. 49, forms a part of the printed Bk. III, ch. xi, the significant portions of the latter chapter represent materials added after 1510, and the whole of ch. xii, the discussion of the new form of the divine name, is missing from the earlier version.

[34] *De occulta philosophia*, Bk. I, ch. xi, p. xv (Würzburg MS., Bk. I, ch. 5). Cf. Cassirer, *op. cit*, I, 191-93.

other sources. The supercelestial and celestial as well as the terrestrial realms have their real being in the mind of God. When man discovers an apparent relation between things, that relation is really between the ideas of the things. Hence the ideas are the cause of occult virtues, for instance, of the ability of the magnet to attract iron, or of the fish echina to hold a ship fast. If the idea of matter is closely associated with the idea of a living being, he thinks, its occult virtues cease at death; if it is not so associated, the creature retains its virtues after death.[35] Likewise Agrippa teaches that ideas can affect the material world, as illustrated by the effect of passions of the soul on the body. Thus when we think of eating something sour we grit our teeth. Thus also Cyppus, King of Italy, fell asleep while thinking of a bullfight and awoke horned, because the power of the imagination had driven the horn-bearing humors to his head.[36] Clearly, Agrippa attributes great reality and great effects to ideas.

Furthermore, he believes, words or other symbols which express these ideas possess the power of the ideas themselves. Words which represent the greatest things, the intellectual, the celestial, or the supernatural, have the greatest power, for as symbols of these higher things they attract their power. He distinguishes two sources of the power of words. One of these is the power of the mind of the person who uses the word. The other is a correspondence between the word and the divine idea which it expresses. When both significations concur, he thinks, the word has a double virtue and becomes far more powerful, especially if it is uttered at a suitable time and place and over a material which is apt to receive its influence.[37] The power of a word is greater if it comes from a nobler language and greatest if it comes from Hebrew, which for part of his life, at least, he regarded as the one pure and unchanging language, instituted by God and having great affinity to the relation between things in the universe.[38] Words have their greatest power when joined together to form incantations. To compose such an incanta-

[35] De occulta philosophia, Bk. I, ch. xxi, pp. xxvii-xxviii (MS., Bk. I, ch. 15).
[36] Ibid., Bk. I, ch. lxiv, pp. lxxxiiii-lxxxvi. The corresponding chapter of MS., Bk. I, ch. 40, lacks the story about Cyppus. Montaigne uses this same anecdote in his "Apology for Raymond Sebond."
[37] De occulta philosophia, Bk. I, ch. lxix-lxx, pp. xc-xci. Only a portion of ch. lxix, and none of lxx, occurs in MS. (Bk. I, ch. 46).
[38] Ibid., Bk. I, ch. lxxiv, pp. xcv-xcvi (not found in MS.). Here Agrippa calls Hebrew letters the foundation of all creation and of all magic. This faith in the special permanency of Hebrew letters is lacking in De vanitate, ch. ii.

THE MAGICAL WORLD 275

tion intended to attract the power of some star or spirit, one should select a star or spirit which has the power required and then should invoke that star or spirit, extolling it for possessing the desired power. Such incantations, he says, work by a most pure harmonic spirit which bears along the intention of the speaker. One may further enhance the power of words by inscribing them as well as pronouncing them.[39] Agrippa assigns the various letters of the Hebrew, Greek, and Latin alphabets to the seven planets, the twelve signs of the zodiac, and the elements.[40]

But letters have a further power because in many systems of notation, such as the Roman numerals, they also represent numbers, according to which, he teaches, all things were made and by which all things are ruled. The *magus* who knows natural philosophy and mathematics will be able to. do many things apparently but not really beyond the power of nature. Agrippa notes that in this way the wise men of earlier times were able to build structures which the common people now think are the works of demons, like certain "great citadels and heaps of rocks such as I saw in Britain. . . ."[41] He then expounds the great powers in various numbers, explaining, however, that he means not merchants' numbers but pure or formal numbers, such as the cabalists use.[42] He gives inventories of the powers of the numbers up to ten, and also examples of the powers of certain larger numbers. Six, for example, is the number of perfection. The Pythagoreans apply it to generation and marriage. The world was finished on the sixth day. On the sixth day Christ suffered for our redemption. The Hebrew bondservant served for six years. There are six tones in all harmony.[43] And so on.

[39] *De occulta philosophia*, Bk. I, ch. lxxi-lxxiii, pp. xci-xciiii. These chapters, all of which deal with incantations, are lacking from Würzburg MS., though MS. does have other chapters on this subject (Bk. II, ch. 34-48). For Renaissance magicians, "spirit" generally performed the function of linking the intellectual and nonmaterial with the material world. See Walker, *Spiritual and Demonic Magic*, especially pp. 3-4, 12-13, 52-53, 75.

[40] *De occulta philosophia*, Bk. I, ch. lxxiiii, pp. xcvi-xcvii (MS. lacks this chapter).

[41] *Ibid.*, Bk. II, ch. i, p. c: ". . . arces saxorumque moles, cuiusmodi ego in Britannia uidi uix credibili arte congestas." Stonehenge, perhaps? (MS. lacks this chapter.)

[42] *Ibid.*, Bk. II, ch. iii, pp. cii-ciii. This qualification about pure number is not in the corresponding chapter of MS. (Bk. II, ch. 29).

[43] *Ibid.*, Bk. II, ch. ix, p. cxiii. Many, but not all, of these examples of the powers of six occur in MS., Bk. II, ch. 23. A concise and suggestive account of the origins and character of this number symbolism is Vincent Foster Hopper, *Medieval Number Symbolism: Its Sources, Meaning, and Influence*

Certain symbols express these numbers. One of the most mysterious is magical gesticulation. Agrippa explains that the strange gesticulations which magicians use are not signals to demons, as many critics charge, but rather are symbolical representations of the numbers whose virtues are needed for the particular work in hand.[44] There are also more easily comprehensible symbols for numbers; and he discusses in some detail the various Latin, Greek, Arabic, Hebrew, and Chaldean systems of numerical notation. Again he attributes highest worth to the Hebrew systems. These numerical symbols may be assigned, he says, to letters, to gods, to planets, and to elements. Thus if one wishes to cast a person's horoscope, a good way to begin is by finding the numerical value of his name and the names of his parents, although Agrippa adds that this applies only in countries where names are chosen according to nativity and not at random.[45] The virtues of a planet may be attracted by inscribing on a material subject to that planet the magic square which represents its number. The puzzling symbols which Agrippa appends to the chapters that expound this theory are, as recent research has shown, mnemonic devices to guide the magician in constructing the magic square of each planet. Another example of the influence of such ideas in the sixteenth century occurs in Albrecht Dürer's famed engraving "Melencolia I." The magic square of Jupiter on the wall in the engraving is intended to counteract excessive melancholy resulting from the influence of the planet Saturn, which shines in the background.[46]

Numbers are not the only symbols to which Agrippa attributes magical power. Symbolical figures have their power because they express some higher reality, ultimately because they express a divine idea.[47] Thus geometrical figures have magical power because they express pure number: for instance, the circle stands for unity; the

---

on Thought and Expression (New York, 1938), *passim*, especially p. 105, where he calls Agrippa's *De occulta philosophia* the most elaborate development of medieval numerological symbolism. Agrippa wrote down many of the details of numerological relationships discussed by Hopper on pp. 38-46.

[44] *De occulta philosophia*, Bk. II, ch. xvi, pp. cxxxviii-cxxxix (not in MS.).

[45] *Ibid.*, Bk. II, ch. xx, p. cxliii-cxliiii (not in MS.).

[46] Aby Warburg, "Heidnisch-antike Weissagung in Wort und Bild zu Luthers Zeiten," in his *Gesammelte Schriften* (2 vols.; Leipzig, 1932), II, 530-31; Erwin Panofsky and Fritz Saxl, *Dürers "Melencolia I": Eine Quellen- und Typengeschichtliche Untersuchung* (Leipzig, 1923), pp. 51-53.

[47] *De occulta philosophia*, Bk. II, ch. xxiii, pp. cliiii-clv (Würzburg MS., Bk. II, ch. 30).

pentagon, five. Music, too, has its great curative powers because its harmony symbolizes the harmony of celestials and so can draw down planetary influences. The human body itself, Agrippa says, symbolizes numerical relationships by the harmony and numerical proportion of its parts. This is why a well-proportioned soul requires a well-proportioned body.[48] The soul itself has harmony and proportion if it is well ordered. There are many other symbols, he believes, with similar magical power because they represent divine ideas. The power of superior ideas, for instance, may be invoked by making images after the likeness of the effect desired, or after the model of the celestials which govern the projected operation.[49] These symbols stand for the ideas so completely that they have the power of those ideas.

Having thus studied the importance of number, proportion, and harmony, Agrippa can now treat in detail the use of planetary, demonic, and even divine names in magic. His study of number is a necessary prelude because he faces the problem of how to learn these names. The best way, he feels, involves mathematics. Names expressing the true essence of things are the most magically efficacious, but man cannot ordinarily discover such names by reason. Unless divine revelation informs him of such names, man must attempt to derive efficacious names. In the case of God, the only names which revelation shows to express the divine essence are the Tetragrammaton, *JHVH*, and its new form, *Jesus*. One can derive names of certain intelligences from the effect desired; and most of the angelic names in Hebrew, he teaches, have precisely this derivation.[50] One can also derive such names from the planets which govern the proposed magical operation. But the most efficacious derived names, whether divine, demonic, or celestial, he believes, are those which are extracted from Scripture according to the art of the cabalists. One of the chief cabalistic methods is numerical, involving the substitution for one word of another having the same numerical value. To this procedure, known as *gematria*, Agrippa refers by name. He likewise names another method, *notarikon*,

[48] *Ibid.*, Bk. II, ch. xxiiii-xxviii, pp. clvii-clxxi. (MS., Bk. II, ch. 32-33, has some of this, but no equivalent to ch. xxvii-xxviii.)

[49] *Ibid.*, Bk. II, ch. xlix-lii, pp. cxci-cxcvii. (MS., Bk. II, ch. 15, 16, 31; MS. lacks an equivalent for Bk. II, ch. lii.)

[50] *Ibid*, Bk. III, ch. xxiv, pp. ccliiii-cclvi (not in MS., which, however, has plenty of material on angelic names, as in Bk. II, ch. 44-45; Bk. III, ch. 50).

which finds hidden words from Scripture by taking the initial or final letter or by regarding the letters of a word as abbreviations for a phrase.[51] He gives tables for the derivation of the names of the seventy-two good and seventy-two evil angels of the Schemhamphoras, derived from a short passage in Exodus by the process of *notarikon*.[52] All these angelic names, like all angelic and celestial names, draw all their power from the divine name which is their origin. Such cabalistic derivations are, in Agrippa's opinion, merely the deciphering of occult wisdom placed in the sacred text by inspired writers desirous of keeping certain knowledge from the masses. In harmony with this belief that the deepest wisdom is not for the eyes of the vulgar, he adds to this section of *De occulta philosophia* an exposition of several types of secret writing, most of them in Hebrew characters.[53]

There are also certain other symbols for higher spirits which come only from special revelation. One example would be the vision of the cross shown to Constantine. Agrippa notes that Iamblichus and Porphyry give numerous examples of such symbols and that they lay great stress on the need to address each divinity by its proper name.[54]

The importance of all these symbols in Agrippa's occult system is that, representing the divine ideas and even the attributes of God Himself, they have the ability to summon the power for which they stand. Thus the magician, in addition to purging his soul, using a time and a place where celestial influences are favorable, and using suitable incenses and other materials suited to the particular work or particular power, will above all use the proper divine, angelic, or astral name, the proper verse, formulary, or other incantation, and even the proper written symbols and physical gesticulations. All

---

[51] *Ibid.*, Bk. III, ch. xi, pp. ccxxvii-ccxxxii. The corresponding chapter of MS. (Bk. III, ch. 49) lacks the relevant matter. See Joseph Leon Blau, *The Christian Interpretation of the Cabala in the Renaissance* (New York, 1944), pp. 8-9. The numerical systems which Agrippa described in Book II generally express numbers by means of letters (as in ordinary Roman numerals). Such systems of notation facilitated these cabalistic practices, for words containing letters could be assigned a numerical value.

[52] *De occulta philosophia*, Bk. III, ch. xxv, pp. cclvi-cclxv (not in Würzburg MS.).

[53] *Ibid.*, Bk. III, ch. xxix-xxx, pp. cclxxii-cclxxvi. This idea of the importance of secrecy is a commonplace of Agrippa's thought and is a point on which he followed Trithemius. See Trithemius' letter of 8 April 1510 to Agrippa, printed in *De occulta philosophia*, fol. a4r [*sic;* should be aa4r]. Würzburg MS. lacks these chapters illustrating types of secret writing.

[54] *Ibid.*, Bk. III, ch. xxxi, pp. cclxxvi-cclxxvii (not in MS.).

these symbols will have such a hold over the spirits that the work will succeed.[55]

Yet Agrippa does make three reservations about use of these symbols. One is that evil spirits may appear in place of good ones and may harm the *magus* if he is careless in his preparations and if his intention is impure. A second is that he who without firm faith uses the new form of the perfect divine name, Jesus, will accomplish nothing, for one must invoke this name in the Holy Spirit.[56] A third reservation is that no human efforts can really compel spirits, which are pure intellects and quite incorporeal. Rather it is that we, ignorant of their essence, from their names, works, or other properties, devise symbols "not by which we can in any way compel them to us, but by which we lift ourselves up to them. . . ."[57] Again, as always, Agrippa returns to the mystical ascent of the soul for his final explanation.

What really made Agrippa's world view magical, rather than merely another expression of the widely held Neoplatonic picture of a hierarchically ordered world, was the position he assigned to man. The preceding chapter has shown that man was the *magus* —not just a helpless object on which influences play, nor even just an interested observer of the action of cosmic forces. Potentially, man was what he had been before the fall of Adam: under God, lord and master of Creation. This exaltation of man as the *magus* was a special form of the Renaissance tendency to glorify man. Hence the Agrippan picture of the universe assigned an important position to man as center of all being, link between the material and spiritual worlds, and master of all the forces of the created world.

[55] Obviously, Agrippa fully shared the tendency of Renaissance Neoplatonists to recognize a real, not just a conventional, relationship between object and symbol. This tendency was expressed quite clearly in cabalism, the very basis of which was the belief that words had a real and essential relation to the objects for which they stood, not just a conventional one. Ludovico Lazzarelli believed this, and concluded therefrom that the words themselves can exert power. See Walker, *Spiritual and Demonic Magic*, pp. 68-69. For an illuminating discussion of the new ontological element in Ficino's use of metaphor and symbol, see Paul Oskar Kristeller, *The Philosophy of Marsilio Ficino*, trans. Virginia Conant (New York, 1943), pp. 93-94.

[56] *De occulta philosophia*, Bk. III, ch. xii, p. ccxxxiii (not in MS.). Cf. *ibid.*, Bk. III, ch. xxxvi, p. cclxxxviii: "Omnis itaque sermo noster, omnia uerba, omnis spiritus et uox nostra, nullam uirtutem habent in magia, nisi quatenus diuina uoce formentur." (This passage does not appear in the corresponding chapter of MS., Bk. III, ch. 22.)

[57] *Ibid.*, Bk. III, ch. xxx, p. cclxxvi (not in MS.): "non quibus illos ad nos ullo modo compellere possimus, sed quibus nos ad illos adsurgimus. . . ."

Man is the microcosm, says Agrippa, taking up a favorite Neo-platonic theme. He is called microcosm because he contains all the components of the universe: an elementary body, a celestial spirit, vegetative life, brute sense, reason, an angelic mind, and the simili-tude of God. He has commerce with all the planets. Because of this position, man is the image of God and the absolute consummation and the center of the greater world. All particular worlds, the in-tellectual, celestial, and elementary, serve him. Yet man is not God, even though like God he includes all components of Creation. God includes all things as the principle of all; man, as the middle or con-nection of all. Before his fall, man's mind contained the ideas of all things; and all creatures gladly served him. Now, however, his mind is veiled and darkened; and he must turn to occult traditions, derived ultimately from an act of divine grace, to overcome his limitations and recover his power.[58]

Agrippa suggests that man was not created directly by God, for that would have made him immortal. Intermediate deities per-formed the act of creation.[59] The Nettesheimer believes that even Adam was mortal by nature, but that a divine light prevented the decay of his compounded (and so inherently perishable) body until the sin of Adam caused God to withdraw that light.[60]

The human soul according to Agrippa has three parts, *mens*, which does not act except when itself illumined by God; *ratio*, which is subject to error unless illumined by *mens*; and *idolum*, the power which is the origin of the senses and which rules the body. The *idolum* consists of the imaginative and cogitative powers. The body and this lowest portion of the soul are subject to fate and to the rule of celestials; but *mens* is in the order of providence and so is above fate and is affected by neither celestial influences nor

[58] *Dialogus de homine*, Lyons, Bibliothèque Municipale, MS. No. 48, fols. 44v-51r [*sic;* should be 45v-52r]. Cf. *De vanitate*, "Peroratio," fols. a5v-a6r of ed. 1531 used for this study; also *De triplici ratione cognoscendi Deum*, in *Opera*, II, 480-86, and *De occulta philosophia*, Bk. III, ch. xl, pp. ccxciii-ccxciiii (not in Würzburg MS.).

[59] *De nobilitate et praecellentia foeminei sexus*, in appendix to *De vanitate* (Hagae-Comitvm, 1662), pp. 510-11 (also printed in *Opera*, II, 518-42). This use of intermediate deities or emanations from God was commonplace among Neoplatonists and even made its way into Judaism, especially through the Cabala.

[60] *Dialogus de homine*, Lyons, Bibliothèque Municipale, MS. No. 48, fol. 55r-v [*sic;* should be 56r-v]. Unlike the cabalistic *Zohar*, Agrippa believed in the material nature of creation before the fall of Adam. See Scholem, *op. cit.*, pp. 224-25.

the qualities of natural things.[61] Although he does not explicitly say so, Agrippa may have regarded *mens* or intellect as the same in all men, a doctrine which the Averroists of Paris and northern Italy openly taught in his lifetime. At least he does not flatly deny the Averroist position. *Ratio*, or reason, is the middle portion of the soul, for it is intermediary between the divine and imperishable *mens* and the material and perishable *idolum*. In a sense, *ratio* is the most important part of the soul, for its fate, unlike that of *mens* and *idolum*, is not predetermined. It is free to choose whether it will follow the divine light streaming into the soul through the *mens* or whether it will descend to the *idolum* and so will be over-whelmed by material things. Thus the character of the human soul really depends on the choice made by the *ratio*. Agrippa's habit of loosely writing "soul" (*anima*) when he obviously means *ratio* shows that in practice he regards *ratio* as the truly individual and personal part of the soul.

Closely linked with his beliefs about the human soul is his practice of alluding to two other intermediary entities, the ethereal vehicle of the soul (*aethereum animae vehiculum*) and the *spiritus*. Agrippa nowhere wrote down a detailed and direct discussion of these two entities, but he refers to them repeatedly, especially to the latter. *Vehiculum animae* is apparently not a part of the soul, but an aerial or celestial thing which bears the soul and is the medium by which God diffuses the soul from the middle of the heart through all parts of the body. It is the means by which the soul is shut up in this coarse and material body. This ethereal vehicle shares the immortality of the soul. At death, at least in the case of a virtuous man, it accompanies the soul to the choirs of the blessed.[62]

[61] This distinction between the order of fate and the order of providence appears in Ficino, *Theologia platonica de immortalitate animorum*, Bk. XIII, ch. ii, in his *Opera omnia* (2 vols. in 4; Turin, 1959 [a photo-reprint of edition Basileae, ex officina Henricpetrina, 1576, which was in two volumes, consecutively paginated; henceforth cited as Ficino, *Opera omnia* (reprint)]), I¹, 288-90. See especially pp. 289-90: "Anima igitur per mentem est supra fatum, in solo prouidentiae ordine. . . . Per idolum est in ordine fati similiter, non sub fato. . . . Per naturam quidem corpus est sub fato, anima in fato naturam mouet. Itaque mens super fatum in prouidentia est, idolum in fato super naturam, natura sub fato, supra corpus. Sic anima in prouidentiae fati, naturae legibus, non ut patiens modo ponitur, sed et ut agens." Cf. Kristeller, *Philosophy of Marsilio Ficino*, p. 313.

[62] *De occulta philosophia*, Bk. III, ch. xxxvii, xli, xliii, corresponding to Würzburg MS., Bk. III, ch. 23, 24 (which, however, lacks the discussion of *vehiculum animae*), and 25 (which refers to "etheroum idoli vehiculum," while the printed text speaks of "aethereum animae uehiculum").

This Neoplatonic concept also appears in the writings of Ficino, who regarded its substance as identical with the substance of the heavens, and who occasionally identified it with the glorified body of departed souls. Ficino also associated the *vehiculum* with the lowest part of the soul, the *idolum*, which was "nothing but the image of the rational part [of the soul] communicated to the etheric body. . . ." This astral body, or *vehiculum animae*, was a potentially dangerous concept, for in its origin it was associated with belief in pre-existence of the soul and metempsychosis. Ficino himself, like most Platonists of the Renaissance, avoided use of the term *vehiculum* and explicitly denied the astral descent of the soul. Agrippa was less cautious, for he wrote quite fully and rather recklessly about metempsychosis, though without endorsing the doctrine; and he explicitly used the term *vehiculum animae*.[63] On the relation of this vehicle to the stars, he remained vague, though he did call it ethereal.

The second intermediary between soul and body was the *spiritus*, which Agrippa, like Ficino, regarded as a very subtle but material substance, much like the air, or as a subtle vapor of the blood, generated by the heat of the heart, permeating the whole body, just as the *spiritus mundi* permeates the universe. As the preceding chapter shows, Ficino tried to found a whole new system of purified, nondemonic magic on this concept of *spiritus*, while Agrippa took up the same idea but was far less careful to exclude the action of demons. As in the case of *vehiculum animae*, Agrippa nowhere discussed this intermediate entity in detail, but he referred to it much more often. Agrippa's discussions are not clear on the actual relation between *vehiculum* and *spiritus*. Apparently the vehicle is immaterial; certainly the *spiritus* is material, though extremely refined and subtle. Agrippa attributes the magical effect of incenses, collyria, unguents, philtres, and similar substances to their ability to affect the *spiritus*, or to transmit its influence through the air to the *spiritus* of other persons. In particular, that whole group of magical effects known as fascinations, ligations, or enchantments, is the result of the ability of the *spiritus* to attract celestial and natural powers, and then to transmit its influence through the air, much as the poison of infectious disease spreads by affecting the air. Incantations

---

[63] Kristeller, *Philosophy of Marsilio Ficino*, p. 371; Walker, *Spiritual and Demonic Magic*, pp. 39-40. *De occulta philosophia*, Bk. III, ch. xli, pp. ccxciiii-ccciiii (the corresponding chapter of MS., Bk. III, ch. 24, lacks any reference to metempsychosis); Bk. III, ch. xliv, p. cccix (not in MS.).

also act through the *spiritus*. Through it, a *magus* can incite love, hate, or disease, or can make the shades of demons appear in the air.[64] Both the *vehiculum animae* and the *spiritus* were concepts used by Neoplatonists in an effort to bridge the sharp gap between material and nonmaterial being, between body and soul.

When Agrippa discusses the fate of the soul after death, he applies his tripartite division of it. *Mens* is free from all sin and so returns to the heavens whence it came. He does not discuss whether *mens* thereupon loses its individuality, as the Averroists taught. But his discussion shows pretty clearly, despite the presence of heterodox influences, that he continued to believe that the human soul eternally retains its personal identity and its memory of the acts of its earthly life.[65] Hence even though he does not explicitly affirm the separate individual existence of the *mens* of each soul after death, there is no hint that he adopted the Averroist position. In fact, he flatly states that the soul (apparently the total entity) is individual and that it surpasses all corporeal and material things.[66] The *ratio* (for though he writes soul, this is what he means) shares the fate of *mens* if it has functioned well: it enjoys the divine vision. If it has been virtuous but not Christian, it goes to Elysian fields where perhaps it is converted to Christianity and so is saved in the end. If it has been truly evil, *mens* may condemn it to wander the earth as a ghost or to be tortured by devils. Agrippa wavers concerning the fate of souls after death. At times he seems inclined to believe that evil souls are long-lived but die eventually just as the *idolum* and the body die. Thus he may have accepted the mortality of the soul until the Resurrection. He knows of metempsychosis from Hellenistic and cabalistic sources but gives no evidence of endorsing this teaching. His final position appears to be that the saintly soul gains immortality. Those who lived an ordinary life attain not divine intelligence but an image of it, and wait in pleasure or in pain for the Last Judgment. About the evil soul, his position remains unclear. Perhaps he means to leave it a wandering, demon-tormented spirit. Perhaps

---

[64] On the *spiritus*, see *De occulta philosophia*, Bk. I, ch. vi-vii (neither is in MS.), xliii (MS., Bk. I, ch. 32), xlv (MS., Bk. I, ch. 35), and l (MS., Bk. I, ch. 34). See also Kristeller, *Philosophy of Marsilio Ficino*, pp. 372-73, and Walker, *Spiritual and Demonic Magic*, pp. 3-4, 12-13, 47, 75-78.

[65] *De occulta philosophia*, Bk. III, ch. xli, pp. ccxciiii-ccciiii. Only a small part of this lengthy discussion appears in MS., Bk. III, ch. 24.

[66] *Ibid.*, Bk. III, ch. xxxvii, pp. cclxxxix-ccxc. MS., Bk. III, ch. 23, contains much but not all of the same material.

284 AGRIPPA AND THE CRISIS OF RENAISSANCE THOUGHT

he means to leave it mortal.[67] Much of his unclarity may stem from his desire to leave the way open for his discussion of demons and ghosts and for his chapter on necromancy, yet not to stray too far from orthodox Christian beliefs on the fate of the soul. He flatly asserts that this whole question is full of uncertainties. Citing St. Augustine, he pleads that it is better to leave such questions open, and not to argue about uncertain matters.

The important thing about this doctrine of the tripartite soul for his magical world is that it provides a basis for mystical illumination. Divine light flows through the *mens* into the *ratio*, which if it chooses is then illumined by that light and made capable of great magical works. If the soul attempts such works without preparing for and receiving such illumination, if it acts while still immersed in the cares of the flesh and while dominated by *idolum* rather than *mens*, then it will at the very least fail to elicit any result from its works, while there is reason to fear that if it tries to summon spirits, those spirits may inflict harm.[68] Persons born under certain celestial signs are more apt for this illumination than others, but Agrippa believes that other persons can compensate for this want by training and careful procedure. Once the soul has attained illumination, it returns to something like the condition before the fall of Adam, when the seal of God was upon it and all creatures feared and revered man.[69]

Once illumined by God or by celestial powers, the soul can ac-

[67] *Ibid.,* Bk. III, ch. xxxvii, xli-xliv. MS., Bk. III, ch. 23-25, presents fundamentally the same doctrine of the soul and its fate after death, but without the frequent references to transmigration. Agrippa says that the cabalists opposed belief that human souls transmigrate into the bodies of brute animals. Scholem, *op. cit.,* pp. 241-43, calls this objection a distinctive trait of the *Zohar,* as contrasted with earlier cabalistic texts. Agrippa's tripartite doctrine of the soul and the ensuing discussion of immortality is very like that of the *Zohar* and also shows resemblances to Ficino. According to Scholem, *op. cit.,* pp. 239-41, *Neshamah,* like *mens,* cannot sin and is free from punishment; *Nefesh,* like *idolum,* and sometimes *Ruah,* the counterpart of *ratio,* suffer punishment for sin. Ficino's doctrine of the threefold nature of the soul, and his subsequent discussion of immortality, must also have influenced Agrippa. In particular, his term *idolum* is a characteristic Ficinian term, derived from Plotinus. See Kristeller, *Philosophy of Marsilio Ficino,* pp. 359-91. For the original Latin text of some aptly chosen illustrations of Ficino's views, see the Italian edition of Kristeller's study of Ficino, *Il pensiero filosofico di Marsilio Ficino* (Florence, 1953), pp. 407-8.
[68] *De occulta philosophia,* Bk. III, ch. i, p. ccxi, and ch. iii, p. ccxv (Würzburg MS., Bk. III, ch. 1, 4). Cf. *ibid.,* Bk. III, ch. xxxviii, p. ccxci (not in MS.).
[69] *Ibid.,* Bk. III, ch. xl, pp. ccxciii-ccxciiii (not in MS.).

complish great things in magic. It can attract astral virtues and use them. It can understand divine and angelic names and how to use them for its purposes. It can summon and command spirits. It can employ the power of numbers. In general, the illuminated soul has the power of impressing itself on other things and other persons. This procedure is what Agrippa calls *ligatio*, or binding. Such bindings, fascinations, or enchantments receive aid from potions, suffumigations, unguents, rings, and other preparations made of substances whose elementary or occult properties or celestial affinities make them suited for a certain kind of action on a certain individual.[70] But such action can also take place without such material instruments, merely by emanations from the eyes, with the *spiritus* acting as the medium of transmission. If used to cause illness, this would be the evil eye.[71] So important is the soul in such works that without intentness and firm belief, little can be done. Agrippa uses as an example the fact that a patient's trust in his doctor often does at least as much for the cure as the medicine does.[72] He is not quite clear whether the real source of this power of fascination lies in the human soul or in the celestial virtues which it attracts. Probably he thought that it was in both, but the former alternative would harmonize better with his general position.

The ability to fascinate or enchant another person is by no means the only power of the purified and illuminated soul. The inspired soul can also foretell the future. Not all the forms of divination which Agrippa discusses give the central place to the soul. Auspices and auguries, for example, depend on natural causes. Yet even in auspices, he regards seeing a man as the most efficacious omen, of far greater power than seeing a bird or other animal, for, he says, more light is granted to men than to other creatures.[73] This power of giving auguries comes to living things from the celestial realm; and interpretation of auspices taken from an animal depends not only on the quarter where the omen appears but also on the planet which governs that animal. Divination from the elements (geomancy, hydromancy, aeromancy, and pyromancy) also depends

[70] *Ibid.*, Bk. I, ch. xl-xlvii, pp. xlv-lv (MS., Bk. I, ch. 32-37, 47-51). Cf. Bk. III, ch. iii (not in MS.).
[71] *Ibid.*, Bk. I, ch. l-li, pp. lix-lxi. (MS., Bk. I, ch. 34, is equivalent to Bk. I, ch. l.)
[72] *Ibid.*, Bk. I, ch. lxvi, p. lxxxviii (MS., Bk. I, ch. 42).
[73] *Ibid.*, Bk. I, ch. liv, p. lxviii. This chapter is not in MS., which lacks all the chapters on auspices and auguries that were printed as Bk. I, ch. liii-lvi.

largely on nonhuman powers, although Agrippa's special treatise on geomancy attributes great power to the mind of the person who casts the lots.

The major impression left by Agrippa's writings on divination, however, is that the enlightened soul is the great factor. Although no divination is perfect without astrology, the soul has the greatest power because it can choose a time and a place when the celestial influences will subserve its own ends.[74] Since all things obey the soul when it is filled with a strong desire, it can also govern the casting of lots. Furthermore, by certain rites the soul can summon celestial intelligences to help it direct the outcome of lots and auguries. Sometimes the soul attains prophetic powers because a melancholy humor fills it, and it can render itself more apt for such prophetic frenzy by obtaining help from the influence of Saturn. This doctrine of melancholy frenzy probably came from Ficino, but Agrippa has introduced one important change: melancholic frenzy can influence not just the intellect or *mens* but also the *ratio* and *idolum*.[75]

But the form of soothsaying which Agrippa discusses at greatest length is that which arises from the illapsion (as the Platonists call it) of a superior soul into the human soul. The prerequisite for such an illapsion is that the soul be not intent on some work, but empty. There are three conditions in which the soul is thus empty: frenzy (*furor*), rapture or ecstasy, and dream.

Frenzy is the illumination of the soul by gods or demons. The first type of prophetic frenzy comes from the Muses, or presiding intelligences of the nine celestial spheres, each of which governs certain classes of prophecy. A second type proceeds from Dionysus, being preceded by certain rites which direct the soul (*anima*) into its highest part, the intellect (*mens*), and so make it a fit temple of the gods. A third type comes from Apollo, the mind of the world, and grants sudden infusion of learning, knowledge of the future, and immunity from bodily harm. The fourth and last type of prophetic frenzy comes from Venus. By fervent love it makes the soul an

---

[74] *Ibid.*, Bk. II, ch. liii-liiii, pp. cxcviii-cc (neither chapter appears in MS.).

[75] *Ibid.*, Bk. I, ch. lx, pp. lxxviii-lxxx (cf. MS., Bk. III, ch. 31-32). Erwin Panofsky, *Albrecht Dürer* (2 vols.; Princeton, 1943), I, 168-70, shows that Agrippa's concept of three types of melancholic *furor* is a major source of Dürer's famed engraving "Melencolia I." He thinks that Dürer knew *De occulta philosophia* in one of the manuscript copies which circulated long before the book was printed.

image of God, or God Himself, elevated above the intellect by the touch of divinity. The mind thus elevated can perform things surpassing any power of nature, in alchemy, for example. This whole discussion of frenzy is clearly a fruit of Agrippa's reading of the Platonists, both ancient and modern.[76]

Contemplation of divine things makes the soul capable of the second great kind of prophecy, rapture or ecstasy. The soul, freed from the body, flies to the supercelestial realm and is filled with a divine light. In this ecstatic state, the soul "knows not by acquired species, but by contemplation of ideas; and it knows all things in the light of the ideas." A related but inferior type of prophetic ecstasy arises from an excess of some passion, such as love or sadness. The power to comprehend all things in this way always exists in the soul potentially but is normally impeded "by the darkness of the body and of mortality" until death releases the soul from the body. This is why persons on the point of death, or very aged persons, often possess prophetic powers.

The third and last great type of prophecy comes from dreams. It arises from a pure and tranquil mind which receives prophecy either through a union of the imagination and the intellect, or through illumination of the mind by the active intellect, or by simple revelation from some divine spirit. The most reliable prophetic dream is that which concerns what a carefully prepared dreamer was thinking of when he went to sleep. Agrippa expresses greater doubts about dreams than about other forms of prophecy. If the dreamer is oppressed by cares of the flesh, or if the imagination is dull, he warns, dreams have no prophetic value. If one's mind is troubled or if he has not prepared by fasting, likewise his dreams have no worth. Furthermore, interpretation of another's dreams is

[76] On types of frenzy, De occulta philosophia, Bk. I, ch. lx, pp. lxxviii-lxxx (Würzburg MS., Bk. III, ch. 31-32); Bk. III, ch. xlv-li, pp. cccxi-cccxx (MS., Bk. III, ch. 30-38). The fourfold classification of frenzy and the identification of each with a pagan deity comes from Plato, Phaedrus, 265B, though Agrippa adds much new material on the relation between the deities and the specific materials which the magus uses to induce the proper frenzy. His identification of these deities with the celestial intelligences (the Muses with the presiding intelligences of the nine celestial spheres, and Apollo with the mind of the world) comes from Ficino, Theologia platonica de immortalitate animorum, Bk. IV, ch. i (in Ficino, Opera omnia [reprint], I¹, 131). The practice of identifying the pagan deities with celestial bodies was common in the Middle Ages, according to Jean Seznec, The Survival of the Pagan Gods: The Mythological Tradition and Its Place in Renaissance Humanism and Art, trans. Barbara F. Sessions (New York, 1953), pp. 16-17, 37, 48.

difficult and depends more on trial and error than on sure principles. Finally, even true prophetic dreams almost always have an admixture of error, some element which will not come true.[77]

The result of such prophetic frenzies, ecstasies, and dreams is not only the power to foretell the future. It also includes knowledge of all things and of all sciences, and the power to perform things in magicaι arts (alchemy, for example) which are above the power of nature. This is why his discussion, although foreshadowed by the chapter on melancholic prophecy in Book One (which deals with natural magic), appears in Book Three (which has to do with ceremonial, religious, or supernatural magic). The mind of man can perform the greatest works imaginable; but no one should forget that the mind does so not through discursive reason but through illumination from the celestial and supercelestial realms, in the last analysis through illumination from God.

Although this illumination comes by a free act of God, there are still ways in which man can render himself more apt for these divine and celestial influences. In a general sense, the aim of Book Three of De occulta philosophia is to teach man to fit himself to receive these gifts. This is why the book discusses the nature of God and of the angels, and the way to derive and use their names. In this broad scheme, from which Agrippa makes continual digressions, the final chapters of the book and thus of the entire work assume special significance as the guide to practical application of what has gone before. The concluding major theme of De occulta philosophia is the practical question of how to prepare the soul to receive illumination, and hence also to receive power.

Agrippa's dualistic interpretation of human nature of course made him regard the freeing of the soul from the body as the only way to become capable of receiving illumination. The highest part of the soul, mens or intellect, alone can receive divine light, alone can

---

[77] The passages quoted on ecstasy are both in De occulta philosophia, Bk. III, ch. l, p. cccxvii ("intelligit non per species acquisitas, sed per inspectionem ad ideas, omniaque in idearum lumine cognoscit") and p. cccxviii ("caligine corporis et mortalitatis"). MS., Bk. III, ch. 37, contains much of the material printed in this chapter, but lacks the passages quoted. The Agrippan chapter shows strong influence from Ficino, Theologia platonica de immortalitate animorum, Bk. XIII, ch. ii (in Ficino, Opera omnia [reprint], I¹, 292-95), which discusses the themes of vacatio of the soul and of resultant prophecies. Agrippa treats dreams in Bk. I, ch. lix, pp. lxxvii-lxxviii (not in MS.). Although there are enough correspondences to prove that Agrippa knew this section of Ficino's works, he has much other material and does not organize his treatment of ecstasy and dreams as Ficino does.

work miracles. Hence the sensory part of the soul, *idolum*, must be held in restraint, while *mens* fills and rules the soul. In other words, he who wants to prepare to receive divine gifts must do two things: seek to be rid of carnal desires and seek to ascend to the realm of pure intellect. Celestial influences aid this preparation, for by taking advantage of favorable celestial circumstances, man makes this ascent easier. But more important is knowing how to observe certain ritual acts of purification.

Purgation of the soul is attained by cleanliness of body and soul and surroundings; by partaking only of light, dry, and temperate foods; by seeking solitude and freedom from bodily needs; by penitence for one's misdeeds; by almsgiving, a way of purgation unknown to pagans but taught by Christianity; and by certain positive rites such as baptisms, aspersions, oblations, and sacrifices. In this whole process of purgation, Agrippa gives high valuation to external acts of Christian piety: continence; abstinence from food and drink; the sacrament of penance; alms; baptism; use of consecrated objects like relics and holy water; and the only truly acceptable sacrifice, the mass. All these liberate the soul from the body. The only alien element is ritual cleanliness, probably a borrowing from medieval Jewish mystics, the cabalists. The others are specifically Christian, though not exclusively so except for the mass.[78]

A further problem, once the soul has been prepared, is the attraction of celestial and supercelestial powers, that is, the powers which actually illumine the soul. Agrippa teaches that adorations, vows, and prayers, especially those which are not external but inward, put the human soul in touch with God. Such adorations of lesser deities are permissible only insofar as these deities draw their power from the Creator. Sacrifices are also of use in attracting divinity, with various types suited to various deities; but of course the Christian sacrifice, the mass, is most efficacious of all. Various suffumigations

[78] The preparation of the soul is discussed in *De occulta philosophia*, Bk. III, ch. liii-lvii (MS., Bk. III, ch. 39-44). Cf. Bk. III, ch. iii (not in MS.) and ch. xliii (MS., Bk. III, ch. 25-27). On ritual cleanliness in the preparation of the mystical cabalist Abulafia, see Scholem, *op cit.*, pp. 135-37. Many of Agrippa's acts of ritual purification, especially the parts on diet and environment, are strongly reminiscent of Ficino. But Ficino in *De vita coelitus comparanda* was not giving advice on how to purge the nonmaterial soul; he was prescribing a regimen designed to refine and improve the subtle material thing known as *spiritus*, and to make it more receptive to celestial influences. See Walker, *Spiritual and Demonic Magic*, pp. 5-6, 13-14.

are able to "open the gates of the elements and of the heavens, so that through them man can see and know the secrets of the Creator. . . ." A firm belief in what one is doing also strengthens the power of the soul to attract divine gifts, while the use of a time and place consonant to one's nativity conduces to success; and the powers of words and incantations also help. But the most important, the final, bit of advice is still: "Finally, in all things have God before your eyes. . . ." [79]

This careful preparation and mystical ascent will fit the soul for the reception of divine power and for the performance of great works in natural, celestial, and ceremonial magic once the soul has been illuminated. But, Agrippa warns, this illumination does not come at will. Step by step through careful preparation, purgation, and prayer, the soul will win freedom from involvement in mundane, sensual, carnal affairs, and will rise through the hierarchy of being. Then it will not need rational demonstration, but like the angels, "not in succession, not in time, but in a sudden moment it attains what it wants." [80] In other words, a sudden flash of mystical union and illumination, dependent ultimately not on man's preparation but on God's will, consummates the soul's ascent and makes man the true image of God, even makes him God, as Agrippa dares to write.[81]

[79] *De occulta philosophia*, Bk. III, ch. lvii-lxiiii (MS., Bk. III, ch. 45-48, 51-53, 56-57). The two quotations are from ch. lxiiii, p. cccxlii ("aperiunt portas elementorum atque coelorum, ut per illas homo possit uidere et cognoscere secreta creatoris. . . .") and p. cccxliiii ("In omnibus denique deum prae oculis habe. . . ."). MS., Bk. III, ch. 57, contains the first but not the second of these passages, but it expresses the same idea as the second. This chapter clearly illustrates the recklessness with which Agrippa applied religious rites to the conjuring of demons.

[80] *Ibid.*, Bk. III, ch. liii, p. cccxxiii: "non successione, non tempore, sed subitaneo momento quod cupit assequitur." (MS., Bk. III, ch. 40.) This is reminiscent of Ficino, *Theologia platonica de immortalitate animorum*, Bk. XIII, ch. ii, in his *Opera omnia* [reprint], I¹, 290: "Mens autem illa quae est animae caput, et auriga, suapte natura angelos imitata, non successione, sed momento quod cupit assequitur. . . ."

[81] Letter of Agrippa to Aurelius ab Aquapendente, Lyons, 19 November 1527, printed in *De occulta philosophia*, p. cccxlvii: ". . . te scire uolo, quod omnium rerum cognoscere opificem ipsum deum, et in illum tota similitudinis imagine (ceu essentiali quodam contactu siue uinculo) transire, quo ipse transformeris efficiareque deus. . . ." Also his *Oratio in praelectione convivii Platonis*, in *Opera*, II, 1073: ". . . Perfectus ad Deum amor, animam nostram ad Deum convertit et transmutat, efficitque Deo penitus similem, tanquam propriam Dei imaginem, et haec est summa hominum foelicitas, Deum scilicet fieri." Agrippa shared this belief in the deification of man with Marsilio Ficino. See Robb, *op. cit.*, pp. 67-68.

This mystical consummation of magic appears most fully in the third book of *De occulta philosophia*, but it is not confined to that work. Although *De triplici ratione cognoscendi Deum* is quite different in general development, the doctrines of the purification of the soul, the illumination of the purified soul by divine light, and the miraculous power of the illuminated soul form a basic presupposition of this whole treatise.[82] The stress on mystical union also appears in *Oratio in praelectione convivii Platonis*. And although the confidence in human preparatory acts and in the value of external rituals is missing from *De vanitate*, the ultimate resolution which that book offers for man's quest for God is also mystical union with God for those who have been so blessed by Him, and reverent trust in the Scriptures, the writings of men thus enlightened, for those lesser souls which remain incapable of mystical experience.[83] Only through union with God can the veil of material distractions, the result of original sin, be lifted from the soul. Despite extensive changes in the manner of its expression, this mystical resolution of the problems of the soul is one of the constants in Agrippa's intellectual world.[84]

From the beginning of his development to the end, Agrippa remained true to his insistence on divine action through grace as the only hope for mankind. All the power, all the glory of man as *magus* rested, in last analysis, on this assistance from God. Without such aid, man had neither power nor glory. Natural, profane man, the man who depended on his own powers, his own reason, and his own sciences, was powerless and inglorious. Agrippa believed this just as fully in his youth as in the dark period when he wrote *De vanitate*. Pursuing such ideas of natural man's weakness, Agrippa constructed in *De vanitate* a dark and almost hopeless view of man's life, a picture which stood in apparent contrast to the world view of *De occulta philosophia*, but which in reality showed many of the same fundamental attitudes. This dark side of Agrippa's thought forms the subject of the following chapter.

[82] *Opera*, II, 491-93.
[83] *De vanitate*, ch. xcix, and "Peroratio," fols. a5v-a7v.
[84] The occultist Lewis Spence, *Cornelius Agrippa, Occult Philosopher* (London, 1921), pp. 49-50, is in a sense correct when he insists on the persistence of the mystical element in Agrippa's thought.

CHAPTER ELEVEN

AGRIPPA AND THE END OF A WORLD

Despite Agrippa's failure to carry through consistently the exposition of his magical world view, and despite the fact that pessimism about human reason dominated his thinking even in his early years, the universe portrayed in *De occulta philosophia* is an orderly one. If man is unable by reason to comprehend all its secrets, Agrippa felt, still he may be able to find in the divinely revealed traditions of ancient sages, especially of Hermes and the cabalists, the key to mastery of his surroundings. The idea of a closely interconnected world, a world every part of which is alive, and the idea that the divinely illuminated soul can draw down superior powers, celestial, angelic, and even divine, do not represent a break on Agrippa's part with the cultural heritage of either the remote or the more immediate past.[1] His aim of restoring magic to its ancient purity did not at all prevent him from drawing freely on such medieval magical writers as Albertus Magnus, Arnold of Villanova, Roger Bacon, Pietro d'Abano, and *Picatrix*. The organic, animistic, aesthetic

[1] Guido de Ruggiero, *Storia della filosofia*, Part III, *Rinascimento, Riforma e Controriforma* (2nd ed.; 2 vols.; Bari, 1937), I, 159-60.

world view which Agrippa shared with these men was not, after all, alien even to the thought of the greatest minds of the Middle Ages, such as Thomas Aquinas.[2]

Yet some elements in the thought of Agrippa were destructive and disintegrative of the medieval world view in particular and, in general, of all culture. This chapter will consider these anarchical elements, which appear not only in Agrippa's speculative thought but also in his ethical, political, and social doctrines. This side of his thought found its chief expression in *De incertitudine et vanitate scientiarum declamatio invectiva*, just as his magical thought was expressed principally and most completely in *De occulta philosophia*; but elements of this tendency appear in other works as well.

It is one of the peculiarities of intellectual history that later generations have found elements of skepticism in the thought of a man who on one occasion wrote that of the three chief modes of philosophizing, the Peripatetic, the Academic, and the Skeptical, he sometimes followed the first and sometimes the second, but always shunned the Skeptics, "among whom nothing is certain that they may follow, but all things are indifferent to them, and so they dispute on both sides concerning all things. . . ."[3] Yet such is the case with Agrippa. Almost all the standard histories of philosophy mention the presence of skeptical elements in his thought, although they generally class him among Neoplatonic occultists or theosophists, and although they agree that his skepticism is only fragmentary and not of much significance.[4] One of the few writers who

[2] See Aquinas' short treatise, *De occultis operibus naturae ad quemdam militem*, in his *Opera omnia* (25 vols.; New York, 1948-50), XVI, 355-57. On astral influences, see *Summa theologica*, I, 115, 4 (Editio Instituti Studiorum Medievalium Ottaviensis; 5 vols.; Ottawa, 1941-45), I, 687b: "Dicendum quod corpora caelestia in corpora quidem imprimunt directe et per se. . . . In vires autem animae quae sunt actus organorum corporeorum, non directe quidem sed per accidens. . . ." In short, the stars influence the body but do not determine the will. On Aquinas, cf. the authorities cited above, Chapter Nine, n. 6.

[3] *Oratio in praelectione . . . Trismegisti*, in Agrippa's *Opera* (2 vols.; Lugduni, n.d.), II, 1082: "quos penes nihil certum est quod sequantur, sed omnia illis indifferentia sunt, ideoque de omnibus in utranque partem disputant. . . ."

[4] Ruggiero, *op. cit.*, II, 167. Émile Bréhier, *Histoire de la philosophie* (2 vols.; Paris, 1926-32), I, 760. Friedrich Ueberweg, *Grundriss der Geschichte der Philosophie: Die Philosophie der Neuzeit bis zum Ende des XVIII Jahrhunderts*, ed. Max Frischeisen-Köhler and Willy Moog (Berlin, 1924), p. 161, admits that *De vanitate* contains the principal skeptical arguments but adds that the renewal of ancient skepticism is generally ascribed to the French, especially Montaigne, and then discusses Agrippa elsewhere (pp. 138-39) as a precursor of the theosophy of Jakob Boehme. Ernst Cassirer, *Das Erkenntnisproblem in*

have taken the skeptical side of his thought seriously, Rossi, explains this apparent contradiction by assuming a fundamental change of attitude in the eleven years between the quoted statement and the composition of *De vanitate* in 1526.[5] Actually, however, there was no major change. The context of the earlier statement makes it clear that what Agrippa had in mind when he attacked the skeptics was those who, often pretending to give rational demonstration of Christian dogmas, often even sincerely intending to do so, actually weakened Christian faith by seeking to confine faith within the bounds of human reason. This attitude, which is strongly reminiscent of the Scotist and Occamist denial of the power of reason to grasp ultimate, divine truths, was the basis of the criticism of scholastic philosophy which fills much of *De vanitate*.[6] For Agrippa, the essence of the skepticism which he denounced was failure to acknowledge the limitations of human reason in religious matters. He would have agreed with the statement of his contemporary, Giovanni Francesco Pico della Mirandola, that the skeptics' arguments properly ought not to have any force when turned against Christian doctrines, since those doctrines rest solely on faith and revelation and are subject neither to proof nor to disproof.[7]

---

der *Philosophie und Wissenschaft der Neuzeit* (3 vols.; Berlin, 1906-20), I, 162, 181, takes Agrippa's skepticism more seriously. Rudolf Stadelmann, *Vom Geist des ausgehenden Mittelalters: Studien zur Geschichte der Weltanschauung von Nicolaus Cusanus bis Sebastian Franck* (Halle, 1929), demonstrates Agrippa's connection with the skeptical tendencies of late scholasticism and the mystics such as Cusanus. See especially pp. 79-86. Luigi Credaro, *Lo scetticismo degli Accademici* (2 vols.; Rome, 1889-93), I, 320-21, denies that Agrippa presented a fully developed skepticism, as do Paola Zambelli, "A proposito del 'De vanitate scientiarum et artium' di Cornelio Agrippa," *Rivista critica di storia della filosofia*, XV (1960), 166-80, Richard H. Popkin, *The History of Scepticism from Erasmus to Descartes* (Assen, 1960), pp. 22-25, and Erwin Metzke, "Die 'Skepsis' des Agrippa von Nettesheim," *Deutsche Vierteljahrsschrift für Literaturwissenschaft und Geistesgeschichte*, XIII (1935), 407-20, and "Die 'Skepsis' des Agrippa von Nettesheim: Eine Studie zur Geschichte des deutschen Geistes im ausgehenden Mittelalter," in his *Coincidentia oppositorum: Gesammelte Studien zur Philosophiegeschichte*, ed. Karlfried Gründer (Witten, 1961).

[5] G[iuseppe]. Rossi, *Agrippa di Nettesheym e la direzione scettica della filosofia nel Rinascimento* (Turin, 1906), pp. 61-62.

[6] Maurice de Wulf, *History of Medieval Philosophy*, trans. P. Coffey (3rd ed.; London, 1909), p. 418. For Agrippa's insistence on the danger of reason when it fails to recognize its limitations, see his *De incertitudine et vanitate scientiarum declamatio inuectiua* (Coloniae, 1531), ch. xcvii, ci, and "Ad Lectorem" (fols. A6r-A7r). This work is henceforth cited as *De vanitate*.

[7] See the younger Pico's *Examen vanitatis doctrinae gentium, et veritatis christianae disciplinae* (Mirandulae, 1520), Bk. II, ch. 20, fols. L^v-LI^r. Cf. *ibid.*, Bk. III, ch. 14, fols. CVIII^r-CX^r.

Even Rossi admits that Agrippa's approach to skepticism was inductive, that is, that his main line of argument was to show that all sciences as now taught are full of contradictions and so cannot be regarded as certain.[8] It is certainly true that quantitatively speaking, Agrippa based most of his declamation against the sciences on points which are only peripheral to the main problem of human knowledge. The lines of attack are several. The most important is that a given science is uncertain because all the authorities are at odds with one another. Unlike many of his contemporaries, in particular unlike his favorite modern authors, Ficino and Pico, Agrippa appears to delight in emphasizing the disunity of the various philosophical schools. He also shows a strong inclination to discredit the great authorities of the past, most notably in his repeated aspersions against the moral and intellectual integrity of Aristotle.[9] A second major line which his so-called inductive skepticism follows is to show that the various arts and sciences are often or even usually the source of sin, evil, and heresy. Architecture, for example, is in itself praiseworthy but has led to excessive ornateness in the design of churches and has been employed in construction of engines of war. Rhetoric, to take another instance, is unsure of its principles, subject to misuse in the interests of injustice and untruth, infamous and disgraceful, and a source of heresies such as the apostasy of the Emperor Julian or, more recently, the outbreak of the Lutheran heresy, whose heads only a few years ago were everywhere lauded for their skill in rhetoric. Painting has been misused to depict obscene and inflammatory subjects.[10] Further, if he can think of no other accusation against a science, Agrippa calls it useless for human salvation and happiness, as in the case of mathematics or cosmography.[11] This, of course, is completely to confuse

[8] Rossi, *op. cit.*, pp. 85-86.

[9] A good example of Agrippa's emphasis on disunity is *De vanitate*, ch. lii, "De anima," including a sharp denunciation of Aristotle, who is also attacked *ibid.*, ch. liv. Agrippa mocks at the differences among the philosophers: *ibid.*, ch. xlix: "Cunque de singulis philosophia disputat et opinatur, de nullis certa est. Vnde philosophos an inter bruta, an inter homines numerem plane nescio: brutis siquidem praestare videntur, eo quod rationem habent et intelligentiam, homines autem quomodo erunt, quorum ratio nihil constans persuadere potest, sed semper in lubricis opinionibus vacillat, quorum intellectus ad omnia incertus non habet quod teneat, aut sequatur. . . ." G.-F. Pico also attacked Aristotle, but less savagely, and with less emphasis on his personal failings. See *Examen vanitatis*, Bk. IV, ch. 1-10, 12; Bk. V, ch. 2; Bk. VI, *passim*.

[10] For architecture, *De vanitate*, ch. xxviii; for rhetoric, ch. vi; for painting, ch. xxiv-xxv.

[11] *Ibid.*, ch. xi, xxvii.

the issue, to divert discussion from the validity of human knowledge to the question of human beatitude and salvation. Finally, Agrippa repeats the common objection that human life is too short to master even one science well, even though he himself had often advised students to master all fields of learning.[12]

Certain aspects of this attack on the individual sciences possess considerable intrinsic interest. There is, for example, his appeal to the reports of Spanish and Portuguese navigators in order to show how baseless were the authoritative opinions of all earlier geographers. This appeal to brute fact to undermine accepted theories shows an empirical side to his thought quite in harmony with the widespread empiricism of the later sixteenth century.[13] It is also a rather early instance of the disturbing effect of the discoveries on the European world view. The chapters on astronomy and astrology have high intrinsic interest in their own right, one of the many interesting ideas being the disquieting possibility that unknown planets and stars may exist, thus vitiating any astrological science based on present knowledge. The whole argument is an example of the influence of Pico della Mirandola north of the Alps.[14] Agrippa's general practice of collecting the opinions of the various philosophical schools on a given point is an example of the spread of knowledge about ancient philosophy and of the unsettling effect which acquaintance with ancient philosophical controversy might have.

But if there were nothing more than these immediately apparent lines of argument in Agrippa's thought, the historians of philosophy would have the best of Rossi on the question of the significance of Agrippa's skeptical tendencies. The most one could make of such statements would be an additional instance of the widespread dissatisfaction with late medieval learning.[15] De vanitate would remain nothing but a flashy bit of paradox without much significance for the history of European thought and with greatly reduced significance even for study of Agrippa's own development. Agrippa

[12] Ibid., ch. i.
[13] Ibid., ch. xxvii. On this empiricism of brute fact in the later sixteenth century, see Hiram Haydn, The Counter-Renaissance (New York, 1950), pp. 190-223, especially 202-3, 222. On the unsettling impact of the discoveries on sixteenth-century thought, see Geoffroy Atkinson, Les nouveaux horizons de la Renaissance française (Paris, 1935).
[14] De vanitate, ch. xxx-xxxi.
[15] Christoph Sigwart, Kleine Schriften (2nd ed.; 2 vols.; Freiburg-i-B., 1889), I, 5, regards expression of this dissatisfaction as the chief significance of De vanitate.

would be just Agrippa the Magician or perhaps Agrippa the Charlatan.

In reality Agrippa has at least the germ of a far more thorough-going skeptical development than anyone, even Rossi, has realized. He is quite aware of the skepticism of the Academics and the Pyrrhonists concerning the ability of man to know causes.[16] He sees as the weakness of Peripatetic logic the fact that the force of any argumentation depends on the truth of the premises, which must come from earlier demonstrations of no greater validity, or else from an accepted authority.[17] He had always known this fact, even in his more optimistic treatise on the Lullian art;[18] but by 1526 he was ready to deny not only in specific cases but also in the most general terms the ability of the human mind in any way to arrive at truths which can form adequate premises for truthful as well as formally valid syllogisms: "But so great is the ample liberty of truth, and its free amplitude, that by the speculations of no science, by no urgent judgment of the senses, by no arguments of logical artifice, by no evident proof, by no demonstrating syllogism, and by no discourse of human reason can it be seized upon, but only by faith. . . ."[19] In short, what he is arguing, and this in the most explicit terms, is that "all sciences are nothing but decisions and opinions of men. . . ."[20] If any science is used to good purpose, the goodness comes from its inventor or its user, not from the science itself.[21] He flatly states that anything can be disproved just as easily as it can be proved, that there is no argument so strong that a stronger cannot be presented to overturn it.[22]

[16] De vanitate, ch. i.

[17] Ibid., ch. vii, where he charges that logicians either depend on authority or else are guilty of the fallacy of circular reasoning. Only authority or sense perception of singulars can furnish terms (and those uncertain ones) for a syllogism. Agrippa also pursues this point ibid., ch. i.

[18] For Agrippa's In artem brevem Raymundi Lullii commentaria, see Raymundus Lullius, Opera (Argentinae, 1598), p. 839. This work is also printed in Agrippa's Opera, II, 334-436.

[19] De vanitate, ch. i. "Tanta autem est veritatis ampla libertas, liberaque amplitudo, vt nullius scientiae speculationibus, non vllo sensuum vrgenti iudicio, non logici artificij argumentis, nulla probatione euidente, nullo syllogismo demonstrante, nec vllo humanae rationis discursu possit deprehendi, nisi sola fide. . . ."

[20] Ibid.: "Praeterea omnes scientiae, nil nisi decreta et opiniones hominum sunt. . . ."

[21] Ibid.

[22] Ibid., ch. c: "Quodcunque enim (vt ait Gregorius) ab eo [verbo Dei] autoritatem non habet, eadem facilitate contemnitur qua probatur. . . ."

These are not mere bald statements unsupported by argumenta-tion. How is man by his own powers to grasp truths from which to construct logical chains of reasoning? The way obviously would be by sensory means. But although Agrippa does not name any source, he here applies arguments ultimately derived from ancient skepticism and later developed, with help from Sextus Empiricus, at much greater length by Michel de Montaigne. Agrippa observes that all knowledge comes from the senses and that the test of a true proposition is whether it corresponds to the sensed object. From this source alone we get all knowledge that is possible. But in the first place, it is evident that the senses are often deceived and hence that they can give no great degree of certitude. What is more, the senses are unable to reach intellectual nature and so can teach us nothing of the causes of lower things, from which must be demonstrated their natures, effects, and properties. The most we can know from the senses is individual objects. So all higher sciences founded on sensory knowledge can be only fallacious, since sensa-tion cannot give us any general principles.[23]

A way out of this dilemma should have been available to one so strongly influenced by Platonism as Agrippa; but he fails to discuss it at this point because his own doctrine of original sin had already closed this way to him. The obvious solution was to teach that the ideas of all things already pre-existed in the soul. This would at least bridge the gap between the sensory and intellectual realms. But by teaching that original sin had veiled these ideas in the human soul by causing the departure of the divine light that had once made man know all truth, Agrippa effectively blocked this means of escape from skepticism.[24] Of course, as demonstrated in previous chapters, he clearly and consistently taught that mystical illumina-

[23] *Ibid.*, ch. vii: "Iam enim cum sensus omnes saepe fallaces sint, certe nullam nobis synceram probare possunt experientiam. Praeterea cum sensus intellec-tualem naturam nequeant attingere, et rerum inferiorum causae ex quibus illarum naturae, effectus, et proprietates seu passiones demonstrari deberent, sint omnium consensu nostris sensibus penitus ignotae, nonne conuincitur veritatis viam sensibus esse praeclusam, quare etiam omnes illae deductiones et scientiae quae in ipsis sensibus radicibus fundatae sunt, omnes incertae erunt et erroneae et fallaces." Agrippa's critique of sensation is somewhat reminiscent of Sextus Empiricus, *Outlines of Pyrrhonism* (Loeb Classical Library edition; London, 1933), Bk. I, sect. 91-99; Bk. II, sect. 72-75; but the relation is not close.

[24] This effect of original sin is developed in *Dialogus de homine*, Lyons, Bibliothèque Municipale, MS. No. 48, fol. 55 [*sic*; should be 56], as far as loss of the divine light is concerned; in *De originali peccato, ibid.*, fols. 4r-6v; and especially in *De vanitate*, "Peroratio," fols. a5v-a6r. Cf. *De occulta philosophia libri tres* (Coloniae, 1533), Bk. III, ch. xl (not in the unprinted manuscript text

tion could restore the original condition and grant all knowledge and true wisdom to man. But this doctrine leads out of the realm of epistemology and into the field of religious experience and grace. Although never systematically stated in his earlier writings, this skeptical attitude is intimately associated with his doctrine of mystical illumination. His general message had always been that man needs grace before he can attain ultimate reality.[25]

The theoretical presentation of true skepticism in *De vanitate* is small in bulk, far smaller than the space devoted to specific and "empirical" attacks on various sciences. When compared to this latter element, the critical analysis of the foundations of human certitude seems hurried, sketchy, and incomplete. Agrippa's declamation against human learning certainly does not mark the systematic introduction of ancient Pyrrhonism into modern philosophical discussion, an introduction foreshadowed by the younger Pico and really accomplished by Montaigne and his disciples only much later in the century. So brief is the Nettesheimer's discussion of truly epistemological issues and so small the evidence of direct contact with the works of Sextus Empiricus, that the author of an important recent work on the growth of skepticism in the Renaissance refuses to call his standpoint skeptical and prefers the phrase "fundamentalist anti-intellectualism."[26] Whether one chooses to apply the term *skeptic* to Agrippa depends, of course, on how strictly one wishes to limit the term. Certainly Agrippa did not offer the detailed presentation of ancient Pyrrhonist arguments that one will find in Montaigne and his followers. Whether he drew directly on the principal ancient skeptical source, Sextus Empiricus, is debatable. But although his book does indeed give far more space to gibes against learning than to philosophical analysis (the same is true, in lesser degree, even of Montaigne's "Apology for Raymond Sebond"), his work is not entirely innocent of the profounder philosophical questions. Small in bulk though it is, he does present a brief but effective analysis, framed in terms of broad reference to the problem of man's ability to know. This general consideration

of 1510, Würzburg, Universitätsbibliothek, MS. M.ch.q.50). The surviving fragment of *Dialogus de homine* has been edited by Paola Zambelli in *Rivista critica di storia della filosofia*, XIII (1958), 47-71. *De originali peccato*, with some textual changes, appears in Agrippa's *Opera*, II, 553-64.
[25] In addition to the citation of *De originali peccato* in the preceding note, see *De triplici ratione cognoscendi Deum*, in *Opera*, II, 480-81, 486, 489-500.
[26] Popkin, *op. cit.*, pp. 22-25.

of the basis of human knowledge explains why he found so much uncertainty in each of the special sciences which he studied. Furthermore, he made specific reference to the Academics and Pyrrhonists when he wrote his short general discussion of the foundations of human knowledge. This evidence suggests that alongside late medieval disdain for learning, which was reinforced in his lifetime by the tendency of humanists and Reformers to adopt a fundamentalist anti-intellectualism, Agrippa did feel some influence of truly skeptical nature. It is not entirely wrong, therefore, to call him a skeptic, even though strictly skeptical considerations form only a very small portion of *De vanitate*.

The fundamental inability of unaided human reason to gain valid scientific knowledge of course applies also to man's knowledge of God, the highest form of knowledge. God reveals Himself in three ways, which Agrippa describes as the Book of Nature, the Book of the Law, and the Book of the Gospel. Only from the first of these does man read by use of his own cognitive powers. But the knowledge of God from creatures, while clear enough to make inexcusable anyone who does not know and honor God, cannot attain His essence as He is in Himself, separated from all things. Thus even if man were capable of forming a valid science from created things, the real essentials of a knowledge of God are not discoverable in those created things.[27] Dialectic and philosophy are simply unable to rise to true knowledge of God. Only the purified soul, filled with grace, love, and faith, can do this. In other words, knowledge of God occurs only in the realm of grace, not in that of reason.

As early as 1516, this belief in the inability of reason to comprehend the divine nature had led Agrippa to attack contemporary theology for trying to bend divinity to human reason. Reasoning in divinity, he argues, is the source of all error. It even led to the fall of Adam, since by reasoning with the Serpent instead of blindly obeying God's commandment, Eve made it possible for him to deceive her.[28] Reason does nothing but destroy the simplicity of

[27] *De triplici ratione cognoscendi Deum*, in *Opera*, II, 482-85, 490-91.

[28] *Ibid.*, II, 494-95, and *De originali peccato*, Lyons, Bibliothèque Municipale, MS. No. 48, fols. 4r-6v. The clash between reason and faith is pungently summarized in a work of 1519, *De beatissimae Annae monogamia ac unico puerperio* (n.p., 1534), fol. G4v: "Dic mihi o perditissime hominum, quid commercij Christo et Aristoteli? quid logicis argutijs cum diuinae sapientiae mysterijs? Christus illa docet non Aristoteles, gratia non ratiocinatio, afflatus non syllogismus."

faith, trying to take heaven by storm, questioning and so undermining the most sacred beliefs. The Schoolmen, Agrippa charges,
while criticizing freely all others, themselves debate the most shocking propositions imaginable.[29] The only theology which he praises
is that of the Church Fathers.[30] Needless to say, Agrippa's study of
the writings of Luther and other Reformers did not weaken this
antischolastic predilection, a fact which appears clearly from *De
vanitate*. It is true that much of his invective is directed against
symptoms of scholastic decadence, such as the involved and over-
subtle terminology of the later Scotists or the blind and narrow
sectarianism of the various schools, Thomists, Albertists, Scotists,
Occamists, and others.[31] Yet he clearly believes that even in the less
decadent age, the age of Albert, Thomas, and Scotus themselves,
when at least it might have been useful to refute heretics, scholastic
theology was a monstrous combination of philosophical reasons and
divine revelation. He expressly compares it to a centaur. Rational
proof of dogmas may be clever, he admits, but it is not pious.[32] The
only theology which he can approve is that which depends on
divine illumination or which plainly expounds the text of Scripture,
which itself is a product of divine illumination, not of human
reasoning.[33]

What this rejection of scholastic theology really amounts to is
a restatement by Agrippa of the fideistic attitude of late medieval
thinkers, especially the followers of William of Ockham. Man should
not proudly strive to know by rational powers, but rather should
fervently believe in revelation. In itself, fideism does not necessarily
imply a thoroughgoing skepticism, only a sharper division between
the realm of grace and the realm of reason than that posited by
the Thomists. But Agrippa united this partial skepticism of the
fideists with a more general skepticism concerning all human
knowledge. This more general skepticism shows traces of a re-
thinking of the works of ancient skeptics as they were known to
the Middle Ages; it also shows the influence of potentially skeptical
elements in the thought of Nicholas of Cusa, who believed that all
human knowledge is more or less árbitrary, and who compared the

---

[29] *Apologia adversus calumnias, propter declamationem de vanitate scientiarum, et excellentia verbi Dei, sibi per aliquos Lovanienses theologistas intentatas*, in *Opera*, II, 297. Henceforth cited as *Apologia*.
[30] *De triplici ratione cognoscendi Deum*, in *Opera*, II, 489-500.
[31] *De vanitate*, ch. viii, and "Ad Lectorem," fol. A7r.
[32] *Ibid.*, ch. xcvii; *Apologia*, in *Opera*, II, 321.
[33] *De vanitate,*·ch. xcviii.

relation between human statements and actual truth to that between a polygon and the circle in which it is inscribed.[34] Fideism could easily employ general skeptical arguments if these terminated in counsels to follow probability in daily living and so left the way open for an act of faith. This, for instance, was the teaching of Giovanni Francesco Pico della Mirandola, nephew of the famous Pico.[35] This late-medieval fideism not only survived into the sixteenth century but became accentuated with the appearance of Protestantism. Indeed, this union of skepticism and fideism, already foreshadowed in certain late medieval thinkers and in the younger Pico, became a prime characteristic of French Roman Catholic disciples of Montaigne, and formed a major element in the anti-Calvinist religious polemic of the Catholic Reformation in France.[36]

Not only theology, however, but every field of human learning came in for attack by the restless and pessimistic mind of the Nettesheimer, for his epistemological doubts seriously questioned the conformity between the abstractions of the human mind and the external objects for which they stood. Thus such abstractions as the cycles, epicycles, and spheres of the astral world became for Agrippa mere figments of the astronomer's mind. Similarly, he denied any objective existence to the abstractions of metaphysics and to those of mathematics.[37] The same anarchy of uncontrolled opinion exists in natural philosophy, where philosophers freely put forth opinions, all equally valid and invalid, concerning all questions, ranging from the theoretical problems of the principle of all being or the plurality of worlds to the practical question of the immediate causes of observable phenomena such as earthquakes.[38] Little remained to Agrippa but unreliable sense experience

[34] Stadelmann, op. cit., p. 51. This is not to say that Cusanus was a skeptic, for the simile of the inscribed polygon symbolizes gradual approach to truth, not skepticism. Nevertheless, it also implies that except when the number of sides attains infinity, the polygon never truly becomes a circle; and that similarly, the human statement never in the realm of finite existence fully expresses truth. Certainly Agrippa understood Cusanus in this sense.

[35] Haydn, op. cit., p. 101.

[36] Ibid., pp. 98-104; Popkin, op. cit., pp. 66-83. De Wulf, op. cit., p. 418, shows that the fideists were not skeptics in any full sense. On the lack of true skepticism among Ockham's followers, see Gerhard Ritter, "Romantische und revolutionäre Elemente in der deutschen Theologie am Vorabend der Reformation," Deutsche Vierteljahrsschrift für Literaturwissenschaft und Geistesgeschichte, V (1927), 342-80.

[37] For astral figures, De vanitate, ch. xxx; for metaphysical constructs, ch. liii; for mathematical abstractions, ch. xi.

[38] Ibid., ch. xlix-li.

of singulars and arbitrary constructs of the human mind. In later thinkers, this attitude was eventually destined to grow into the modern theory of scientific hypothesis and its subjection to the test of facts; and Agrippa's thought contains hints that he himself was groping blindly in this direction. Chapter Eight above has already discussed this tendency. But the general effect of Agrippa's thought, and especially of De vanitate, the most widely circulated of his writings, was to present only the negative moment of this philosophical development. The message of De vanitate was overwhelmingly destructive in nature.

A further line of attack on human learning hit not so much at the intellectual validity of the sciences as at their significance. This kind of argument, as noted above, was only peripheral to Agrippa's expression of true skepticism. Yet this argument, that even if true the sciences have no significance for the happiness and well-being of man, was in its own right a disquieting, though hardly original, element in the man's thought. Orthodox Christianity had never given ultimate value to human learning in its own right, but the moderately humanistic tendency represented by Thomas Aquinas had recognized a value, secondary but still real, in secular learning. Now Agrippa denied not only the validity of the sciences as sciences but also their relevance to man's welfare in any case.[39] Man's true happiness, he argued, does not consist in knowledge of any sort but in a good life and a connection with God which unaided human powers cannot achieve. Not a clever mind but a virtuous will is important.[40] Repeatedly Agrippa introduced the question of value.[41] His chief interest regularly seems to be less in the validity of a science than in its significance for man's happiness and salvation.[42]

[39] Ibid., ch. i: "Vera enim beatitudo non consistit in bonorum cognitione, sed in vita bona, non in intelligere sed in intellectu viuere. . . ." For a good example of how Agrippa appeals from the uselessness of human learning to faith and to the Bible, ibid., "Peroratio," fols. a6v-a7v: "Sed reuocate vosmetipsos qui veritatis cupidi estis, discedite ab humanarum traditionum nebulis, adsciscite verum lumen. . . . Indeficiens enim est diuina scientia, cui nihil elabitur, nihil accedit, sed comprehendit omnia. Scitote ergo nunc, quia non multo labore istic opus est, sed fide et oratione: non longi temporis studio, sed humilitate spiritus, et munditia cordis: non librorum multorum sumptuosa supellectile, sed expurgato intellectu. . . . In vno sacro bibliorum volumine omnia continentur, et traduntur. . . ." This discussion, except for an apology for writing so long a book, is the concluding portion of De vanitate.
[40] Apologia, in Opera, II, 213.
[41] Thus in judging mathematics, De vanitate, ch. xi; in judging cosmography, ch. xxvii.
[42] Apologia, in Opera, II, 282-85.

He did not ask whether a science makes a man more knowing but whether it makes him morally better and whether it grants him true wisdom. In his pessimism he was certain that at best human arts and sciences are irrelevant for this purpose, while more often than not they are positively harmful. Sciences do not illumine the Bible but are illumined by it.[43] Any goodness that may be in any human science comes not from the science itself but from the goodness of its founder or of him who uses it in a given instance.[44]

Agrippa did not try to escape this intellectual anarchy by pushing aside all philosophical considerations and stressing the value of ancient literature for its aesthetic and moral content. Despite his broad general acquaintance with classical literature and the writings of such modern authors as Petrarch, Valla, Ficino, and Pico, he was not a humanist in any broad sense of the term. He believed that Roman law should be stripped of medieval accretions; he urged students to study ancient literature; he praised the study of languages; he criticized the barbarisms of the terminology of professional philosophers. But none of these traits of humanism gave him a way out of the intellectual anarchy he had wrought. If he praised the idea of trilingual (Latin, Greek, and Hebrew) learning, it was solely for the sake of Bible study. If he praised the study of ancient authors, it was not with confidence that any ancient philosophical school would provide a system of great value,[45] and it was almost always with an admonition about the greater value of studying sacred letters. If he himself studied ancient texts with avidity, he did so in the belief that they enshrined a secret revelation from God to man. What is more, in addition to becoming disillusioned with Hermetic and cabalistic writings as a source of divine revelation, the later Agrippa reserved some of his sharpest barbs for those who upheld the value of polite letters. He accused some of the proud literary men of scorning the Bible because of its lack of literary adornment.[46] He denied any validity to grammar because it depends on usage rather than on reason; and he pointed out the hypercritical tendency of all grammarians. Grammarians, he said, have shown that not only George of Trebizond and Lorenzo Valla but even

[43] Ibid., II, 286; De vanitate, ch. c, ci.

[44] De vanitate, ch. i.

[45] De beatissimae Annae monogamia, fols. K5v-K7r. Agrippa ad Amicum, Geneva, 7 October 1522, Epistolarum Liber III, xxxi, in Opera, II, 797-99. This correspondence is henceforth cited as Epist.

[46] De vanitate, "Ad Lectorem," fol. A7r.

Cicero, Ovid, and other ancient writers have committed faults of grammar. He attacked such fields of literature as poetry and history because they tell tales both untrue and depraving, such as the stories of Arthur, Lancelot, and Tristan.[47] Ovid to him was nothing but a teller of bawdy tales, as were Aeneas Sylvius, Dante, Petrarch, Pontano, Leon Battista Alberti, and, above all, Boccaccio.[48] Finally, when he said that pride in learning is the source of all heresies, when he noted that Christendom was tranquil and devout when Alexander Gallus was the only grammarian, Petrus Hispanus dominated dialectic, Laurentius Aquilegius ruled rhetoric, the ecclesiastical calendar was all the mathematics studied, and Isidore sufficed for all the rest of learning,[49] was he not striking almost as hard against the humanists as against the Schoolmen? He concentrated more on the latter because he regarded them as the more pressing danger, but he did not leave humanistic studies and their proponents untouched by any means.

Since Agrippa had left little basis for science except the authority of the past, his readers must have found it still more disconcerting to see how everywhere he assailed the accepted authorities. This was true not only of the medieval Schoolmen and their favorite philosopher, Aristotle, but also of every ancient author. He showed that even Cicero, Demosthenes, Ovid, and the other great ancient writers erred often.[50] If study of Plato makes a man impious, yet study of Aristotle and his followers makes one superstitious, while would-be Ciceronians become pagans.[51] Even such revered authorities as Hippocrates in medicine came under Agrippa's attack.[52] Even the Church Fathers, the only theologians whom he praised, erred on individual points in spite of all their sanctity.[53] A recurring refrain in Agrippa's works is: "Every man is a liar: but only Christ, man and God, never was and never will be found untruthful. . . ."[54] Only divine grace and revelation offer hope of release from human weakness and ignorance.

[47] *Ibid.*, ch. iii-v.   [48] *Ibid.*, ch. lxiii and lxiv.
[49] *Ibid.*, ch. ci.
[50] For more attacks on accepted authorities, *ibid.*, ch. vi, and *De beatissimae Annae monogamia*, fol. K7v.
[51] *De vanitate*, ch. vi. One would expect the roles of Plato and Aristotle here to be reversed, but this is how Agrippa puts it.
[52] *Ibid.*, ch. lxxxii.
[53] *Ibid.*, ch. xcviii, and *De beatissimae Annae monogamia*, fol. L1v.
[54] *De vanitate*, ch. xcix: "Omnis homo mendax: Solus autem CHRISTVS deus et homo, nunquam repertus est, nec reperietur mendax. . . ."

Thus Agrippa denied the ability of man to know the external world or its Creator, and cast doubt on the arts and sciences which man had constructed on the presumption that he could know reality. Agrippa cast doubt on all past authorities and so could not find satisfactory refuge in any form of ipsedixitism. And he had little use for mere external sensory knowledge of singulars. What the present chapter has shown, in short, is his denial of any congruity between human reason and reality. The only way in which he softened this discord was by giving a high position to the power of the divinely illuminated mind and to the Bible as the greatest of all products of divine inspiration.

Yet such denial of the powers of human reason does not necessarily call into question the orderly nature of the universe itself. A further question is whether from being a mystical romantic, as Hiram Haydn would call him,[55] Agrippa passed on to become a disillusioned naturalist: in other words, whether he denied that there is any order in creation to begin with. His attack on the power of the human mind was consciously, clearly, and pungently worked out. There was no comparable assault on the idea that the universe is orderly and meaningful. Yet there were hints in this direction. Most of these occurred as an underlying and scarcely conscious element in his treatment of specific problems, especially in the realm of practical affairs.

In one sense, of course, the magical world view which he never wholly abandoned was itself a challenge to belief in an orderly universe. The action of the *magus* and of the multitude of natural, occult, celestial, and spiritual forces which he employs represented an unruly, disorderly principle which broke through the usual hierarchical structure of reality, bending and twisting that order to make it subject to the will of man. Yet at the same time, magic depended on the sympathetic interrelationship of all ranks of being, an interrelationship which was no less real merely because human reason could not grasp it but could only learn it from experience. So in a higher sense, Agrippa's acceptance of a magical world view did not really contradict belief in the goodness and orderliness of God's creation. There was still an orderliness in the world, but the order was that of a living, growing, feeling, and even intelligent animal, endowed at once with material body, intermediate spirit,

[55] Haydn, *op. cit.*, pp. 15-17, a definition based on Lovejoy.

and nonmaterial soul, rather than that of cold, dead matter divided into rigid, easily classified categories. The order was hidden from man's reason, at least since the sin of Adam had robbed the soul of divine illumination. But it was known to the Creator, and also known to glorified, purified man—to Adam before his fall, and to man after the action of divine grace and his own self-purification had restored the light of God to his soul.

In most respects, one must conclude that Agrippa's universe still seemed orderly even though beyond the power of human comprehension. Hence he felt that if only divine illumination would lift the veil of fleshly cares from the soul, man could attain all knowledge by immediate intuition. Such divinely inspired knowledge would also enable man to perform wondrous works, beyond the ordinary powers of nature. The belief in an orderly and interconnected universe thus had not disappeared, if only man could learn the order and connection between things and so make use of them. In criticizing alchemy, Agrippa blamed the alchemists for seeking by art to overcome nature, when art could only follow nature from afar.[56] Its effort to make gold was not only fraudulent but also wicked, for it sought to upset a divine law in nature instituted after the fall of Adam: that man should eat his bread in the sweat of his brow. Still in lesser matters, where it has not done violence to nature but only followed it, alchemy has produced many useful things, such as dyestuffs, metallic alloys, cannon, and glass. There are also something of orderliness and a suggestion of primitivism in Agrippa's treatment of the various branches of agriculture in De vanitate, for although he has criticisms to make, the simpler, more natural agrarian society does not suffer the scathing criticism to which he subjects courtly and urban life.[57] Likewise his strong preference for simples and his distaste for foreign remedies in medicine, attitudes soon to be emphasized in far greater detail by Paracelsus,[58] are based on a confidence that if any drug were really suited to the treatment of persons living in a given climate, nature would have provided a source for it in some native plant.[59] Belief in an orderly universe also appears in Agrippa's definition of natural magic as the highest part of natural philosophy, inspecting the sympathetic

[56] De vanitate, ch. xc.   [57] Ibid., ch. lxxiv-lxxvi, lxxviii.
[58] Henry M. Pachter, Magic Into Science: The Story of Paracelsus (New York, 1951), p. 87.
[59] De vanitate, ch. lxxxiv.

bonds between things and so understanding and using occult powers to perform apparently miraculous works. Its major failing, he
thought, is that it is so easily and so often contaminated by superstition.[60] Agrippa's world even after 1526 was peopled by good and
evil spirits, which the *magus* could summon; but even more than
in his earlier period, he warned of the danger of such practices,
since evil spirits often appear in the guise of good ones. The only
statement which might seriously shake belief in the existence of an
orderly world is Agrippa's ridiculing of the notion of the music
of the spheres.[61] This is only a peripheral matter, however. Agrippa
had far too much faith in divine wisdom to teach that the universe
created by God was disordered and imperfect.

Religion was no guard, however, against a contrary view in the
realm of human affairs, for the doctrine of original sin could always
serve as a theoretical justification for belief that society was disordered, selfish, and cruel. There are strong traces of just such a
view in Agrippa's thought. The key to this belief in the anarchy of
society is the chapter on moral philosophy in *De vanitate*. Here,
while assuming of course that there is an absolute moral law in the
realm of grace, the Nettesheimer seriously questions the existence
of a moral order in the purely human sphere. Moral philosophy, he
charges, "depends not so much on the reasons of philosophers as on
varying usage, custom, observation, and frequent use of daily living,
and is changeable according to the opinion of times, places, and
men. . . ."[62] He defends this statement first of all with reference to
the varying moral standards of different peoples. Like Montaigne
half a century later, he says "that what once was a vice is even
regarded as virtue, and what is here a virtue is elsewhere vice."[63]
For example, the ancient Hebrews and modern Turks permitted
polygamy and concubinage, a practice regarded as execrable among
the Christians. The Greeks found nothing wrong, he says, with
homosexuality and appearance on the stage, both held shameful by
the Romans. The Romans let their wives appear in public, while the
Greeks did not. The Lacedemonians and Egyptians regarded theft

[60] *Ibid.*, ch. xlii-xlvi.   [61] *Ibid.*, ch. xvii.
[62] *Ibid.*, ch. liv, fol. K2r ("non tam philosophorum ratiunculis quam vario
vsu, consuetudine, obseruatione, ac communis vitae conuersatione consiare, ac
pro temporum, locorum, hominumque opinione mutabilem esse. . . .")
[63] *Ibid.*, fol. K2v ("vt quod aliquando vitium fuit, modo virtus habeatur, et
quod hic virtus est, alibi vitium sit. . . .")

as honorable, while we punish it. Agrippa also explains the existence of moral relativism on the grounds of different national characteristics, which in this case he attributes to the stars. This attribution, not wholly consonant with his doubts about astral influences earlier in the same work, was more happily explained as the result of climatic conditions by Jean Bodin later in the same century. Agrippa's denunciation of the wickedness of moral philosophers, especially the depraved and miscreant Aristotle, does not add much to buttress his belief in moral relativism. More effective is his argument that even ethicians are still disagreed about the nature of the *summum bonum*, some placing it in pleasure, some in virtue, and some elsewhere. He insists on the fundamental disharmony between the teachings of moral philosophy and the teachings of Christ. Beatitude, he says, is attained "not by Stoic virtue, Academic purgation, or Peripatetic speculation but by faith and grace in the Word of God." Agrippa makes a radical contrast between the wisdom of the world and the foolishness of Christ: "Christ teaches to do good to all, to love even one's enemies, to lend freely, to take revenge on no one, to give to every one who asks; on the contrary the philosophers [teach one to aid] only those who repay benefit with benefit; besides, that it is permissible to be wrathful, to hate, to contend, to wage war, to take interest." [64] In conclusion, Agrippa charges that those who trust in the dictates of right reason are tending toward the heresy of Pelagianism. All moral philosophy is false and vain.

Accompanying this belief in moral relativism is a picture of human nature which shows strong traces of what students of sixteenth-century thought, referring to writers like Machiavelli and Guicciardini, call an animalistic view of human nature.[65] Anyone who reads the bitter social criticisms contained in *De vanitate* must be well aware that they are not the work of a man who believed in the goodness of human nature. Every rank of society, according to Agrippa, depends on cruelty and deceit for its being. The nobility have risen to power by warfare, another name for murder, by pros-

[64] *Ibid.*, fol. K5v ("non acquiri per virtutem Stoicam nec per purgationem Academicam, nec per speculationem peripateticam, sed per fidem et gratiam in verbo dei.") and fol. K6r ("Docet Christus de omnibus benemerendum esse, etiam inimicos diligendos, libere mutuum dandum[,] de nullo vindictam sumendam, omni petenti tribuendum: contra philosophi non nisi his qui beneficium compensant beneficio: caeterum liceat irasci, odisse, contendere, belligerare, foenerari.").

[65] Haydn, *op. cit.*, p. 408.

tituting their wives and daughters to the lusts of the monarch, or by the basest flattery and most abject servitude to the great and powerful; and they live by oppressing the lower classes, by cheating the crown, and by selling their influence at court. Their life is a mass of vices of every sort. Most members of religious orders regard their vocation as nothing but a means to win a subsidized and idle life and a shield against prosecution for their crime and immorality. Medical doctors are ignorant charlatans who do more harm than good. Lawyers are shysters who distort good laws and worm their way into the inner councils of princes, displacing the rightful and hereditary councillors. Merchants are cheats and usurers.[66] This sharp social criticism, of which these are but a few instances, by no means implies any truly democratic element in Agrippa's thought. If the upper classes are vicious and oppressive, he regards the lower classes as stupid, superstitious, and crude. The gnostic scorn for the rabble which underlay Agrippa's insistence on the need to conceal occult philosophy never left him.[67] The unforgivable sin of the monks is the way in which they expose the debates of the learned to the vulgar by their vituperative sermons. Their greatest folly was, by denouncing Luther in their sermons, to force him to write in the vernacular and so to infect the common herd with his heresy. The most desperate threat which Agrippa could make was that he might write in the vulgar tongue and so carry his anticlerical attack among the masses.[68]

There is more to Agrippa's naturalistic view of man than mere denunciation of the injustice and vice of every rank of society. His attack on human nature also passes to the theoretical sphere, though not in any single coherent expression. What is the law of nature of which political theorists prattle so greatly? It is, he says, "not to go hungry, not to go thirsty, not to be cold, not to torment oneself with vigils or labors: it places Epicurean pleasure in the place of the highest felicity, pushing aside all the penitence of religion and

---

[66] For the nobles, De vanitate, ch. lxviii-lxxi, lxxx; for religious, ch. lxii; for physicians, ch. lxxxii-lxxxiii; for lawyers, ch. xcv; for merchants, ch. lxxii.

[67] For example, De occulta philosophia, Bk. III, ch. lxv, pp. cccxlv-cccxlvi.

[68] De beatissimae Annae monogamia, fol. A6r-v. Apologia, in Opera, II, 295. Querela super calumnia, ob editam declamationem, de vanitate scientiarum, atque excellentia verbi Dei, sibi per aliquos sceleratissimos sycophantas, apud Caesaream majest. nefarie ac proditorie intentata, in Opera, II, 481. Henceforth cited as Querela.

works of penitence." [69] Taking up a characteristic theme of the extreme ethical pessimists of the sixteenth century, Agrippa says that "even man himself (as it is in the proverb) is a wolf to man," [70] a judgment amply borne out by his detailed picture of the abuses of society. Elsewhere he returns to the same theme by noting that when noblemen choose animals for their coats of arms, they never choose useful beasts but always fierce and predatory ones.[71] His view of human nature is hardly optimistic.

Moral relativism and the animalistic view of natural man almost necessarily implied the shaking of all those social institutions which made for orderliness in human affairs. Politics, a branch of applied moral philosophy, fell into ruin under Agrippa's criticism. He discussed the usual three forms of government, monarchy, aristocracy, and democracy, and showed some tendency to favor a mixed constitution combining two or more of the pure forms. But no type of constitution, he concluded, has any real value. All depends on the moral character of ruler and ruled. All forms of government are equally good in good hands, equally bad in bad hands.[72] Thus there is no true order in the state itself; there is really no science of politics.

If Agrippa's view of political science depends chiefly on his ethical relativism, his view of law derives also from his pessimistic view of human nature. Agrippa knew quite well the many definitions of justice and expressed them fully in his *Oratio pro quodam doctorando*.[73] But what came to his mind when he wrote on law in *De vanitate* was the harsh realities of law and government. Noting papal and imperial claims to plenitude of power, he traced the origin of all law to arbitrary acts of will on the part of lawmakers, who then cleverly gave their statutes divine sanction among the vulgar masses by pretending to have received their codes from a god. At this particular point he used only examples from gentile history, but in another place in the same chapter he discussed Moses' foundation of Jewish law in terms identical to those he used to describe the origin of gentile legal systems. Thus he seems to hint at the doctrine of the

[69] *De vanitate*, ch. xci: "Denique lex naturae est, non esurire, non sitire, non algere, non vigilijs, non laboribus macerari: Quae omnem religionis poenitentiam poenitentiaeque opera depellens, Epicuream voluptatem pro summa statuit felicitate."
[70] *Ibid.*, ch. lxxviii: "ipse etiam homo (vt est in prouerbio) homini lupus est. . . ." Haydn, *op. cit.*, pp. 405-6, for the significance of *homo homini lupus*.
[71] *De vanitate*, ch. lxxx-lxxxi.
[72] *Ibid.*, ch. lv.   [73] *Opera*, II, 1084-90.

political origin of religious laws which was to become a major theme of seventeenth-century libertinism.[74] Agrippa did not explicitly state it, however, and may not have consciously intended to include the Mosaic code among those laws whose divine sanction is the result of mere imposture. His denunciation of laws as a source of strife and contention was less weighty; but then he proceeded to analyze the binding power of laws, a power which according to him derives solely from the consent of the people, or from the consent of a prince on whom this popular power has been conferred. If an error is made, the error may itself become good law. "Hence we now know that all the prudence of the civil law depends on the mere opinion and will of men, no other reason being active except honesty of manners, or convenience of living, or the authority of the prince, or force of arms." [75] If made for a good purpose by a good prince, a law is good; otherwise not. What is more, pettifogging lawyers and glossators often succeed in distorting even a good law, while lustful princes pervert all the laws to pander to their own unclean desires. There is no law so carefully written that lawyers cannot overturn it. And legal remedies are weak and ineffective unless the plaintiff is strong enough to assert his rights. Agrippa did not spare the canon law either, for he regarded it as arbitrary and oppressive and subject to the greatest abuse by sharp practitioners and unworthy clerics.[76] Much of the social criticism contained in the middle chapters of *De vanitate* concerns perversion of the law by the mighty, and he made effective use of the venality of the university law faculties which pronounced in favor of the divorce of Henry VIII.[77]

Agrippa did not accept these conditions with the coolness of a Machiavelli or a Guicciardini, although his attitude is otherwise reminiscent of the amoral view of the state which appears in the writings of the two great Florentine political theorists. The difference is partly in the passion with which Agrippa denounced the

[74] *De vanitate*, ch. lvi, xci. For the background of the libertines, Giorgio Spini, *Ricerca dei libertini: La teoria dell' impostura delle religioni nel Seicento italiano* (Rome, 1950), pp. 15-21.

[75] *De vanitate*, ch. xci: "Hinc ergo scimus iam omnem iuris ciuilis prudentiam, ex sola hominum opinione voluntateque dependere, nulla alia ratione vrgente, quam vel honestate morum, vel commoditate viuendi, vel autoritate principis, vel vi armorum." Derivation of the authority of law from popular sovereignty, either exercised by the people or devolved upon the *princeps*, is a commonplace of Roman law.

[76] *Ibid.*, ch. xcii-xcv.   [77] *Querela*, in *Opera*, II, 452.

conditions which grow out of this political relativism and this bestiality of the great and powerful. But it lies mainly in the persistence in his thought of the other realm of being, the other standard of morals, that of the world of grace. All this disorder just described exists in the natural and unsanctified world, which original sin has cut off from contact with the world of the ideal. The Nettesheimer was unable and unwilling to push into the background the insistent moral imperative of Christianity. The power of the state still ideally derives from God. The holders of political power are under obligation to punish those who offend against the divine law: for instance, to repress houses of prostitution instead of favoring them and profiting by them.[78] Similarly the claims of princes to be mortal gods are not in contradiction to man's obligation to obey the divine law. Their power derives from God, and part of man's religious duty is to obey them. The ability of kings to cure disease by touch illustrates their divine institution. Agrippa's argument that kings and nobles first arose from violence and bloodshed, that the Lord was angry with the Israelites for desiring a king, and that royal power corrupted even virtuous men, does not really contradict this ultimate derivation of authority from God. There is some inconsistency in his praising tyrannicide, but this still is not contradictory to the divine origin of authority. The unclear question is rather whether one may licitly kill the ruler who abuses the divinely instituted power.[79] Thus one cannot say that there is no moral order in the intellectual world of Agrippa; but the order is in the realm of grace, not that of nature. The natural world is disordered and animalistic. The major positive message of De vanitate is that to end all these abuses in the intellectual realm and in the secular and ecclesiastical worlds, man must stop depending on his own depraved nature and instead must humbly rely on the Word of God as expressed in the illuminated soul and in the Bible. The ideal Christian is symbolized by the humble and patient ass, by the idiota, an ideal quite reminiscent of the docta ignorantia of Nicholas of Cusa, to whose work De docta ignorantia Agrippa expressly appealed in his defense of De vanitate.[80]

---

[78] Apologia, in Opera, II, 297.

[79] De occulta philosophia, Bk. III, ch. xxxv, pp. cclxxxiii-cclxxxiiii. Cf. De vanitate, ch. lxxx, on tyrannicide.

[80] De vanitate, ch. cii, "Ad encomium asini digressio." For the reference to Cusanus and the ideal of learned ignorance, see Apologia, in Opera, II, 288.

De vanitate was a disturbing book. The Sorbonne and the Louvain theological faculty both condemned it, though their condemnations missed much of the point of the entire argument. The radical denial of the power of the human mind to grasp reality was one of the chief disturbing elements. Villey, although he regards the book as a mere *jeu d'esprit*, admits that it was an important source of the skepticism of Michel de Montaigne.[81] All that survived the wreckage of human science, aside from supernatural mysticism, was sense perception of singulars, which Agrippa thought unsuited to the foundation of a science, and the authority of the past masters of Antiquity. Even the great authorities of the past came in for attack, not only Aristotle and the medieval scholastics, but also Plato, Hermes, the Alexandrian school, the cabalists, and even, with far greater limitations, the Church Fathers. These two elements of *De vanitate*, the attack on reason and the repudiation of past authorities, undermined faith in the ability of the mind to know reality. A third major theme of the book was the shaking of belief in the orderly nature of the universe. This attack struck not at the physical world but at the moral world, where original sin provided a theoretical justification for it. A pessimistic view of human nature combined with moral relativism to undermine the rational foundations of human institutions. The prolonged and embittered social criticism which fills much of the book was really an extended demonstration of this principle of moral anarchy in the natural world. A final disturbing element was the rabid anticlericalism which the book reflects. Despite the obvious exaggeration of many of the statements, the book is a valid expression of the author's intellectual and emotional rejection of all human arts and sciences.

It is not hard to picture the consternation which Agrippa himself must have felt at the results of his formulation of doubt. The position which he had reached could hardly have satisfied him, for his tone was not the cool mockery of a Montaigne, nor the matter-of-fact attitude of a Machiavelli, but rather the impassioned invective of a Jean-Jacques Rousseau.[82] One can see him shrinking back from the chaos he had wrought.

[81] Pierre Villey, *Les sources et l'évolution des Essais de Montaigne* (2nd ed.; 2 vols.; Paris, 1933), II, 166-70. He notes the close textual dependence of many parts of the "Apology for Raymond Sebond" on *De vanitate*.

[82] The comparison to Rousseau is common enough and, as far as the emotional quality in Agrippa is concerned, quite justifiable. See, for example, H. Follet, "Un médecin astrologue au temps de la Renaissance, Henri Cornelius Agrippa," *Nouvelle revue*, XCVIII (1896), 330.

His declamatory little book itself contains elements of an effort to save something out of the ruin of all learning. Most important in Agrippa's own mind was the mystical escape from intellectual anarchy. As the present study has repeatedly shown, the mystical solution ran through his thought consistently from his earliest to his latest years. If only the mind of man, having been freed from the bonds of the flesh by careful preparation, can attain mystical illumination, then all knowledge and so all power will be its own. Since Agrippa himself did not claim personal experience of this sort, he had to provide a way out for those like himself who were not mystics. This way was to follow the lead of those who had gained such union, that is, simply and humbly to follow the Bible, which is the work of such illuminates. Even for a profound understanding of Scripture, illumination is necessary; but the humbler believer can gain beatitude by merely following the letter of Holy Writ carefully, believing the essentials of the teaching of the universal church (whatever those essentials were, a point on which he was not clear, though he certainly included the two great commandments and the Apostles' Creed), and reverently praying to God. God, he was sure, will not fail such a believer.[83] Mysticism and skepticism, far from being opposed, here exist together.

Agrippa also groped, although far less surely, toward a solution of the problem of skepticism on an intellectual plane. Sense knowledge of singulars did not perish in his attack, although he seriously questioned its accuracy in any given case. This was the empirical side of his thought. His suspicion that somehow the great authorities of Antiquity could not have been so wrong as they seemed was an effort to salvage the principle of authority by accepting allegorical interpretations. Both his attempt to return to Antiquity and his empiricism really amounted to authoritarianism, the authority of bald statement and the authority of brute fact. At the same time, the belief that all higher generalizations were equally arbitrary made it possible for him to accept any scheme of explanation provisionally as long as it seemed useful, that is, as long as it stood the test of facts. Here was an adumbration of the function of scientific hypothesis, but without any program for controlled observation or

---

[83] *De vanitate,* "Peroratio," fol. a6r: "Dicetis forsan paucissimis admodum haec [illuminatio] contigisse. Et pauci quos aequus amauit Iupiter, aut ardens euexit ad aethera virtus, Dijs geniti potuere. Sed nolite desperare, non est abbreuiata manus domini omnibus inuocantibus eum, qui illi fidele praestant obsequium." The sentence "Et pauci . . . potuere" is from Vergil, *Aeneid,* Bk. VI, ll, 129-31, and was frequently quoted by Ficino.

planned experiments, and of course without any idea of quantitative, mathematical expression. Here was also an invitation to question and rethink all scientific generalizations, a process which was far more important in the scientific revolution that was about to begin than was any accumulation of new data. The least that such a book could do was to encourage people to explore any new idea, however absurd it might seem. All of this later development, of course, was outside the scope of Agrippa's thought, but he stood at the threshold of it. Ernst Cassirer has long since noted that skepticism was the first great step toward modern philosophical reconstruction.[84] Consciously or unconsciously, this is how Agrippa was able to continue his alchemical operations and his search for recondite literature after 1526, and how he was able to publish *De occulta philosophia* as a book containing many errors of the past but also much useful information.

His own and succeeding generations were unable to see this, and for them *De vanitate* remained either a pungent and sometimes witty paradox or a very unsettling book. His complete separation of the ideal and real worlds, for instance, was intended for the disparagement of the latter, not of the former. But all now depended on an act of faith, for he had ruled out on principle any rational demonstration of religious or other significant truth. Suppose one did not choose to take the leap of faith. What remained was an unknowable world, and, as far as the moral realm was concerned, a brutal, disorderly, and amoral one. This was the danger latent in the fideists' sharp separation of the realm of grace from the realm of nature. Even John Calvin felt some alarm at the tendency of certain naturalists to exalt animal instinct and appetite in man, a tendency which recent Roman Catholic apologists have called a natural outcome of the radical split which the Protestants made between the world of grace and the world of nature.[85]

The present chapter has already shown the possible germ of the libertine belief that all religious laws, even that of Moses, were the products of clever impostors who gained respect for their codes among the masses by pretending to have written at the dictate of a god. This teaching was one of the major ingredients of that seventeenth-century Italian libertinism which attracted the *esprits forts*

---

[84] Cassirer, *op. cit.*, I, 162, 181, and more recently, Popkin, *op. cit.*, *passim.*
[85] Haydn, *op. cit.*, p. 416. Cf. Jacques Maritain, *Trois Réformateurs: Luther —Descartes—Rousseau* (2nd ed.; Paris, 1925), pp. 12-19.

of every part of Europe. It is by no means clear that Agrippa meant the idea to apply to anyone but the founders of gentile religious laws, and there is not the slightest hint anywhere in his writings that he regarded Jesus Christ as such an impostor. This was, of course, a common enough theme in medieval literature, expressed in the tale of the three impostors, Moses, Jesus, and Mohammed.

De vanitate also shows other traits of the later libertine teachings. One is the notion that all religions are subject to the stars in their origin, rise, and fall, though Agrippa mentioned it only to denounce it as an example of the impiety to which astrology has led.[86] He was also well aware of the heterodox interpretation of Aristotle by the Averroists and the school of Alexander of Aphrodisias; and apparently he believed that these doctrines of the unity of the intellect, the mortality of the individual soul, and the eternity of the world represented the real teaching of Aristotle.[87] It was precisely for this reason that he so bitterly detested and denounced the Stagirite. Still this heterodox interpretation of Aristotle was available for readers of De vanitate, as it was in the works of many writers of that period, most notably Pietro Pomponazzi. Agrippa also approximated Machiavelli's amoral view of the world, another ingredient of the libertine teachings. His suggestion that contradiction and error exist even in Scripture [88] might encourage the greatest disorders among persons who did not, like him, submit the interpretation and the canon of Scripture ultimately to the judgment of the institutional church. He also knew and partly adopted the notion of natural causation of such supposedly miraculous phenomena as the stigmata of St. Francis, although he specifically refuted the idea that Christ's miracles were of this sort.[89] The gnostical scorn for the canaille, which Spini regards as one of the chief proofs of the un-Christian mood of the Italian Seicento, was certainly not lacking

[86] De vanitate, ch. xxxi: "Iam vero et haereses et infidelitates perniciosissimas docere non verentur, videlicet dum donum prophetiae, vim religionum, arcana conscientiae, imperium in daemones, virtutem miraculorum, efficaciam supplicationum, et futurae vitae statum, omnia pendere ab astris . . . ex illis cognosci impia temeritate fatentur."

[87] Ibid., ch. lii, liv; and, for the eternity of the world, ch. li.

[88] Ibid., ch. xcix.

[89] For the natural causation of the stigmata, De occulta philosophia, Bk. I, ch. lxiv, p. lxxxv. For rejection of the idea that all miracles were of this sort, ibid., Bk. I, ch. xiii, p. xviii. The explaining away of all mysteries, including Christian miracles, was a subtly concealed danger of all systems of natural, nondemonic magic, according to Walker, Spiritual and Demonic Magic, pp. 82-84, 108-9, 111.

from Agrippa's thought, although it was tempered by some compassion for their suffering at the hands of their upper-class oppres-
sors, a compassion which even grew into a positive program of
indoor poor relief as a means of suppressing sturdy beggars while
aiding the impotent poor, a scheme which drew an approving marginal comment from his Elizabethan translator.[90]

A recently discovered Agrippan imprint, known in only one
copy, has raised the further question whether Agrippa was not
himself the central figure of a group of libertines, who combined a
truly dangerous degree of free thought with the occultist enthusiasms that characterized Agrippa's circle of friends wherever he
lived. This document, discovered in the Biblioteca Colombina at
Seville, is a small piece of four leaves printed in blackletter type,
without indication of place or date, and entitled *Prognosticon vetus
in Agrippinarum archivis inventum*. It consists of a prefatory letter
entitled "Henricus Cornelius Agrippa Lectori S.D.," the *Prognosticon* itself, with an appended verse referring to Revelations 22, a
French translation of the main text of the *Prognosticon* and the
verse, and three Italian-language quatrains appended to the French
verses. Its discoverer suggests a French origin for it, and the period
1515-1530 for date of publication. She also defends its authenticity
as a work of Agrippa. For one thing, the *Ad Lectorem* or prefatory
letter is textually almost identical to a letter which Agrippa wrote,
probably in 1526, to an unnamed friend. In this letter, he attacked
the validity of astrology. Furthermore, the same text, with only
minor verbal changes, forms part of his chapter "De astrologia
iudiciaria" in *De vanitate*.[91] In his letter, the Nettesheimer himself
wryly referred to a prognostication with twofold commentary
which he sent so that those who demand predictions from him "may
know that I, whom they think to be such an astrologer, am also such
a prophet, and know how to profit by their folly."[92] The same

---

[90] *De vanitate*, ch. lxv. The translation is *Of the Vantitie and Vncertaintie
of Artes and Sciences*, trans. Ja[mes]. San[dford]. (London, 1569), pp. 104-5.
For the libertines' scorn for the masses, see Spini, *op. cit.*, pp. 40-41.

[91] *De vanitate*, ch. xxxi, and *Epist.* IV, viii. The text of the *Prognosticon* is
in Paola Zambelli, "Umanesimo magico-astrologico e raggruppamenti segreti
nei platonici della preriforma," in *Umanesimo e esoterismo: Atti del V convegno internazionale di studi umanistici, Oberhofen, 16-17 settembre 1960*, ed.
Enrico Castelli (Padua, 1960), p. 168; cf. *ibid.*, pp. 157-58, for discussion of
this document.

[92] *Epist.* IV, viii: "ut sciant, qualem me opinantur astrologum, talem esse
prophetam, et me scire eorum frui stultitia." Cf. *Prognosticon*, in Zambelli,
"Umanesimo magico-astrologico," p. 168.

prophecy is surely mentioned in another letter which he sent to a friend named Conrad living at Chambéry in Savoy on 18 April 1526. Here he enclosed his *De matrimonio*, the Latin text for his friend and a French text for the friend's wife, together with "a certain prognostication, and that my own, from which you can judge what a noteworthy astrologer I have become." [93] This letter, and especially the ironic tone in which it is written, strongly confirms Agrippa's authorship of the *Prognosticon* and makes it possible that either he or his Savoyard friend also prepared the French translation.

The *Prognosticon* itself consists of a short prophetic statement concerning four kings who are to come from the four corners of the world, and the horrors and prodigies which are to ensue. It is obviously meant to be typical of the obscure prophecies of doom which circulated frequently in Agrippa's time, and about which he himself often received requests for interpretations.[94] Then he has added a twofold marginal interpretation, one of them speaking in a serious tone and one in a tone of folly. The serious interpretation refers the prophetic words to a great war, a terrible conqueror, religious reforms, and other favorite topics of contemporary prophecy. The jocular interpretation refers the same words to a description of a carouse by a pack of gamblers (the four kings, for instance, are in a deck of cards). Obviously, this newly discovered work is a fine example of prophetic parody, a genre which was quite popular in the early Reformation period and which had reached a climax after the dire but unfulfilled predictions of floods which were expected to result from the great planetary conjunction in the sign of Pisces in 1524. Such parody became a favorite propaganda device of humanists, and Agrippa's *Prognosticon*, probably a work of his year of crisis and disillusionment, 1526, is akin to the jocular prophecies of Rabelais just a few years later, or the anticlerical *Judicio over pronostico di mastro Pasquino quinto evangelista per l'anno 1527* by Pietro Aretino, with its delightful spoof of astrological pomposity: "Secondo la opinione di moderni interpreti dei pianeti . . . lo introito del Sole sarà ne la prima taverna ch'egli troverà. . . ." [95]

---

[93] *Epist.* IV, iv: "prognosticum quoddam, idque meum, ex quo judicabis, quam egregius evaserim astrologus." For Conrad's reply, *Epist.* IV, v.

[94] E.g., *Epist.* III, lvii; IV, xii, xxix, xxx, and several subsequent letters of the year 1526, especially IV, lv, lxx.

[95] Quoted by Zambelli, "Umanesimo magico-astrologico," p. 161. For this whole discussion, *ibid.*, pp. 158-63, 169-70.

The significance of this new Agrippan document needs to be carefully weighed. Its discoverer concludes that the publication of this document and the preservation and eventual publication of Agrippa's correspondence much later in the century were both the work of a secret brotherhood of disciples, perhaps the "Agrippans" denounced by André Thevet later in the century.[96] Yet there is danger in pushing this argument too far. For instance, Agrippa himself preserved his own letters, as is shown not only by the publication of a few of them as appendices to his books published during his lifetime, but also by his threat to retaliate against Louise of Savoy by publishing his correspondence with various courtiers, in order to demonstrate to the world how shabbily she had treated him.[97] Second, although there can be no doubt that the Nettesheimer was linked to an extensive network of fellow students of the occult, there is no real proof that this group was an institutionalized brotherhood, a conventicle.[98] Perhaps his friends really did preserve his letters and were responsible for their eventual publication. On the other hand, Agrippa left several children; and one of them, at least, was a man of some learning and reputation who might well have preserved his father's papers. The phrase from the new-found *Prognosticon*, "ex archivis Agrippinarum," need not be taken too literally. Finally, the real influence of Agrippa on later libertinism did not derive chiefly from circulation of his collected letters, only a few of which betray the mocking tone and corrosive doubt of the libertines.[99] The principal influence of Agrippa on later free thought was not a secret one exercised through secret channels, but a public one exercised through his widely circulated, much-translated, and highly popular book, *De vanitate*, a work which as late as the eighteenth century could still unsettle the youthful optimism of a Goethe. What the new Agrippan document really does, is to confirm still further a point already evident from the Nettesheimer's known works: that even at the height of his doubts about occultism and all sciences, he still preserved a belief, or at least a tentative half-

[96] *Ibid.*, pp. 153-56.

[97] Agrippa ad Amicum [Jean Chapelain], Lyons, 5 February 1527, *Epist.* V, ii.

[98] Zambelli, "Umanesimo magico-astrologico," pp. 153-55, carries this point perhaps somewhat further than the evidence justifies. For a general warning against interpreting such academies as full-fledged conventicles, see Edgar Wind, *Pagan Mysteries in the Renaissance* (New Haven, 1958), p. 18, n. 1.

[99] As Zambelli herself indirectly admits, in "Umanesimo magico-astrologico," p. 155.

belief, in such basic occultist concepts as the emanation of mysterious influences from the stars.[100] Like *De vanitate*, like a few letters
from the same period, the *Prognosticon* reflects a serious spiritual
crisis on the part of the author himself, and also, in a more general
sense, on the part of the Renaissance culture in which he was so
deeply learned.

Although many hints of familiarity with the doctrines of later
libertine groups abound in his works, Agrippa flatly rejected most
of these teachings. He was no libertine, though he was interested in
all viewpoints, even the most dangerous. One is not justified in calling his rejection of libertinism insincere, for it by no means ran
counter to the main stream of his thought. Nor ought one to exag-
gerate the role of his works, chiefly *De vanitate*, in the development
of unbelief at the end of the century. The book was certainly much
edited and much translated in the sixteenth and seventeenth centuries
and doubtless made its contribution to the growth of such ideas not
only in Italy but north of the Alps as well; but Spini has shown that
these ideas were widely spread even before the sixteenth century.[101]
In any case, the writings of Agrippa von Nettesheim furnish an
example of acquaintance with some of these libertine ideas in germ
north of the Alps, and so suggest a third major way in which *De
vanitate*, even though unintentionally in this instance, helped shatter
the rational and orderly world view of the great medieval intellectual syntheses. The other two ways were the epistemological pessimism and the moral anarchism discussed in the preceding sections
of this chapter.

[100] This point is made admirably clear, *ibid.*, pp. 142-53, 163-67. Dr. Zambelli,
however, misinterprets my own association of Agrippa's position with what
Hiram Haydn labels "the Counter-Renaissance," since although I find Haydn's
book stimulating and suggestive, I do not really regard the evidence there
presented as constituting proof of a separate "Counter-Renaissance" movement,
but rather as demonstrating an important aspect of Renaissance culture which
most interpretations of the period tend to underestimate or even ignore. See
my article, "Magic and Skepticism in Agrippa's Thought," *Journal of the
History of Ideas*, XVIII (1957), 161-82. My other reservations about Dr. Zambelli's interpretation concern: 1) the above-mentioned tendency to make
Agrippa's *sodalitium* of occultist friends into a too definitely organized and
institutionalized group, and 2) her tendency to attribute a too limited significance to the skeptical element in *De vanitate* and to its influence on later
thought. On *De vanitate*, cf. her article, "A proposito del 'De vanitate scientiarum et artium' di Cornelio Agrippa," *Rivista critica di storia della filosofia*,
XV (1960), 166-80. Nevertheless, her position on this subject is not extreme,
and her interpretation retains high value.

[101] Spini, *op. cit.*, p. 15.

CHAPTER TWELVE

FACT AND FANTASY: AGRIPPA'S POSITION IN INTELLECTUAL HISTORY

Agrippa von Nettesheim is now a forgotten figure in the intellectual history of the West. Yet both as a real man and as a legend he made his contribution to the development of the modern mind; and there is besides the intrinsic interest of the picture of the European mentality in the early sixteenth century which one can form from his numerous treatises and his hundreds of surviving letters. This analysis of his intellectual world will be complete when it has suggested his influence in his own day and after, discussed the legends that grew up around his figure and their contribution to that great symbol of western man, Faust, and then related the main elements of Agrippa's thought to the general intellectual movement of his age.

Only a handful of his contemporaries had a reputation for erudition and for boldness of thought and expression that could be compared to Agrippa's during the sixteenth and seventeenth centuries, and even well into the eighteenth century. His biography shows that he was able to attract, though not to hold, the attention of the greatest princes of his age. Even the reserved and cautious Erasmus, though thinking him rash and ill-advised, still admitted his erudition and wit. Juan Luis Vives called him "the wonder of letters and of literary men," while the elder Scaliger esteemed him for his learning.[1] Rabelais knew of him and did him the honor of satirizing him as the ridiculous astrologer and cuckold Her Trippa of his *Tiers Livre*, a book wherein he also lampooned such figures as Lefèvre d'Étaples, Lemaire de Belges, and Tiraqueau.[2] Agrippa's doctrine of the three types of melancholy strongly influenced his great contemporary Albrecht Dürer in his famous engraving "Melencolia I." [3] Agrippa's pupil Johann Wier, one of the few outspoken opponents of the witchcraft delusion later in the sixteenth century, wrote respectfully of his master and refuted some of the wild legends which already were gathering around this strange figure.[4] Paracelsus, or one of his followers writing under his name, when boasting of his knowledge of magic, claimed to surpass Agrippa, as if he were an acknowledged master. Cardan attacked *De vanitate* as a mere literary trifle but admitted that many of his contemporaries admired it.[5]

The generation which flourished near the end of the sixteenth century had not forgotten Agrippa. The continued re-editing of his books would suggest this fact even if there were no other evidence. In 1572, the landgrave of Hesse quoted an opinion of Agrippa's on astronomy in a letter to Caspar Peucer; and although both

[1] Thomas Pope Blount, *Censura celebriorum authorum* . . . (Londini, 1690), p. 387, gives the opinions of Julius Caesar Scaliger and Juan Luis Vives. The latter's words are given thus: "literarum literatorumque omnium miraculum."
[2] François Rabelais, *Tiers Livre*, ch. xxv, in *Oeuvres*, ed. Burgaud des Marets and E. J. B. Rathery (2 vols.; Paris, 1856-58), I, 538-44. See also Abel Lefranc, "Rabelais et Cornelius Agrippa," in *Mélanges offerts à M. Émile Picot* (2 vols.; Paris, 1913), II, 477-86, where he shows that the two men may even have been house guests of the same person at the same period of 1535.
[3] Erwin Panofsky, *Albrecht Dürer* (2 vols.; Princeton, 1943), I, 168-70.
[4] Johann Wier, *Opera omnia* (Amstelodami, 1660), pp. 108-11, 260, 625-29.
[5] Theophrastus Paracelsus, *Sämmtliche Werke*, ed. Karl Sudhoff (14 vols.; Munich, 1922-33), XIV, 513-14. Sudhoff denies that this particular treatise, *De philosophia occulta*, is genuine; it first appeared in print in 1570. Lynn Thorndike, *A History of Magic and Experimental Science* (8 vols.; New York, 1923-58), V, 138, gives Girolamo Cardan's opinion on Agrippa, citing the former's *Opera* (1683), V, 491, for the treatise *De exemplo centum genitura-rum*. There is a passing and unfavorable reference to Agrippa in Cardan's *De rervm varietate libri XVII* (Basileae, 1581), Bk. XII, ch. lxi, p. 781: "Fuit uir paulo ante nostram aetatem mendacior Agrippa, inanior Raymundo Lullio, Abbas Trithemius. . . ."

the latter and Tycho Brahe discounted this authority, they did so perhaps as much because of his reputation for impiety as because of the error of his opinions in astronomy.[6] Giordano Bruno's general view of the universe was much like the Nettesheimer's magical world, and was partly derived from it. Of course the great Nolan philosopher drew on other sources also; but he took much of the detail of his *De monade* straight from *De occulta philosophia*, which was perhaps the chief source for his knowledge of Cabala. He also knew *De vanitate*, which in a negative sense was the source of his satirical treatment of asininity as the chief human virtue.[7] Earlier chapters of the present study have shown repeatedly that *De vanitate* was an important source for the skeptical thought of Michel de Montaigne, who based extensive passages of his "Apology for Raymond Sebond" on the earlier work. Montaigne also borrowed some illustrative details from *De occulta philosophia*.[8] One French writer of the late sixteenth century, André Thevet, wrote that there was a whole school of atheists who claimed to follow Agrippa,[9] while John Calvin earlier had classed him as a mocker at religion.[10] One need not take these complaints as accurate reflections of Agrippa's own intentions; but the preceding chapter has shown that *De vanitate* contained ideas with an affinity for the thought of later groups of libertines and freethinkers. Furthermore, if *De vanitate* became a favorite of those who mocked at all learning and even at religion, *De occulta philosophia* in both printed and manuscript forms be-

[6] Tycho Brahe, *Opera omnia*, ed. I. L. E. Dreyer (15 vols.; Hauniae, 1913-29), III, 114-27.

[7] J. Lewis McIntyre, *Giordano Bruno* (London, 1903), pp. 131, 148-49. Cf. William Boulting, *Giordano Bruno: His Life, Thought, and Martyrdom* (London, n.d.), pp. 26, 168, 237, and Dorothea Waley Singer, *Giordano Bruno, His Life and Thought* (New York, 1950), pp. 69, 141.

[8] Pierre Villey, *Les sources et l'évolution des Essais de Montaigne* (2nd ed.; 2 vols.; Paris, 1933), I, 61-62; II, 154-55, 166-71.

[9] André Thevet, *Les vrais povrtraits et vies des hommes illustres* (Paris, 1584), p. 544: "Et, pleut à Dieu, que tout seul il se fust noyé en ce goulphre d'impieté, auiourd'huy nous n'aurions vn tas d'Athees, de mesdisans et brocardeurs, comme ce siecle les nous a produict." P. 545: "I'ay honte qu'il faille que ie ramentoyue les malheurs de nostre France, qui encores pour le iourdhuy soustyent des Agrippins, esquels soubs quelques traicts estranges et espouuentables font estat de prendre la lune auec les dents, taillent, roignent, retranchent, moderent, partissent et despiecent la puissance de l'Eternel, lequel ils veulent assubiectir aux niaiseries, qu'asses sottement ils s'impriment dans la ceruelle."

[10] Josef Bohatec, *Budé und Calvin: Studien zur Gedankenwelt des französischen Frühhumanismus* (Graz, 1950), pp. 149-50, 162-65, based on Calvin's *De scandalis*.

came a standard text for students of magic in the sixteenth and seventeenth centuries, although perhaps the spurious Fourth Book, with its numerous formulae and detailed instructions for conjuring spirits, was more influential than the three genuine books.[11] It was chiefly as an infamous sorcerer that Jean Bodin denounced the Nettesheimer, though the occasion of the attack was rather the tendency of Agrippa and the open effort of his pupil Wier to throw discredit on the prosecution of witches.[12]

[11] Will-Erich Peuckert, *Pansophie: Ein Versuch zur Geschichte der weissen und schwarzen Magie* (Stuttgart, 1936), pp. 119-201, especially pp. 186, 193, speaks of Agrippan, Faustian, and Rabellinian schools among northern magicians; and though he thinks Agrippa's effort to purify magic vain, *De occulta philosophia* became the standard text for all later magicians because it collected so much earlier material. As late as 1895, he says, a German sorcerer was arrested and was found to have formularies drawn from Agrippa in his book of enchantments (p. 195). Thorndike, *op. cit.*, V, 136, grudgingly admits the important position which *De occulta philosophia* had among later magicians, though he is at a loss to understand why. The use of Agrippa's book by wizards began very early. On 30 December 1532, William Neville, perhaps the minor poet and son of Sir Richard Neville, second baron Latimer, confessed that he had consulted a wizard named Johns at Oxford and had heard various personal and political prophecies, among them a prediction that he was to become earl of Warwick. Said Johns had spoken to him about Agrippa's *De occulta philosophia*. See *Letters and Papers, Foreign and Domestic, Henry VIII*, V, 694 (No. 1679). The *Index to the Sloane Manuscripts in the British Museum*, ed. Edward J. L. Scott (London, 1904), p. 5, lists at least seven pieces which are seventeenth-century extracts of portions of *De occulta philosophia*, chiefly from the spurious Fourth Book. Quite recently, Helda Bullotta Barracco, "Saggio bio-bibliografico su Enrico Cornelio Agrippa di Nettesheim," in the *Rassegna di filosofia* published by the Instituto di Filosofia of the University of Rome, VI (1957), 237-43, attempted to rebut Johann Wier's denial of Agrippa's authorship of the Fourth Book of *De occulta philosophia*. But many of the presuppositions there made are questionable, and the parallel passages used to justify a part of the argument are not strikingly similar. She also attributes to Agrippa the authorship of the pseudo-*Heptameron* which appears (together with the "Liber Quartus dictus spirius" and several works of other magical authors) in Volume I of Agrippa's *Opera*. But her argument is not convincing. Interest in Agrippa during the sixteenth century is also suggested by Additional Manuscript No. 36,674 of the British Museum, which includes a lengthy extract from the spurious Fourth Book. This piece once belonged to Gabriel Harvey, and before him to Dr. John Caius, master and refounder of Gonville and Caius College at Cambridge. See *Catalogue of Additions to the Manuscripts in the British Museum in the Years MDCCCC-MDCCCCV* (London, 1907), p. 183. Agrippa was still the famous magician in the early nineteenth century. In her famous horror novel, *Frankenstein*, Mary Wollstonecraft Shelley made Agrippa's *De occulta philosophia* the book which first aroused in Frankenstein the curiosity that led to his destruction. (See the edition printed in 1897 at London by Gibbings and Company, pp. 32-33.)

[12] Jean Bodin, *De la demonomanie des sorciers* (Antwerp, 1593), pp. 403-7. Cf. D. P. Walker, *Spiritual and Demonic Magic from Ficino to Campanella* (London, 1958), p. 174.

Another important author who felt Agrippa's influence, far more strongly and positively than Bodin, was Sir Philip Sidney, whose well-known *Apologie for Poetrie* (written about 1579-1580 and posthumously published in 1595) not only referred directly to *De vanitate* but also, more important, modeled its fundamental arguments in defense of poetic fiction along lines obviously suggested by the recently translated declamation. Many other Elizabethan and Jacobean authors in England read and referred to Agrippa, including Christopher Marlowe, Francis Bacon, and Thomas Nashe.[13]

The seventeenth century saw frequent mention of Agrippa, but in the most various ways: as an enlightened opponent of the witchcraft delusion during his residence at Metz; as a Protestant hero who had been slandered by the Papists; as a wicked sorcerer or an equally wicked mocker at religion.[14] Few of the numerous collections of lives of scholars failed to present him in one of these guises. The mystical writer and magician Thomas Vaughan in mid-century gave to Agrippa perhaps the most extravagant praise he ever received: "He indeed is my Author, and next to God I owe all that I have unto Him." His twin brother, the poet Henry Vaughan, drew from *De vanitate* at least the symbol of the ass as the humble Chris-

[13] Sir Philip Sidney, *An Apologie for Poetrie*, ed. Evelyn S. Shuckburgh (Cambridge [Eng.], 1891), pp. 35-47, and the article by A. C. Hamilton, "Sidney and Agrippa," *Review of English Studies*, n. s., VII (1956), 151-57, an article which also lists Agrippan references by Marlowe, Nashe, Harington, and Gabriel Harvey. For Bacon's attack on Agrippa, "that trivial buffoon," with whom he regretted to find his own attacks on traditional learning compared, see F. H. Anderson, *The Philosophy of Francis Bacon* (Chicago, 1948), p. 110. Nashe, in his episodic tale *The Unfortunate Traveller*, in *The Works of Thomas Nashe*, ed. Ronald B. McKerrow (5 vols.; London, 1904-10), II, 252-55, makes Agrippa accompany the narrator and his master, Henry Howard, Earl of Surrey, in Germany, and conjure up visions for Erasmus, Sir Thomas More, Thomas Cromwell, and Charles V, as well as the famous vision of the fair Geraldine who appeared to Surrey. The latter legend eventually found its echo in the writings of Sir Walter Scott, as noted below.

[14] Indeed, all these themes go back to the late sixteenth century. For Protestant interpretation and defense of Agrippa as an opponent of witchcraft, see Reginald Scot, *Discovery of Witchcraft* (London, 1651), pp. 24-33 [*sic*; should be pp. 24-25], 144, 153, 327, 345. This book was first printed in 1584. See also John Webster, *The Displaying of Supposed Witchcraft* (London, 1677), pp. 58-59. Gabriel Naudé, *Apologie pour les grands hommes soupçonnez de magie* (Amsterdam, 1712), pp. 285-306 (ch. XV), defends Agrippa from the charge of sorcery and calls him less superstitious than his accusers, but claims that he was a charlatan who pretended to be a magician. See also Pierre Bayle, *Dictionnaire historique et critique*, ed. Des Maizeaux (4th ed.; 4 vols.; Amsterdam, 1730), I, 107-9.

tian believer, and in part perhaps his stress on humility as a Christian ideal.[15]

Such instances could be multiplied; but these, together with the continued re-editing of Agrippa's books, should at least show that there was something in his writings and in the figure of the man himself to attract the attention of his own and succeeding ages. Even well into the eighteenth century, although Agrippa had begun to be regarded as rather quaint, his *De vanitate* could still shake the youthful optimism of Goethe and cause him to pass through an intellectual crisis.[16]

The Nettesheimer survived in the European mind, however, as a legend as well as a real man. The legends began accumulating within a very few years after his death. The earliest to find written expression was that wherever he went, a devil in the form of a black dog accompanied him, and that on his deathbed, he removed from the neck of this dog a collar bearing magical emblems and said, "Depart, damned beast, who hast wholly ruined me," whereupon the dog ran and leaped into the river Saône and was never seen again. This devil supposedly kept him informed of news, so that even though he spent long periods without ever leaving his study, he knew all that had happened even in distant places.[17] This tale of Paolo Giovio reappears in Thevet and many later authors. Thevet also records (but denies) early tales that Agrippa's magical practices were responsible

[15] [Thomas Vaughan:] Eugenius Philalethes, *Anthroposophia theomagica; or, A Discourse of the Nature of Man and his state after death. . . .* (London, 1650), p. 50. The same author, writing under the same pseudonym, defends Agrippa's reputation in *Anima magica abscondita; or, A Discourse of the universall Spirit of Nature, With his strange, abstruse, miraculous Ascent, and descent* (London, 1650), "To the Reader," fols. A2v–A7v. For the Agrippan influence on him and on his brother Henry, see Alexander C. Judson, "Cornelius Agrippa and Henry Vaughan," *Modern Language Notes*, XLI (1926), 178-81.

[16] See Goethe's *Dichtung und Wahrheit*, Part I, ch. 4, where, speaking of one of the older men who influenced him, Huisgen, he adds, "Eins seiner Lieblingsbücher war *Agrippa de vanitate scientiarum*, das er mir besonders empfahl, und mein junges Gehirn dadurch eine Zeitlang in ziemliche Verwirrung setzte."

[17] Paolo Giovio, *Elogia doctorvm virorvm ab avorvm memoria publicatis ingenij monumentis illustrium* (Basileae, 156?), pp. 236-37. This work was first published in 1546 at Venice. Wier, *Opera omnia*, p. 111, attributes this tale to his former teacher's excessive fondness for dogs, especially a black dog which he called Monsieur. He also says that Agrippa's great correspondence kept him so well informed of distant events that many people thought that a spirit must keep him posted.

for the military victories of Charles V; and he attributes Agrippa's many travels to repeated expulsions caused by his practice of magic.[18] Writing no later than 1599, the Jesuit Del Rio repeated the latter claim and added two new tales. According to him, Agrippa and Faust were both notorious for paying innkeepers with coins which after their departure turned into leaves or filth. The second tale is that a curious boarder once stole into the Nettesheimer's study and, by chance repeating a phrase found in a magical book that lay open on the desk, conjured up a devil. This devil fell upon the unskillful conjurer and killed him. Shortly afterward, Agrippa returned home and, fearing prosecution for murder, made the devil enter the victim's body and transport it to the public square, where, after strolling for a time as if alive, it collapsed, apparently the victim of a natural death.[19] To these tales an eighteenth-century polyhistor added two more, that Agrippa was able to read in the moon distant events such as the outcome of the military operations of Francis I in Italy, and that he was able to lecture from nine to ten o'clock at Fribourg (or Freiburg-im-Breisgau) and at ten to begin his lecture at Pont-à-Mousson in Lorraine.[20] In *The Lay of the Last Minstrel*, Sir Walter Scott preserves a legend—either invented or first written down by Thomas Nashe—that the alchemist Cornelius Agrippa allowed Henry Howard, Earl of Surrey, to see his deceased sweetheart in a magic mirror.[21]

To the European mind of the sixteenth century and after, then, Agrippa represented several things. Above all, as these legends show, and as the widespread use of *De occulta philosophia* confirms, he was the great magician who had sought out the wisdom of the remote past and had expressed some (but not all) of what he knew in *De occulta philosophia*, leaving much, however, to the conjecture of the reader or to private instruction which was handed down only

[18] Thevet, *op. cit.*, pp. 542-45.

[19] Martinus Antonius Del Rio, *Disquisitionum magicarum libri sex* (Coloniae, 1679), pp. 283, 164, 339-40. Despite a marked personal credulity about supernatural occurrences, Del Rio was an important critic of various magical traditions handed down by the Renaissance. He regarded Agrippa as the *Archimagus*, the very personification of evil sorcery. See Walker, *Spiritual and Demonic Magic*, pp. 180-83.

[20] Johann Georg Schelhorn, ed., *Amoenitates literariae* (14 vols. in 7; Francofurti, 1726-30), II, 588-89.

[21] Sir Walter Scott, *The Lay of the Last Minstrel: A Poem* (London, 1805), Canto VI, xvi, and his commentary on p. 307. He does not tell his source for this legend, but cf. n. 13, above.

by word of mouth. As later generations saw him, he was expert in the secret wisdom of the ancients, as expressed in the Orphic hymns and in the Hermetic writings. Not only Hellenistic but also Jewish culture excited the imagination of later decades, however; hence his contemporaries saw in him not just an expert in the writings of the magicians but also a rediscoverer of the still more sacred lore of the cabalists. His reputation for great learning, moreover, was not confined to these occult traditions. His works, which are rich in quotations, showed his readers that he also had a command of the ancient classics, especially the Latin ones, and of more recent authors. References to Italian authors of the fourteenth and fifteenth centuries are not uncommon in his books; and of these Italians, at least one, Pico della Mirandola, had influenced the structure of his thought considerably. The authority of Agrippa as a magician was doubtless enhanced by this familiarity with classical writings and with Italian humanistic literature.

The Agrippa who lived on in the awareness of following centuries, however, was not merely the magician and cabalist, the author of *De occulta philosophia*. He was also the radical doubter who passionately questioned the worth of all human learning, the author of *De vanitate*. Chapter Eight of this study has already shown that these two books are not so incompatible as they seem; but the appearance of these two elements in the thought of the Nettesheimer was nevertheless profoundly disturbing to an age which felt that all the old certainties (the unity of Christendom, the organic balance of the three traditional classes of society, the validity of human reason, the authority of accepted intellectual heroes such as Aristotle) were falling in ruin. In Agrippa the succeeding generations saw one of the greatest scholars of his age pursue and master not only the usual classical masterpieces but also the rarest works known, works enshrining the profound wisdom of ancient Greece, ancient Egypt, ancient Israel. Here they saw a man deeply versed in all the four faculties (liberal arts, medicine, law, and theology) and claiming academic degrees in all but the latter. And then they saw this same man turn against all arts and sciences, whether rational or occult, against all classes in society, even, it was whispered despite his final appeal to the unadulterated Gospel, against Christianity itself. Here these succeeding ages saw not just a man but also a symbol of disgust with all culture, with all values, with the whole

condition of man in the universe. Agrippa von Nettesheim personified all the many doubts and uncertainties of his epoch.

It is small wonder that his century made of him and of other
figures like him a legend, though it was Agrippa's misfortune that
men named this legend, this symbol of their own intellectual despair
and struggle, after a more shadowy figure, Faust. The Jesuit Del
Rio classed Agrippa and Faust together as wicked sorcerers and
swindlers who paid innkeepers in false gold. Christopher Marlowe
expressed this same association between the two men, for his Dr.
Faustus, after denouncing all human learning, explicitly takes
Agrippa for his ideal:

> Philosophy is odious and obscure,
> Both Law and Physic are for petty wits;
> Divinity is basest of the three,
> Unpleasant, harsh, contemptible, and vild:
> 'Tis Magic, Magic that hath ravished me.
> Then, gentle friends, aid me in this attempt;
> And I that have with concise syllogisms
> Gravelled the pastors of the German Church,
> And made the flowering pride of Wertenberg
> Swarm to my problems, as the infernal spirits
> On sweet Musaeus when he came to hell,
> Will be as cunning as Agrippa was,
> Whose shadows made all Europe honour him.[22]

The poet knew, as scholars long did not, that rejection of all learning
was the prelude to an appeal to magic, not the product of dissatisfaction with it.

The influence of Agrippa on the other great recension of the
Faust legend, that of Goethe, is even more obvious and more thoroughly established by literary scholarship. Here there is more than
the general parallel between the intellectual bankruptcy of Faust
and Agrippa's views in De vanitate. It is true that the name of
Agrippa does not occur in Goethe's Faust; but Goethe knew De
vanitate as a youth, when it caused him an intellectual crisis; and
surely during his prolonged study of magic, the poet must have
come across Agrippa's name time and time again. Certain details
of the Faust character are clearly Agrippan in origin, such as
the schwarze Pudel who attaches himself to Faust not long before

[22] Christopher Marlowe, The Tragical History of Dr. Faustus, Scene II, ll.
104-116, in The Works of Christopher Marlowe, ed. A. H. Bullen (3 vols.;
London, 1885), I, 218.

the latter's first encounter with Mephistopheles. This element is the product of Giovio's legend about Agrippa's black devil-dog and of Wier's factual account of his master's fondness for a black dog called Monsieur. Like Agrippa, Goethe's Faust mastered and came to loathe all four faculties of university learning. Both of them were supposedly makers of gold; both of them supposedly offered to enrich the Emperor Charles V. Like Agrippa in the first chapter of *De vanitate*, Goethe's Mephistopheles gives an ironic twist to the phrase "Eritis sicut Deus, scientes bonum et malum" which he writes in the young scholar's book. One authority even suggests that Goethe changed Faust's first name from the Johann of earlier versions to Heinrich because Agrippa bore the latter name. This writer concludes that although Goethe drew on numerous figures, among them the real Faust and Paracelsus, no other individual united so many of the traits of his Faust as Agrippa did.[23] Faust's opening speech sounds almost like a summary of *De vanitate*.

The matters so far discussed represent things which the contemporaries and successors of Agrippa could see. He was the magician, the cabalist, the Faustian doubter, the living embodiment of many of the enthusiasms and most of the gnawing doubts and uncertainties and fears of his age. There were other sides to his thought which his contemporaries could not see.

Agrippa's contemporaries could not, for instance, see his interest in magic and Cabala against its proper historical background. Such an appeal to occult traditions of Antiquity should not cause the modern student to speak grandly of interest in magic or Cabala as a passing fad of no great significance, as some have done.[24] What could be more natural, in a civilization which for centuries had

[23] Anton Reichl, "Goethes Faust und Agrippa von Nettesheim," *Euphorion: Zeitschrift für Literaturgeschichte*, IV (1897), 287-301. Cf. Gerhard Ritter, "Ein historisches Urbild zu Goethes Faust (Agrippa von Nettesheym)," *Preussische Jahrbücher*, CXLI (1910), 300-5. On the other hand, Harold S. Jantz, *Goethe's Faust as a Renaissance Man: Parallels and Prototypes* (Princeton, 1951), pp. 55, 58, 124-27, while admitting such connections on points of detail between Faust and a number of Renaissance men (Agrippa among them), argues that the real source of Goethe's conception of Faust was not any single individual, but a dominant mood of seeking (through rejection of traditional learning and through exploration of subjects such as magic) for a new all-inclusive synthesis of learning. Even so, however, the thought of Agrippa remains a likely source for much of Goethe's understanding of this mood of sixteenth-century men.

[24] For example, Joseph Leon Blau, *The Christian Interpretation of the Cabala in the Renaissance* (New York, 1944), p. vii.

looked back with respect and awe to the cultural achievements of Antiquity and which was experiencing a great revival of interest in classical literature, than to look backwards for the solution of its intellectual problems? That it looked backwards not only for literary models and moral philosophies but also for magical lore should not be surprising, for even the main stream of ancient literature contained strong elements of magical belief.[25] Furthermore, the Neoplatonic philosophy, which was the first great philosophical rediscovery of the humanists, was highly receptive to magic; and from it Agrippa's magical world view ultimately derives.

Not only Hellenistic but also Jewish culture had its contribution to make to the age; the revival of Hebrew studies led to a search for recondite Jewish literature. This interest in Cabala, too, was a natural outgrowth of the intellectual atmosphere of the century. It was natural for a humanistic age to look back to Greek and Roman literature for a shortcut to solution of its intellectual problems. It was just as natural for a Christian age to look back to the Hebrew texts that were its sources for a solution of religious and also general intellectual problems. This meant first of all study of the Hebrew Old Testament, but interest in Jewish Biblical commentary was a natural outgrowth of this study. Development of interest in Cabala and in the Talmud was aided by the fact that these writings often took the form of Biblical commentaries, and also by the pseudepigraphical character of much of the *corpus* of Cabala: it appeared to go back to very early times and to enshrine traditions handed down from the foundations of Judaism, even from Abraham and Moses themselves. It claimed, therefore, to be presenting not a Neoplatonizing philosophy of Alexandrian origin but the true and deeper meaning of divine revelation, as preserved from the most remote times. Christians would of course be interested in writings which presented themselves in this guise, especially since the gnostic and Neoplatonic influence on the actual authors of the cabalistic texts had led them to include materials which seemed to support such Christian doctrines as the Trinity.

Another matter which Agrippa's own age could not really understand was his relation to the Reformation, for men in the sixteenth and seventeenth centuries could not see that he stood quite apart

[25] Lynn Thorndike, *The Place of Magic in the Intellectual History of Europe* (New York, 1905), *passim.*

from the movement initiated by Luther, neither wholly approving nor wholly condemning. The nearest approach to a correct understanding was that of Bayle, who felt that Agrippa like Erasmus first welcomed Luther but then felt disappointment with the Lutheran movement.[26] Most Protestants in the sixteenth and seventeenth centuries regarded him as a man of Protestant convictions who lacked the courage to avow them openly. Few in either religious camp could realize that his bitter attacks on the institutional church were accompanied by a refusal to disavow the institution, which he wanted to see purified of abuses and reduced in temporal power, but not shattered and broken.

Contemporaries also could not see that much of the destructive portion of his thought was an outgrowth of the fideism of late scholasticism and of the skeptical tendencies found in the thought of Nicholas of Cusa and perhaps in ancient philosophical writings. These contemporaries certainly felt the insufficiency of scholastic philosophy to meet their own intellectual needs; but they could not trace the growth of these antischolastic elements as, in part, scholars like Rudolf Stadelmann, Gerhard Ritter, Ernst Cassirer, and Richard H. Popkin have done in our own century. So they could not relate Agrippa to this more general movement which was producing a sense of debility, cultural decline, and decadence, a feeling that western society was passing through a terrible crisis, perhaps through its death agony, and that the Last Day was at hand.

Finally, even Agrippa himself had no glimpse of how the European mind was preparing to rise like the legendary Phoenix from the ashes of its despair to a new sense of mission, of self-confidence, of purposeful striving for progress. So he could not see his own doubt and despair as a preparation for a synthesis on a new and higher plane. He could not realize that his emphasis on sense knowledge of singulars could ever help create a new science, or even that it was in harmony with the crude empiricism of the rising generation. He could not see that the effect of books like *De vanitate* would be to encourage a bold questioning of accepted authorities and accepted beliefs in every field of endeavor and so would prepare men's minds to accept or at least to explore new patterns of explanation for old facts. Yet this inquisitive attitude, far more than the accumulation of new data, was the key to the rise of modern science later in the

[26] Bayle, *op. cit.*, I, 106.

334 AGRIPPA AND THE CRISIS OF RENAISSANCE THOUGHT

sixteenth and in the seventeenth centuries.[27] Above all, Agrippa could have had only the dimmest awareness, if any at all, of the elements of future scientific reconstruction which existed in his later thought. As earlier chapters have suggested, his half-hearted acceptance of sense perception of singulars and his doctrine that all higher patterns of explanation are arbitrary constructs of human reason, joined to his appeal to a principle of utility to justify his continued study of magic, put him on the threshold, logically speaking, of the modern notion of scientific hypothesis and its subjection to the test of facts. He did not cross this threshold; that was the work of later generations. But his history illustrates how European thinkers were beginning to grope in the direction of the seventeenth-century resolution of the problem of human knowledge. Agrippa himself stood amid the ruin of medieval thought, a ruin which he himself did much to advance; but he also pointed tentatively and unknowingly in directions which, for some centuries to come, European mankind was to find fruitful and satisfying.

[27] Herbert Butterfield, *The Origins of Modern Science, 1300-1800* (London, 1951), p. 1.

BIBLIOGRAPHY [1]

I. PRIMARY SOURCES

A. *Manuscripts*

Grenoble, Bibliothèque Municipale. MS. No. 35. Documents of the sixteenth and seventeenth centuries relative to the history of Dauphiné, collected by Nicolas Chorier and Guy Allard. Fols. 199-202 contain a petition by Henry Corneille Agrippa, son of Agrippa von Nettesheim, alleging noble rank and claiming tax exemption. (Microfilm in University of Illinois Library.)

Lyons, Bibliothèque Municipale. MS. No. 48, Collection of the Palais des Arts. Manuscript of the sixteenth century on paper, sixty leaves. Delandine, *Manuscrits de la Bibliothèque de Lyon*, item no. 179, dates it 1528. Miscellany of treatises and letters of Agrippa, including *De originali peccato*, the fragment of *Dialogus de homine*, the first sketch of *Contra pestem antidota*, and correspondence of Agrippa with Theodoricus Wichwael, Bishop of Cyrene, Augustinus

---

[1] I have listed works pertaining to the subject of this study even in cases where I have not found occasion to cite them in the notes. In listing early printed books, I have given only a short-title entry, not a complete transcription of their sometimes inordinately long titles. In many cases, the publication data appear not on the title page but in a colophon. In the case of rare-book materials, I have given the location of the copy or copies used in the present study.

335

Ritius, and Guiliermus, Marquis of Monferrato. (Microfilm in
University of Illinois Library; duplicate microfilm in possession of
author.)
Paris, Bibliothèque Nationale. MS. Lat. 598. Paulus Riccius, *Portae lucis*.
Written in 1513 by Egidio da Viterbo. (Photostatic copy in University of Illinois Library.)
Paris, Bibliothèque Nationale. MS. Lat. 16,625. Agrippa, *De triplici
ratione cognoscendi Deum*. Manuscript of the sixteenth century, on
paper, thirty-three numbered leaves, written in a clear, humanistic
hand. (The present author has a microfilm copy, which he hopes to
use in preparing a critical edition.)
Rome, Vatican Library. Vat. Lat. 6937. Index librorum selectorum ex
bibliotheca Reverendissimi Cardinalis Hieronymi Archiepiscopi
Brundusini, nuper bibliothece Apostolice donatorum, Die xxvi Julij.
M.D.xxxij. (Microfilm, Knights of Columbus Foundation, St. Louis
University, Roll No. 857.)
Wrocław, University Library (*olim* Breslau). MS. Rehdigeriana, 254.4.
Holographic letter of Agrippa to Erasmus, dated 17 March 1532.
(Microfilm in University of Illinois Library; microfilm and photo-
copy in possession of author; both are based on a photocopy made
before the original manuscript was lost or damaged during World
War II.)
Würzburg, Universitätsbibliothek. MS. M.ch.q.50. Agrippa, *De occulta
philosophia*. 137 leaves, on paper, numbered in a modern hand, cor-
rectly up to fol. 123; 123 is then repeated, and all subsequent numbers should be raised by one. This represents the earliest known
version of *De occulta philosophia*, quite clearly distinct from the
text printed partially in 1531 and completely in 1533. This is probably the presentation copy which Agrippa sent to Trithemius of
Sponheim in 1510. (Microfilm in University of Illinois Library;
duplicate microfilm in possession of author.)

B. *Agrippa's Printed Works* [2]

Agrippa von Nettesheim, Heinrich Cornelius. *Opera*. 2 vols.; Lugduni,
per Beringos fratres, n.d. This imprint is probably fictitious and
appears on several similar but not identical (except in contents)
editions. The card catalog of Harvard College Library suggests
Eberhard Zetzner of Strasbourg as publisher, on the basis of a wood-
cut on the title page, and suggests *ca.* 1620 as the date of one issue,
and *ca.* 1630 as the date of another, almost identical, issue. I have
used a microfilm of the copy in the Newberry Library at Chicago
and have inspected other copies of this or a very similar edition at
Harvard, the University of Chicago, the University of Missouri, and
the American Antiquarian Society. (Microfilm in University of Illinois Library; duplicate in possession of author.)

[2] I have included only those editions of Agrippan works which I have
actually used and cited in this book, and have made no attempt to list the
scores of other Agrippan editions which I have inspected but not cited.
Ordinarily, I have used the earliest and best edition available to me.

————. *De beatissimae Annae monogamia, ac unico puerperio proposi-tiones abbreuiatae et articulatae, iuxta disceptationem Iacobi Fabri Stapulensis in libro de tribus et una, intitulato. Eiusdem Agrippae defensio propositionum praenarratarum contra quendam Dominicas-trum earundem impugnatorem, qui sanctissimam deiparae uirginis matrem Annam conatur ostendere polygamam. Quaedam epistolae super eadem materia atque super lite contra eiusdem ordinis haereti-corum magistro habita.* N.p., 1534. (Microfilm in University of Illi-nois Library, based on Rés. Z 2500(2) of the Bibliothèque Nationale at Paris; duplicate film in possession of author.)

————. *De incertitudi[n]e et vanitate scientiarum declamatio inuectiua.* Coloniae, M[elchior]. N[ovesianus]. excudebat, 1531. This is the text cited for *De vanitate.* (University of Illinois Library.)

————. *De incertitudine et vanitate omnium scientiarum et artium liber, lectu plane jucundus et elegans: et De nobilitate et praecellentia foeminei sexus, ejusdemque supra virilem eminentia libellus, lectu etiam jucundissimus.* Hagae-Comitum, ex typographia Adriani Vlacq, 1662. (University of Illinois Library.) Used for text of *De nobilitate et praecellentia foeminei sexus.*

————. *Of the vanitie and vncertaintie of artes and sciences.* Englished by Ia[mes]. San[dford]. Gent. London: Imprinted by Henry Wykes dwelling in Fleete Streat, at the signe of the blacke Elephant, 1569. English translation, one of two, of *De vanitate.* Issued in several editions. (University of Illinois Library.)

————. *Die Eitelkeit und Unsicherheit der Wissenschaften, und die Verteidigungsschrift,* ed. Fritz Mauthner. 2 vols.; Munich: Georg Müller, 1913. A modern German translation, with introductory essay, of *De vanitate* and *Apologia.*

————. *Paradoxe svr l'incertitvde, vanité et abus des sciences. Traduit en françois, du latin de Henry Corneille Agr. Oeuure qui peut profiter, et qui apporte merueilleux contentement à ceux qui frequentent les cours des grands seigneurs, et qui veulent apprendre à discourir d'vne infinité de choses contre la commune opinion.* N.p., 1608. Transla-tion by Louis Turquet de Mayerne. (Newberry Library, Chicago.) Originally published, under a slightly different title (*Déclamation sur l'incertitude,* etc.), at Paris by J. Durand in 1582.

————. *De occulta philosophia libri tres.* N.p. [Coloniae], 1533. The first complete edition. There are two almost identical editions, dis-tinguishable only by line-endings. Apparently identical are the copies used at the University of Illinois Library (which, however, lacks the title page and preliminary matter) and at the Chapin Library at Williams College. The second family of copies is repre-sented by the copy at the University of Chicago.

————. *Dialogus de homine,* ed. Paola Zambelli, in *Rivista critica di storia della filosofia,* XIII (1958), 47-71. Critical edition based on Lyons, Bibliothèque Municipale, MS. No. 48. Also gives this manu-script's variant readings for its other Agrippan materials.

Lull, Ramon. *Opera ea quae ad adinventam ab ipso artem vniversalem, scientiarvm artivmque omnium breui compendio . . . pertinent.* Argentinae, sumptibus Lazari Zetzneri, 1598. Contains Agrippa's *In artem brevem Raymundi Lullii commentaria.* (University of Illinois Library.)

C. *Writings of Agrippa's Contemporaries and Sources* [3]

Bellievre, Claude. *Souvenirs de voyages en Italie et en Orient; Notes historiques; Pièces de vers,* ed. Charles Perrat, Geneva: Librairie E. Droz, 1956.

Castellesi [or Castellense], Adriano, Cardinal. *De vera philosophia libri IIII.* Coloniae, ex officina Melchioris Nouesiani, 1540. (Microfilm from New York Public Library.)

Champier, Symphorien. *De triplici disciplina.* Lugduni, expensis . . . Simonis Vincentii: arte vero et industria Claudii Dauost alias de Troys, 1508. (Houghton Library, Harvard University.)

Diogenes Laertius. *Lives of Eminent Philosophers,* ed. and trans. R. D. Hicks. Loeb Classical Library edition; 2 vols.; London: W. Heinemann, 1925.

Erasmus, Desiderius. *Opus epistolarum Des. Erasmi Roterodami,* ed. P. S. Allen [and H. M. Allen and H. W. Garrod]. 12 vols.; Oxonii, in typographeo Clarendoniano, 1906-58.

Ficino, Marsilio. *Commentaire sur le Banquet de Platon,* ed. Raymond Marcel. Paris: Les Belles Lettres, 1956.

————. *Opera.* 2 vols.; Parisiis, apud Gvillelmvm Pelé, 1641. (University of Illinois Library.)

————. *Opera omnia.* 2 vols.; Basileae, ex officina Henricpetrina, 1576. (Harvard College Library.) (I also consulted the recent photo-reprint of this edition: 2 vols. in 4; Turin: Bottega d'Erasmo, 1959.)

————. *Supplementum Ficinianum: Marsilii Ficini florentini philosophi platonici Opvscula inedita et dispersa,* ed. Paul Oskar Kristeller. 2 vols.; Florentiae: L. S. Olschki, 1937.

Galen, Claudius. *Galeni medicorvm principis exhortatio ad bonas arteis, praesertim medicinam, de optimo docendi genere, et qualem oporteat esse medicum, D. Eras. Roter. interprete.* Basileae, apud Ioan. Frob[en]., Mense Maio, 1526. (University of Illinois Library.)

Garin, E[ugenio]., et al., eds. *Testi umanistici su l'Ermetismo: Testi di Ludovico Lazzarelli, F. Giorgio Veneto, Cornelio Agrippa di Nettesheim.* Rome: Fratelli Bocca, 1955.

Gikatilla, Joseph ben Abraham. *Portae lucis: Hec est porta Tetragrammaton[,] iusti intrabunt per eam,* [trans. Paulus Riccius]. Augustae Vindelicorum, excusa in officina Millerana, 1516. (Houghton Library, Harvard University.)

---

[3] I have excluded the books of patristic writers whose works I have consulted only incidentally in tracing the sources of Agrippa's thought, such as St. Augustine, St. Jerome, and Dionysius the Areopagite. I have generally used such works in the standard modern editions, such as the *Patrologia graeca* and *Patrologia latina* of J.-P. Migne, or the *Corpus scriptorum ecclesiasticorum latinorum.*

Hermes Trismegistus. *Corpus Hermeticum,* ed. A. D. Nock, trans. A. J. Festugière. 4 vols.; Paris: Société d'Édition "Les Belles Lettres," 1945-54.
———. *Asclepius,* in *Iamblichvs de mysteriis Aegyptiorum.* . . . Lugduni, apud Ioan. Tornaesivm, 1570. (University of Illinois Library.)
———. *Liber de potestate et sapientia Dei* [i.e., the *Pimander*]: *Per Marsilium Ficinum traductus: ad Cosmum Medicem.* Impressum in alma Parisiorum academia . . . Impressore vuolffgango hopyl in pago diui Iacobi et apud insigne sancti Georgij, 1494. (Chapin Library, Williams College.)
Majrītī: see *Picatrix.*
Paracelsus, Theophrast von Hohenheim. *Sämmtliche Werke,* 1. Abteilung: *Medizinische, naturwissenschaftliche und philosophische Schriften,* ed. Karl Sudhoff. 14 vols.; Munich: R. Oldenbourg, 1922-33. (Pseudo-Paracelsus, *De occulta philosophia,* is printed in vol. XIV.)
Picatrix [i.e., pseudo- al-Majrītī, Maslamah ibn Ahmad]. *Das Ziel des Weisen,* ed. Hellmut Ritter, vol. I, Arabischer Text. Studien der Bibliothek Warburg, vol. 12. Leipzig: B. G. Teubner, 1933.
———. *"Picatrix": Das Ziel des Weisen von Pseudo-Magriti,* trans. [from Arabic into German] Hellmut Ritter and Martin Plessner. Studies of the Warburg Institute, vol. 27. London: The Warburg Institute, University of London, 1962.
Pico della Mirandola, Giovanni. *De hominis dignitate, Heptaplus, De ente et uno, e scritti vari,* ed. Eugenio Garin. Florence: Vallecchi, 1942.
Pico della Mirandola, Giovanni Francesco. *Examen vanitatis doctrinae gentium, et veritatis Christianae disciplinae.* Mirandulae, Ioannes Maciochivs bundenius, 1520. (Microfilm of copy in Columbia University Library.)
Plotinus. *Opera omnia,* trans. Marsilio Ficino. Florentiae, Antonivs Miscominvs, 1492. (Chapin Library, Williams College.)
Rabelais, François. *Oeuvres,* ed. Burgaud des Marets and E. J. B. Rathery. 2 vols.; Paris: Librairie de Firmin Didot Frères, Fils et Cⁱᵉ, 1856-58.
Reuchlin, Johann. *De accentibus, et orthographia, linguae hebraicae.* Hagenoae, in aedibus Thomae Anshelmi Badensis, 1518. (Houghton Library, Harvard University.)
———. *De arte cabalistica libri tres Leoni X. dicati.* Hagenau, apud Thomam Anshelmum, 1517. (University of Illinois Library.)
———. *Liber de verbo mirifico.* Tubingae, ex aedibus Thomae Anshelmi Badensis, 1514. (University of Illinois Library.)
Ricci, Agostino [i.e., Augustinus Ritius]. *De motu octaue sphere: opus mathematica atque philosophia plenum, vbi tam antiquorum quam iuniorum errores luce clarius demonstrantur: in quo et quamplurima platonicorum et antique magie (quam cabalam hebrei dicunt) dogmata videre licet intellectu suauissima.* . . . *Item eiusdem epistola de astronomie auctoribus.* . . . Impressum in oppido Tridini dominij Illustrissimi et inuictissimi domini domini Gullielmi Marchionis

Montisferrati, in edibus domini Ioannis de ferrarijs: alias de Iolitis, 1513. (Library of Congress.)

Vigneulles, Philippe de. *La chronique de la ville de Metz*, ed. Charles Bruneau. 4 vols.; Metz: Société d'Histoire et d'Archéologie de la Lorraine, 1927-33.

Wier, Johann. *Opera omnia*. Amstelodami, apud Petrum van den Berge, 1660. (University of Illinois Library.)

[Zohar:] *The Zohar*, trans. Harry Sperling and Maurice Simon. 5 vols.; London: The Soncino Press, 1931-34.

D. *Documentary Collections*

Cologne, Universität. *Die Matrikel der Universität Köln, 1389 bis 1559*, ed. Hermann Keussen. 3 vols.; Bonn: H. Behrendt, 1892-1931. ("Publikationen der Gesellschaft für rheinische Geschichtskunde," vol. VII.)

[Cronica:] *Die Cronica van der hilliger stat van Coellen 1499*, in *Die Chroniken der deutschen Städte*, ed. Karl von Hegel, vol. XIV. Leipzig: S. Hirzel, 1877.

Geneva, Conseil Général. *Registres du Conseil de Genève*. 12 vols.; Geneva: H. Kundig, 1900-36.

Great Britain, Public Record Office. *Letters and Papers, Foreign and Domestic, of the Reign of Henry VIII*. 21 vols.; London: [H. M. Stationer's Office], 1862-1910.

Herminjard, Aimé Louis, ed. *Correspondance des Réformateurs dans les pays de langue française*. 9 vols.; Geneva: H. Georg, 1866-97.

Memorie e documenti per la storia dell'Università di Pavia e degli uomini più illustri che v'insegnarono. 3 vols.; Pavia: Bizzoni, 1878.

E. *Literary and Other Evidences of Agrippa's Influence*

Belot, Jean. *Oeuvres*. Lyon: Claude de la Riverie, 1654. (University of Illinois Library.)

Blount, Thomas-Pope. *Censura celebriorum authorum*. Londini, impensis Richardi Chiswel, 1690. (University of Illinois Library.)

Bodin, Jean. *De la demonomanie des sorciers*. Antwerp: Arnould Coninx, 1593. (University of Illinois Library.)

Brahe, Tyge. *Opera omnia*, ed. I. L. E. Dreyer. 15 vols.; Hauniae, in libraria Gyldendaliana, 1913-29.

Burnet, Gilbert. *The History of the Reformation of the Church of England*. 2 vols.; London: Printed by T. H. for Richard Chiswell, at the Rose and Crown in St. Paul's Church-Yard, 1681-83. (University of Illinois Library.)

Del Rio, Martinus Antonius. *Disquisitionum magicarum libri sex*. Coloniae Agrippinae, Sumptibus Hermanni Demen, 1679.

Gesner, Konrad. *Bibliotheca vniuersalis, siue Catalogus omnium scriptorum locupletissimus*. Tigvri, apud Christophorvm Froschouerum, 1545. (University of Illinois Library.)

Giovio, Paolo. *Elogia doctorvm virorvm ab avorvm memoria publicatis ingenij monumentis illustrium*. Basileae [no printer, no date, but probably in the 1560's]. (University of Illinois Library.)

Goethe, Johann Wolfgang von. *Aus meinem Leben: Dichtung und Wahrheit.* 2 vols..; Frankfurt-am-Main: Frankfurter Verlags-Anstalt A. G., 1921-22.

Marlowe, Christopher. *The Works of Christopher Marlowe,* ed. A. H. Bullen. 3 vols.; London: J. C. Nimmo, 1885.

Nashe, Thomas. *The Works of Thomas Nashe,* ed. Ronald B. McKerrow. 5 vols.; London: A. H. Bullen, 1904-10.

Naudé, Gabriel. *Apologie pour les grands hommes soupçonnez de magie.* Amsterdam: P. Humbert, 1712. (University of California Library, Berkeley.)

Scot, Reginald. *Scot's Discovery of Witchcraft.* [London]: Printed by R. C. and are to be sold by Giles Calvert, dwelling at the Black Spread-Eagle at the West-end of Pauls, 1651. (University of Illinois Library.)

Scott, Sir Walter. *The Lay of the Last Minstrel: A Poem.* London.: Longman, Hurst, Rees, and Orme, 1805.

Shelley, Mary Wollstonecraft. *Frankenstein; or, The Modern Prometheus.* London: Gibbings and Company Limited, 1897.

Sidney, Sir Philip. *An Apologie for Poetrie,* ed. Evelyn S. Shuckburgh. Cambridge [England]: Cambridge University Press, 1891.

Thevet, André. *Les vrais povrtraits et vies des hommes illvstres, grecz, latins, et payens, recveilliz de levrs tableaux, liures, medalles antiques et modernes.* Paris: Par la vefue I. Keruert et Guillaume Chaudiere, 1584. (Two volumes bound as one, and consecutively numbered like a single-volume work; University of Illinois Library.)

Vaughan, Thomas [using pseud. Eugenius Philalethes]. *Anima magica abscondita; or, A Discourse of the universall Spirit of Nature, With his strange, abstruse, miraculous Ascent, and descent.* London: Printed by T. W. for H. Blunden, 1650. (University of Illinois Library.)

———. [using same pseud. as above]. *Anthroposophia theomagica; or, A Discourse of the Nature of Man and his state after death.* London: Printed by T. W. for H. Blunden at the Castle in Cornhill, 1650. (University of Illinois Library.)

Webster, John. *The Displaying of Supposed Witchcraft.* London: J. M., 1677. (University of Illinois Library.)

Zwinger, Theodor. *Theatrum vitae hvmanae.* Parisiis, apud Nicolaum Chesneau, 1572. (University of Illinois Library.)

II. Secondary Sources

A. *Books on Agrippa*

Bernárdez, Antonio. *Enrique Cornelio Agripa, filósofo, astrólogo y cronista de Carlos V. Traducción al castellano de la Historia de la doble coronación del emperador en Bolonia, escrita en latín.* Madrid: Espasa-Calpe, S. A., 1934. Contains a biographical essay.

Halm, Erich. "Die Stellung des H. C. Agrippa von Nettesheim in der Geschichte der Philosophie." Unprinted Ph.D. dissertation, Munich,

1923. Cited by Thorndike, *History of Magic and Experimental Science*, V, 128, but recently reported missing from the Munich library since the end of World War II. If a copy still exists, I have no knowledge of it.

Meurer, Johann. *Zur Logik des Heinrich Cornelius Agrippa von Nettesheim.* "Renaissance und Philosophie: Beiträge zur Geschichte der Philosophie," ed. Adolf Dryoff, vol. XI. Bonn: P. Hanstein, 1913. Mainly a study of his commentary on Ramon Lull, but also gives valuable material on the intellectual traditions at Cologne.

Morley, Henry. *Cornelius Agrippa: The Life of Henry Cornelius Agrippa von Nettesheim, Doctor and Knight, Commonly Known as a Magician.* 2 vols.; London: Chapman and Hall, 1856. Contains much material but is unreliable because of the author's propensity to let his imagination outrun his evidence.

Mullerus, Ioannes Iacobus. *Ex historia literaria de Henrici Cornelii Agrippae eruditorvm portenti vita fatis et scriptis.* Vitembergae Saxonum: Typis Schroederianis, [1726]. This dissertation is commonly but incorrectly attributed to the professor who directed it, Georgius Fridericus Ravius (or Rau). (Microfilm in University of Illinois Library, based on the copy in the Bibliothèque Nationale at Paris.)

Orsier, Joseph. *Henry Cornélis Agrippa, sa vie et son oeuvre d'après sa correspondance (1486-1535).* Paris: Chacornac, 1911. A French translation of some of Agrippa's letters, preceded by a biographical sketch which relies chiefly on Prost.

Prost, Auguste. *Les sciences et les arts occultes au XVI siècle: Corneille Agrippa, sa vie et ses oeuvres.* 2 vols.; Paris: Champion, 1881-82. Hypercritical and on some points wrong-headed, but by all odds the best earlier biography of Agrippa. Also valuable for archival documents printed in the Appendices at the end.

Rossi, G[iuseppe]. *Agrippa di Nettesheym e la direzione scettica della filosofia nel Rinascimento.* Turin: Paravia, 1906.

Spence, Lewis. *Cornelius Agrippa, Occult Philosopher.* London: W. Rider & Son, Ltd., 1921. Occultist in outlook, but has some insight into Agrippa's development.

B. *Other Books*

Adam, Melchior. *Dignorum laude virorum, quos musa vetat mori, immortalitas, seu Vitae theologorum, jure-consultorum, et politicorum, medicorum, atque philosophorum, maximam partem germanorum, nonnullam quoque exterorum.* 3rd ed.; Francofurti ad Moenum: J. M. à Sande, 1706.

[Adelung, Johann Christoph]. *Geschichte der Philosophie für Liebhaber.* 3 vols.; Leipzig: Bey Johann Friedrich Junius, 1786-87.

Anderson, F[ulton]. H[enry]. *The Philosophy of Francis Bacon.* Chicago, Illinois: The University of Chicago Press, c1948.

Andreas, Willy. *Deutschland vor der Reformation: Eine Zeitenwende.* 2nd ed.; Stuttgart: Deutsche Verlags-Anstalt, 1934.

Arnold, Gottfried. *Unpartheyische Kirchen und Ketzer-Historie vom*

Anfang des neuen Testaments biss auf das Jahr Christi 1688. 2 vols.; Frankfurt-a.-M.: Bey Thomas Fritschens sel. Erben, 1729.

Atkinson, Geoffroy. *Les nouveaux horizons de la Renaissance française.* Paris: Librairie E. Droz, 1935.

Axenfeld, Alexandre. *Jean Wier et la sorcellerie.* Paris: G. Ballière, 1866.

Bainton, Roland Herbert. *Here I Stand: A Life of Martin Luther.* New York: Abingdon-Cokesbury Press, [1950].

Ballesteros y Beretta, Antonio. *Historia de España y su influencia en la historia universal.* 2nd ed.; 12 vols.; Barcelona: Salvat Editores, S. A., 1943-63, 1941.

Bayle, Pierre. *Dictionnaire historique et critique,* ed. Des. Maizeaux. 4th ed.; 4 vols.; Amsterdam: P. Brunel *et al.,* 1730.

Beaune, [François Bénigne] Henri, and J. d'Arbaumont. *Les universités de Franche-Comté, Gray, Dôle, Besançon: Documents inédits publiés avec une introduction historique.* Dijon: J. Marchand, Éditeur, 1870.

Bianco, Franz Joseph von. *Die alte Universität Köln und die späteren Gelehrten-Schulen dieser Stadt.* Cologne: Commissions-Verlag von J. M. Heberle, 1856.

Blau, Joseph Leon. *The Christian Interpretation of the Cabala in the Renaissance.* New York: Columbia University Press, 1944. A standard work on this subject; but see the criticism by François Secret in his book listed below.

Bohatec, Josef. *Budé und Calvin: Studien zur Gedankenwelt des französischen Frühhumanismus.* Graz: Verlag Hermann Böhlaus Nachf., 1950.

Boulting, William. *Giordano Bruno: His Life, Thought, and Martyrdom.* London: Kegan Paul, Trench, Trubner & Co. Ltd., n.d.

Bréhier, Émile. *Histoire de la philosophie.* 2 vols.; Paris: F. Alcan, 1926-32.

Bridge, John S[eargeant]. C[yprian]. *A History of France from the Death of Louis XI.* 5 vols.; Oxford: The Clarendon Press, 1921-36. Helpful in investigating the background of Agrippa's years in Italy.

Brucker, Johann Jakob. *Historia critica philosophiae a mundi incunabilis ad nostram usque aetatem deducta.* 4 vols. in 5; Lipsiae: B. C. Breitkopf, [1742-44].

————. *Institutiones historiae philosophicae usui academicae iuventutis adornatae.* 2nd ed.; Lipsiae, impensis B. C. Breitkopfi, 1756.

Buhle, Johann Gottlieb. *Geschichte der neuern Philosophie seit der Epoche der Wiederherstellung der Wissenschaften.* 6 vols.; Göttingen: Bey Johann Georg Rosenbusch's Wittwe, 1800-05.

Butterfield, H[erbert]. *The Origins of Modern Science, 1300-1800.* London: G. Bell and Sons Ltd., 1951.

Carriere, Moriz. *Die philosophische Weltanschauung der Reformationszeit in ihren Beziehungen zur Gegenwart.* 2nd ed.; 2 vols.; Leipzig: F. A. Brockhaus, 1887.

Cassirer, Ernst. *Das Erkenntnisproblem in der Philosophie und Wissenschaft der neueren Zeit.* 3 vols.; Berlin: Verlag von Bruno Cassirer, 1906-20. I have also seen the second edition, 3 vols.; Berlin: B. Cassirer, 1911-23.

Clément, David. *Bibliothèque curieuse historique et critique; ou, Catalogue raisonné de livres difficiles à trouver.* 9 vols.; Göttingen: J. G. Schmid, 1750-60.

Constant, Abbé Alphons Louis [using pseud. Eliphas Levi]. *Geschichte der Magie.* 2 vols. in 1; München-Planegg: Otto Wilhelm Barth Verlag G.M.B.H., 1926.

Credaro, Luigi. *Lo scetticismo degli Accademici.* 2 vols.; Rome: Hoepli, 1889-93. Devoted mainly to ancient skepticism, but contains some discussion of Agrippa and his period.

Encausse, G[érard]. *L'occultisme et le spiritualisme: Exposé des théories philosophiques et des adaptations de l'occultisme.* Paris: Félix Alcan, Éditeur, 1902.

Eubel, Conradus, ed. *Hierarchia catholica medii aevi.* 3 vols.; Monasterii, sumptibus et typis librariae Regensbergianae, 1898-1910. A valuable reference for identifying bishops.

[Farel: Comité Farel]. *Guillaume Farel, 1489-1565.* Neuchâtel: Éditions Delachaux et Niestlé S.A., 1930. A co-operative work, collecting the monographic scholarship of a large group of historians. Valuable for the background of Agrippa's residence at Geneva and also at Metz.

Festugière, André Marie Jean. *La révélation d'Hermès Trismégiste.* 4 vols.; Paris: J. Gabalda, 1949-54.

Freher, Paul. *Theatrum virorum eruditione clarorum,* [ed. Carl Joachim Freher]. Noribergae, impensis J. Hofmanni, & typis haeredum Andreae Knorzii, 1688. (Newberry Library, Chicago.)

Gams, Pius Bonifacius. *Series episcoporum ecclesiae catholicae.* 2nd ed.; Leipzig: K. W. Hiersemann, 1931. Valuable for identifying bishops and their sees.

Garin, Eugenio. *Giovanni Pico della Mirandola: Vita e dottrina.* Florence: Felice LeMonnier, Editore, 1937.

———. *Medioevo e Rinascimento: Studi e ricerche.* Bari: G. Laterza, 1954. A collection of essays; the ones used for this study deal with the significance of magic in Renaissance culture.

Geanakoplos, Deno John. *Greek Scholars in Venice: Studies in the Dissemination of Greek Learning from Byzantium to Western Europe.* Cambridge [Massachusetts]: Harvard University Press, 1962.

Geiger, Ludwig. *Johann Reuchlin: Sein Leben und seine Werke.* Leipzig: Verlag von Duncker & Humblot, 1871.

Gilmore, Myron P. *The World of Humanism, 1453-1517.* New York: Harper & Brothers Publishers, c1952.

Hauser, Henri, and Augustin Renaudet. *Les débuts de l'âge moderne.* 3rd ed.; Paris: Presses Universitaires de France, 1946.

Haydn, Hiram. *The Counter-Renaissance.* New York: Charles Scribner's Sons, 1950. A highly stimulating interpretation of certain currents in Renaissance culture, giving considerable attention to Agrippa.

Hefele, Charles-Joseph, and J[oseph Adam Gustav]. Hergenroether. *Histoire des conciles d'après les documents originaux,* trans. H[enri]. Leclercq. 11 vols. in 21; Paris: Librairie Letouzey et Ané, 1907-52.

Valuable for tracing the movements of the Council of Pisa in the period when Agrippa may have attended.

Henry-Bordeaux, Paule. *Louise de Savoie: Régente et "Roi" de France.* Paris: Librairie Plon, c1954.

Holborn, Hajo. *Ulrich von Hutten and the German Reformation,* trans. Roland H. Bainton. New Haven: Yale University Press, 1937.

Hopkin, Charles Edward. *The Share of Thomas Aquinas in the Growth of the Witchcraft Delusion.* Philadelphia, 1940. A Ph.D. dissertation at the University of Pennsylvania; no publisher's name is given.

Hopper, Vincent Foster. *Medieval Number Symbolism: Its Sources, Meaning, and Influence on Thought and Expression.* New York: Columbia University Press, 1938.

Horst, Georg Konrad. *Zauber-Bibliothek.* 6 vols. in 3; Mainz: F. Kupferberg, 1821-26. A heterogeneous collection of magical texts, none by Agrippa; but it does contain a short discussion of both Agrippa and Paracelsus.

Höss, Irmgard. *Georg Spalatin, 1484-1545: Ein Leben in der Zeit des Humanismus und der Reformation.* Weimar: H. Böhlaus Nachfolger, 1956.

Hyma, Albert. *The Christian Renaissance: A History of the "Devotio Moderna."* Grand Rapids, Michigan: The Reformed Press, 1924.

Imbart de la Tour, Pierre. *Les origines de la Réforme.* 4 vols.; Paris: Hachette et Cie, 1905-35. A general work of great importance for nearly all aspects of pre-Reformation France.

Iongh, Jane de. *Margaret of Austria, Regent of the Netherlands,* trans. M. D. Herter Norton. New York: W. W. Norton & Company, c1953.

Jantz, Harold Stein. *Goethe's Faust as a Renaissance Man: Parallels and Prototypes.* Princeton, New Jersey: Princeton University Press, 1951.

Jedin, Hubert. *Geschichte des Konzils von Trient,* vol. I. 2nd ed.; Freiburg: Verlag Herder, 1951.

Jöcher, Christian Gottlieb. *Allgemeines Gelehrten-Lexicon.* 11 vols.; Leipzig [*et alibi*]: J. F. Gleditsch [*et al.*], 1750-1819, 1897.

Jourda, Pierre. *Marguerite d'Angoulême, Duchesse d'Alençon, Reine de Navarre: Étude biographique et littéraire.* 2 vols.; Paris: Librairie Ancienne Honoré Champion, 1930.

Kaser, Kurt. *Deutsche Geschichte zur Zeit Maximilians I. (1486-1519).* Stuttgart: J. G. Cotta'sche Buchhandlung Nachfolger, 1912.

Kiesewetter, Karl. *Faust in der Geschichte und Tradition.* 2nd ed.; 2 vols.; Berlin: Hermann Barsdorf Verlag, 1921.

———. *Geschichte des neueren Okkultismus: Geheimwissenschaftliche Systeme von Agrippa von Nettesheym bis zu Carl du Prel.* Leipzig: W. Friedrich, [1891]. An occultist book.

Kisch, Guido. *Erasmus und die Jurisprudenz seiner Zeit: Studien zum humanistischen Rechtsdenken.* Basel: Helbing & Lichtenhahn, 1960.

———. *Humanismus und Jurisprudenz: Der Kampf zwischen mos italicus und mos gallicus an der Universität Basel.* Basel: Helbing & Lichtenhahn, 1955.

Kristeller, Paul Oskar. *Il pensiero filosofico di Marsilio Ficino*. Florence: G. C. Sansoni, Editore, [1953]. Italian translation of the following book.

———. *The Philosophy of Marsilio Ficino*, trans. Virginia Conant. New York: Columbia University Press, 1943.

———. *Studies in Renaissance Thought and Letters*. Rome: Edizioni di Storia e Letteratura, 1956. A collection of articles and short studies. The essays on Mercurio da Correggio and Ludovico Lazzarelli were particularly helpful for this book.

Labbey-de-Billy, Nicolas-Antoine. *Histoire de l'université du comté de Bourgogne et des différens sujets qui l'ont honorée*. 2 vols.; Besançon: Claude-François Mourgeon, 1814-15.

Lavisse, Ernest, ed. *Histoire de France depuis les origines jusqu'à la Révolution*. 9 vols.; Paris: Hachette et Cⁱᵉ, 1900-11. Vol. V, parts 1 and 2, were helpful in this book.

LeClerc, Daniel. *Histoire de la medicine*. 2nd ed.; The Hague: I. Van der Kloot, 1729.

Legge, F[rancis]. *Forerunners and Rivals of Christianity: Being Studies in Religious History from 330 B.C. to 330 A.D.* 2 vols.; Cambridge [England]: Cambridge University Press, 1915.

Lehmann, Alfred. *Aberglaube und Zauberei von den ältesten Zeiten an bis in die Gegenwart*, trans. [from Danish] Dr. Petersen [perhaps R. H. Pedersen]. 2nd ed.; Stuttgart: Verlag von Ferdinand Enke, 1908.

Maritain, Jacques. *Three Reformers: Luther—Descartes—Rousseau*. London: Sheed & Ward, [1928]. An English translation of the following book.

———. *Trois réformateurs: Luther—Descartes—Rousseau*. 2nd ed.; Paris: Librairie Plon, c1925.

Martin, Alfred von. *Sociology of the Renaissance*, trans. W. L. Luetkens. New York: Oxford University Press, 1944.

Mattingly, Garrett. "Eustache Chapuys and Spanish Diplomacy in England (1488-1536): A Study in the Development of Resident Embassies." Unprinted Ph.D. dissertation, Harvard University, 1935; bound in three consecutively paged volumes.

McIntyre, J. Lewis. *Giordano Bruno*. London: Macmillan and Co., Limited, 1903.

Meiners, Christoph. *Lebensbeschreibungen berühmter Männer aus den Zeiten der Wiederherstellung der Wissenschaften*. 3 vols.; Zürich: Orell, Gessner, Füssli und Compagnie, 1795.

Merriman, Roger Bigelow. *The Rise of the Spanish Empire in the Old World and in the New*. 4 vols.; New York: The Macmillan Company, 1918-34.

Metzke, Erwin. *Coincidentia oppositorum: Gesammelte Studien zur Philosophiegeschichte*, ed. Karlfried Gründer. Witten: Luther-Verlag, 1961. A collection of essays, including "Die 'Skepsis' des Agrippa von Nettesheim: Eine Studie zur Geschichte des deutschen Geistes im ausgehenden Mittelalter."

Mommsen, Theodore E. *Medieval and Renaissance Studies*, ed. Eugene F. Rice, Jr. Ithaca, N.Y.: Cornell University Press, [1959]. A collection of essays, including "Petrarch's Conception of the Dark Ages."

Naef, Henri. *Les origines de la Réforme à Genève: La cité des évêques—L'Humanisme—Les signes précurseurs*. Geneva: Librairie Alex. Jullien, 1936. A valuable study of the Genevan background, covering the period when Agrippa resided there.

Nelson, John Charles. *The Renaissance Theory of Love: The Context of Giordano Bruno's Eroici Furori*. New York: Columbia University Press, 1958.

Nicéron, Jean Pierre. *Nachrichten von den Begebenheiten und Schriften berümten [sic!] Gelehrten, mit einigen Zusätzen*, ed. Siegmund Jacob Baumgarten. 24 vols.; Halle: Verlag und Druck C. P. Franckens, 1749-77. Has an article on Agrippa, but not very helpful.

Pachter, Henry M. *Magic Into Science: The Story of Paracelsus*. New York: Henry Schuman, c1951. A popularized biography.

Pagel, Walter. *Paracelsus: An Introduction to Philosophical Medicine in the Era of the Renaissance*. Basel: S. Karger, 1958.

Panofsky, Erwin. *Albrecht Dürer*. 2 vols.; Princeton: Princeton University Press, 1943. Discusses Agrippa's influence on Dürer.

———, and Fritz Saxl. *Dürers "Melencolia I": Eine Quellen- und Typengeschichtliche Untersuchung*. Leipzig: B. G. Teubner, 1923.

Paquier, J[ules]. *L'Humanisme et la Réforme: Jérôme Aléandre de sa naissance à la fin de son séjour à Brindes*. Paris: Ernest Leroux, Éditeur, 1900.

Pastor, Ludwig, Freiherr von. *The History of the Popes, From the Close of the Middle Ages*, ed. Frederick Ignatius Antrobus *et al.* 40 vols.; St. Louis, Missouri: B. Herder, 1894-1953.

Patrick, Mary Mills. *Sextus Empiricus and Greek Scepticism*. Cambridge [England]: Deighton Bell & Co., 1899.

Peers, E. Allison. *Ramon Lull: A Biography*. London: Society for Promoting Christian Knowledge, 1929.

Peuckert, Will-Erich. *Pansophie: Ein Versuch zur Geschichte der weissen und schwarzen Magie*. Stuttgart: Verlag von W. Kohlhammer, 1936. Helpful for its study of Agrippa's influence on later German students of magic.

Popkin, Richard H. *The History of Scepticism from Erasmus to Descartes*. Assen [the Netherlands]: Van Gorcum & Comp. N.V., 1960. A very helpful study, giving considerable attention to Agrippa.

Ranke, Leopold von. *Deutsche Geschichte im Zeitalter der Reformation*. 5th ed.; 6 vols.; Leipzig: Verlag von Duncker und Humblot, 1873.

Rashdall, Hastings. *The Universities of Europe in the Middle Ages*, ed. F. M. Powicke and A. B. Emden. 3 vols.; Oxford: The Clarendon Press, 1936.

Renaudet, Augustin. *Érasme et l'Italie*. Geneva: E. Droz, 1954. A collection of valuable essays.

———. *Préréforme et humanisme à Paris pendant les premières guerres d'Italie (1494-1517)*. Paris: Librairie Ancienne Honoré Champion,

1916. Also 2nd ed.; Paris: Librairie d'Argences, 1953. Extremely valuable on the intellectual background of Agrippa's periods of residence in France.

Ritter, Gerhard. *Die Neugestaltung Europas im 16. Jahrhundert: Die kirchlichen und staatlichen Wandlungen im Zeitalter der Reformation und der Glaubenskämpfe.* 2nd ed.; Berlin: Verlag des Druckhauses Tempelhof, 1950.

Ritter, Heinrich. *Geschichte der Philosophie.* 12 vols.; Hamburg: Bei Friedrich Perthes, 1836-53.

Robb, Nesca Adeline. *Neoplatonism of the Italian Renaissance.* London: G. Allen & Unwin Ltd., [1935].

Rossi, Paolo. *Clavis universalis: Arti mnemoniche e logica combinatoria da Lullo a Leibniz.* Milan: R. Ricciardi, 1960.

Ruggiero, Guido de. *Storia della filosofia,* Part III: *Rinascimento, Riforma e Controriforma.* 2nd ed.; 2 vols.; Bari: Gius. Laterza & Figli, 1937.

Ruska, Julius. *Tabula smaragdina: Ein Beitrag zur Geschichte der hermetischen Literatur.* Heidelberg: Carl Winter's Universitätsbuchhandlung, 1926.

Sancio, [Antonio?]. *Cenno storico intorno ai marchesi del Monferrato di stirpe Paleologa.* Casale: Tipografia F. Maffei, e T. Scrivano, 1835.

Schelhorn, Johann Georg, ed. *Amoenitates literariae, quibus variae observationes, scripta item quaedam anecdota et rariora opuscula exhibentur.* 2nd ed.; 14 vols. in 7; Francofurti, apud Daniel. Bartholomaei & Filium, 1726-30.

Scholem, Gershom Gerhard. *Bibliographia kabbalistica: Verzeichnis der gedruckten die jüdische Mystik (Gnosis, Kabbala, Sabbatianismus, Frankismus, Chassidismus) behandelnden Bücher und Aufsätze von Reuchlin bis zur Gegenwart.* Leipzig: W. Druglin, 1927.

———. *Major Trends in Jewish Mysticism.* New York: Schocken Books, 1946. Extremely valuable for general background on cabalism.

Schwiebert, E[rnest]. G[eorge]. *Luther and His Times: The Reformation From a New Perspective.* St. Louis, Missouri: Concordia Publishing House, c1950.

Secret, François. *Le Zôhar chez les Kabbalistes chrétiens de la Renaissance.* Paris: Librairie Durlacher, 1958. A recent re-evaluation of cabalistic influence, critical of the earlier work by Blau.

Seznec, Jean. *The Survival of the Pagan Gods: The Mythological Tradition and Its Place in Renaissance Humanism and Art,* trans. Barbara F. Sessions. [New York]: Pantheon Books, [1953]. An English translation of the following book; an important work, though of only occasional relevance to the present study.

———. *La survivance des dieux antiques: Essai sur le rôle de la tradition mythologique dans l'humanisme et dans l'art de la Renaissance.* London: The Warburg Institute, 1940.

Sigwart, Christoph. *Kleine Schriften.* 2nd ed.; 2 vols.; Freiburg-i-B.: J. C. B. Mohr, 1889. Volume I contains helpful essays on Agrippa and Paracelsus.

Singer, Dorothea Waley. *Giordano Bruno, His Life and Thought*. New York: Henry Schuman, [1950].

Smith, Preserved. *The Life and Letters of Martin Luther*. Boston: Houghton Mifflin Company, 1911.

Spini, Giorgio. *Ricerca dei libertini: La teoria dell'impostura delle religioni nel Seicento italiano*. [Rome]: Editrice Universale di Roma, [1950]. A valuable study of certain currents of thought which show kinship to Agrippa.

Spitz, Lewis W. *The Religious Renaissance of the German Humanists*. Cambridge, Massachusetts: Harvard University Press, 1963.

Stadelmann, Rudolf. *Vom Geist des ausgehenden Mittelalters: Studien zur Geschichte der Weltanschauung von Nicolaus Cusanus bis Sebastian Franck*. Halle/Saale: M. Niemeyer, 1929. A brilliant and provocative intellectual study of a number of figures, Agrippa among them, tracing their development back to an intellectual tradition founded by Nicholas of Cusa.

Strowski, Fortunat. *Montaigne*. Paris: Félix Alcan, 1906.

Thirion, Maurice. *Étude sur l'histoire du protestantisme à Metz et dans le pays Messin*. Nancy: Imprimerie F. Collin, 1884. A thesis in the Faculty of Letters at Paris, useful for understanding the background of Agrippa's experience in Metz.

Thorndike, Lynn. *A History of Magic and Experimental Science*. 8 vols.; New York: The Macmillan Company, 1923-58.

———. *The Place of Magic in the Intellectual History of Europe*. New York [no publisher named], 1905. Also issued under the imprint of Columbia University Press as Vol. XXIV, No. 1, of *Columbia University Studies in History, Economics and Public Law*.

Ueberweg, Friedrich. *Grundriss der Geschichte der Philosophie des Altertums*, ed. Karl Praechter. 11th ed.; Berlin: Ernst Siegfried Mittler und Sohn, 1920.

———. *Grundriss der Geschichte der Philosophie*, Zweiter Teil: *Die patristische und scholastische Philosophie*, ed. Bernhard Geyer. 11th ed.; Berlin: Verlegt bei E. S. Mittler & Sohn, 1928.

———. *Grundriss der Geschichte der Philosophie*, Dritter Teil: *Die Philosophie der Neuzeit bis zum Ende des XVIII Jahrhunderts*, ed. Max Frischeisen-Köhler and Willy Moog. 12th ed.; Berlin: Verlegt bei E. S. Mittler & Sohn, 1924.

Villey, Pierre. *Les sources et l'évolution des Essais de Montaigne*. 2nd ed.; 2 vols.; Paris: Librairie Hachette et Cⁱᵉ, 1933.

Wadsworth, James B. *Lyons, 1473-1503: The Beginnings of Cosmopolitanism*. Cambridge, Massachusetts: Mediaeval Academy of America, 1962.

Walker, D[aniel]. P[ickering]. *Spiritual and Demonic Magic From Ficino to Campanella*. London: Warburg Institute, University of London, 1958. Extremely valuable study of the relationships between Neoplatonic philosophy and magical thought in Renaissance civilization.

Warburg, Aby. *Gesammelte Schriften*. 2 vols.; Leipzig: B. G. Teubner, 1932. Vol. II, 487-558, contains the essay "Heidnisch-antike Weissagung in Wort und Bild zu Luthers Zeiten," which discusses some valuable analogues to Agrippa's thought.

Wind, Edgar. *Pagan Mysteries in the Renaissance.* New Haven: Yale University Press, 1958.

Wingate, S[ybil]. D[ouglas]. *The Mediaeval Latin Versions of the Aristotelian Scientific Corpus, With Special Reference to the Biological Works.* London: The Courier Press, 1931.

Winters, Roy Lutz. *Francis Lambert of Avignon (1487-1530): A Study in Reformation Origins.* Philadelphia: The United Lutheran Publication House, 1938. An Edinburgh Ph.D. thesis devoted to an acquaintance of Agrippa.

Wulf, Maurice de. *History of Medieval Philosophy,* trans. P[eter]. Coffey. 3rd ed.; London: Longmans, Green, and Co., 1909.

C. *Articles*

Baravalle, Hermann von. "Die geometrischen Figuren des Agrippa von Nettesheim als geometrische Bilder," *Anthroposophie: Zeitschrift für freies Geistesleben,* XV (1932), 61-69.

Baron, Hans. "Erasmus-Probleme im Spiegel des Colloquium 'Inquisitio de fide,'" *Archiv für Reformationsgeschichte,* XLIII (1952), 254-63.

Barracco, Helda Bullotta. "Saggio bio-bibliografico su Enrico Cornelio Agrippa di Nettesheim," in Rome, Università, Instituto di Filosofia, *Rassegna di Filosofia,* VI (1957), 222-48. A general study, advancing some ingenious but sometimes arbitrary conclusions.

Bertrand, Alexis, ed. and trans. "Le mouvement psychologique: Grandeur et suprématie des femmes, manifeste féministe d'Henri-Corneille Agrippa de Nettesheym," *Archives d'anthropologie criminelle, de médecine légale et de psychologie normale et pathologique,* XXV (1910), 112-46. A translation of Agrippa's *De foeminei sexus praecellentia,* with introductory note.

Bielmann, Josef. "Zu einer Handschrift der Occulta Philosophia," *Archiv für Kulturgeschichte,* XXVII (1937), 318-24. A note based on MS. M.ch.q.50 of the Universitätsbibliothek at Würzburg.

Bouwsma, William J. "Postel and the Significance of Renaissance Cabalism," *Journal of the History of Ideas,* XV (1954), 218-32.

Calder, I. R. F. "A Note on Magic Squares in the Philosophy of Agrippa of Nettesheim," *Journal of the Warburg and Courtauld Institutes,* XII (1949), 196-99.

Cazalas, E. [i.e., Jean Jules André Marie Eutrope]. "Le sceau de la lune de C. Agrippa," *Revue de l'histoire des religions,* CXIV (1936), 93-98.

―――. "Les sceaux planétaires de C. Agrippa," *ibid.,* CX (1934), 66-82.

Charvet, Léon. "Correspondance d'Eustache Chapuys et d'Henri-Cornélius Agrippa de Nettesheim," *Revue savoisienne,* XV (1874), 25-30, 33-39, 45-50, 53-58, 61-66, 85-90, 93-98. Still retains some value; but on the attribution of certain letters, see now Mattingly's unprinted thesis (above) on Chapuys.

Daguet, Alexandre. "Agrippa chez les suisses," *Archives de la Société d'histoire du canton de Fribourg,* II (1858), 133-70.

Dannenfeldt, Karl H. "The Pseudo-Zoroastrian Oracles in the Renaissance," *Studies in the Renaissance*, IV (1957), 7-30.

Duncan, Margaret S. "A Famous Magician," *Theosophical Review*, XXV (1899), 105-16.

Fellerer, Karl Gustav. "Agrippa von Nettesheim und die Musik," *Archiv für Musikwissenschaft*, XVI (1959), 77-86.

Ferguson, John. "Bibliographical Notes on the Treatises *De occulta philosophia* and *De incertitudine et vanitate scientiarum* of Cornelius Agrippa," *Proceedings of the Edinburgh Bibliographical Society*, XII (1924), 1-23. A posthumously published fragment of a bibliographical study of editions of Agrippa's works.

Fischer, Karl. "Wanderer im Nebel," *Ethische Kultur*, XLIII (1935), 24-26. Dates Agrippa's death on 18 February 1535, but gives no evidence for this.

Follet, H. "Un médecin astrologue au temps de la Renaissance, Henri Cornelius Agrippa," *Nouvelle Revue*, XCVIII (1896), 303-36.

Geanakoplos, Deno J. "Erasmus and the Aldine Academy of Venice: A Neglected Chapter in the Transmission of Graeco-Byzantine Learning to the West," *Greek, Roman, and Byzantine Studies*, III (1960), 107-34.

Greenwood, Thomas. "L'éclosion du scepticisme pendant la Renaissance et les premiers apologistes," *Revue de l'Université d'Ottawa*, XVII (1947), 69-99.

Gundersheimer, Werner L. "Erasmus, Humanism, and the Christian Cabala," *Journal of the Warburg and Courtauld Institutes*, XXVI (1963), 38-52.

Hamilton, A. C. "Sidney and Agrippa," *Review of English Studies*, n.s., VII (1956), 151-57.

Hauser, Henri. "Le *Journal* de Louise de Savoie," *Revue historique*, LXXXVI (1904), 280-303.

Jaeckle, Erwin. "Paracelsus und Agrippa von Nettesheim," *Nova Acta Paracelsica*, II (1945), 83-109.

Jegel, August. "Die Lebenstragödie des Dr. jur. et med. Heinrich Cornelius Agrippa von Nettesheim," *Jahrbuch des kölnischen Geschichtsvereins*, XX (1938), 15-76.

Judson, Alexander C. "Cornelius Agrippa and Henry Vaughan," *Modern Language Notes*, XLI (1926), 178-81.

Keightley, Bertram. "Agrippa von Nettesheim and Paracelsus," *Theosophical Review*, XXX (1902), 508-14. An occultist lecture, with small mention of Paracelsus and less of Agrippa.

Kleinhans, Arduinus. "De vita et operibus Petri Galatini O.F.M.," *Antonianum*, I (1926), 145-79, 327-56.

Krafft, Karl, and Wilhelm Crecelius. "Mittheilungen über Alexander Hegius und seine Schüler, sowie andere gleichzeitige Gelehrte, aus den Werken des Johannes Butzbach, Priors des Benedictiner-Klosters am Laacher See," *Zeitschrift des bergischen Geschichtsvereins*, VII (1871), 213-88. Contains valuable material on the Canter or Canterius family.

Kristeller, Paul Oskar. "Lodovico Lazzarelli e Giovanni da Correggio, due ermetici del Quattrocento, e il manoscritto II.D.I.4 della Biblioteca Communale degli Ardenti di Viterbo," in *Biblioteca degli Ardenti della Città di Viterbo, Studi e ricerche nel 150° della fondazione.* Viterbo: Agnesotti, 1960.

———. Review of Hiram Haydn's *The Counter-Renaissance,* in *Journal of the History of Ideas,* XII (1951), 468-72.

Lefranc, Abel. "Rabelais et Cornelius Agrippa," in *Mélanges offerts à M. Émile Picot,* II, 477-86. 2 vols.; Paris: Librairie Damascène Morgand, 1913.

Maillet-Guy, Luc. "Henri Corneil Agrippa, sa famille et ses relations," *Bulletin de la Société d'archéologie et de statistique de la Drôme,* LX (1926), 120-44, 201-25.

Mannheimer, E. "Okkultismus bei Agrippa von Nettesheim," *Zentralblatt für Okkultismus,* XXV (1931), 219-23. Occultist.

McIlquham, Harriett. "Agrippa's Appreciation of Women," *Westminster Review,* CLIV (1900), 303-13.

Metzke, Erwin. "Die 'Skepsis' des Agrippa von Nettesheim," *Deutsche Vierteljahrsschrift für Literaturwissenschaft und Geistesgeschichte,* XIII (1935), 407-20.

Montet, Léon. "Études sur quelques hommes de la Renaissance: Henri Corneille Agrippa," *La liberté de penser,* III (1849), 243-58, 471-85.

Murr, Christian Gottlieb von. "Conspectus omnium editionum operum Henrici Cornelii Agrippae ab Nettesheim," *Neues Journal zur Literatur und Kunstgeschichte,* I (1798), 58-86.

Nauert, Charles G., Jr. "Agrippa in Renaissance Italy: The Esoteric Tradition," *Studies in the Renaissance,* VI (1959), 195-222. Includes an apparatus of variant readings offered by MS. Lat. 16,625 of the Bibliothèque Nationale at Paris to the text of Agrippa's *De triplici ratione cognoscendi Deum.* Chapter Two of the present study is a revised form of this article.

———. "Magic and Skepticism in Agrippa's Thought," *Journal of the History of Ideas,* XVIII (1957), 161-82. Chapter Eight of the present study is based on this article.

Nowotny, Karl Anton. "The Construction of Certain Seals and Characters in the Work of Agrippa of Nettesheim," *Journal of the Warburg and Courtauld Institutes,* XII (1949), 46-57.

Orsier, Joseph. "Un aventurier célèbre du XVIᵉ siècle: Cornélis Agrippa," *Revue des idées,* VII (1910), 157-94. An earlier form of the biographical portion of his book on Agrippa.

Philibert-Soupé, A. "Corneille Agrippa," *Annuaire de la Faculté des Lettres de Lyon,* I (1883), 41-60.

Reichl, Anton. "Goethes Faust und Agrippa von Nettesheim," *Euphorion: Zeitschrift für Literaturgeschichte,* IV (1897), 287-301.

Ritter, Gerhard. "Ein historisches Urbild zu Goethes Faust (Agrippa von Nettesheym)," *Preussische Jahrbücher,* CXLI (1910), 300-24.

———. "Romantische und revolutionäre Elemente in der deutschen Theologie am Vorabend der Reformation," *Deutsche Vierteljahrsschrift für Literaturwissenschaft und Geistesgeschichte*, V (1927), 342-80. An important study of German thought in the fifteenth century, including an analysis of the importance of skeptical tendencies within the Occamist tradition.

Rocholl, Rudolf. "Der Platonismus der Renaissancezeit," *Zeitschrift für Kirchengeschichte*, XIII (1892), 47-106.

Röck, Friedrich. "Der Denarzyklus des Agrippa von Nettesheim," *Orientalistische Literaturzeitung*, XVI (1913), cols. 356-62.

Rossi, Paolo. "The Legacy of Ramon Lull in Sixteenth-Century Thought," *Mediaeval and Renaissance Studies*, V (1961), 182-213.

Sandret, L. "Le concile de Pise (1511)," *Revue des questions historiques*, XXXIV (1883), 425-56.

Saulnier, V. L. "Médecins de Montpellier au temps de Rabelais," *Bibliothèque d'Humanisme et Renaissance*, XIX (1957), 425-79.

Scholem, Gershom Gerhard. "Zur Geschichte der Anfänge der christlichen Kabbala," in *Essays Presented to Leo Baeck*. London: East and West Library, 1954.

Schwentner, Ernst. "Agrippa von Nettesheim über Ulfilas," *Wörter und Sachen*, XXI (1940), 227.

Spitz, Lewis W. "Reuchlin's Philosophy: Pythagoras and Cabala for Christ," *Archiv für Reformationsgeschichte*, XLVII (1956), 1-20.

Walker, D[aniel]. P[ickering]. "Orpheus the Theologian and Renaissance Platonists," *Journal of the Warburg and Courtauld Institutes*, XVI (1953), 100-20.

———. "The *Prisca Theologia* in France," *ibid.*, XVII (1954), 204-59.

Wieland, Christoph M. "Nachrichten von Heinrich Cornelius Agrippa von Nettesheim," *Der Deutsche Merkur*, XV (1776), 184-88, 266-72.

Winter, G. "Ein Vorkämpfer geistiger Aufklärung," *Gegenwart*, XXXIV (1888), 229. Discusses Agrippa and Johann Wier as opponents of the witchcraft delusion.

Yates, Frances A. "The Art of Ramon Lull: An Approach to It Through Lull's Theory of the Elements," *Journal of the Warburg and Courtauld Institutes*, XVII (1954), 115-73.

Zambelli, Paola. "A proposito del 'De vanitate scientiarum et artium' di Cornelio Agrippa," *Rivista critica di storia della filosofia*, XV (1960), 166-80.

———. "Umanesimo magico-astrologico e raggruppamenti segreti nei Platonici della Preriforma," in *Umanesimo e esoterismo: Atti del V convegno internazionale di studi umanistici, Oberhofen, 16-17 settembre 1960*, ed. Enrico Castelli. Padua: CEDAM, 1960. Her article is on pp. 141-74.

D. *Articles in Reference Works*[4]

[4] This section includes articles appearing in nineteenth- and twentieth-century works of reference. Older (sixteenth-, seventeenth-, and eighteenth-century) reference books containing notices on Agrippa are listed above under the heading Other Books.

Abt. "Heinrich Cornelius Agrippa von Nettesheim," *Das Staats-Lexikon: Encyklopädie der sämmtlichen Staatswissenschaften*, I, 406-18.

"Agrippa von Nettesheim, Henry Cornelius," *Encyclopaedia Britannica* (1954 edition), I, 435.

Amat, Roman d'. "Arande, Michel d'," *Dictionnaire de biographie française*, III, cols. 227-30.

———. "Bullioud, Symphorien," *ibid.*, VII, col. 663.

Baudrillart, A[lfred]. "Agrippa de Nettesheim, Henri Corneille," *Dictionnaire de théologie catholique*, I, cols. 635-37.

Bonwetsch, N. "Dionysius Areopagita," *Realencyklopädie für protestantische Theologie und Kirche*, IV, 687-96.

Broydé, Isaac. "Zacuto, Abraham ben Samuel," *The Jewish Encyclopedia*, XII, 627.

Dannenfeldt, Karl H. "Hermetica Philosophica," *Catalogus translationum et commentariorum: Mediaeval and Renaissance Latin Translations and Commentaries; Annotated Lists and Guides*, ed. Paul Oskar Kristeller, vol. I, 137-56. Washington, D.C.: Catholic University of America Press, 1960.

———. "Oracula Chaldaica," *ibid.*, I, 157-64.

Delaulnaye. "Finé (Oronce)," *Biographie universelle*, XIV, 542-44.

Delff. "Heinrich Cornelius Agrippa von Nettesheim," *Allgemeine deutsche Biographie*, I, 156-58. (The author, not further identified by the editors, may be the philosopher Heinrich Karl Hugo Delff, d. 1898.)

Denkinger, Henri. "Henri Corneille Agrippa," *Dictionnaire historique et biographique de la Suisse*, I, 125.

Eckstein. "Johannes Caesarius," *Allgemeine deutsche Biographie*, III, 689-91. (The author, not further identified, is probably the historian and educator Friedrich August Eckstein.)

Eisenhart. "Petrus Ravennas," *ibid.*, XXV, 529-39.

Fabro, Cornelio. "Agrippa di Nettesheim, Cornelius Heinrich," *Enciclopedia cattolica*, I, 582-83.

Fonsegrive, G[eorge Pierre Lespinasse]. "Agrippa de Nettesheim, Henri-Corneille," *La grande encyclopédie*, I, 903-4. A good short summary of Agrippa's thought.

Fournier, P. "Agrippa de Nettesheim," *Dictionnaire d'histoire et de géographie ecclésiastiques*, I, 1030-35. A good article.

Geiger, Ludwig. "Aesticampanus, Joh. Rhagius," *Allgemeine deutsche Biographie*, I, 133-34.

———. "Hermann Graf von Neuenar," *ibid.*, XXIII, 485-86.

Godet, P. "Denys l'Aréopagite," *Dictionnaire de théologie catholique*, IV, cols. 429-36.

Grimm, Heinrich. "Agrippa von Nettesheim, Heinrich Cornelius," *Neue deutsche Biographie*, I, 105-6.

Guizot, [François Pierre Guillaume]. "Agrippa de Nettesheim (Henri-Corneille)," *Biographie universelle*, I, 216-17.

Heimsoeth, Heinz. "Agrippa von Nettesheim und Theophrastus Paracelsus," *Handbuch der Philosophie*, I, 17-20.

Herzog. "Wolfgang Fabricius Capito," *Allgemeine deutsche Biographie*, III, 772-75.

Kessler, K. "Mani, Manichäer," *Realencyklopädie für protestantische Theologie und Kirche*, XII, 209-10.

Kirn, O. "Sünde," *Realencyklopädie für protestantische Theologie und Kirche*, XIX, 132-48.

Kleinschmidt, Beda. "Heilige Anna, Mutter Mariä," *Lexikon für Theologie und Kirche*, I, cols. 452-53.

Mirbt, Carl. "Lambert, Franz," *Realencyklopädie für protestantische Theologie und Kirche*, XI, 220-23.

Prevost, M. "Bohier, Henri," *Dictionnaire de biographie française*, VI, col. 782.

————. "Brulart," *ibid.*, VII, col. 487-88.

Rivier. "Claudius Cantiuncula," *Allgemeine deutsche Biographie*, III, 767-68.

Rudge, F. M. "Anthony, Saint, Orders of," *Catholic Encyclopedia*, I, 555-56.

Salomon, Max. "Agrippa von Nettesheim, Heinrich Cornelius," *Biographisches. Lexikon der hervorragenden Ärzte aller Zeiten und Völker*, I, 47-49.

Stöckl. "Agrippa von Nettesheim, Heinrich Cornelius," *Wetzer und Welte's Kirchenlexikon*, I, cols. 364-66.

Tabaraud. "Bullioud" *Biographie universelle*, VI, 259.

Vignola, Bruno. "Agrippa di Nettesheim," *Enciclopedia italiana*, I, 997.

Weizsäcker, C. "Agrippa von Nettesheim," *Realencyklopädie für protestantische Theologie und Kirche*, I, 257-58.

Caius, John, 325n
Calvin, John: opinion of Agrippa, 158, 192, 324; concern over naturalism, 316; mentioned, 74, 161
Campanella, Tommaso, 236
Campeggio, Lorenzo, Cardinal, 53, 107, 109, 113
Candiotus, 38
Canterius, Andreas, 12-13, 217
Cantiuncula, Claudius (Claude Chansonnette): correspondent of Agrippa, 53, 73, 77, 110; career at Basel, 63-64; seeks Agrippa's opinion of his *Topica*, 70; and François Lambert, 74, 170, 171; at French court, 91; attitude toward Reformation, 159, 162; mentioned, 68, 80, 84, 143, 219
Capella, Martianus, 155
Capito, Wolfgang Fabricius: describes Agrippa's education, 53; and Reformation, 97, 160-61; corresponds with Agrippa, 77; and François Lambert, 170, 171; mentioned, 3, 172
Cardan, Girolamo, 323
Carlstadt, Andreas, 167, 169
Caroli, Pierre, 92n
Carondelet, Jean, Archbishop of Palermo, 109
Casale Monferrato, Italy, 37, 39, 40, 51
Cassirer, Ernst, 200, 316, 333
Castellesi, Adriano, Cardinal, 147-48, 207
Catherine of Aragon, Queen of England, 78-79, 108
Catholic Reformation, 302
Catilinet, Jean, 28, 29, 126n
Cecco d'Ascoli, 138, 203
Celsus, 155
Cernole, Ludovico, 51
Chalcidius, 122
Chalendatus, 88n
Chambéry, 52
Champier, Symphorien: connection with Agrippa, 22-23, 24; and French occultism, 43, 228; mentioned, 41, 86, 89

Chansonnette, Claude. *See* Cantiuncula, Claudius
Chapelain, Jehan: as royal physician, 23n; friendship with Agrippa, 88, 93, 100, 102; horoscope cast by Agrippa, 99; attitude toward Reformation, 162; mentioned, 90, 91, 98, 216
Chapuys, Eustache: Agrippa meets him, 52; influence in Geneva, 72-73, 77-78; friend of Genevan humanists, 74; defends Catherine of Aragon, 108; mentioned, 75, 84, 95
Charles V, Emperor: turned against Agrippa, 107; Agrippa's history of his wars, 111; in Agrippa's opinion, 167; in Agrippa legend, 326, 328, 331; mentioned, 84, 108, 110n, 113
Châtelain, Jean, 56, 66, 68
Chicquam, Ginette, 89
Christ. *See* Jesus Christ
Chrysostom of Vercelli, O. Carm., 126n
Church Fathers: cited by Agrippa, 118, 155; as Platonic influence, 128; sources for numerology, 129; used by Castellesi, 148; as models for theology, 301; committed errors, 305, 314; mentioned, 267
Cicero, 142, 203, 305
Closter, Abel, 110
Coct, Anémond de, 92n, 164n
Colet, John, 31, 51, 126n, 145, 152
Cologne, Germany: Agrippa's native city, 8; Agrippa's friends there, 29-30, 69-70; Agrippa's visits, 14-15, 30-31, 68-70, 111
Cologne, University of: intellectual traditions, 11; in opinion of Agrippa, 13, 123, 166, 167; influence on Agrippa, 13-14, 217, 225; attacks Peter of Ravenna, 15; Agrippa's quodlibetical disputations (1510), 32
Colyn, Conrad, O.P., of Ulm, 112
Comparatus the Saracen, 17